iPhoto, iMovie and Other Useful Mac® Programs for SENIORS

Studio Visual Steps

iPhoto, iMovie and Other Useful Mac® Programs for SENIORS

Get acquainted by following easy to understand step-by-step instructions

www.visualsteps.com

This book has been written using the Visual Steps™ method.
Cover design by Studio Willemien Haagsma bNO

© 2012 Visual Steps
With the assistance of Yvette Huijsman
Edited by Jolanda Ligthart, Rilana Groot and Mara Kok
Translated by Irene Venditti, *i-write* translation services and Chris Hollingsworth, *1st Resources*.

First printing: October 2012
ISBN 978 90 5905 138 6

All rights reserved. No part of this publication may be reproduced, stored in a retrieval system or transmitted in any form or by any means, electronic, mechanical, photocopying, recording, scanning or otherwise, except as permitted under Sections 107 or 108 of the 1976 United States Copyright Act, without the prior written permission of the Publisher.

LIMIT OF LIABILITY/DISCLAIMER OF WARRANTY: While the publisher and author have used their best efforts in preparing this book, they make no representations or warranties with respect to the accuracy or completeness of the contents of this book and specifically disclaim any implied warranties of merchantability or fitness for a particular purpose. No warranty may be created or extended by sales representatives or written sales materials. The advice and strategies contained herein may not be suitable for your situation. You should consult with a professional where appropriate. Neither the publisher nor author shall be liable for any loss of profit or any other commercial damages, including but not limited to special, incidental, consequential or other damages.

Trademarks: This book contains names of registered trademarks. Mac is a registered trademark of Apple, Inc. All other trademarks are the property of their respective owners. Visual Steps Publishing is not associated with any product or vendor mentioned in this book.
In the text of this book, these names are not indicated by their trademark symbol, because they are solely used for identifying the products which are mentioned in the text. In no way does this constitute an infringement on the rights of the trademark owners.

Resources used: A number of definitions and explanations of computer terminology are taken over from the *Mac User Guide*.

Do you have any questions or suggestions?
E-mail: info@visualsteps.com

Would you like more information?
www.visualsteps.com

Website for this book:
www.visualsteps.com/iphotomac
Here you can register your book.

Subscribe to the free Visual Steps Newsletter:
www.visualsteps.com/newsletter

Table of Contents

Foreword	11
Visual Steps Newsletter	11
Introduction to Visual Steps ™	12
What You Will Need	13
How to Use This Book	14
Website	15
Test Your Knowledge	15
For Teachers	15
The Screenshots	16
1. Working with Photos	**17**
1.1 Importing Photos with *iPhoto*	18
1.2 Deactivate and Remove the Camera	22
1.3 Rotating a Photo	23
1.4 Creating an Album	25
1.5 Adding Photos To an Album	28
1.6 Removing a Photo From an Album	29
1.7 Creating a Slideshow	30
1.8 Saving a Slideshow	34
1.9 Deleting an Album	36
1.10 Sending a Photo By Email	37
1.11 Viewing Photos with *Preview*	41
1.12 Editing Photos in *Preview*	42
1.13 Rotating a Photo	43
1.14 Enhancing a Photo	45
1.15 Changing the Size of a Photo	47
1.16 Cropping a Photo	48
1.17 Adding Text and Images	50
1.18 Zooming In and Out	53
1.19 Changing the Font	54
1.20 Background Information	56
1.21 Tips	57

2. Working with Video — 69

- 2.1 Downloading and Installing Codecs — 70
- 2.2 Importing Video Files from a Camera (with *iMovie*) — 72
- 2.3 Deactivating and Removing a Camera or SD Card — 77
- 2.4 Creating Videos with *iMovie* — 78
- 2.5 Starting a New Project — 78
- 2.6 Importing a Video File Into a Project — 80
- 2.7 Editing a Video Clip — 83
- 2.8 Adding Multiple Video Files — 87
- 2.9 Moving a Video Clip — 91
- 2.10 Adding a Photo — 92
- 2.11 Adding Titles — 94
- 2.12 Adding a Transition — 95
- 2.13 Adding Music — 97
- 2.14 Creating a Video File — 101
- 2.15 Playing a Video with *QuickTime Player* — 104
- 2.16 Burning a DVD with *iDVD* — 106
- 2.17 Playing a DVD — 112
- 2.18 Background Information — 116
- 2.19 Tips — 118

3. Working with Music — 121

- 3.1 Opening *iTunes* — 122
- 3.2 Importing a CD — 123
- 3.3 Playing Music in *iTunes* — 125
- 3.4 Viewing Information in the *Library* — 128
- 3.5 Modifying the Information on a Track — 129
- 3.6 Rating Tracks — 131
- 3.7 Searching for Songs — 133
- 3.8 Creating a Playlist — 135
- 3.9 Adding Songs to a Playlist — 135
- 3.10 Adding Multiple Tracks At Once — 138
- 3.11 Changing the Order of the Playlist — 140
- 3.12 Removing a Track From the Playlist — 140
- 3.13 Playing a Playlist — 141
- 3.14 Using Smart Playlists — 142
- 3.15 Creating Your Own Smart Playlist — 143

3.16 Deleting a Playlist	145
3.17 Adding Tracks To an iPod	145
3.18 Listening To the Radio	147
3.19 Background Information	150
3.20 Tips	151

4. Practical Applications on the Mac   153
4.1 Removing and Adding Apps in *Launchpad*	154
4.2 Combining Apps into Folders in *Launchpad*	158
4.3 Working with *Disk Utility*	162
4.4 Searching with *Spotlight*	164
4.5 Downloading and Installing an App	166
4.6 Removing an App from the *Mac*	170
4.7 Creating a Backup with *Time Machine*	171
4.8 Background Information	173
4.9 Tips	174

5. Sending Emails and Surfing the Internet Made Easier   175
5.1 Creating Mailboxes in *Mail*	176
5.2 Displaying Conversations	180
5.3 Adding a Signature To an Email Message	182
5.4 Searching for Email Messages	185
5.5 Deleting an Email Message	186
5.6 Organizing Bookmarks in *Safari*	188
5.7 Adding Bookmarks To the Bookmarks Menu	193
5.8 *Top Sites*	194
5.9 Creating a Reading List	197
5.10 Background Information	199
5.11 Tips	201

6. Managing Data — 209

- 6.1 Managing Addresses — 210
- 6.2 Adding an Address — 211
- 6.3 Searching for an Address — 214
- 6.4 Deleting a Card — 215
- 6.5 Keeping a Calendar — 216
- 6.6 Choosing a Calendar — 217
- 6.7 Adding an Event — 219
- 6.8 Editing an Event — 221
- 6.9 Leaf Through a Calendar — 223
- 6.10 Working with Widgets — 224
- 6.11 Adding a Widget — 226
- 6.12 Closing a Widget — 227
- 6.13 Closing the *Dashboard* — 228
- 6.14 Visual Steps — 229
- 6.15 Background Information — 230
- 6.16 Tips — 231

Appendices
- **A. How Do I Do That Again?** — 237
- **B. Download and Install Codecs** — 239
- **C. Download Practice Files** — 245
- **D. Open a Bonus Chapter** — 248
- **E. Index** — 249

Foreword

All *Mac* computers come with an assortment of user-friendly programs that allow you to perform everyday tasks quickly and easily. This book will teach you everything you need to know about these programs in an easy step by step manner. The chapters are divided into small sections, each containing full-color screen shots, thorough explanations, tips and a set of steps to guide you through any task to be performed.

You will learn how to organize and edit your photos with *iPhoto* and how to use *iMovie* to import, arrange and edit your video clips. You will become more proficient with programs you use on a daily basis, such as *Safari* to surf the web and *Mail* to send and receive email messages. You can simplify your life by learning how to manage appointments with *Calendar* and organize contact information with *Addresses*.

The *Mac* also contains a number of useful tools that help to make the *Mac* easier to use. For instance, you can use *Launchpad* to open programs (apps) from a single place. You can add your favorite apps to *Launchpad* yourself and organize similar apps into folders.

We hope you enjoy the multitude of practical and useful programs on your Mac!

Studio Visual Steps

PS We welcome your comments and suggestions.
Our email address is: info@visualsteps.com

Visual Steps Newsletter

All Visual Steps books follow the same methodology: clear and concise step-by-step instructions with screen shots to demonstrate each task.
A complete list of all our books can be found on our website **www.visualsteps.com**
You can also sign up to receive our **free Visual Steps Newsletter**.
In this Newsletter you will receive periodic information by email regarding:
- the latest titles and previously released books;
- special offers, supplemental chapters, tips and free informative booklets.
Also, our Newsletter subscribers may download any of the documents listed on the web pages **www.visualsteps.com/info_downloads**
When you subscribe to our Newsletter you can be assured that we will never use your email address for any purpose other than sending you the information as previously described. We will not share this address with any third-party. Each Newsletter also contains a one-click link to unsubscribe.

Introduction to Visual Steps™

The Visual Steps handbooks and manuals are the best instructional materials available for learning how to work with the computer. Nowhere else can you find better support for getting to know your *Mac* or *PC*, your *iPad* or *iPhone*, the Internet and a variety of computer applications.

Properties of the Visual Steps books:
- **Comprehensible contents**

Addresses the needs of the beginner or intermediate computer user for a manual written in simple, straight-forward English.
- **Clear structure**

Precise, easy to follow instructions. The material is broken down into small enough segments to allow for easy absorption.
- **Screenshots of every step**

Quickly compare what you see on your screen with the screenshots in the book. Pointers and tips guide you when new windows are opened so you always know what to do next.
- **Get started right away**

All you have to do is turn on your computer and have your book at hand. Perform each operation as indicated on your own *Mac*.
- **Layout**

The text is printed in a large size font and is clearly legible.

In short, I believe these manuals will be excellent guides for you.

dr. H. van der Meij
Faculty of Applied Education, Department of Instructional Technology, University of Twente, the Netherlands

What You Will Need

To be able to work through this book, you will need a number of things:

 You must have *Mac OS X Lion* or *Mountain Lion* installed on your computer.

 A connection to the Internet.

The following items will come in handy, but is not a problem if you do not own these devices. Just skip the relevant exercises.

 A digital photo camera, iPad, iPhone or any other portable device with a built-in camera.

 A video camera.

 To burn a movie to DVD you will need a DVD burner and a writable DVD disk.

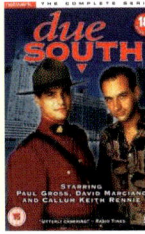 A music CD and a DVD.

How to Use This Book

This book has been written using the Visual Steps™ method. The method is simple: just place the book next to your *Mac.* Open you book and select the desired chapter. Read the instructions and perform each task step by step directly on your own *Mac.* The clear instructions and the multitude of screen shots will tell you exactly what to do. The quickest way of learning how to use the *Mac*, is by working through the exercises.

In this Visual Steps™ book, you will see various icons. This is what they mean:

Techniques
These icons indicate an action to be carried out:

   The mouse icon means you can do something on your *Mac* by using the mouse. The mouse icon is also used for operations that can be done both with the trackpad or the mouse.

   The keyboard icon means you should type something on your *Mac*'s keyboard.

   The hand icon means you should do something else, for example insert a USB stick into the computer. It is also used to remind you of something previously presented in this book.

In addition to these icons, in some areas of this book *extra assistance* is provided to help you successfully work through each chapter.

Help
These icons indicate that extra help is available:

   The arrow icon warns you about something.

   The bandage icon will help you if something has gone wrong.

   Have you forgotten how to do something? The number next to the footsteps tells you where to look it up at the end of the book in the appendix *How Do I Do That Again?*

In separate boxes you will find tips or additional information about the *Mac*.

Extra information
Information boxes are denoted by these icons:

 The book icon gives you extra background information that you can read at your convenience. This extra information is not necessary for working through the book.

 The light bulb icon indicates an extra tip for using the *Mac*.

Website

There is a website accompanying this book: **www.visualsteps.com/iphotomac**
Visit this website regularly and check to see if we have added any additional information or errata for this book. You will also find several bonus chapters and the practice files for use with *iPhoto* and *iMovie* on the website.

Test Your Knowledge

After you have worked through this book, you can test your knowledge online, at the **www.ccforseniors.com** website.
By answering a number of multiple choice questions you will be able to test your knowledge. After you have finished the test, your *Computer Certificate* will be sent to the email address you have entered.
Participating in the test is **free of charge**. The computer certificate website is a free Visual Steps service.

For Teachers

The Visual Steps books have been written as self-study guides for individual use. They are also well suited for use in a group or a classroom setting. For this purpose, some of our books come with a free teacher's manual. You can download the available teacher's manuals and additional materials at:
www.visualsteps.com/instructor

The Screenshots

The screenshots in this book indicate which button, file or hyperlink you need to click on your *Mac*. In the instruction text (in **bold** letters) you will see a small image of the item you need to click. The black line will point you to the right place on your screen. The small screenshots that are printed in this book are not meant to be completely legible all the time. This is not necessary, as you will see these images on your own screen in real size and fully legible.

Here you see an example of such an instruction text and a screenshot of the item you need to click. The black line indicates where to find this item on your own screen:

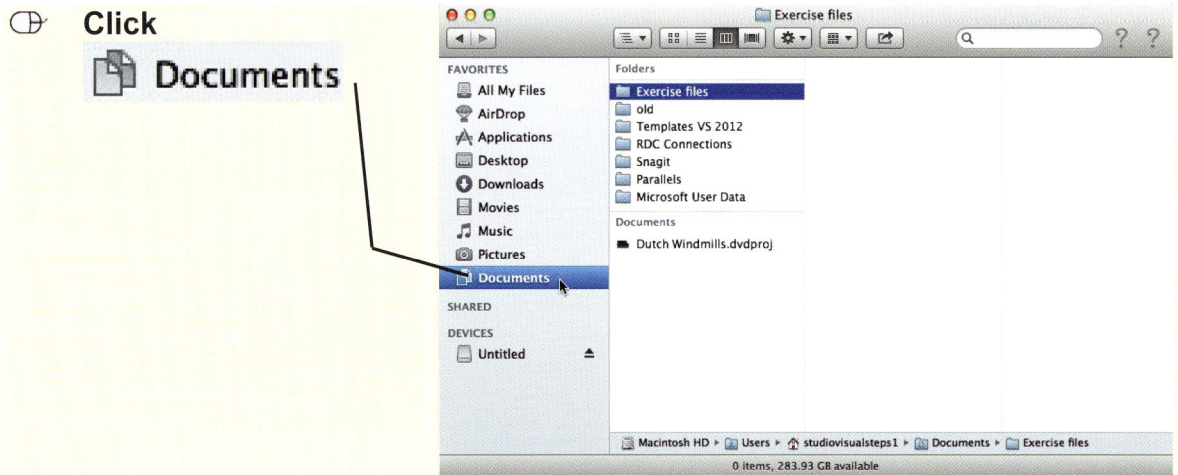

In some cases, the screenshot only displays part of the screen. Below you see an example of this:

At the bottom of the window:

We would like to emphasize that we **do not intend you** to read the information in all of the screenshots in this book. Always use the screenshots in combination with the larger display on your *Mac's* screen.

1. Working with Photos

Your *Mac* comes equipped with an assortment of programs for working with multimedia files, such as photos, video clips and music files. The standard photo editing application is called *iPhoto*.

With the *iPhoto* program you can transfer (import) photos from your digital camera, iPhone, iPad or iPod touch to your *Mac*. You can also import photos from other sources, for instance, an external hard drive, DVD or scanner. Afterwards, you can use *iPhoto* to manage and organize the photos. You can create a photo album, view your photos as a slideshow or send them to someone in an email.

The *Preview* program is primarily intended for viewing pictures. But you can also use this program to add special effects to your photos, as well as additional images, clip art and text balloons.

In this chapter you will learn how to:

- import photos with *iPhoto*;
- rotate a photo in *iPhoto*;
- create an album in *iPhoto*;
- create a slideshow in *iPhoto*;
- send a photo by email with *iPhoto*;
- view photos in *Preview*;
- rotate a photo in *Preview*;
- edit a photo in *Preview*;
- change the size of a photo in *Preview*;
- add additional items to a photo in *Preview*.

 Please note:

If you want to follow the examples in *section 1.1 Importing Photos with iPhoto* and *1.2 Deactivate and Remove the Camera* you will need to have a digital camera or an iPhone, iPad or iPod touch containing a few photos. If you do not own one of these devices, you can read through the following sections. Then continue with the steps in *section 1.3 Rotating a Photo*.

1.1 Importing Photos with iPhoto

Importing means transferring files to your *Mac*, from some kind of device. If you want to import the photos from your digital camera, iPhone, iPad or iPod touch, you will need to connect the device first. You can use a USB cable for this, for example:

☞ **Connect the digital camera to one of the USB ports on your *Mac* with the cable that comes with the camera and then turn the camera on**

If you own an iPhone, iPad, or iPod touch you need to use the white Dock Connector to USB cable (included in the package of your device):

☞ **Connect the broader end of the white Dock Connector to USB cable to your iPhone, iPad or iPod touch**

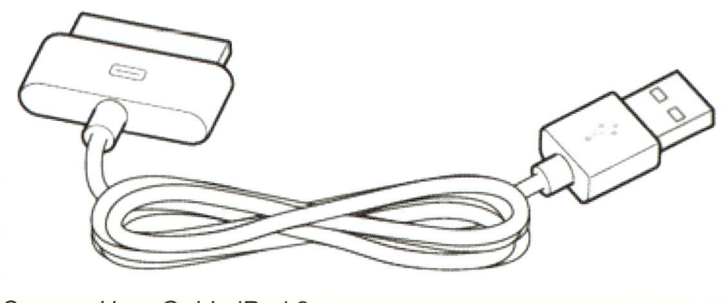

☞ **Connect the other end to one of the USB ports on your *Mac***

Source: User Guide iPad 2

If you are using an iMac and you have a digital camera with a SD memory card, you can also insert the SD card directly into the iMac's card reader.

The SD card slot is located on the right side, below the CD/DVD player:

☞ **Carefully insert the SD card into the slot, with the printed side of the card pointing towards you**

Chapter 1 Working with Photos **19**

As soon as you connect the digital camera or another device containing a digital camera to the computer, the *iPhoto* program should start up right away. If this does not happen, you can open *iPhoto* in two different ways. The first method is through the *Dock*:

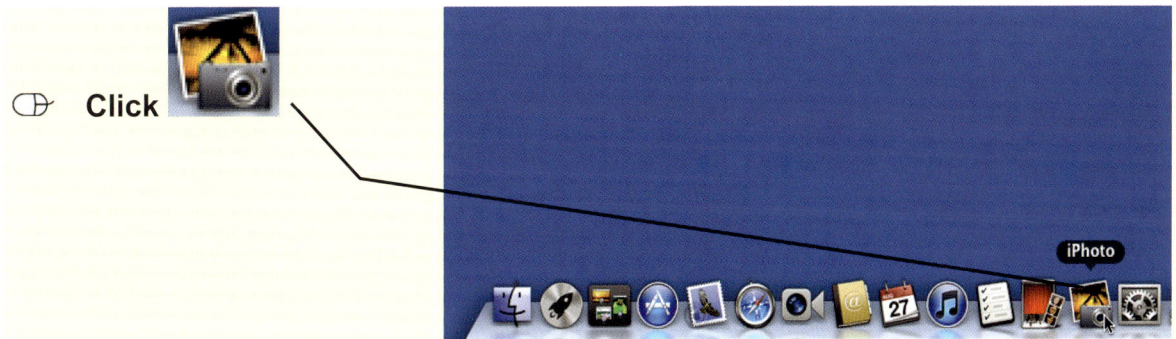

☞ **Click**

If the *Dock* on your computer does not contain the *iPhoto* program, you can also open the program by using *Finder*:

☞ **Open** *Finder* ⚒¹

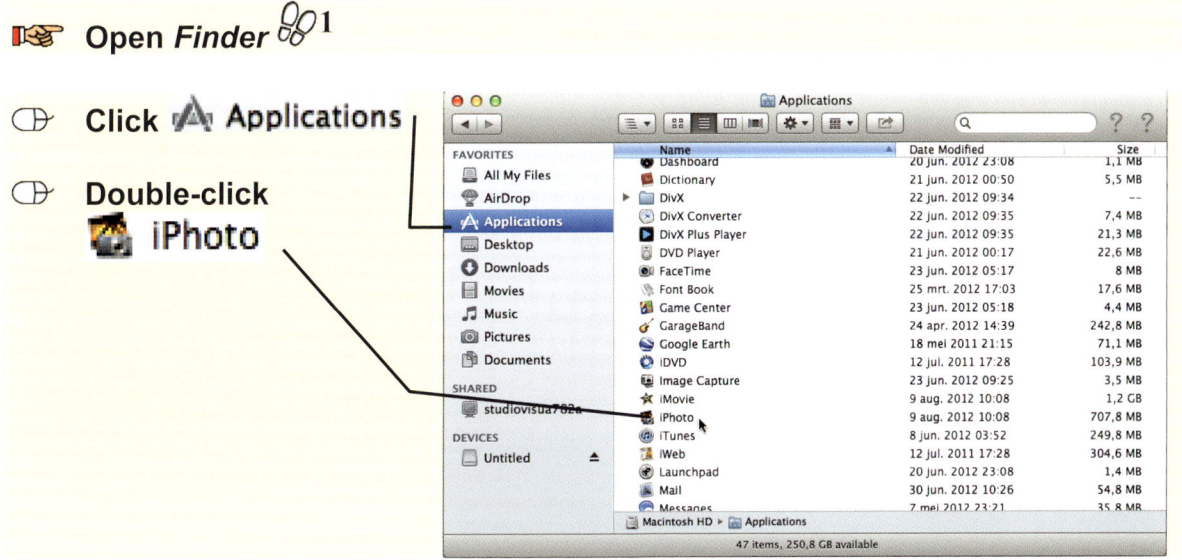

☞ **Click** **Applications**

☞ **Double-click** **iPhoto**

If this is the first time you use *iPhoto*, you will be asked whether you want to start up the program automatically, every time you connect a digital camera (or a device containing a camera):

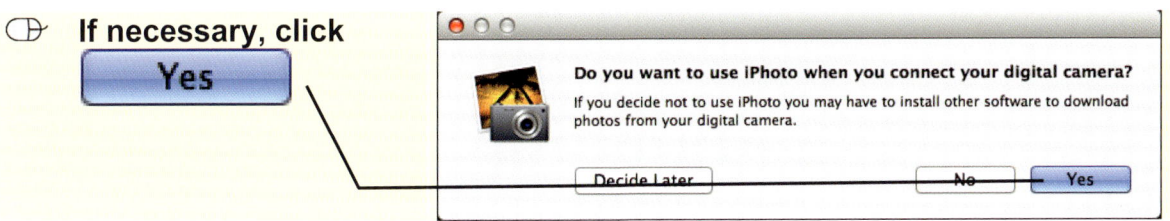

☞ **If necessary, click** **Yes**

You can always change this option later on. In the *Tips* at the end of this chapter you can read how to do this.

Next you will be asked if you want to be able to view the photos on a map. If your digital camera can store GPS coordinates along with the photos, *iPhoto* will be able to find the location where the picture has been taken. We will not be discussing this feature in this book.

 Please note:
Not all cameras are equipped with the option for storing GPS coordinates, so you may not be able to use this setting. However, the iPhone and the iPad will automatically geotag photos for you, if you have set Location Services to 'ON'.

☞ **Click**

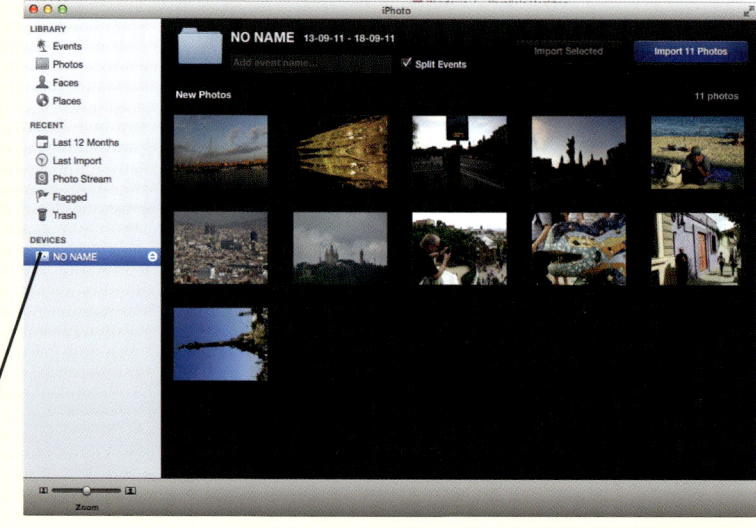

You will see the *iPhoto* window:

You will see different pictures in your own window.

By **DEVICES** you will see the name of the device that contains the photos, in this example the device is called 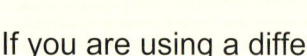.

If you are using a different device, you might see 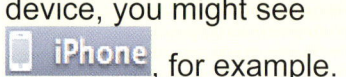, for example.

 HELP! Other programs have been opened too.
If you connect your camera to your computer, another program may open up, usually a program that comes with your camera. You can close that program:

☞ **If necessary, stop the program** ℘²

Chapter 1 Working with Photos **21**

Before you start the importing process, you can enter a name that describes the subject of the pictures. In this example, the digital camera contains a number of pictures taken on a trip to Barcelona:

☞ **Click** Add event name...

⌨ **Type a name for the event:** `Barcelona trip`

Now you can import the photos:

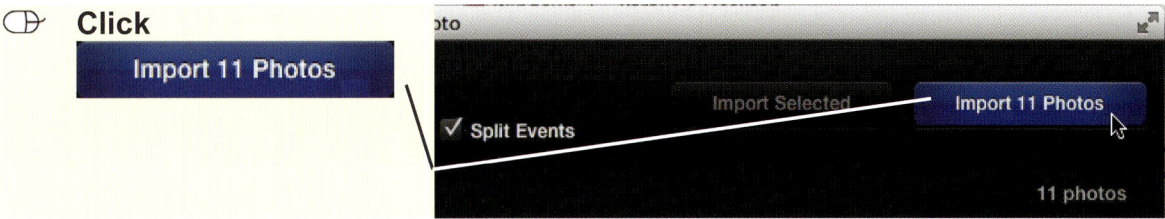

☞ **Click** Import 11 Photos

💡 Tip
Import selected photos
If you do not want to import all of the photos, you can select a number of them use the Command key to do this:

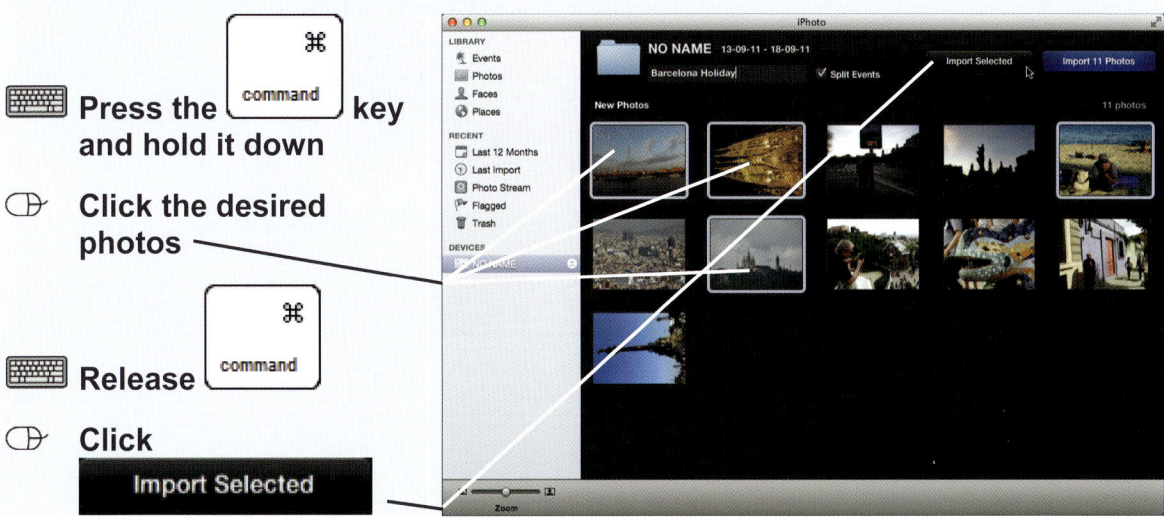

⌨ **Press the** ⌘ command **key and hold it down**

☞ **Click the desired photos**

⌨ **Release** ⌘ command

☞ **Click** Import Selected

You will see the imported photos appear on your screen, one by one:

A blue progress bar indicates the status of the import operation:

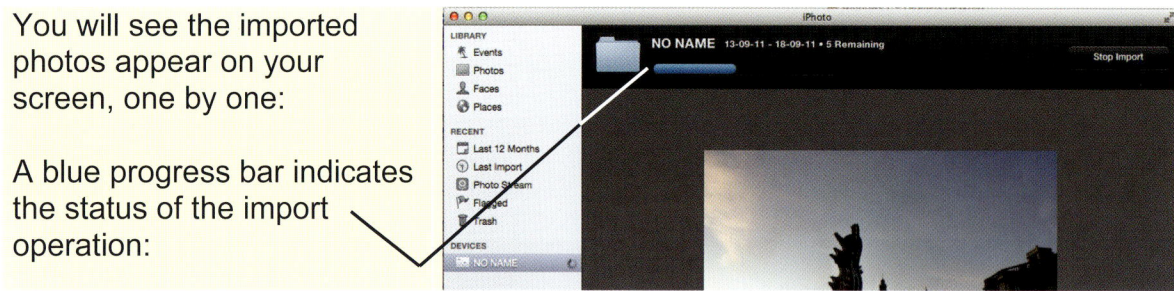

Now the photos have been transferred to *iPhoto*, but they have not been stored in a separate folder in *Finder*. If you want to import photos to a specific folder in *Finder*, you can use *PhotoLoader*. In the *Tips* at the end of this chapter you can read how to use *PhotoLoader*.

1.2 Deactivate and Remove the Camera

After you have finished importing the photos you can deactivate your digital camera (or other device) and safely disconnect it from your *Mac*:

☞ **Click** ⊖ **by the name of your camera, for example** NO NAME **or** iPhone

Or use the Control key:

☞ **Click** control

☞ **Click the camera**

☞ **Click** Eject

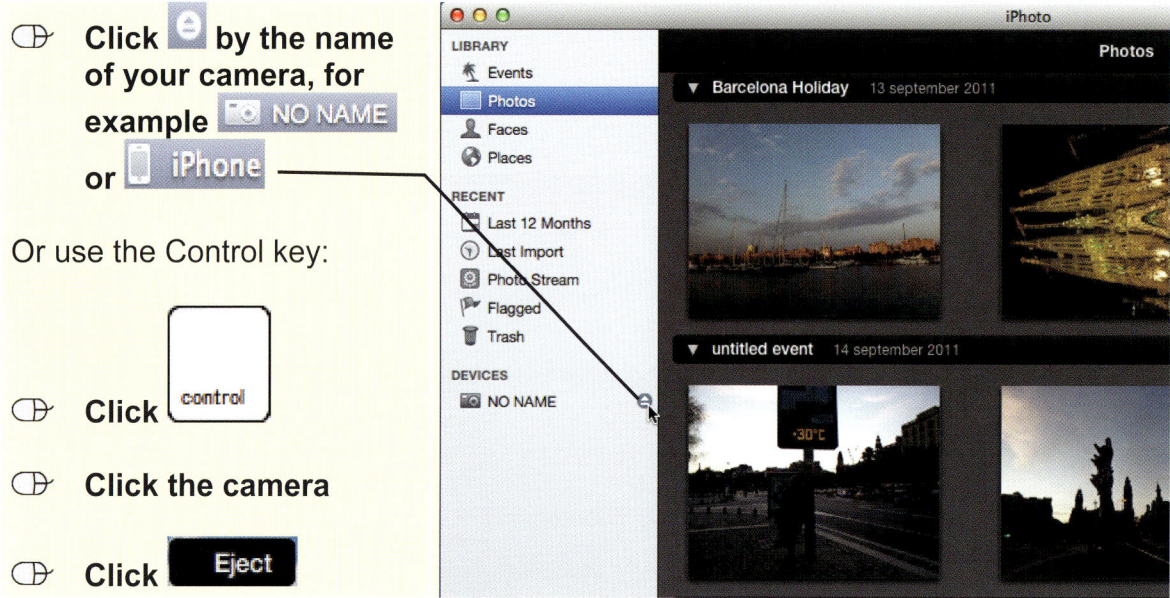

Chapter 1 Working with Photos   23

You will see that the camera has disappeared from the *iPhoto* window:

Now you can safely disconnect the camera from your computer.

☞ **Disconnect the digital camera from your *Mac's* USB port**

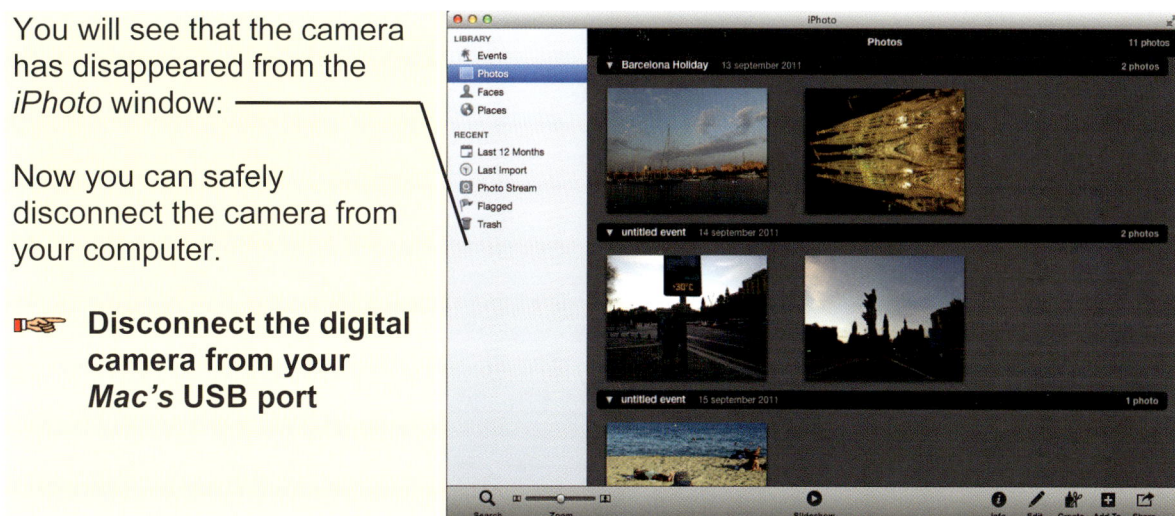

1.3 Rotating a Photo

You can follow the examples in this chapter by using the practice files that go with it. This way, you will see the same images on your screen as in this book. You can download these practice files from the website that accompanies this book and import them into *iPhoto*. In *Appendix C Download Practice Files* you can read how to do this.

☞ **Perform the operations described in *Appendix C Download Practice Files***

⊕ **Click** Photos

You will see the practice files:

Some of the photos are turned the wrong way. You can easily set them upright:

⊕ **Double-click**

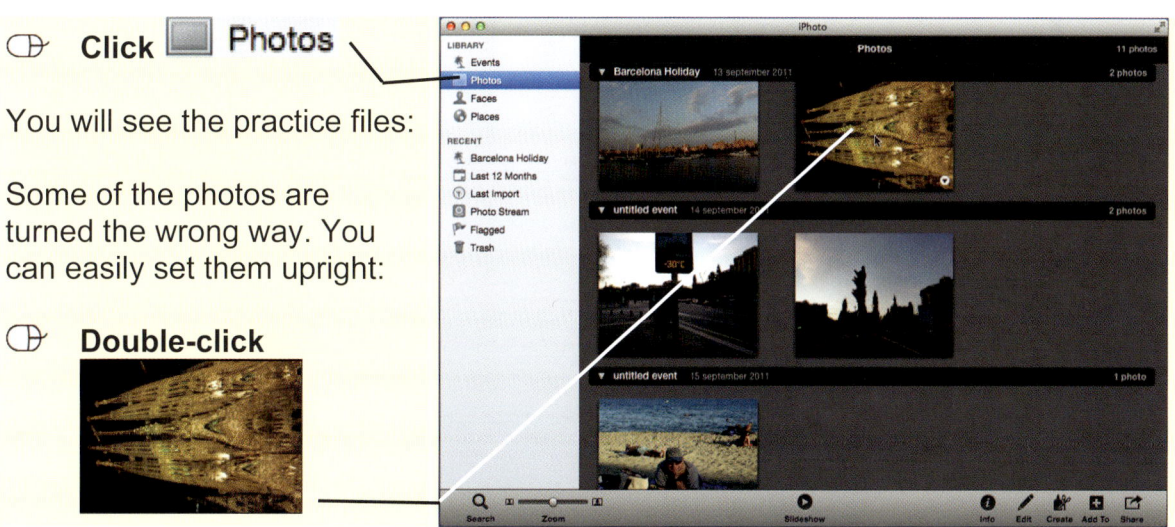

⊕ Click **Edit**

The photo will be opened in the edit window:

⊕ Click **Rotate** three times

Now the photo will be displayed in the right way:

⊕ Click **Photos**

☞ **Rotate the last photo in the same manner** ⚸¹⁷

☞ **Go back to the photo overview** ⚸¹³

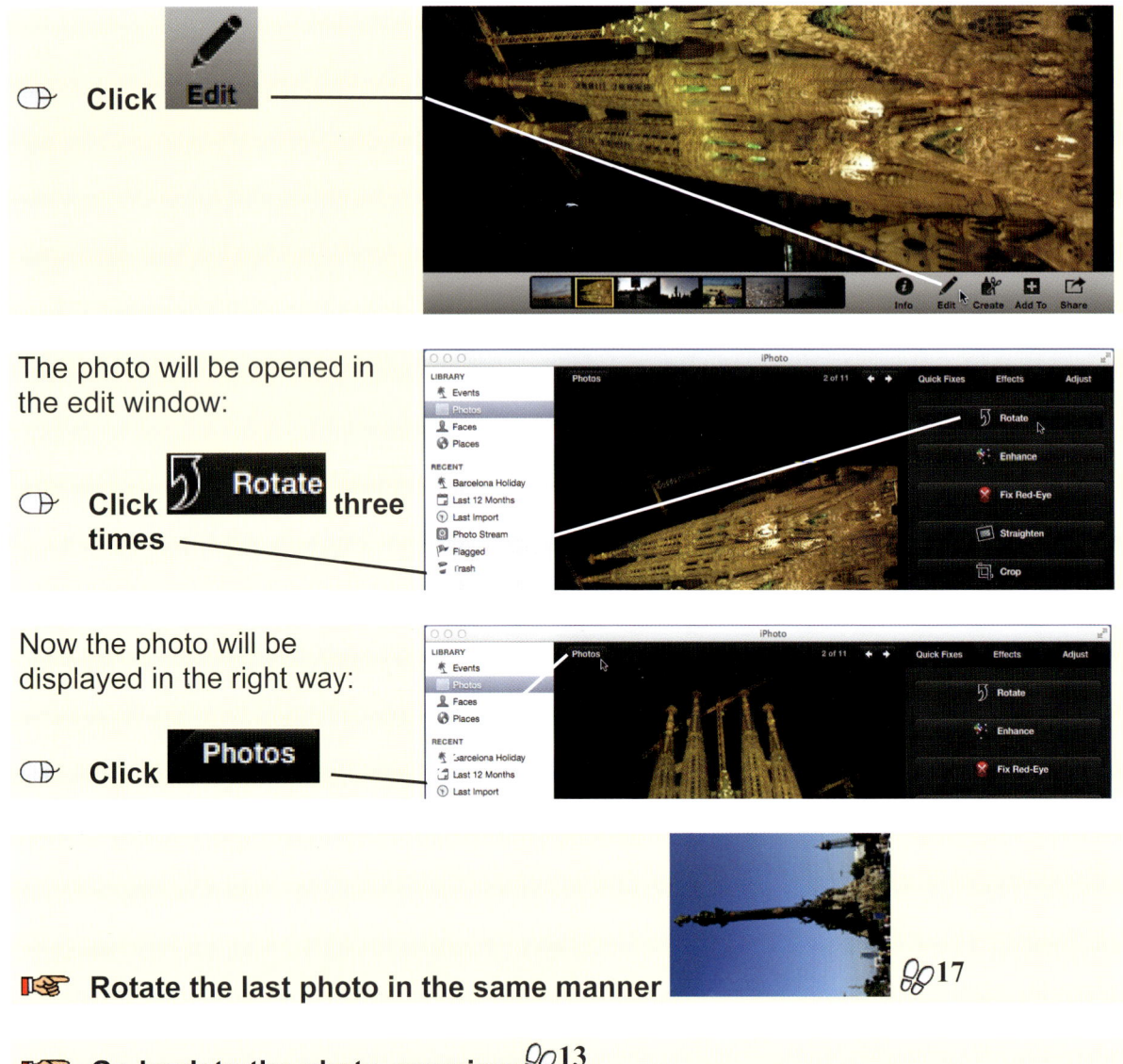

Chapter 1 Working with Photos 25

1.4 Creating an Album

Quite often, the photos you have imported will not all belong together. They may have been taken at different occasions, such as special events or various holidays. You can organize your photo collection by storing the photos in different albums.

This is how you create an album:

First, you select (or *flag*) the photos you want to store in the album:

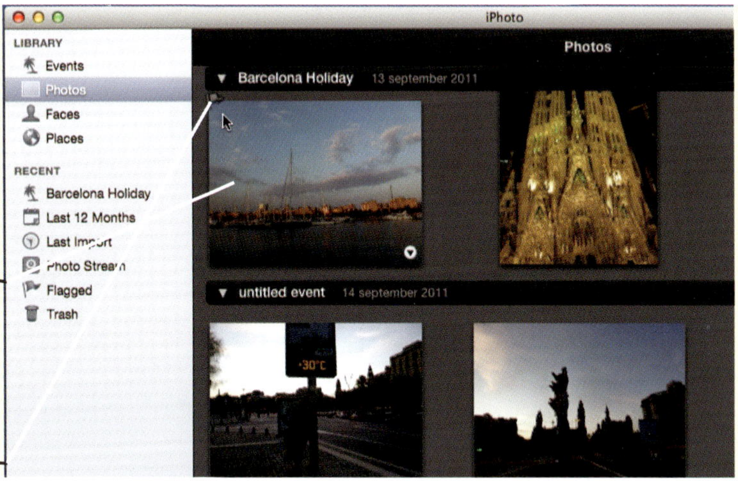

⊕ **Position the mouse pointer on the first photo**

You will see a little grey flag :

⊕ **Click**

Now you will see a little orange flag near the corner of the photo:

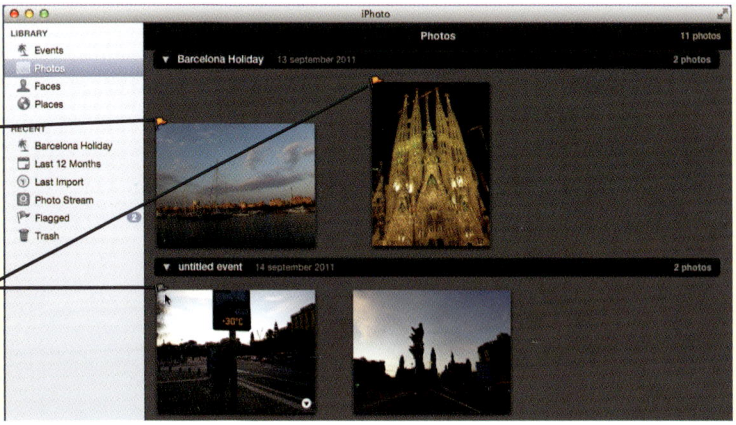

⊕ **By the second and third photo, click**

💡 Tip
Undo the flags
You can undo the flag on a photo by clicking the orange flag in the left-hand corner.

To view only the flagged photos:

⊕ Click **Flagged**

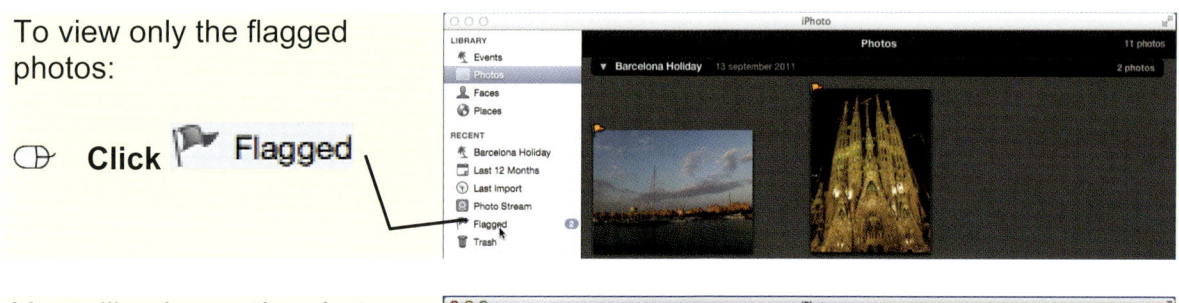

You will only see the photos that have been flagged:

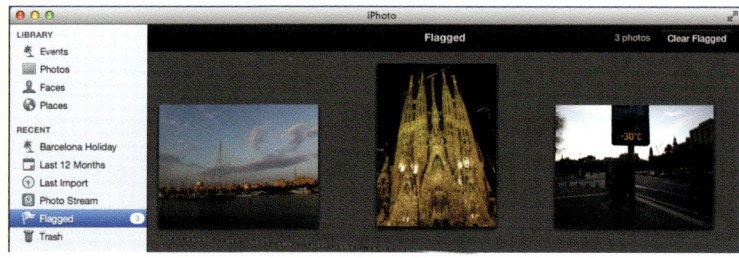

 Tip
Flag in different events
By default, *iPhoto* divides the photos into different events. Pictures that have been taken on the same day are usually combined and stored in the same event. In *iPhoto*, an event is a kind of folder.
By flagging photos you can also combine photos from different events in the same album.

Now you can create an album that contains the photos you have flagged:

⊕ Click **Create**

⊕ Click **Album**

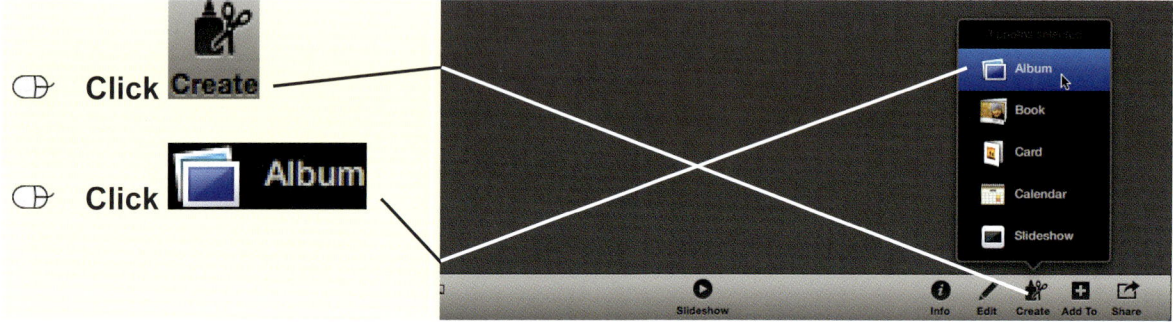

Chapter 1 Working with Photos   27

You have created a new album:

You need to enter a name for this album:

⌨ **Type:** `Barcelona Trip`

⌨ **Press** enter/return

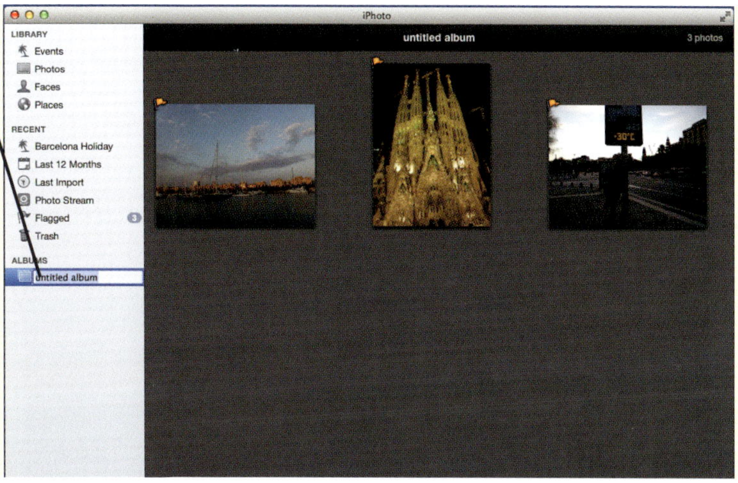

The album has been named:

The markers/flags in the photos are no longer necessary. You can remove them. To do this, you first need to select all the photos with the Command and A keys:

⌨ **Press** ⌘ + A

All the photos in the folder will be selected:

At the top of the window:

☞ **Click Photos**

☞ **Click Unflag Photos**

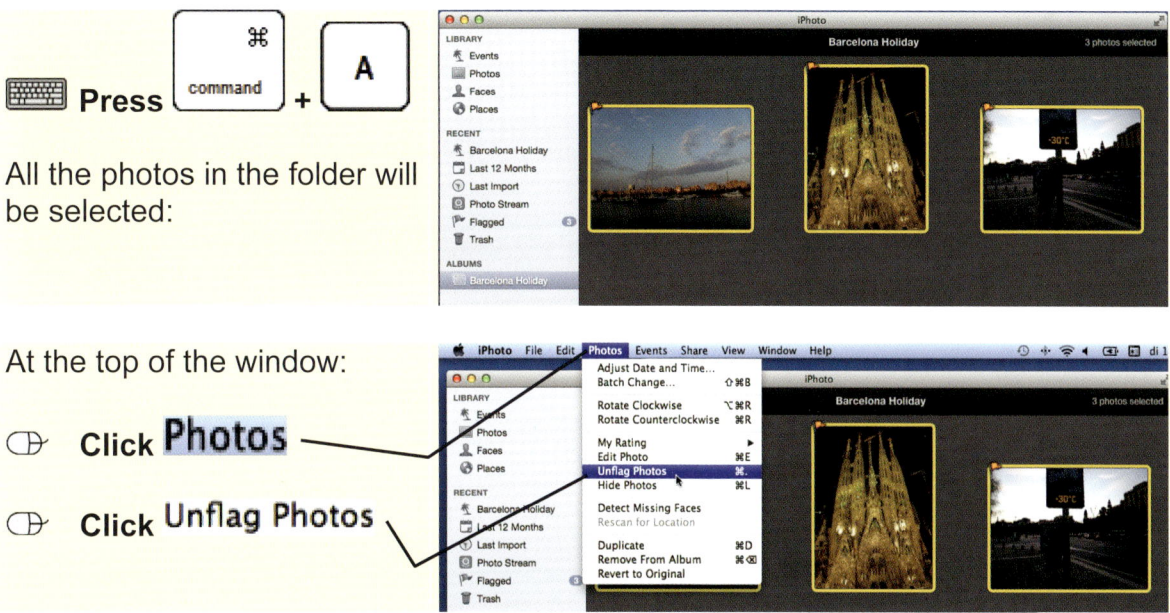

Now the flags have been removed from the photos.

1.5 Adding Photos To an Album

Once you have created an album, you can add more photos to it:

⊕ Click **Photos**

⌨ Press the **command** key and hold it down

⊕ Click the photos no. 4, 5 and 6

⊕ Click **Add To**

⊕ Click **Album**

You will see an overview of the albums in *iPhoto*:

⊕ Click **Barcelona Holiday**

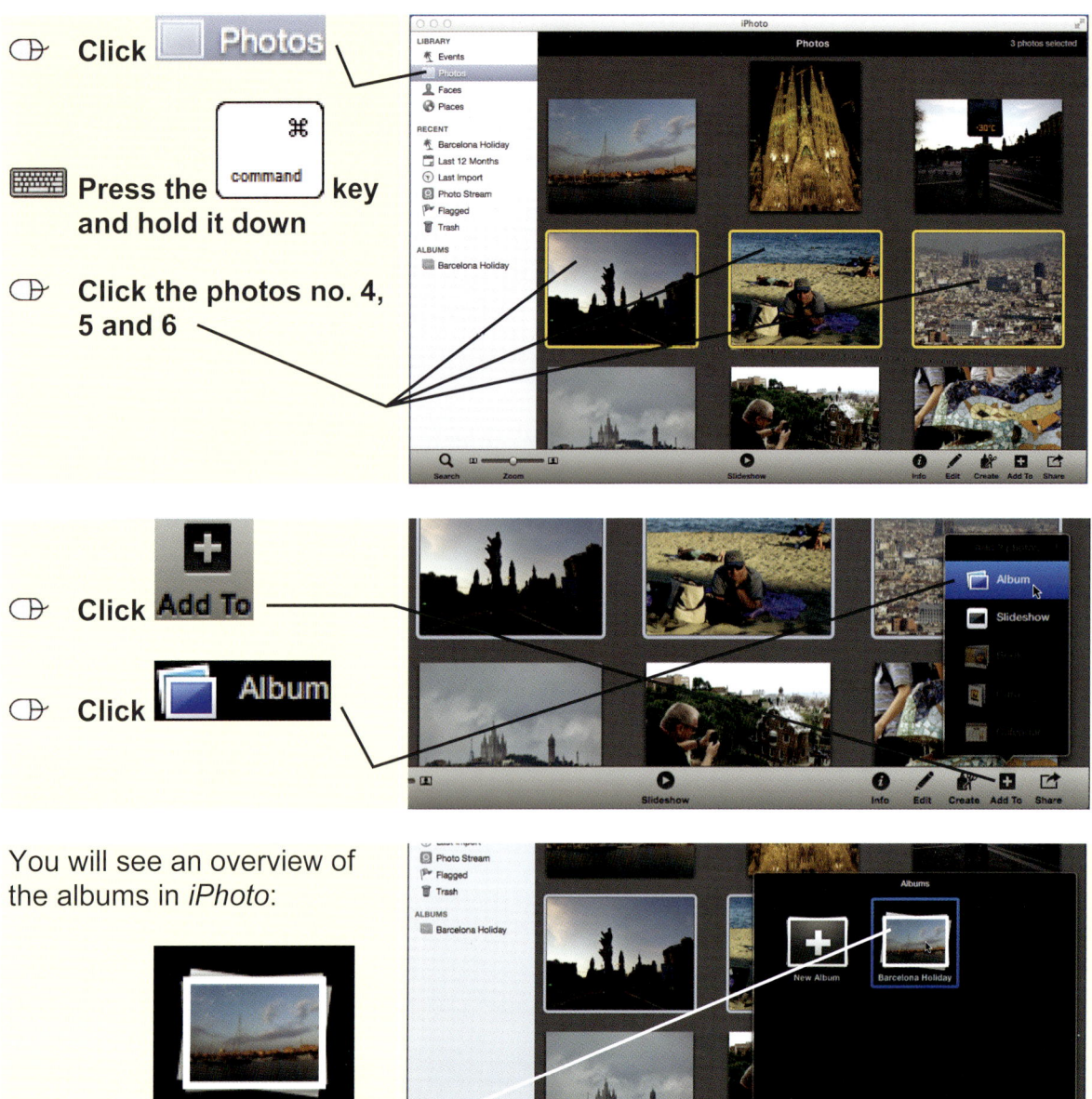

Chapter 1 Working with Photos

⊕ **Click**
▢ Barcelona Holiday

You will see that the photos have been added to the album:

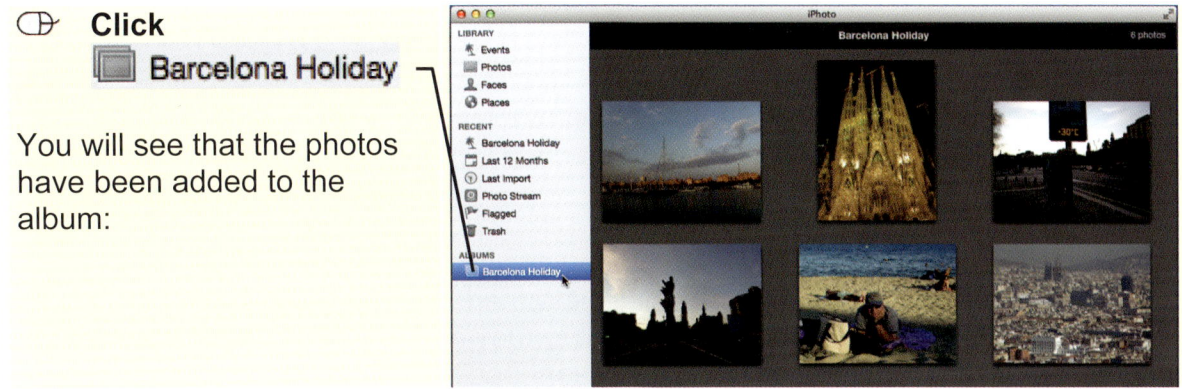

1.6 Removing a Photo From an Album

If you want to remove a photo from an album you need to use a context (pop-up) menu. This menu will be displayed after you have right-clicked an item with the mouse. If you are using a keyboard, you can right-click with the Control key.

⌨ **Press the [control] key and hold it down**

⊕ **Click the first photo**

You will see a menu:

⊕ **Click**
Remove From Album

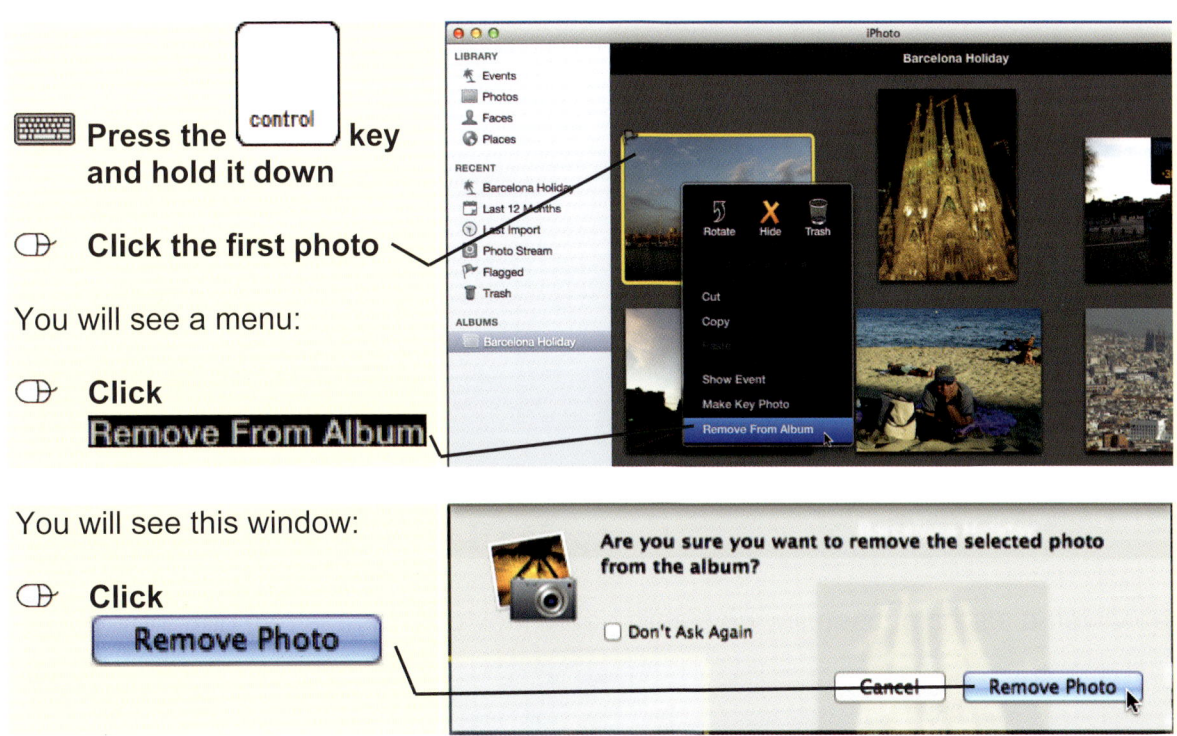

You will see this window:

⊕ **Click**
Remove Photo

The photo has been removed from the album:

But the photo is still stored in the *iPhoto* library on your computer.

 Please note:
Take care when you delete a photo from the library. If you remove a photo from the library, it will be removed from any album in which it was put and from the *iPhoto* library folder as well. All imported photos are stored in this folder by default.

1.7 Creating a Slideshow

You can use the photos on your computer to create a slideshow. When you play this slideshow, the photos will be displayed one by one. This is how you play a slideshow of the photos in an album:

☞ **Click the first photo**

☞ **Click Slideshow**

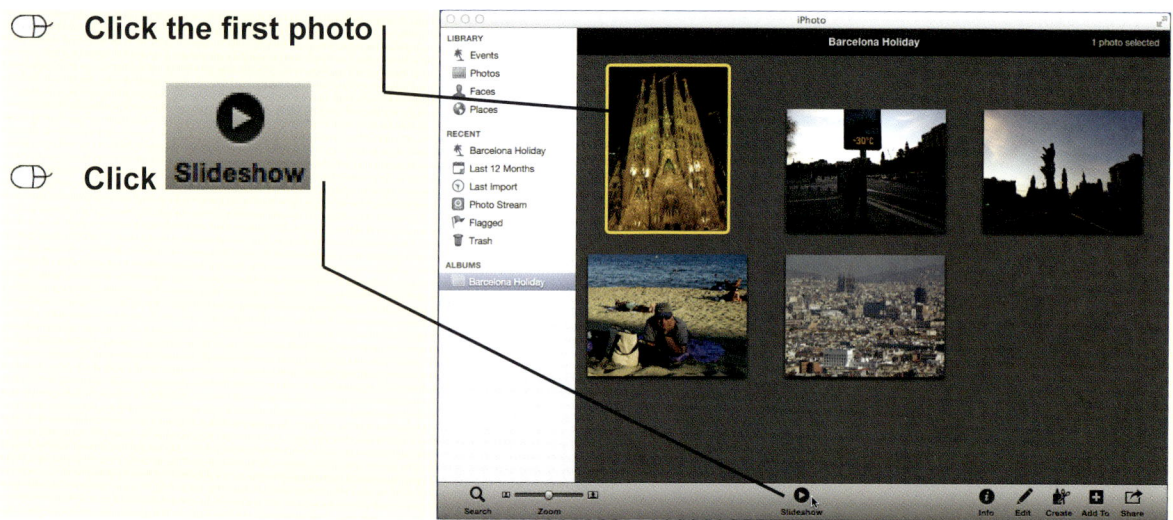

Chapter 1 Working with Photos **31**

Before you start actually playing the slideshow you can set a number of options. You can choose a theme, for example. A theme determines the way in which the photos are displayed:

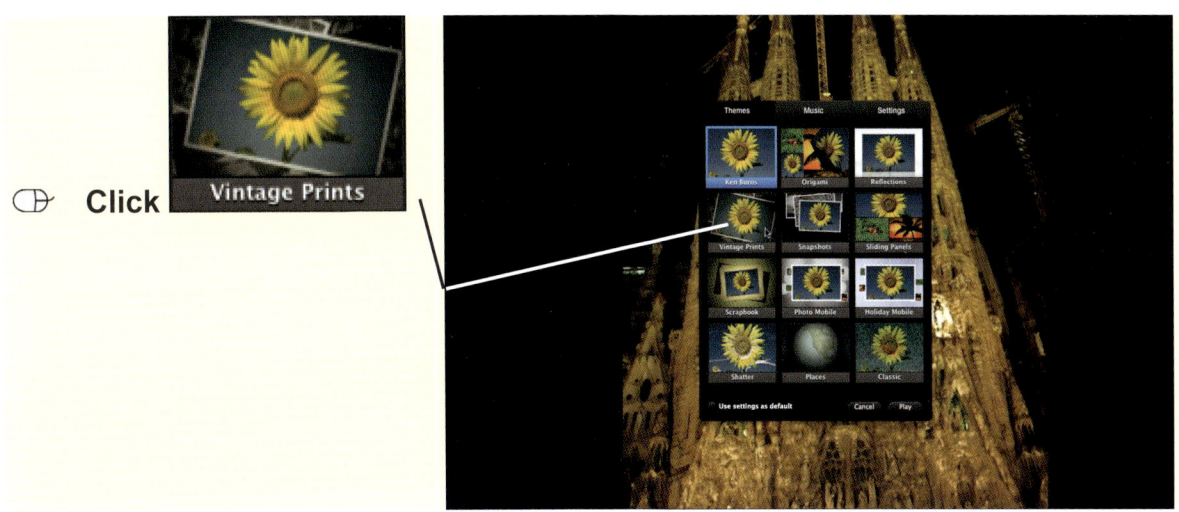

☞ Click **Vintage Prints**

💡 Tip
Viewing a theme
If you position the mouse pointer on a theme, you will see a preview of this theme.

At a later stage you can adapt even more settings for your slideshow. For instance, you can play music during the slideshow:

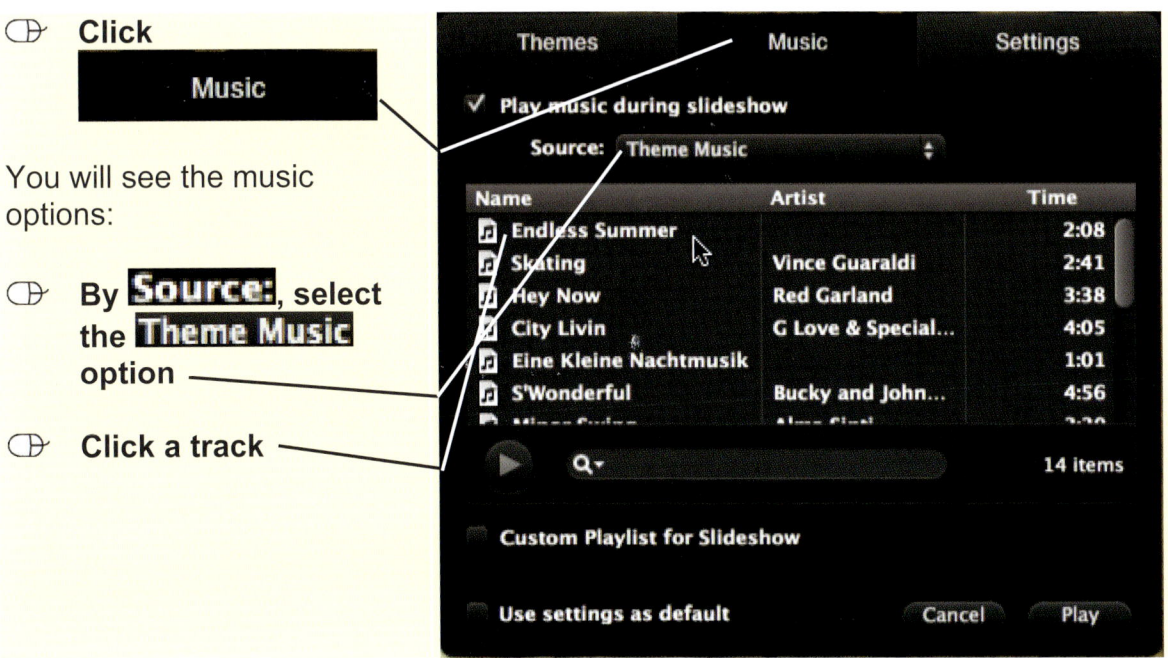

☞ Click **Music**

You will see the music options:

☞ By **Source:**, select the **Theme Music** option

☞ Click a track

32   iPhoto, iMovie and Other Useful Mac Programs for Seniors

 Tip
Music from iTunes
If the *iTunes library* is installed on your computer you can add a track from this library to the slideshow. You can select such a track by Source:.

You can change various other slideshow settings too:

☞ **Click** Settings

You will see the settings tab:

Time period per slide:

Adapt the slideshow to the length of the music track:

Other options:

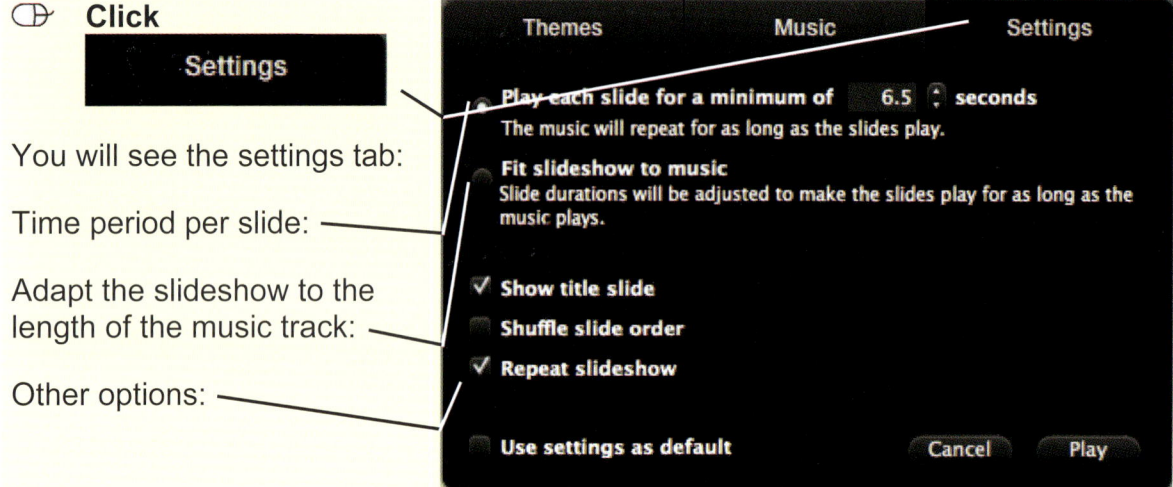

After you have set all the desired options, you can play the slideshow:

☞ **Click** Play

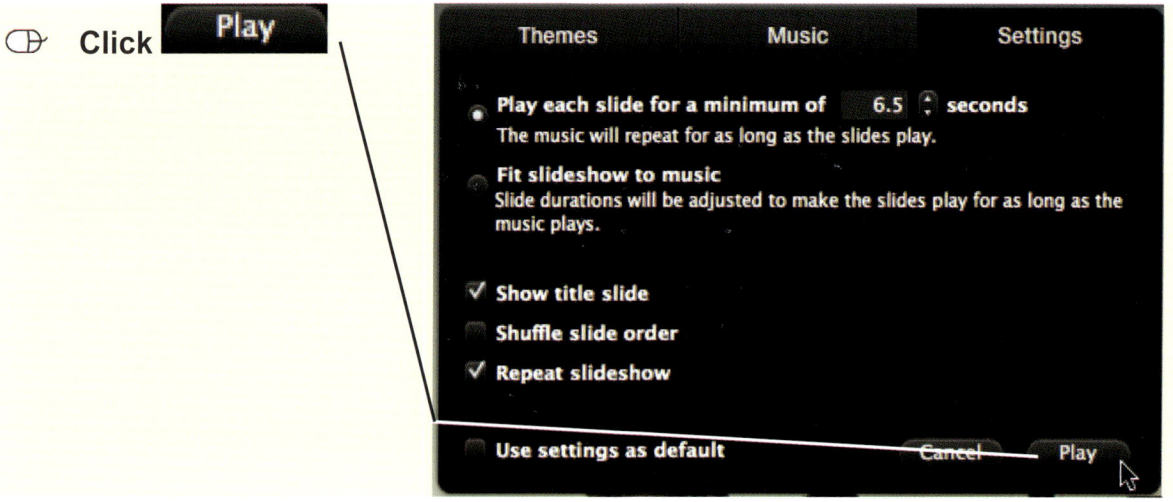

Chapter 1 Working with Photos **33**

The slideshow will be played. You can pause the slideshow whenever you want:

Move the mouse pointer to the bottom of the screen:

You will see the control buttons:

 **Click** ⏸

The slideshow will be paused:

 **Click** ▶

Playback will continue.

There are several control buttons:

⬅ Previous slide.

➡ Next slide.

🖼 Set a theme.

🎵 Set a sound track.

⚙ Select additional settings.

You can stop the slideshow:

☞ Click ⊗

1.8 Saving a Slideshow

Besides creating and playing a slideshow, you can also save it and play the slideshow later on. You can create a slideshow of all the photos in an album and save it. To add all the photos in an album to a slideshow:

☞ **Click next to the photos**

☞ **Click Create**

☞ **Click Slideshow**

Now you can set the properties for the slideshow:

☞ **Click Themes**

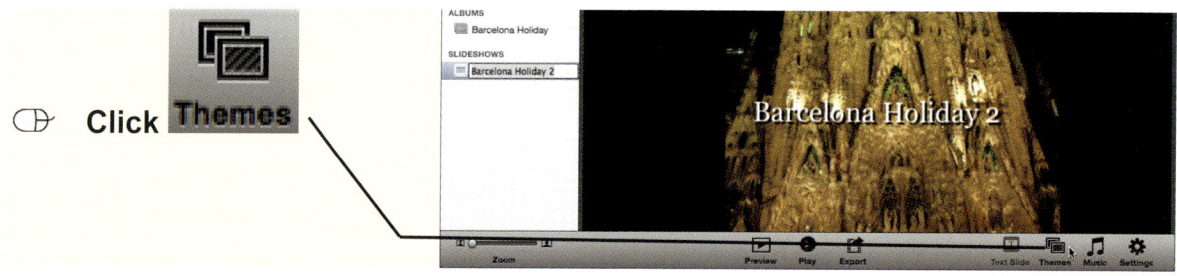

Chapter 1 Working with Photos 35

☞ **Click** Vintage Prints

At the bottom of the window:

☞ **Click** Choose

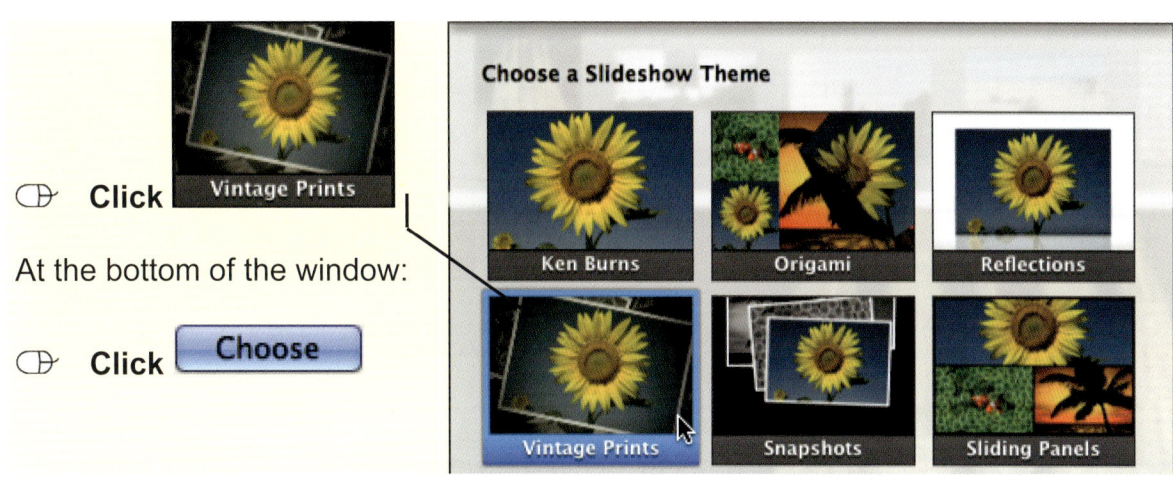

You can change the other settings as well:

👉 **If you wish, you can adjust the options for the Music and Settings**

With the Preview option you can watch a preview of the slideshow:

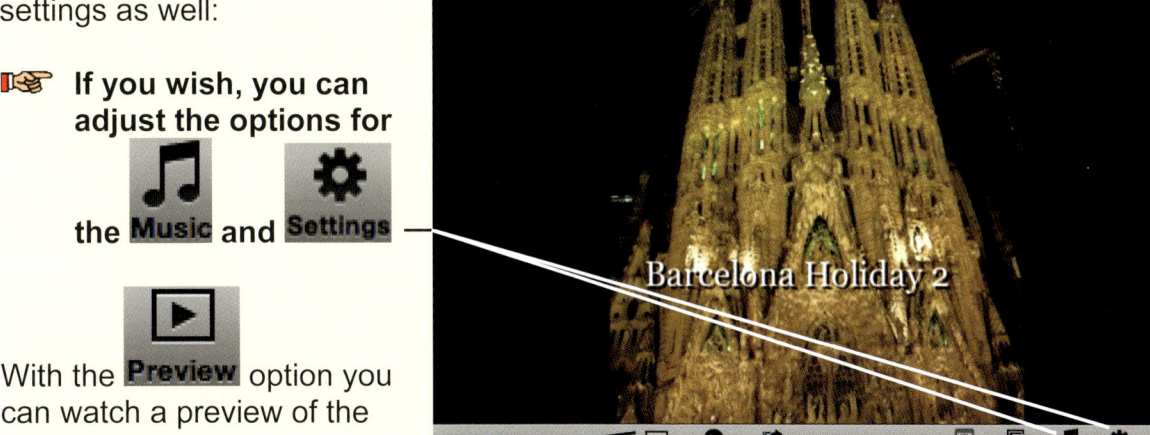

Finally, you will need to enter a name for the slideshow:

⌨ **Type:** Barcelona 2010

⌨ **Press** enter/return

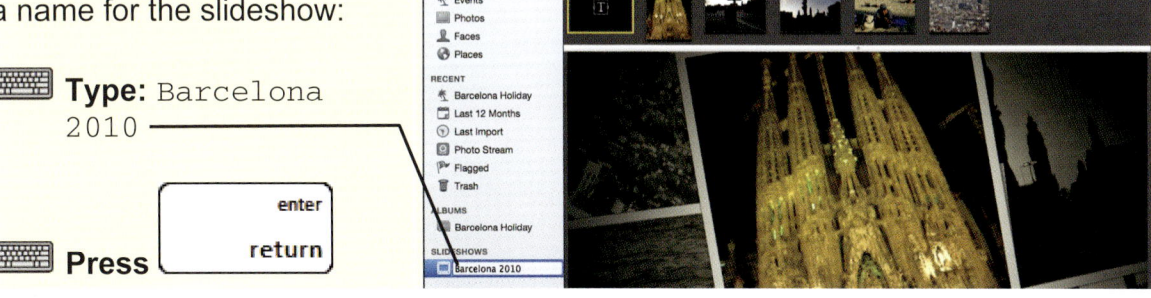

Your slideshow has been saved:

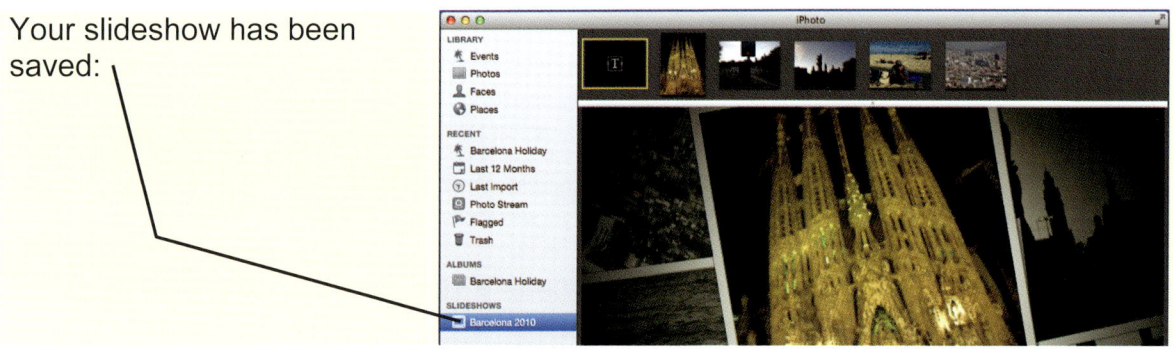

From now on, all you need to do to play this slideshow is select the slideshow and then press  to play it.

 Tip
Select photos for a slideshow
You are not obliged to use all the photos in an album to create a slideshow. You can also select a number of specific photos by flagging them. See *section 1.5 Adding Photos To an Album*.

1.9 Deleting an Album

If you no longer need an album you can delete it. This operation will only delete the album, not the photos that are stored on your *Mac*. You can use the Control key to delete an album.

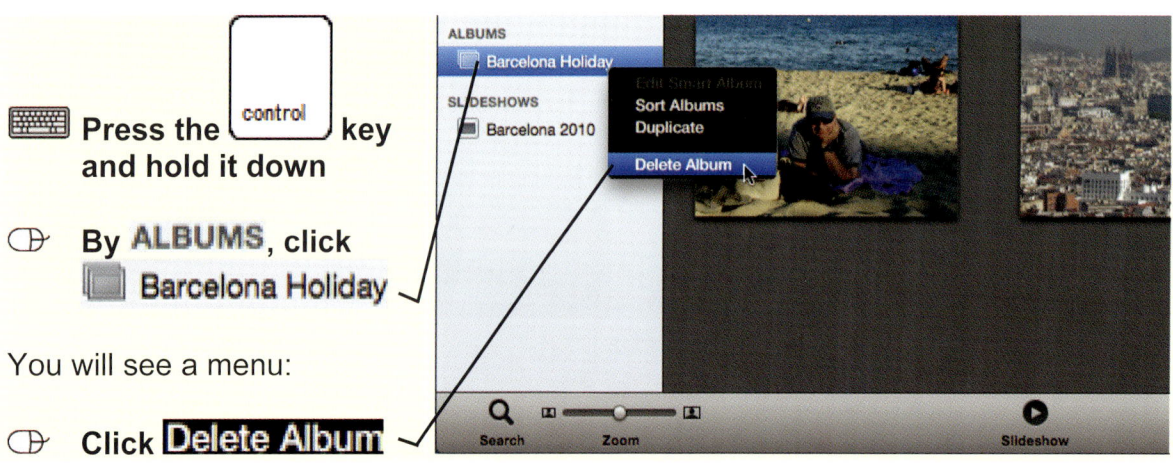

⌨ **Press the** `control` **key and hold it down**

☞ **By ALBUMS, click Barcelona Holiday**

You will see a menu:

☞ **Click Delete Album**

Chapter 1 Working with Photos 37

You will need to confirm the deletion:

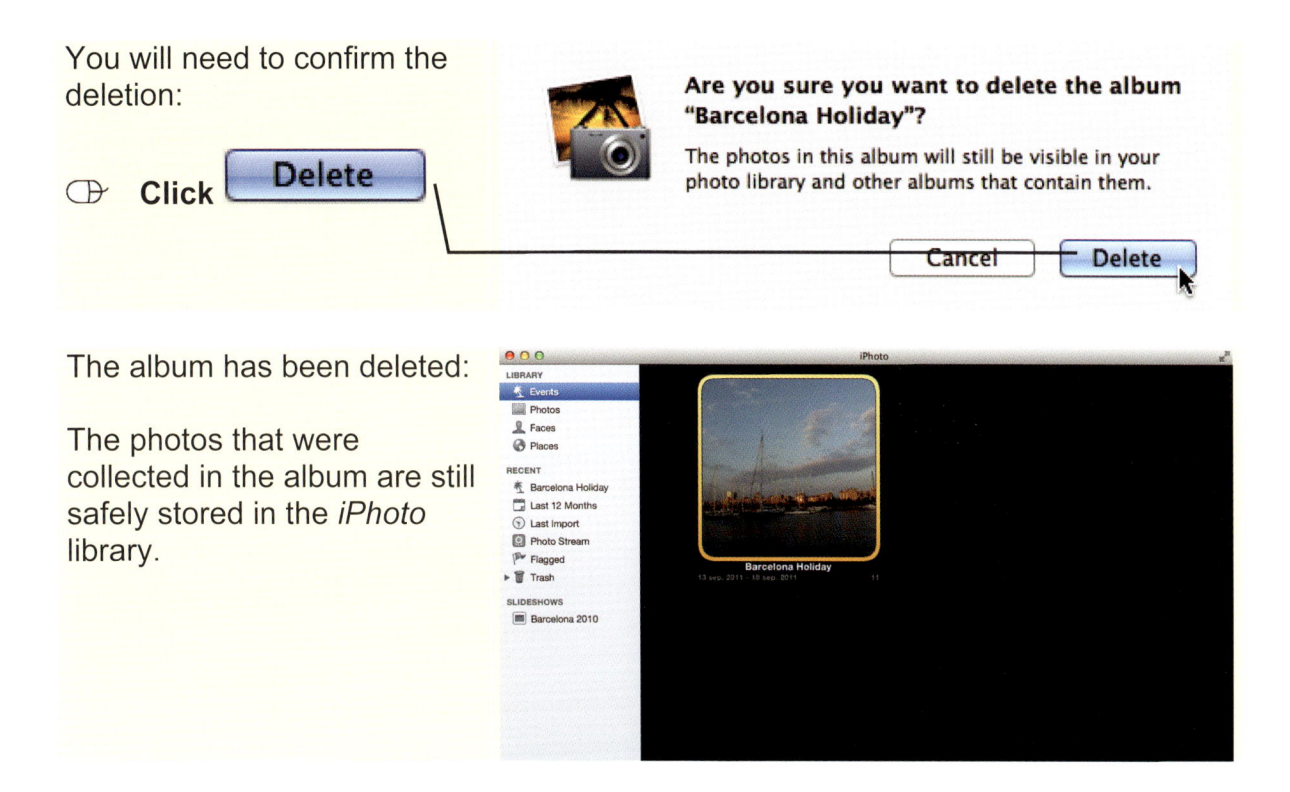

☞ Click **Delete**

The album has been deleted:

The photos that were collected in the album are still safely stored in the *iPhoto* library.

1.10 Sending a Photo By Email

In *iPhoto* you can easily send a photo to someone by email.
When you want to send photos by mail, you need to keep in mind that most email services have size restrictions. You may not be able to send very large picture files or multiple photos at once. Remember that the recipient's mailbox might also overflow due to the size of the files you are sending. This is how you send a photo:

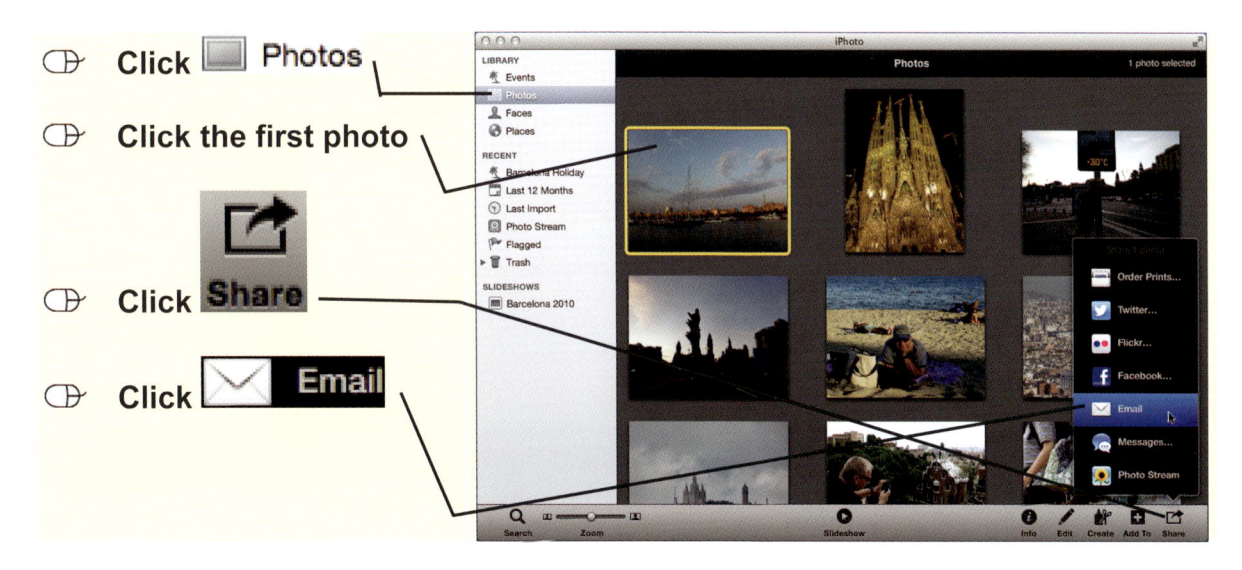

☞ Click **Photos**

☞ Click the first photo

☞ Click **Share**

☞ Click **Email**

If you have an account from an email service such as *Hotmail* or *Gmail*, you can add that account here. You can then send an email message directly from *iPhoto* without the necessity of opening *Mail*. You can present your photos in different themes (frames) and arrange or position them on the page as desired. It is also possible to use *Mail* to send your photos. See the *Tips* section at the end of this chapter to learn how to do this.

If you want to use this option:

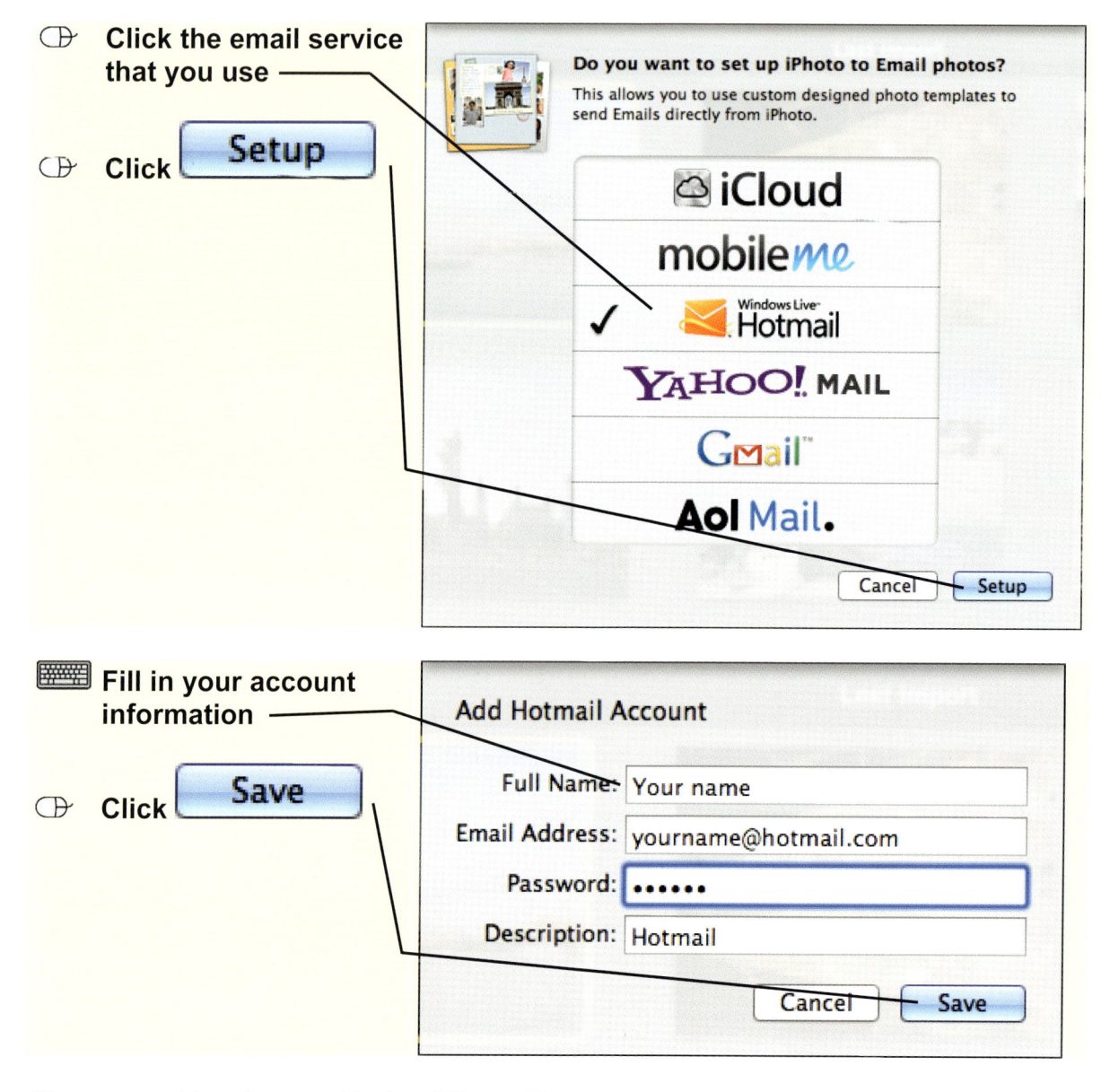

☞ **Click the email service that you use**

☞ **Click Setup**

☞ **Fill in your account information**

☞ **Click Save**

The account has been added to *iPhoto*. The next time you want to send a photo in an email you will not need to fill in this information.

Chapter 1 Working with Photos 39

Your email account has already been entered. You can now select a template for the photo. This template determines how the photo will be displayed:

☞ **Click Snapshots**

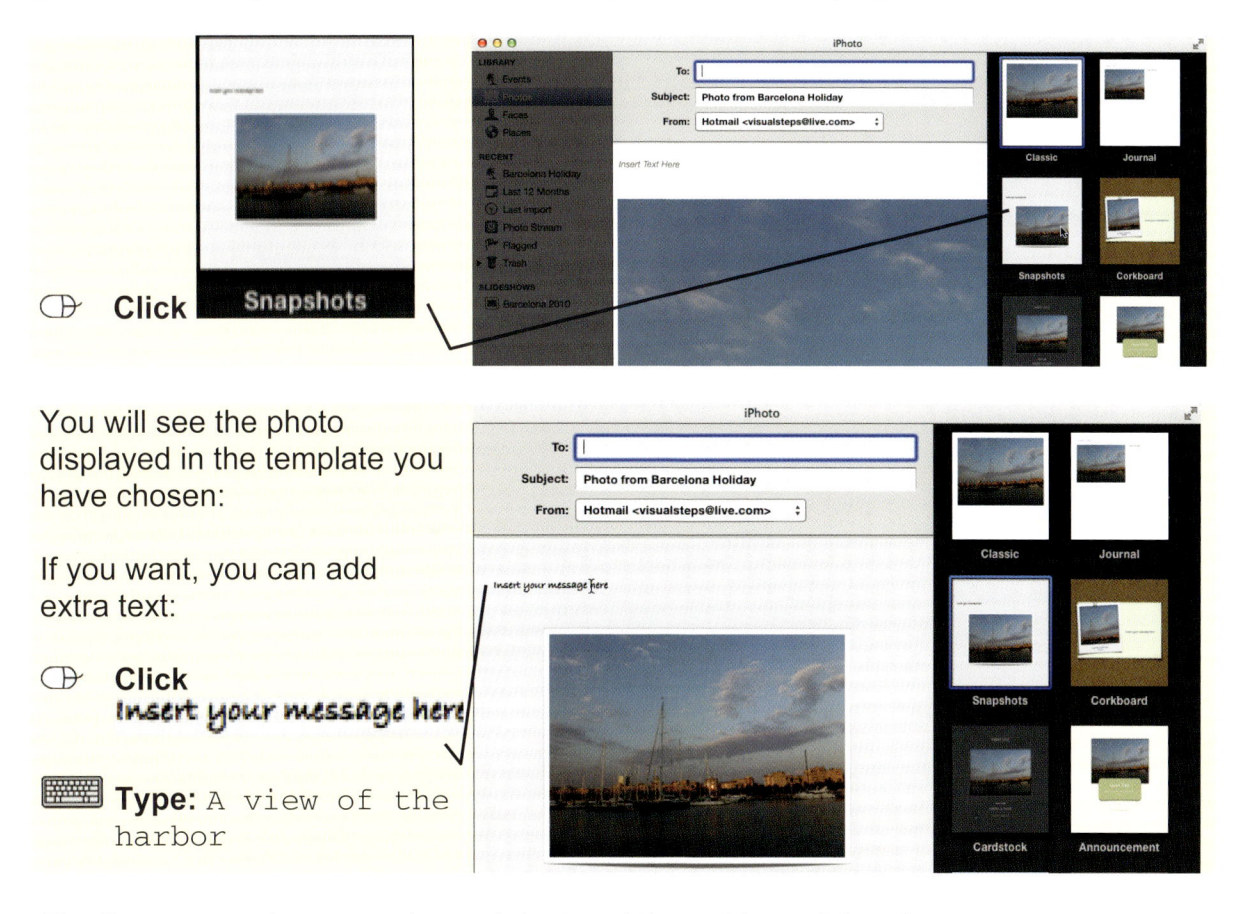

You will see the photo displayed in the template you have chosen:

If you want, you can add extra text:

☞ **Click** *Insert your message here*

⌨ **Type:** A view of the harbor

Finally, you need to enter the recipient and the subject of the photo:

⌨ **By To:, type the recipient's email address**

⌨ **By Subject:, type:** A picture of Barcelona

At the bottom of the window:

☞ **Click Send**

The photo will be sent.

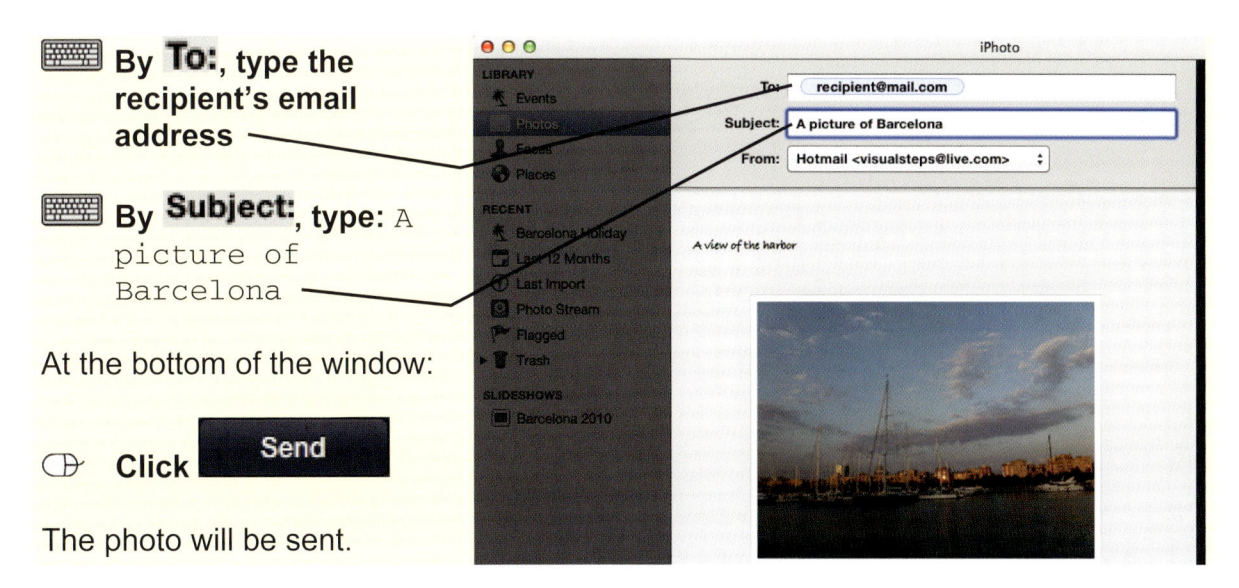

😷 HELP! The photo is not sent.

You will see a message if the photo for some reason or other cannot be sent. This is often caused by the fact that the photos have not been shared or by errors in the settings for the outgoing email:

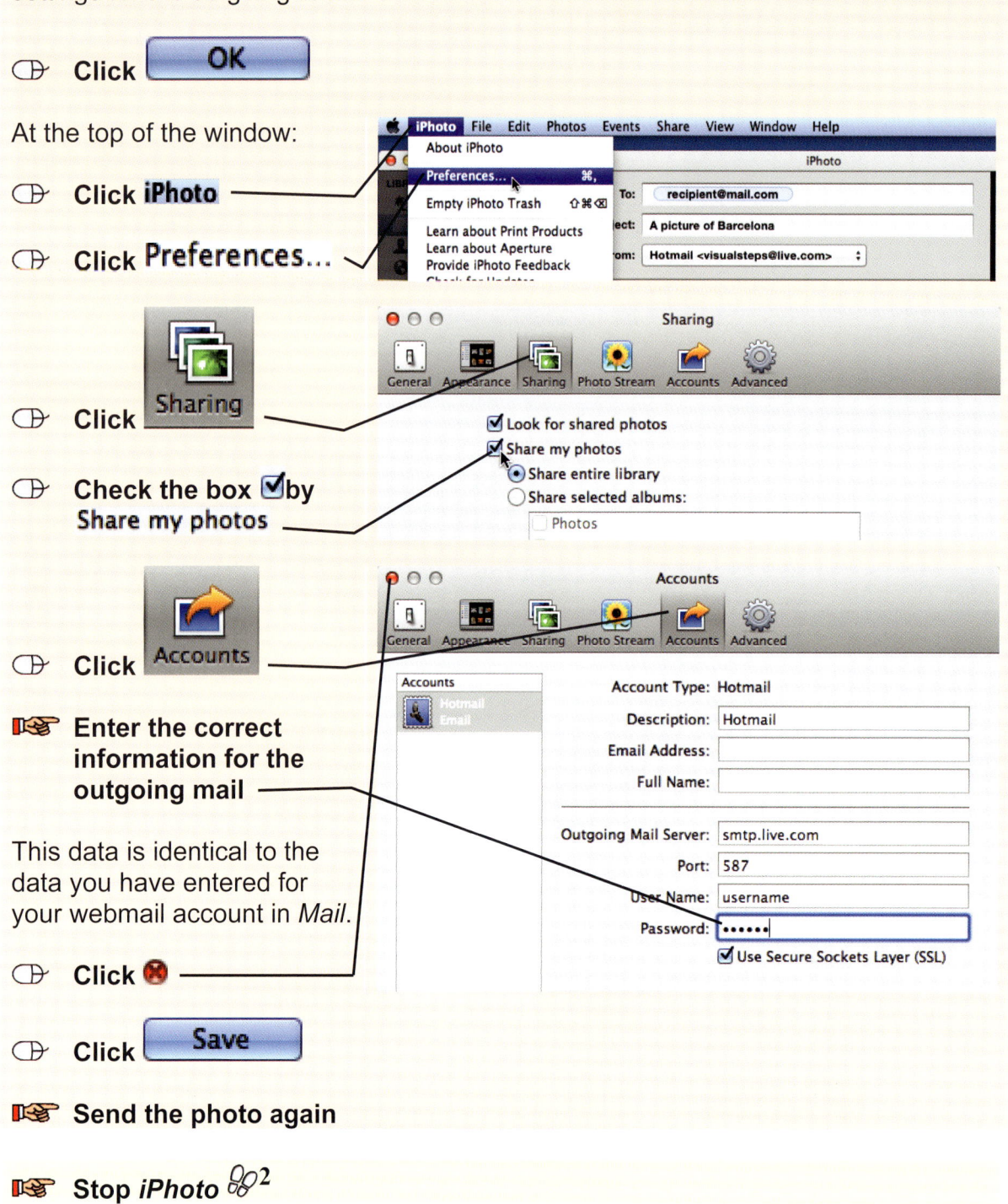

☞ Click **OK**

At the top of the window:

☞ Click *iPhoto*

☞ Click *Preferences...*

☞ Click *Sharing*

☞ Check the box ☑ by *Share my photos*

☞ Click *Accounts*

👉 **Enter the correct information for the outgoing mail**

This data is identical to the data you have entered for your webmail account in *Mail*.

☞ Click ❌

☞ Click **Save**

👉 **Send the photo again**

👉 **Stop *iPhoto* 🐾²**

Chapter 1 Working with Photos **41**

1.11 Viewing Photos with Preview

iPhoto is not the only program that allows you to view photos. *Preview* is another program that lets you view photos. It does not contain as many options but it is quick and easy to use.

By default, *Preview* is opened when you open a photo:

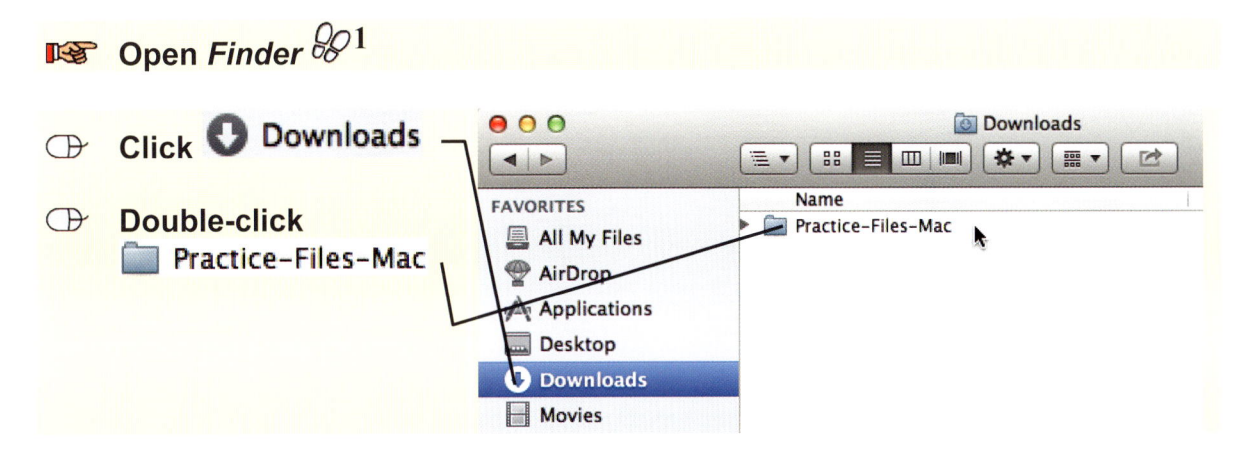

☞ **Open** *Finder* ⅋¹

⊕ **Click** ⬇ **Downloads**

⊕ **Double-click** 📁 **Practice-Files-Mac**

You will see the practice files you have downloaded. You are going to open the photos with the Control key:

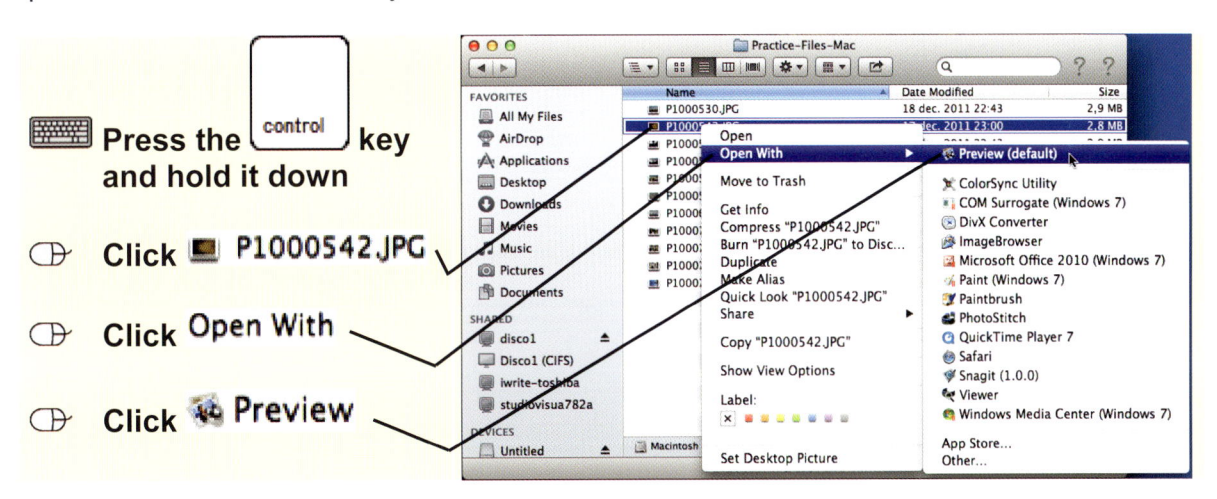

⌨ **Press the** `control` **key and hold it down**

⊕ **Click** 🖼 **P1000542.JPG**

⊕ **Click** **Open With**

⊕ **Click** 🔍 **Preview**

You will see the *Preview* program:

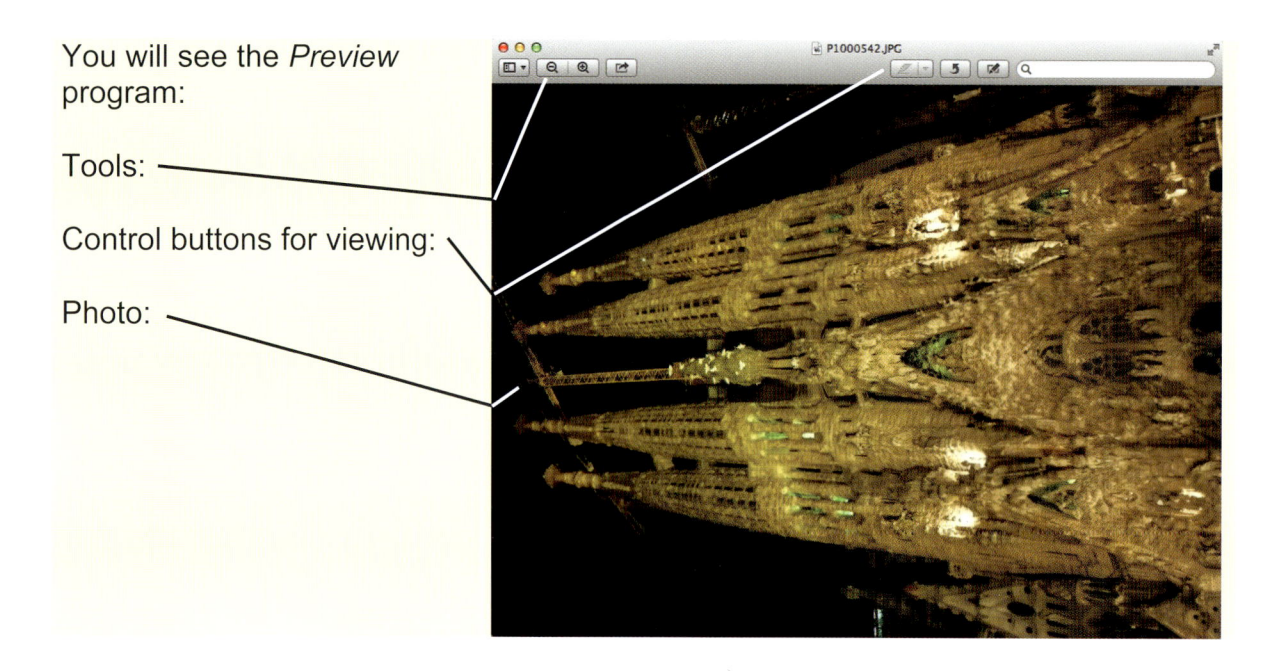

Tools:

Control buttons for viewing:

Photo:

1.12 Editing Photos in Preview

Just like in *iPhoto*, you can edit and adjust photos in *Preview* too. These are some of the things you can do:
- rotate photos;
- enhance photos;
- change the size of a photo;
- crop photos;
- add text and images.

You can try using some of these options with the practice files.

Chapter 1 Working with Photos   **43**

1.13 Rotating a Photo

You can rotate a photo, which is very useful when the photo appears in the wrong orientation:

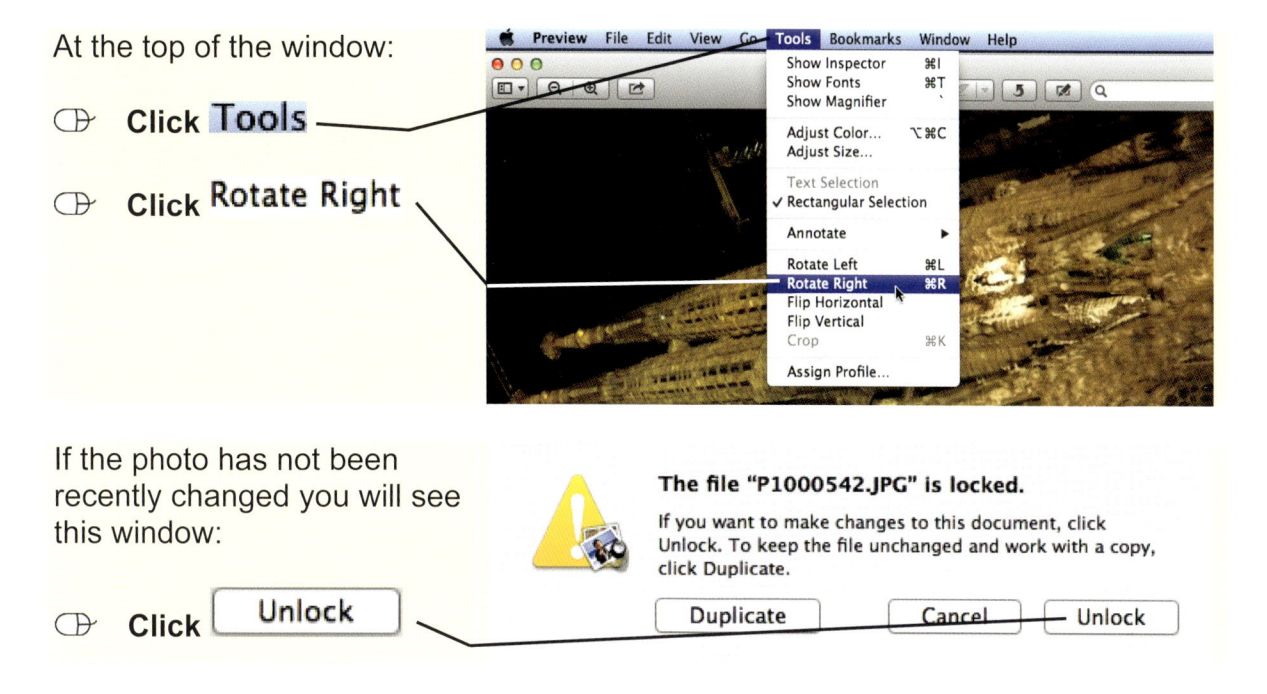

At the top of the window:

☞ Click **Tools**

☞ Click **Rotate Right**

If the photo has not been recently changed you will see this window:

☞ Click **Unlock**

Please note:

If you select **Unlock**, the original photo will be edited. If you prefer to leave the original photo unchanged, you need to click **Duplicate**. This means you will be editing a copy of the original photo.

Now the photo has been rotated and is in the correct position:

💡 Tip
Restore a previous version
In *Preview* you can restore a previous version of the photo. An automatic copy of the photo is already made at regular intervals, but you can also save a particular version of the photo yourself:

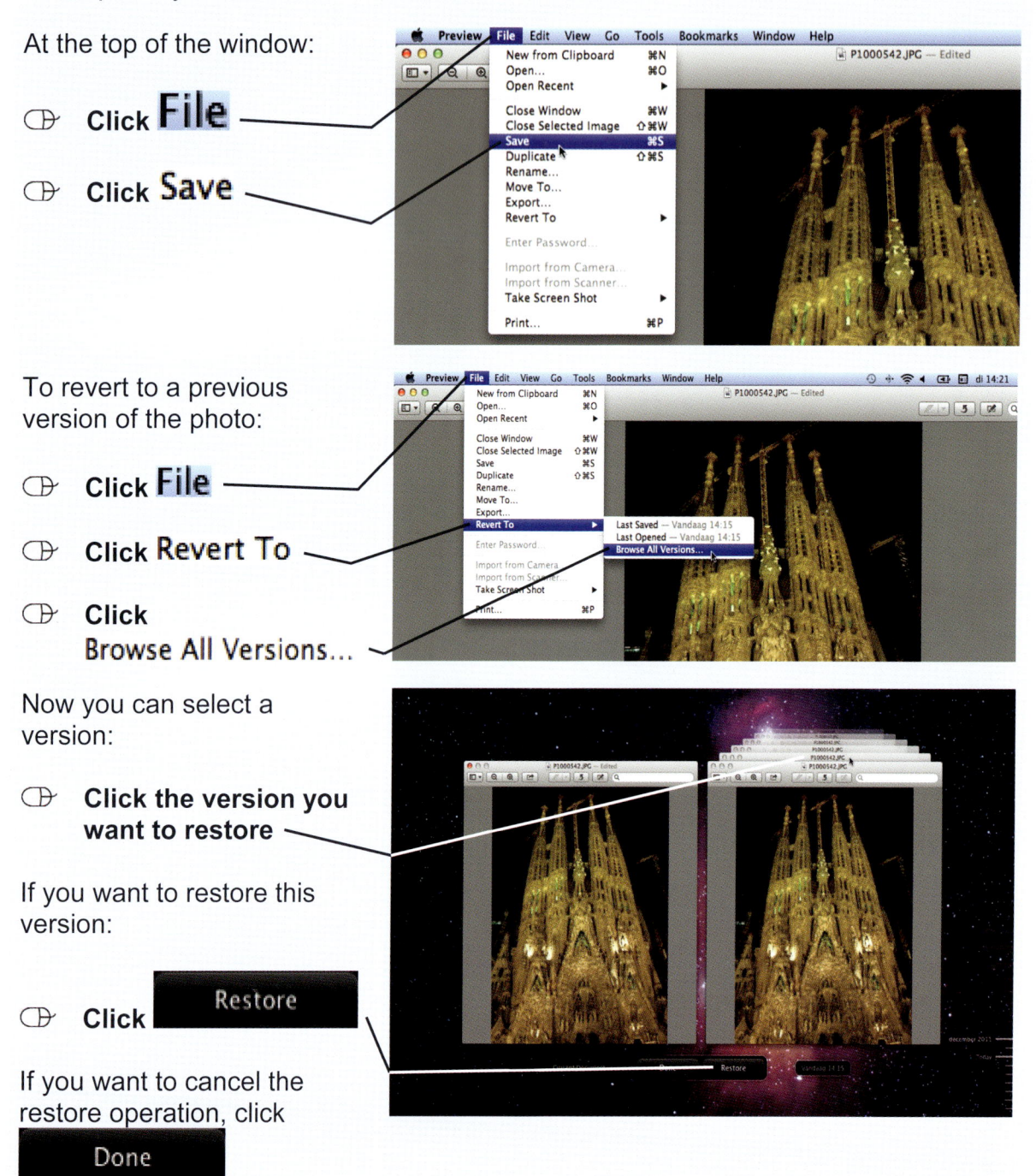

At the top of the window:

☞ **Click File**

☞ **Click Save**

To revert to a previous version of the photo:

☞ **Click File**

☞ **Click Revert To**

☞ **Click Browse All Versions...**

Now you can select a version:

☞ **Click the version you want to restore**

If you want to restore this version:

☞ **Click Restore**

If you want to cancel the restore operation, click **Done**.

1.14 Enhancing a Photo

Sometimes a photo can turn out too dark, while at other times it may be too bright. With the *Adjust colors* option you can enhance a photo that did not turn out the way you expected:

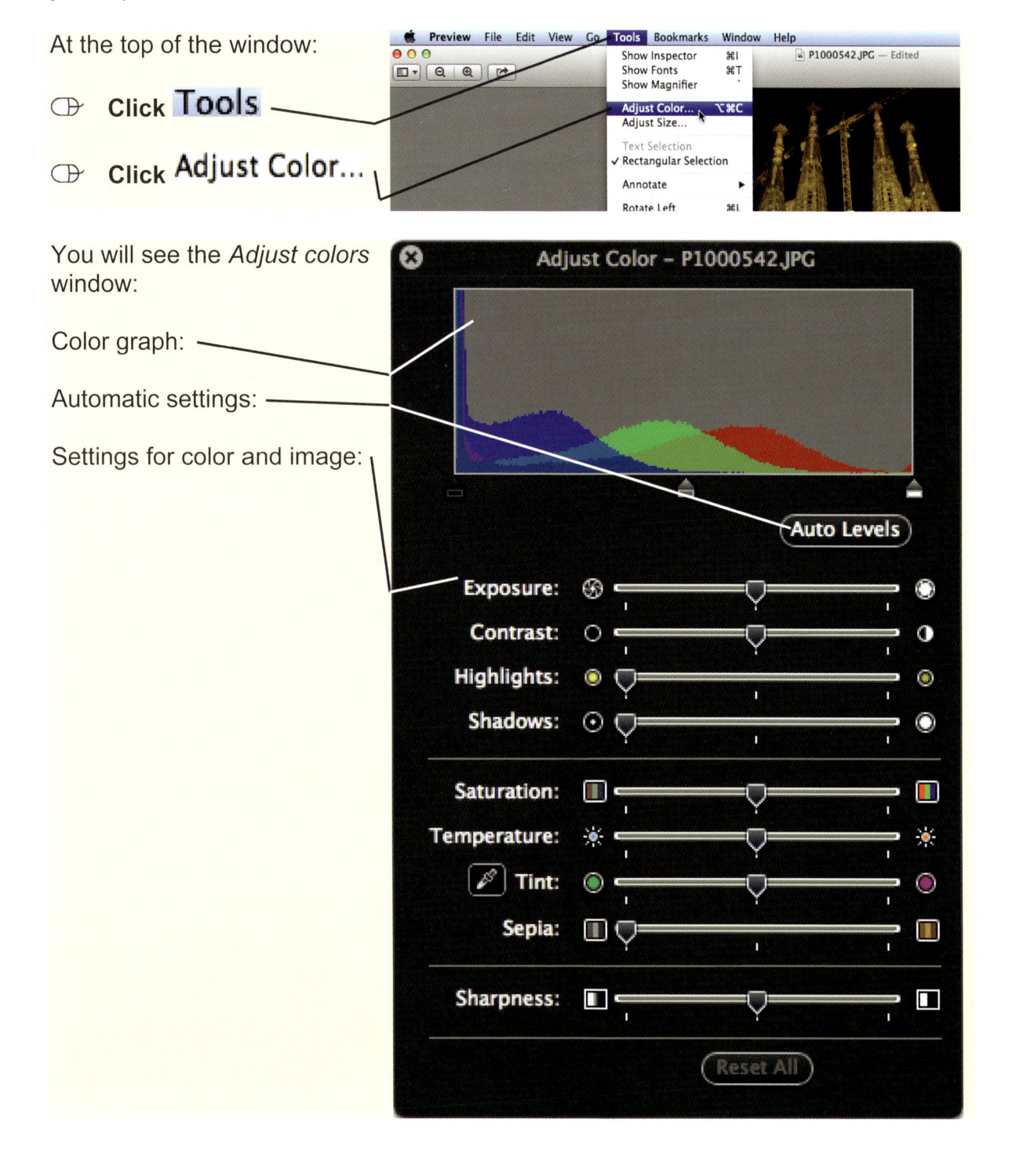

At the top of the window:

☞ Click **Tools**

☞ Click **Adjust Color...**

You will see the *Adjust colors* window:

Color graph:

Automatic settings:

Settings for color and image:

You can move the sliders to change the various color and image settings:

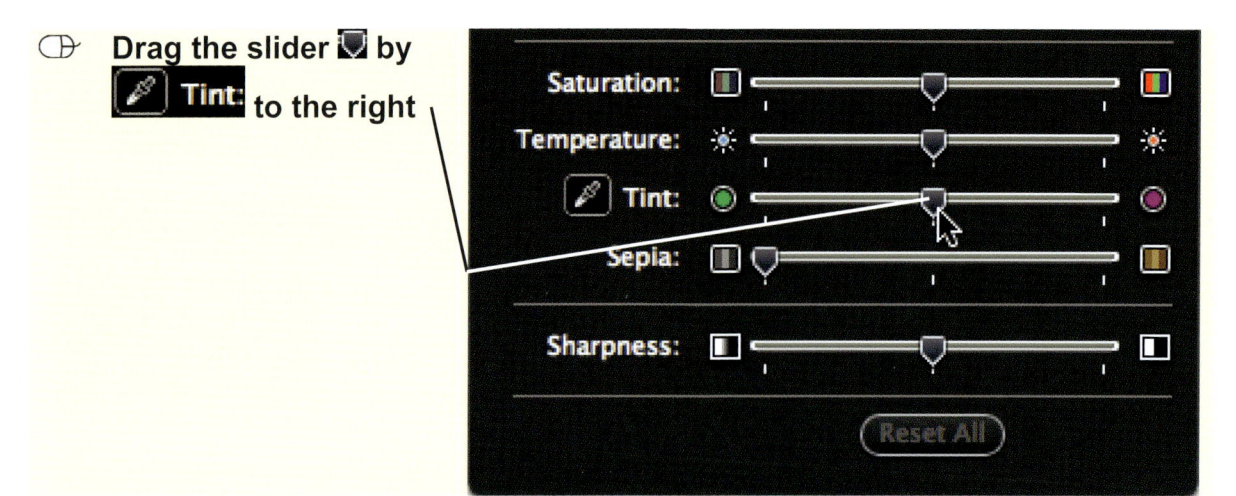

⊕ **Drag the slider ▼ by [Tint:] to the right**

You will see that the hue of the photo has changed a bit (it has become browner):

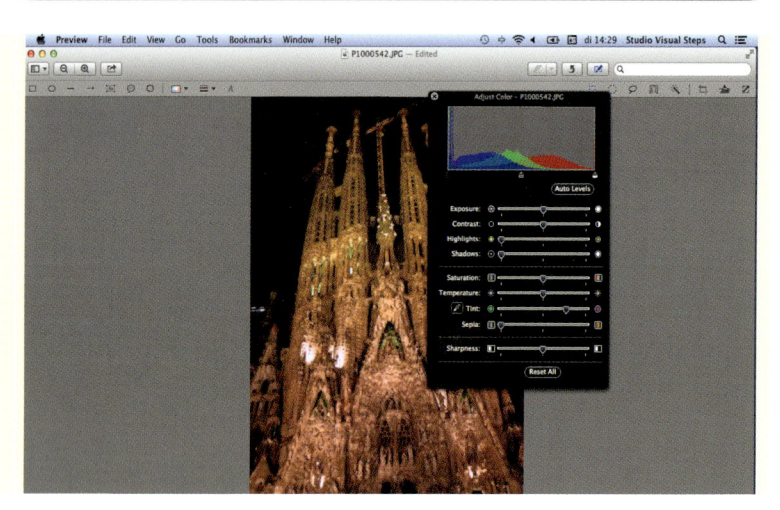

In this way you can also add special effects to a photo. If you find it difficult to decide which settings to use, you can select the option for automatic enhancement:

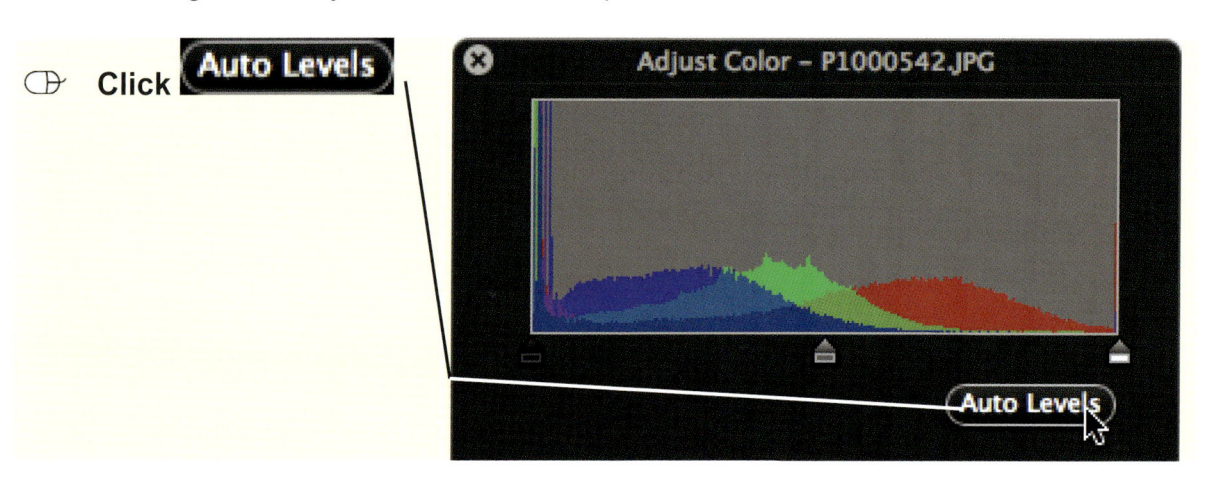

⊕ **Click [Auto Levels]**

Chapter 1 Working with Photos   47

The photo will automatically be enhanced:

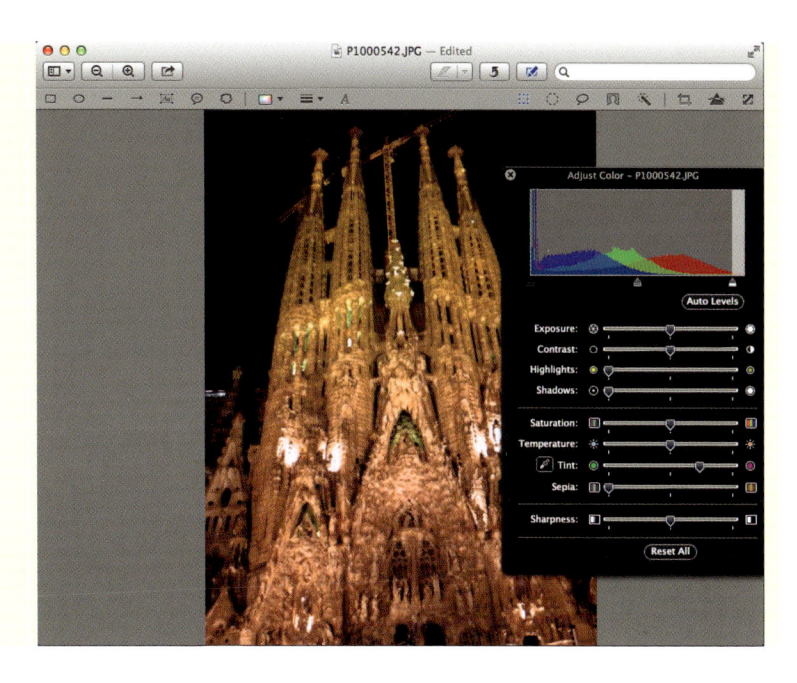

Automatic enhancement will not always guarantee a good result. You may need to improve the photo some more.

☞ **Close the *Adjust colors* window** ⚞³

1.15 Changing the Size of a Photo

If you want to display the photo in a different size, you can set this up in the following way:

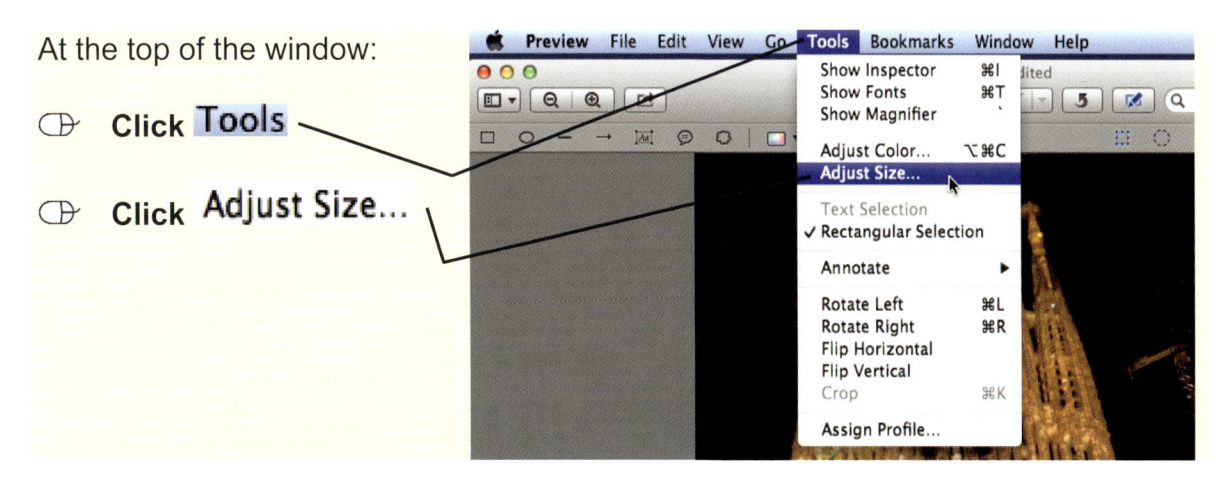

At the top of the window:

⊕ **Click** Tools

⊕ **Click** Adjust Size...

You will see a window in which you can adjust the size:

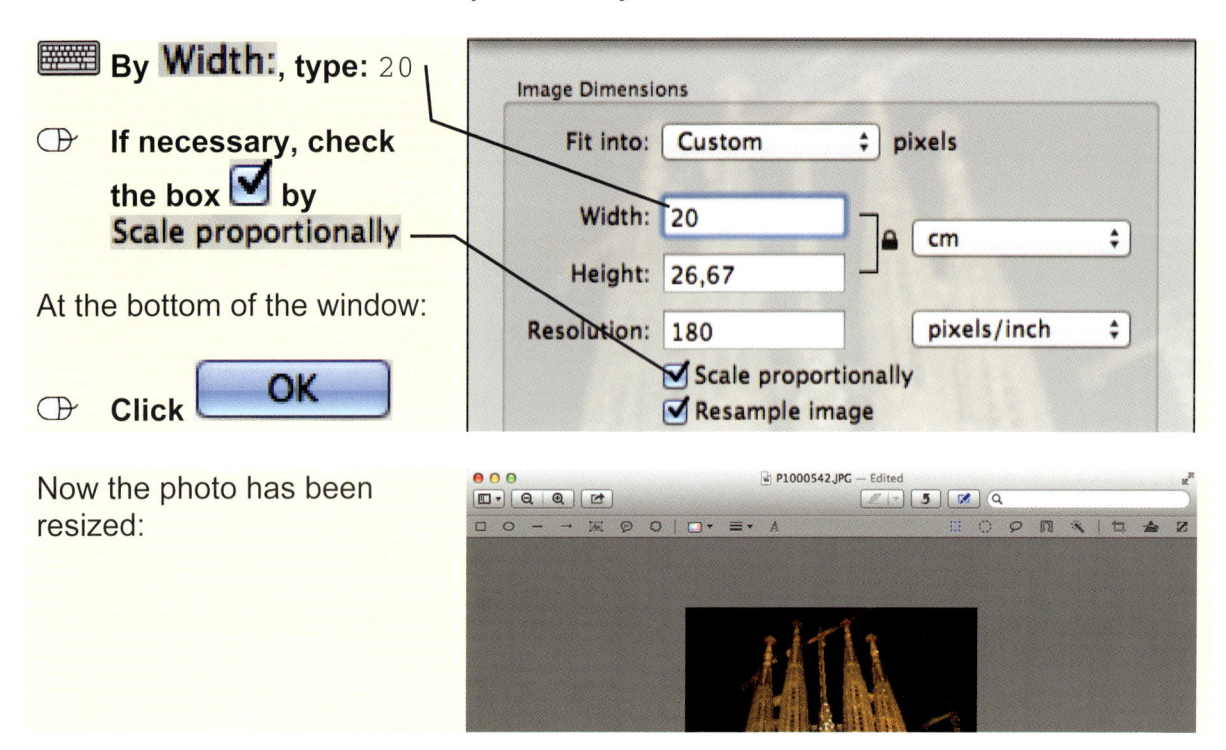

⌨ By **Width:**, type: 20

☞ **If necessary, check the box ☑ by Scale proportionally**

At the bottom of the window:

☞ **Click OK**

Now the photo has been resized:

💡 Tip
Adjust the size proportionally
If you want to adjust the size of a photo, it is wise to adjust the scale proportionally. This means that the horizontal and vertical aspect ratio will remain the same, so the width will be adjusted in proportion to the height of the photo. For example, if the width is decreased by 25%, the height will also be decreased by 25%. This option will make sure the aspect ratio (width to height ratio) of the photo will remain the same, and it will prevent the photo from appearing 'stretched' or 'squished'.

1.16 Cropping a Photo

Sometimes on second thought, you may decide that you want to remove certain items from a particular photo. Or perhaps you want to change the form of the picture. By cropping the photo you can keep the portion you like and remove the rest:

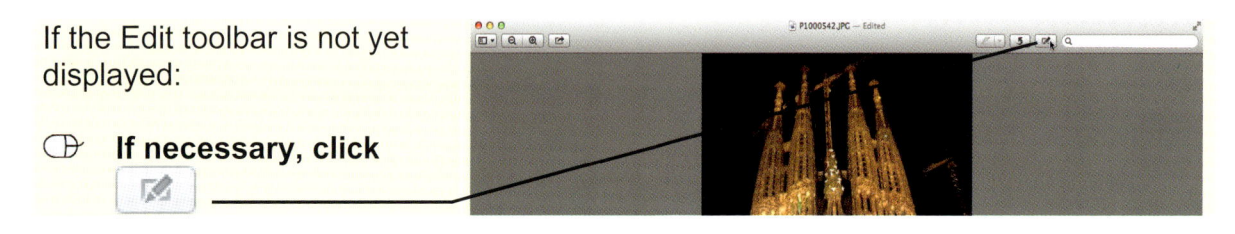

If the Edit toolbar is not yet displayed:

☞ **If necessary, click**

Chapter 1 Working with Photos **49**

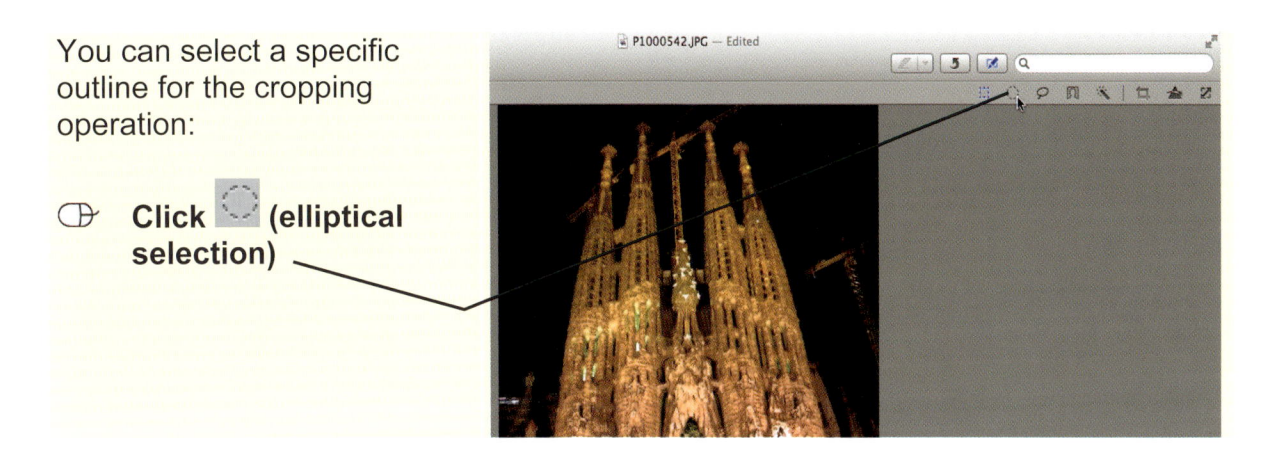

You can select a specific outline for the cropping operation:

☞ **Click** ⬭ **(elliptical selection)**

By dragging the borders of the frame you can select the portion of the photo you want to crop:

☞ **Position the mouse pointer on the top left corner of the photo**

☞ **Press and hold the mouse button down**

☞ **Drag the corner to the bottom right side of the picture**

You will see an elliptical shape:

☞ **Release the mouse button**

If you wish, you can further adjust the selected section by dragging the handles:

Now you can crop the photo:

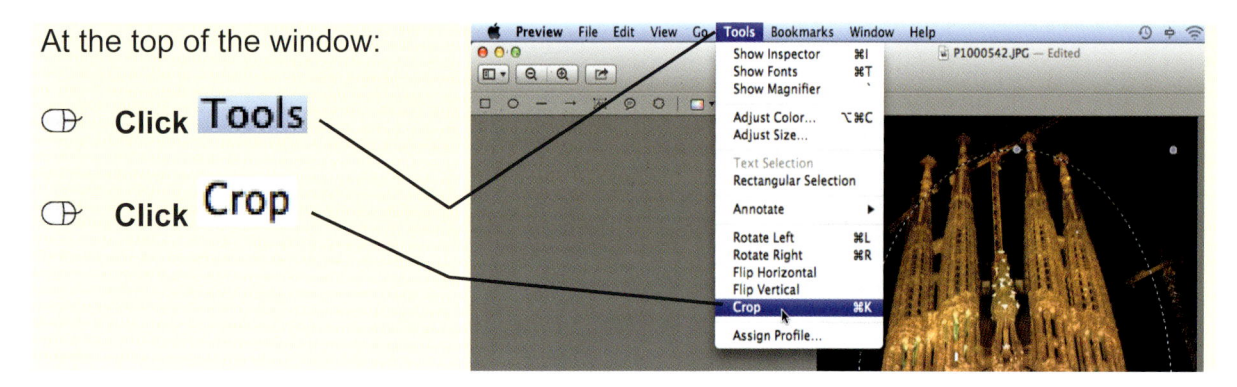

At the top of the window:

☞ Click **Tools**

☞ Click **Crop**

You will see the result.

1.17 Adding Text and Images

In *Preview* you can add text and images to a photo. This is a nice feature if you want to add extra information about a photo, or just make the photo a bit funnier. These additions are called *annotations*. You can easily add annotations to a photo. Just give it a try. Practice first by adding a shape:

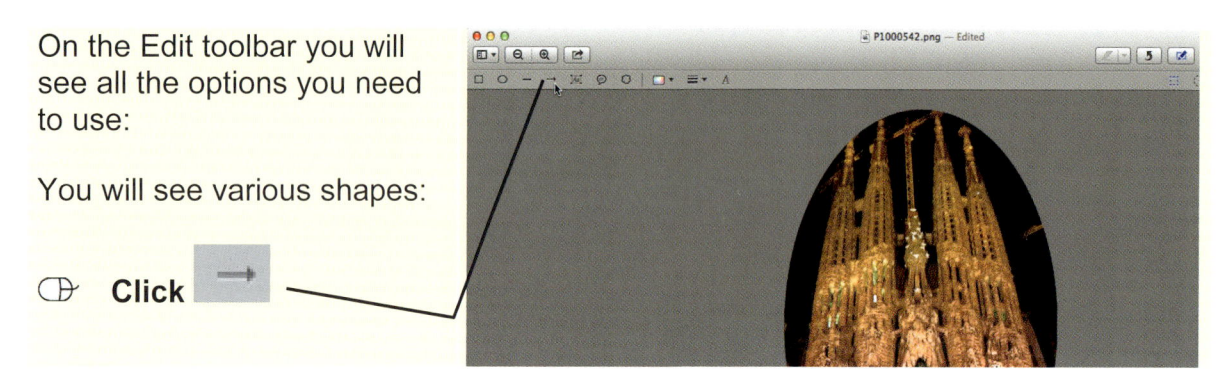

On the Edit toolbar you will see all the options you need to use:

You will see various shapes:

☞ Click **→**

Now you can select the color and width of the arrow:

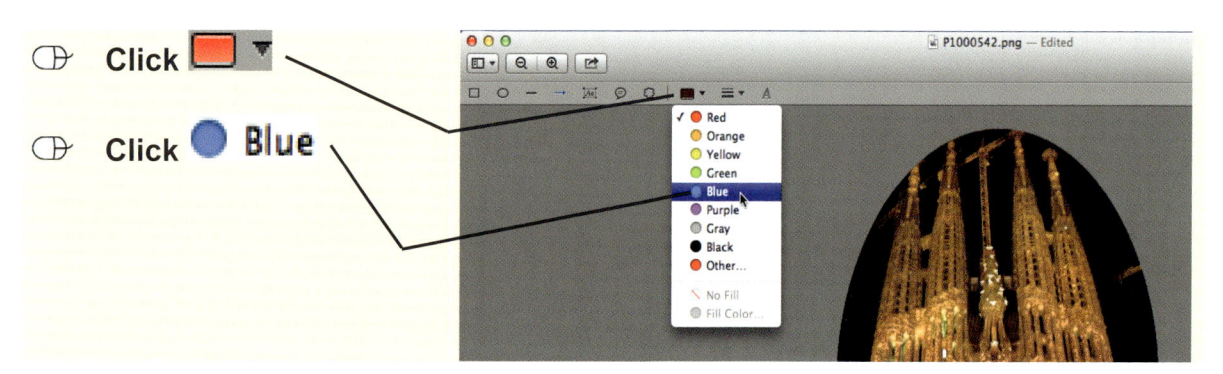

☞ Click 🟥 ▼

☞ Click 🔵 **Blue**

Chapter 1 Working with Photos   **51**

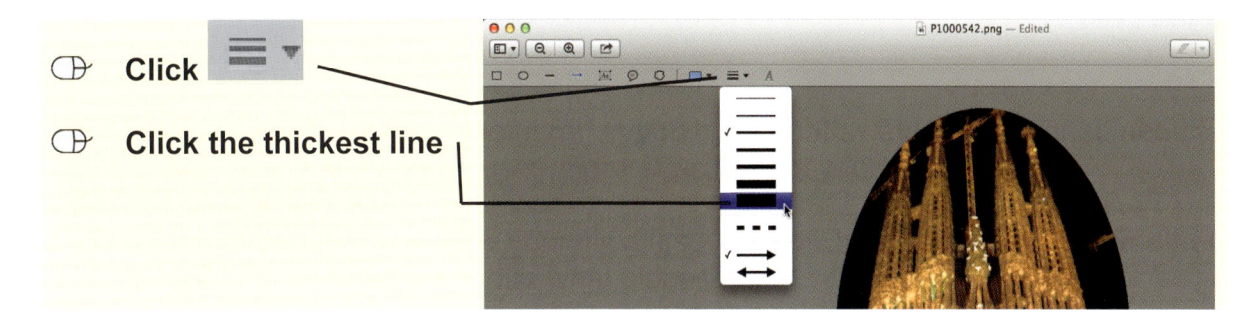

⊕ **Click**

⊕ **Click the thickest line**

Now you can insert the arrow into the photo:

⊕ **Position the mouse pointer somewhat to the left of the center of the picture**

⊕ **Press and hold the mouse button down**

⊕ **Drag the pointer to the top right (point it to the crane)**

⊕ **Release the mouse button**

You can move the shape by clicking it and dragging it to a different spot.

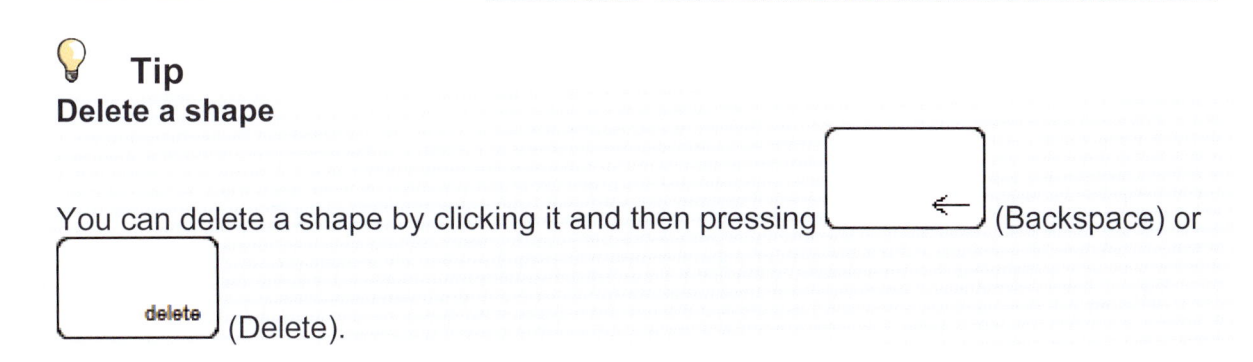

💡 **Tip**
Delete a shape

You can delete a shape by clicking it and then pressing ⌫ (Backspace) or ⌦ (Delete).

Now you can add text to the photo:

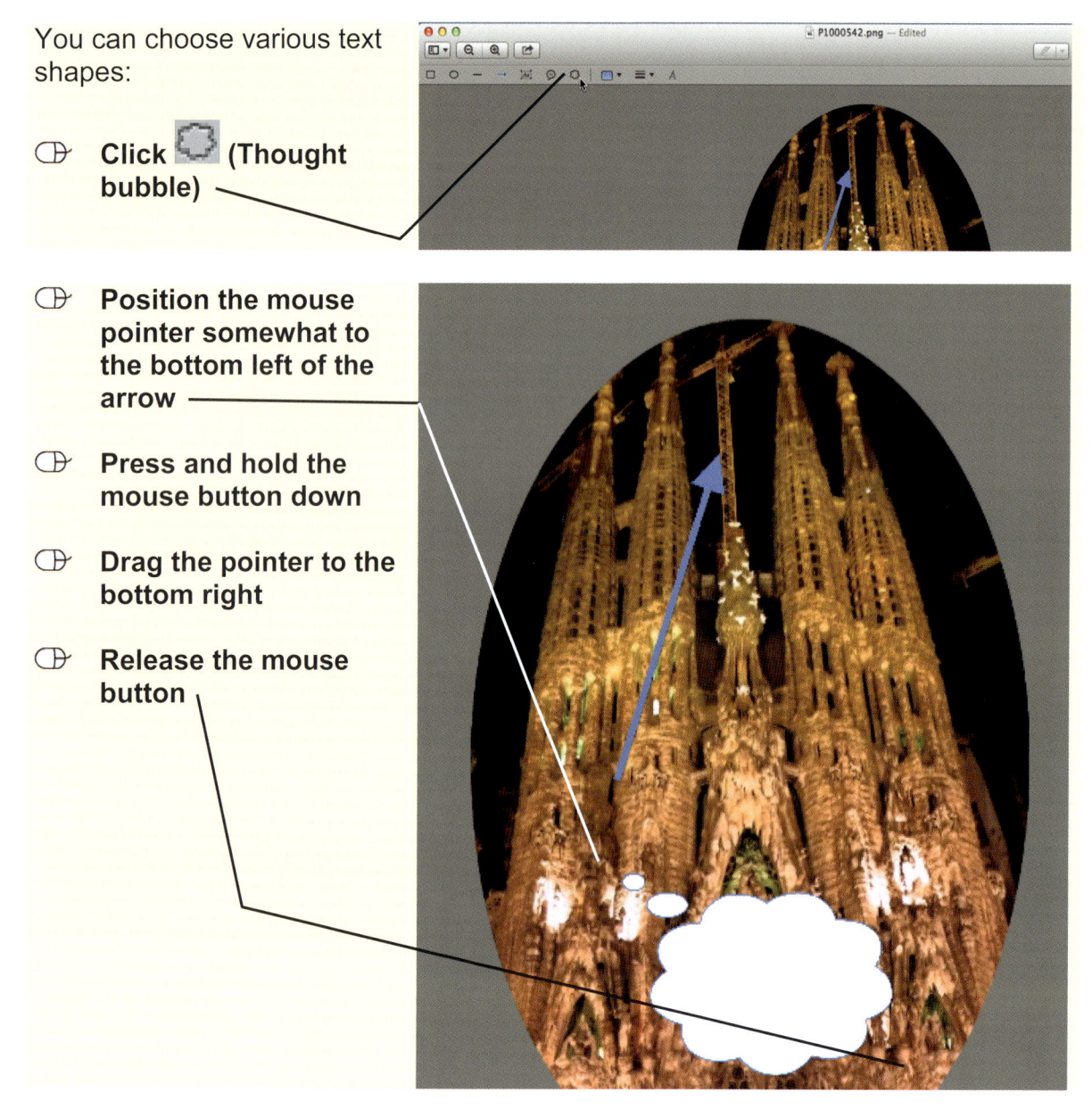

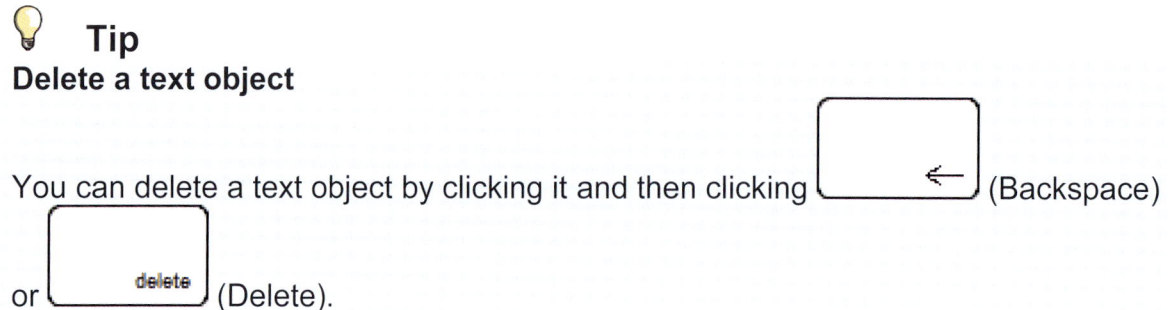

You can choose various text shapes:

☞ **Click ☁ (Thought bubble)**

☞ **Position the mouse pointer somewhat to the bottom left of the arrow**

☞ **Press and hold the mouse button down**

☞ **Drag the pointer to the bottom right**

☞ **Release the mouse button**

💡 **Tip**
Delete a text object

You can delete a text object by clicking it and then clicking ⌫ (Backspace) or [delete] (Delete).

Chapter 1 Working with Photos **53**

Now you can type the text:

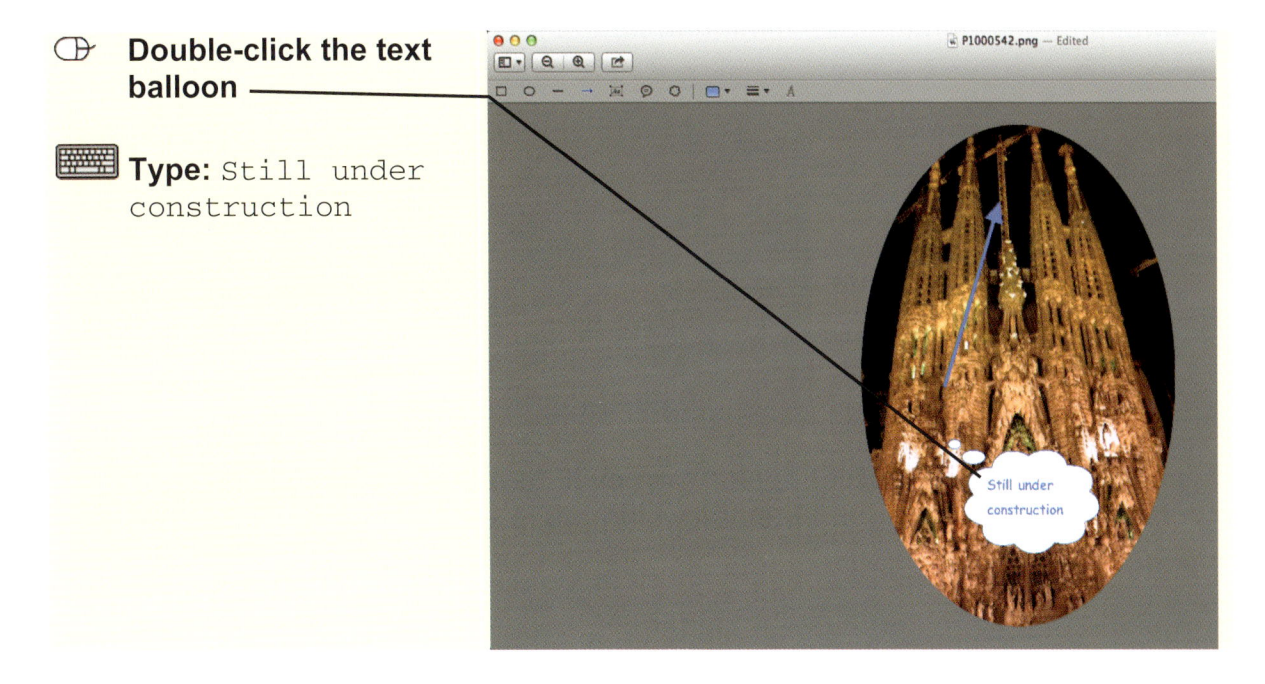

☞ **Double-click the text balloon**

⌨ **Type:** Still under construction

1.18 Zooming In and Out

You may not be able to clearly read the text on your screen. In that case you can zoom in on the photo:

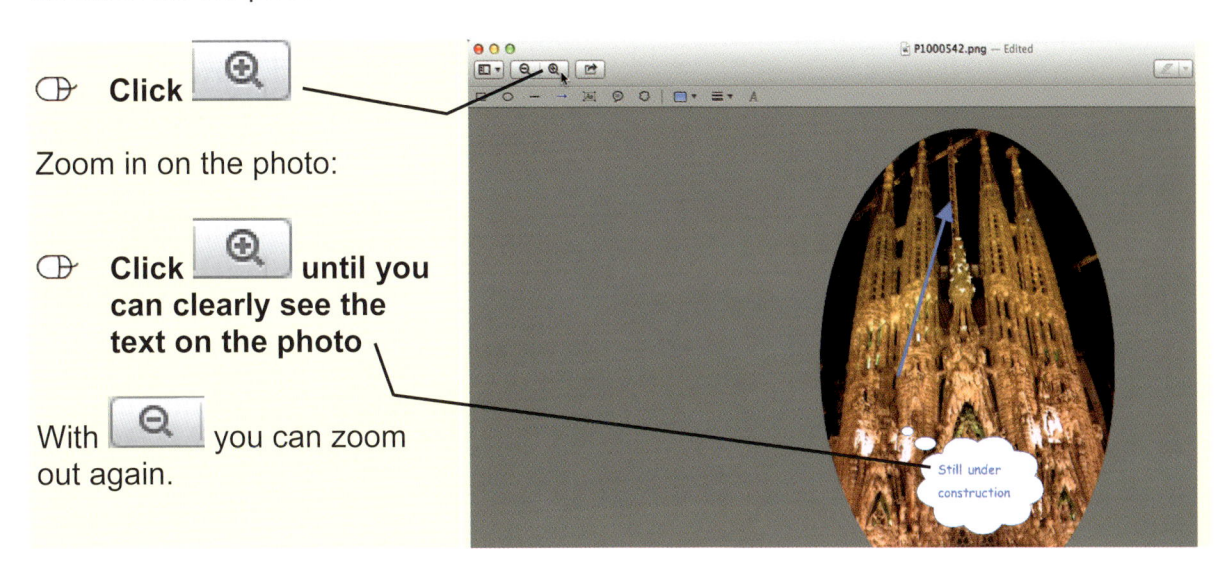

☞ **Click** 🔍

Zoom in on the photo:

☞ **Click** 🔍 **until you can clearly see the text on the photo**

With 🔍 you can zoom out again.

iPhoto, iMovie and Other Useful Mac Programs for Seniors

1.19 Changing the Font

You can change the font size, the font itself and other text properties:

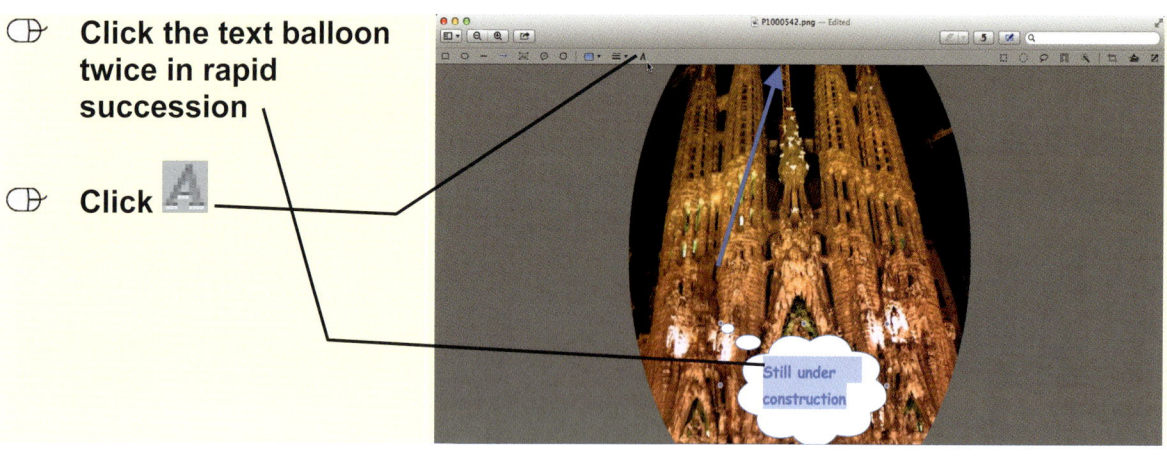

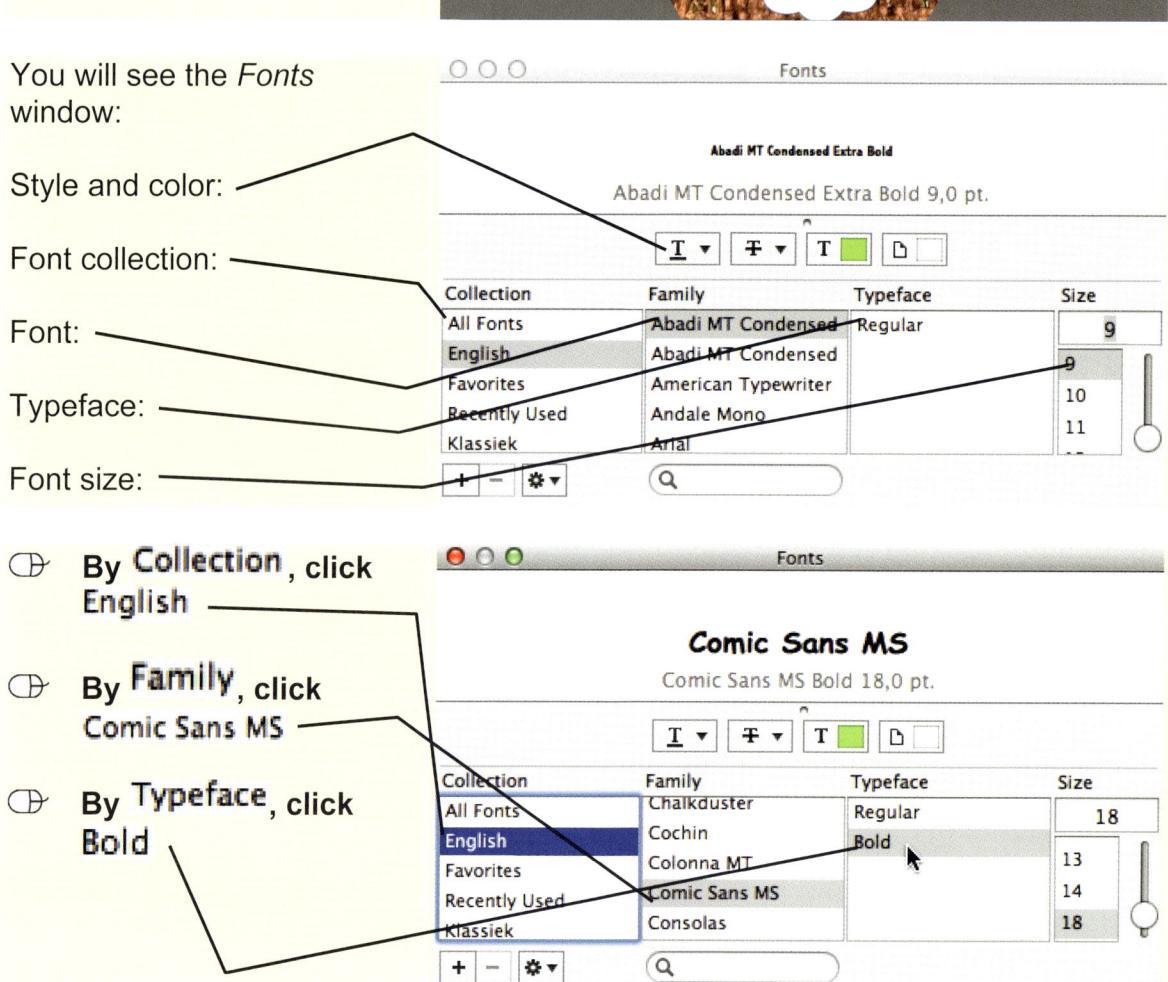

☞ **Click the text balloon twice in rapid succession**

☞ **Click** *A*

You will see the *Fonts* window:

Style and color:

Font collection:

Font:

Typeface:

Font size:

☞ **By** *Collection*, **click** *English*

☞ **By** *Family*, **click** *Comic Sans MS*

☞ **By** *Typeface*, **click** *Bold*

⊕ **By** Size**, click** 48

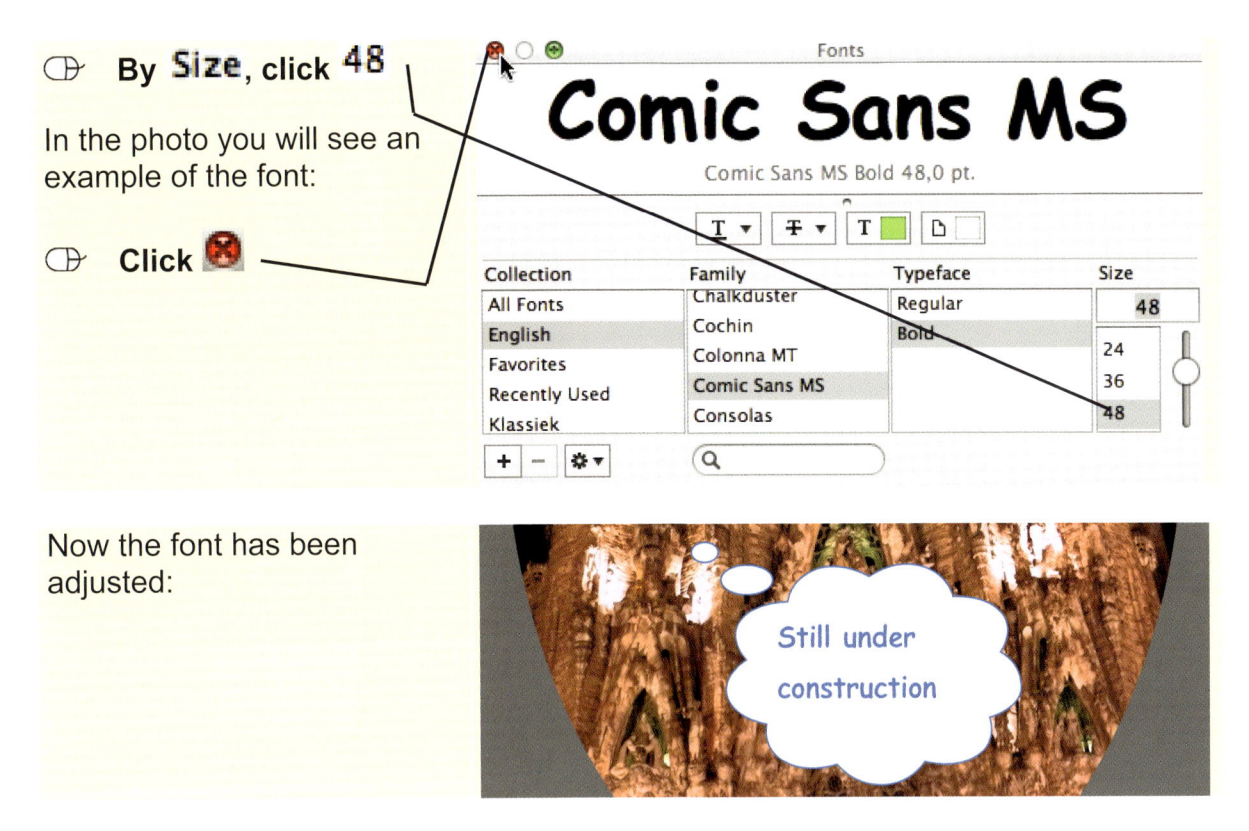

In the photo you will see an example of the font:

⊕ **Click** 🐞

Now the font has been adjusted:

While you were editing the photo in *Preview*, the changes were automatically added to the photo. This means you do not need to save the photo separately.

☞ **Stop** *Preview* 👣²

☞ **Close** *Finder* 👣³

In this chapter, among other things, you have learned how to create an album and a slideshow in *iPhoto*. You have also learned how to edit photos in *Preview*.

1.20 Background Information

Dictionary

Album	A folder in *iPhoto* in which you can collect photos.
Comments	Shapes and texts you can add to a photo in *Preview*.
Email account	The server name, user name, password and the email address used by an email program, or by webmail, in order to send and receive email messages.
Event	The *iPhoto* program organized photos by events. An event contains the pictures that are taken during a certain time period, for instance, at a wedding or a trip to the beach.
GPS coordinates	Data used for pinpointing a location, for example, by a GPS navigation system or a cell phone.
Image Capture	An *Apple* program that lets you transfer photos to your computer, from a digital camera or scanner connected to your computer or network.
Import	Transferring digital photos from your digital camera (or other device with a camera) to your computer.
iPad	A tablet computer made by *Apple*.
iPhone	*Apple's* smartphone.
iPhoto	A program you can use to save, organize and edit digital photos.
Preview	A program that allows you to view and edit digital photos.
Proportional (aspect ratio)	A setting for enlarging or shrinking a photo, while the proportions of height and width of the photo remain unchanged.
SD card	Short for *Secure Digital*. A memory card the size of a stamp, used by digital cameras, tablets and smartphones to store data.
Slideshow	An automatic display of images.
Webmail service	A web service you can use in order to send and receive email messages through a website. For example, *Hotmail* or *Gmail*.

Source: Apple Dictionary, www.apple.com, Wikipedia

Chapter 1 Working with Photos

1.21 Tips

Tip
Image Capture
Apart from *iPhoto*, the *Mac* contains another program you can use to import photos from your digital camera, card reader, smartphone, scanner, multifunction printer or other external device. This program is called *Image Capture* and you can use it to store photos in a specific folder in *Finder*. Within the *Devices* pane you will see any attached devices that are compatible with the application. This is how you open *Image Capture*:

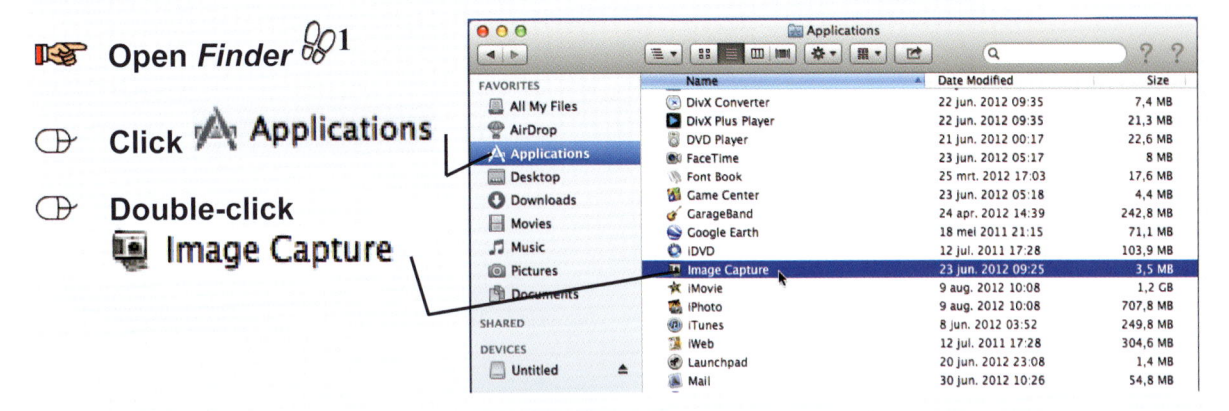

☞ **Open *Finder*** ⁄ ¹

⊕ **Click** Applications

⊕ **Double-click** Image Capture

You will see the *Image Capture* window:

☞ **Connect the digital camera or other device. If it's a camera, turn it on.**

The *iPhoto* program may open automatically:

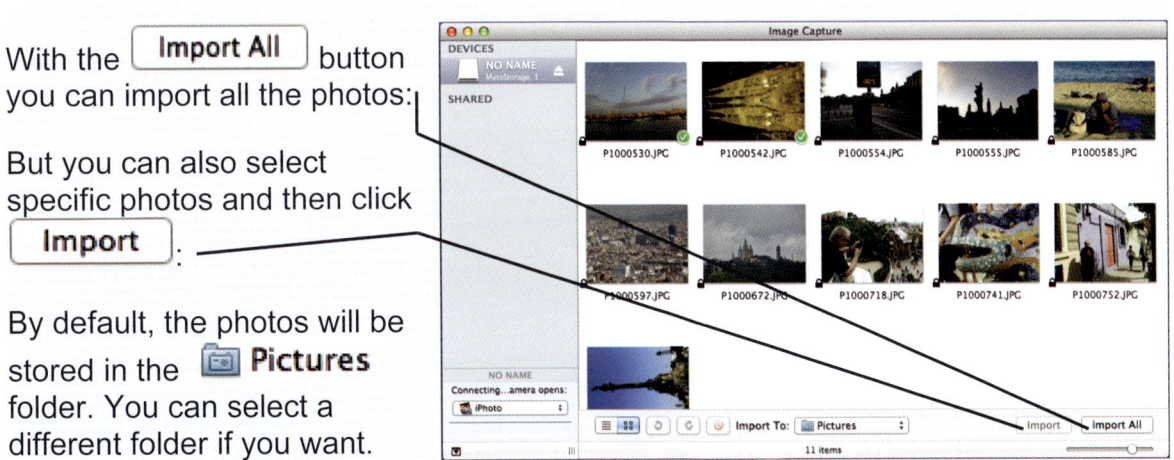

☞ **If necessary, stop *iPhoto*** ⁄ ²

With the **Import All** button you can import all the photos:

But you can also select specific photos and then click **Import**.

By default, the photos will be stored in the **Pictures** folder. You can select a different folder if you want.

- Continue on the next page -

58 *iPhoto, iMovie and Other Useful Mac Programs for Seniors*

At the bottom left of the window, by [iPhoto], you can select which program you want to open when you connect a digital camera to the computer. One of the handiest features in *Image Capture* is that you can set different actions for different devices. If you want *iPhoto* to launch when you connect your digital camera, for example, but do not want anything to pop up when you plug in your iPhone or iPad, *Image Capture* will take care of it. *Image Capture* is one of the easiest ways to grab a full-resolution photo off of your iPhone or iPad.

Tip
Use templates for photos
By using templates in *Mail,* you can easily send an email message with a nice background and a photo:

☞ **Open** *Mail* ⚹⁴

☞ **Open a new email message** ⚹⁵

Open the template pane:

⊕ **Click** [icon]

You will see various email templates:

⊕ **Click Photos**

⊕ **Click Air Mail**

- Continue on the next page -

Chapter 1 Working with Photos **59**

Next, you can replace the text within the template by your own text. By adding your own photos you can personalize your message and create a very special email message. You can replace the photos in the template by your own photos by dragging them from *iPhoto* or *PhotoLoader*:

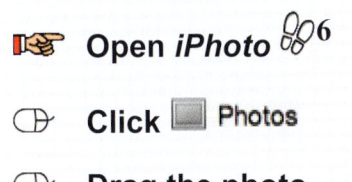

☞ **Open *iPhoto*** 🐾⁶

⊕ **Click 🖼 Photos**

⊕ **Drag the photo towards a photo in the template**

Now the photo has been placed in the template:

In this way you can replace all the photos.

Please note: if you want to send photos you will need to take into account that most email services have size restrictions. You may not be able to send large photo files or multiple photos at once. Also be aware that your photos may cause the recipient's mailbox to overflow.

💡 Tip
Upload photos to the Internet with iPhoto
With *iPhoto* you can easily upload photos to the Internet. This is how you add photos to your *Facebook* account, for example:

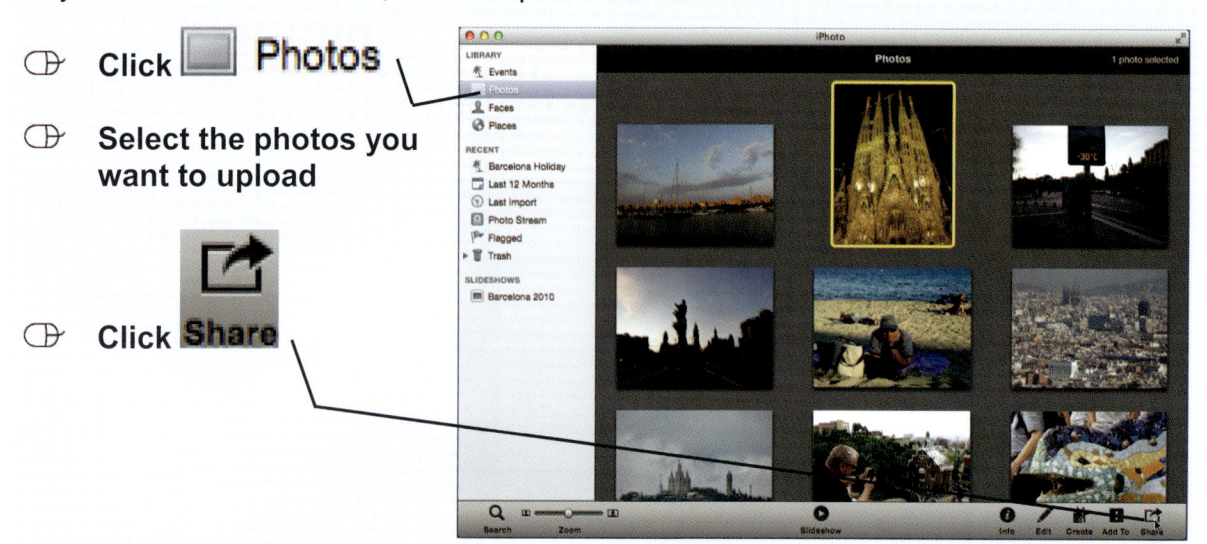

☞ **Click** ▢ **Photos**

☞ **Select the photos you want to upload**

☞ **Click Share**

You will see a menu with various options for uploading data to Internet services:

Before you can upload your photos you will need to have created an account with the relevant Internet service.

To upload a photo to *Facebook*:

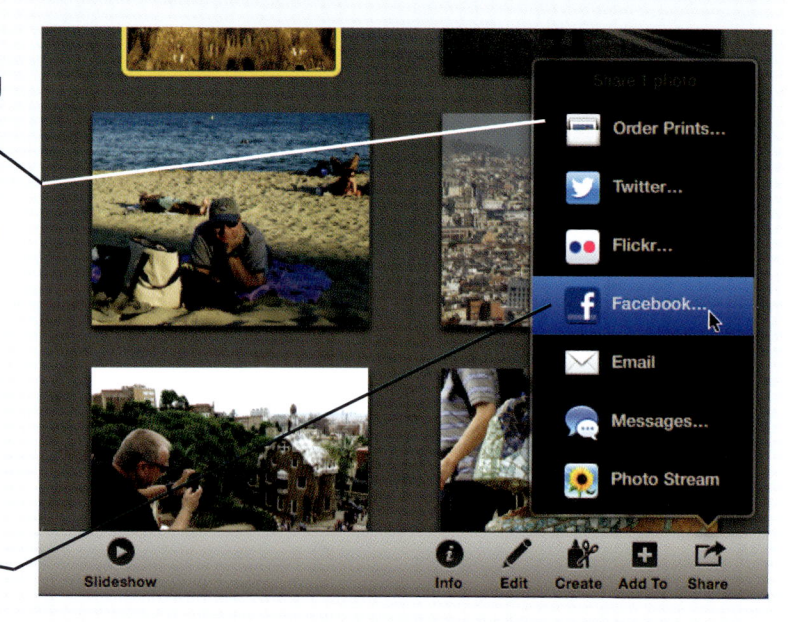

☞ **Click** **[f] Facebook...**

- Continue on the next page -

Chapter 1 Working with Photos

The first time you will see this window:

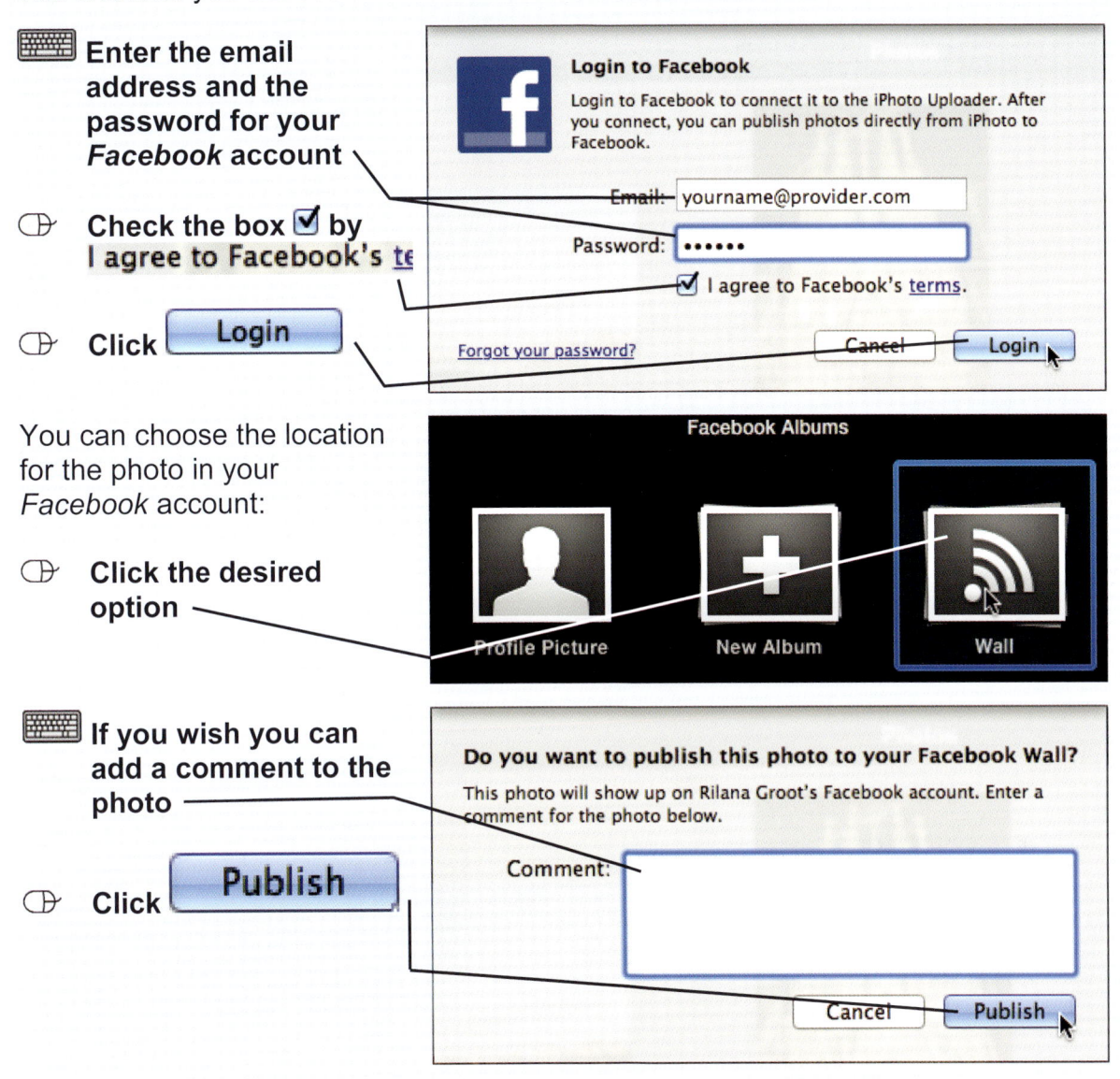

⌨ **Enter the email address and the password for your *Facebook* account**

☞ **Check the box ☑ by I agree to Facebook's te**

☞ **Click Login**

You can choose the location for the photo in your *Facebook* account:

☞ **Click the desired option**

⌨ **If you wish you can add a comment to the photo**

☞ **Click Publish**

Now the photo has been added to your *Facebook* account.

💡 Tip
More about social networks
Do you want to learn more about *Facebook* and other social media networks? Visual Steps has an excellent title that will introduce you to social networking:

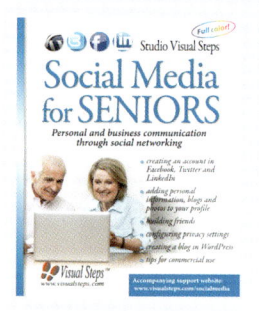

Social Media for SENIORS
Studio Visual Steps
ISBN: 978 90 5905 018 1

Among other things, in this book you will learn how to:
- create an account in *Facebook*, *Twitter* and *LinkedIn*
- add personal information, blogs and photos to your profile
- build friends
- configure privacy settings
- use the tips for commercial use

💡 Tip
Options for iPhoto
You can set various options for *iPhoto*. For example, you can have *iPhoto* start up automatically as soon as a camera is connected to your *Mac*, or you can edit the settings for the email accounts you want to use for sending photos:

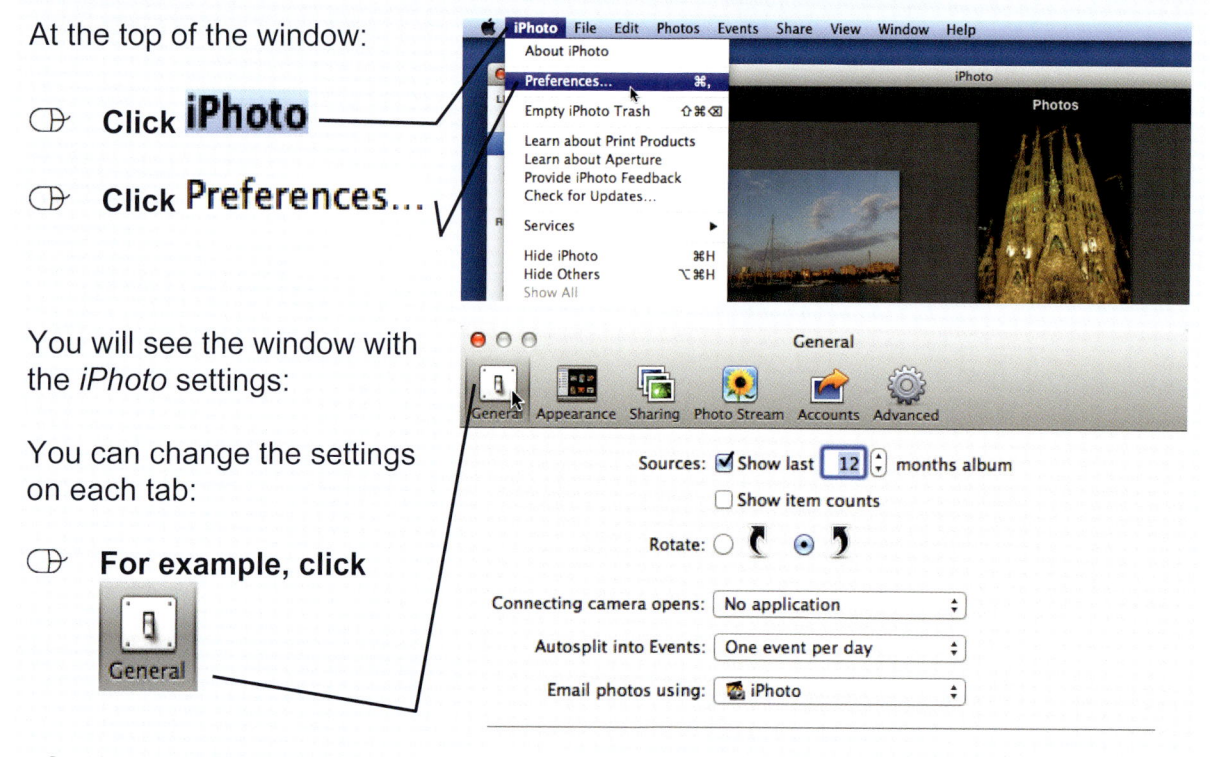

At the top of the window:

☞ Click **iPhoto**

☞ Click **Preferences...**

You will see the window with the *iPhoto* settings:

You can change the settings on each tab:

☞ For example, click **General**

- Continue on the next page -

Chapter 1 Working with Photos 63

If you want *iPhoto* to open automatically when you connect a camera to your computer:

⊕ By **Connecting camera opens:**, click ↕

⊕ Click 🖼 **iPhoto**

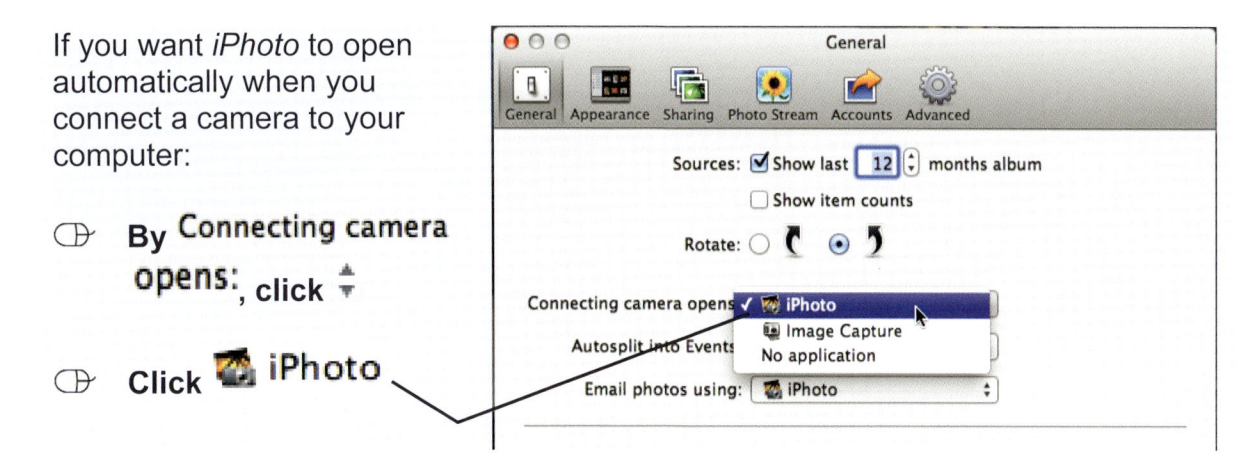

💡 Tip
Send a photo in iPhoto with the Mail program
In *iPhoto* you can always send a photo by using a webmail account. This is the default setting. You can also use the *Mail* program to send a photo in *iPhoto*, without using a template. First, will need to edit a setting in *iPhoto*:

⊕ Click **iPhoto**

⊕ Click **Preferences...**

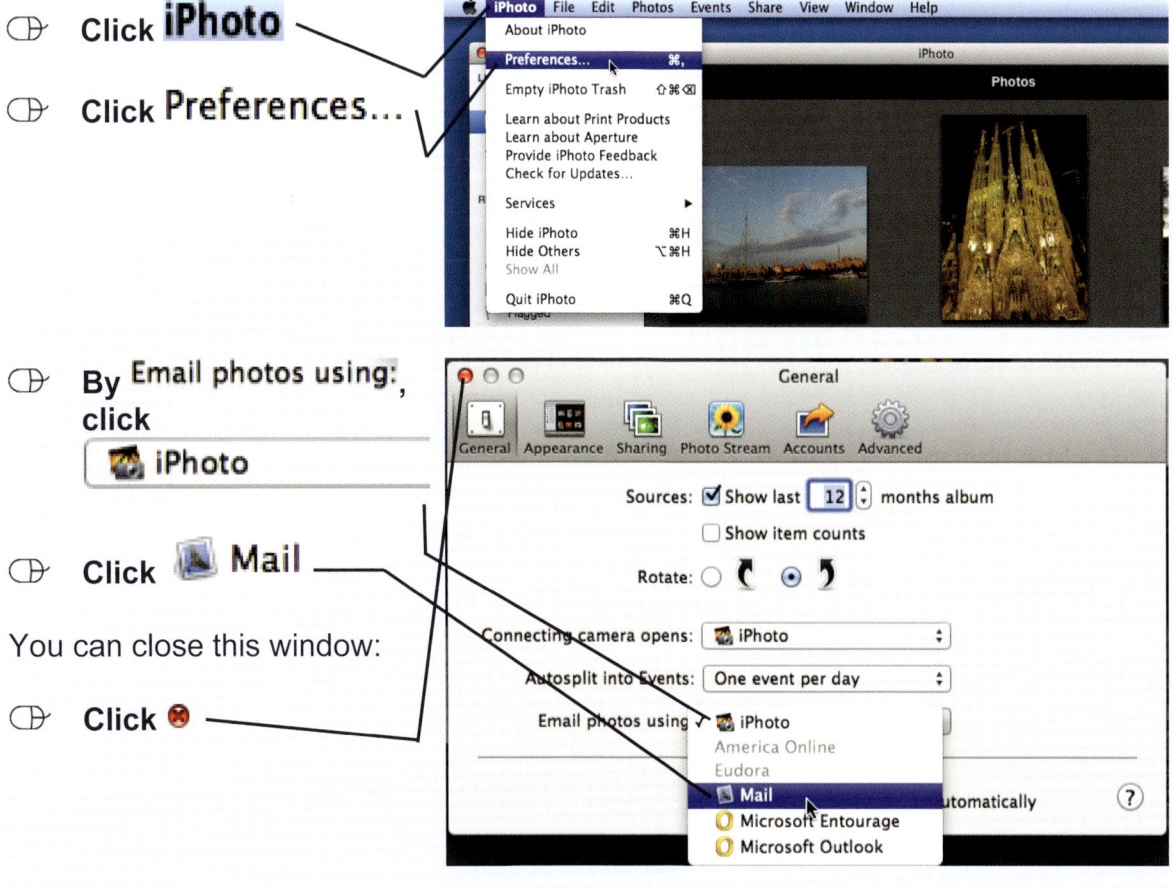

⊕ By **Email photos using:**, click 🖼 iPhoto

⊕ Click 📧 **Mail**

You can close this window:

⊕ Click ⊗

- Continue on the next page -

☞ **Click a photo**

☞ **Click Share**

☞ **Click Email...**

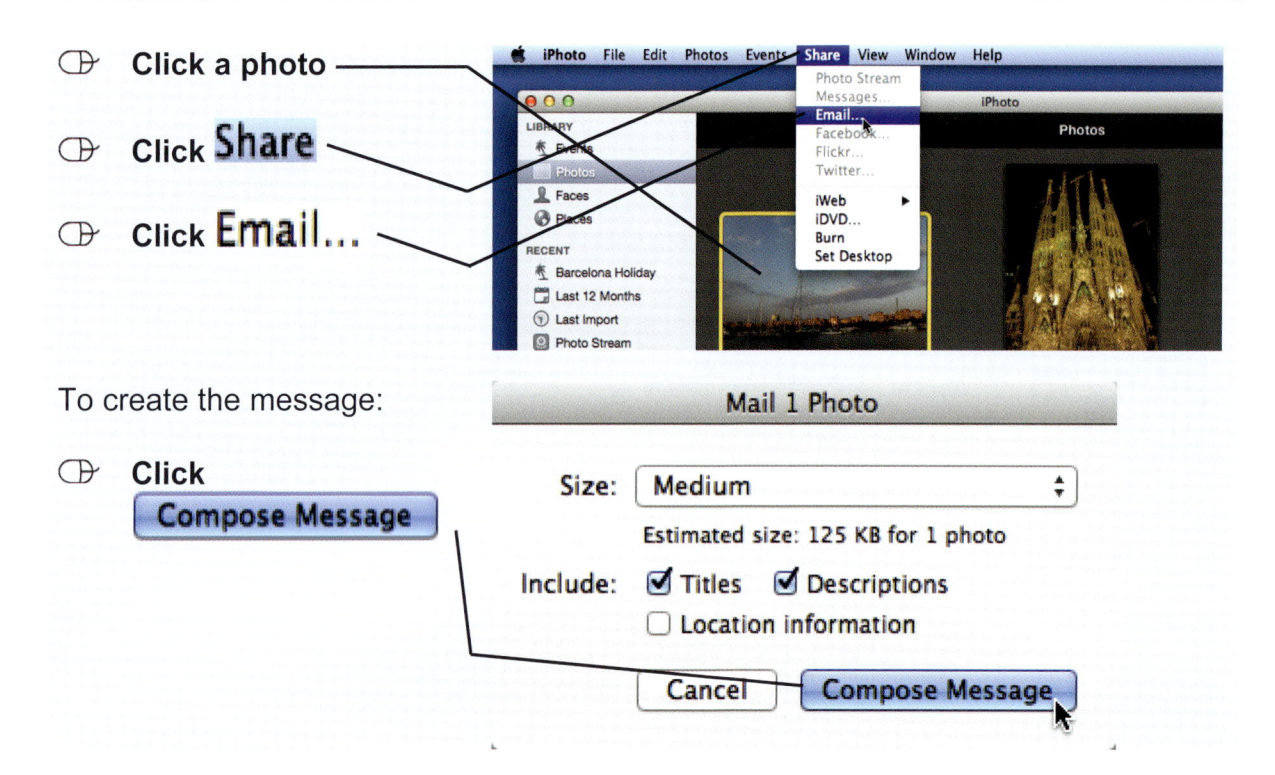

To create the message:

☞ **Click Compose Message**

💡 Tip
View PDF documents with Preview
The *Preview* program is not just suitable for viewing and editing pictures. You can also use it to view PDF documents:

⌨ **Press the control key and hold it down**

☞ **Click a PDF document**

☞ **Click Open With**

☞ **Click Preview (default)**

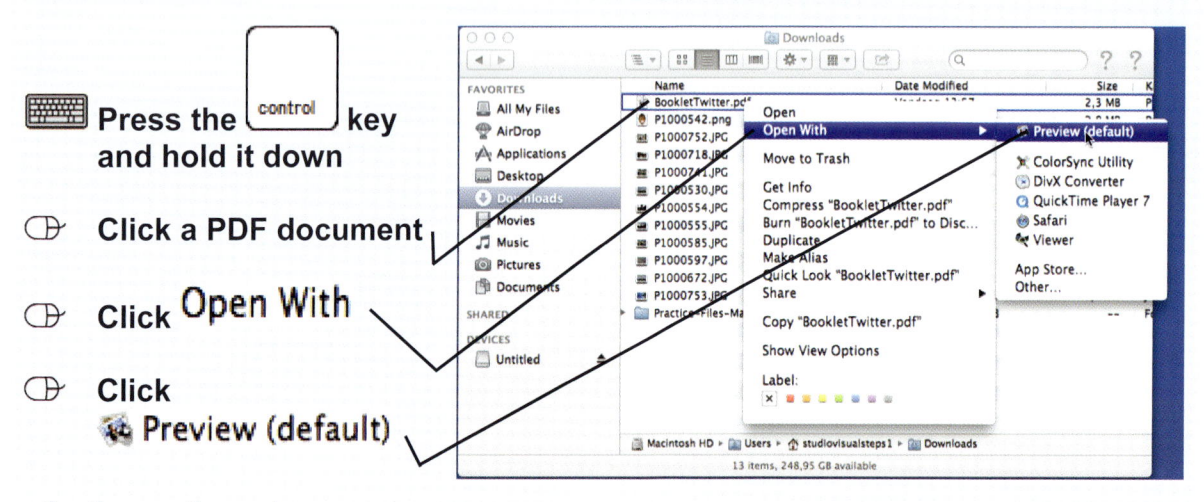

- Continue on the next page -

You will see the *Preview* program:

Now you can leaf through the PDF document in *Preview*.

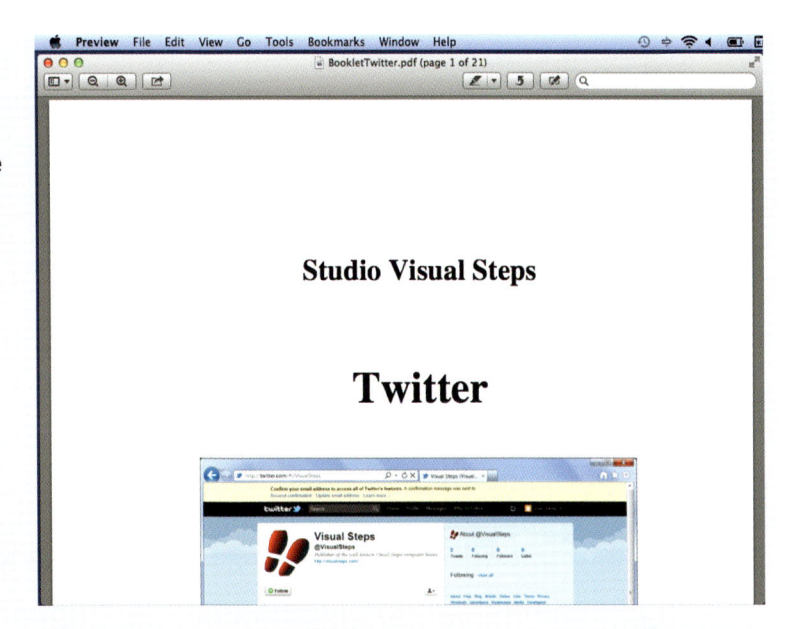

You can search the document for certain keywords:

⌨ **Type the keyword in the search box**

In the pane on the left you will see the pages in which your keyword has been found:

By clicking one of these pages, you will jump automatically to it.

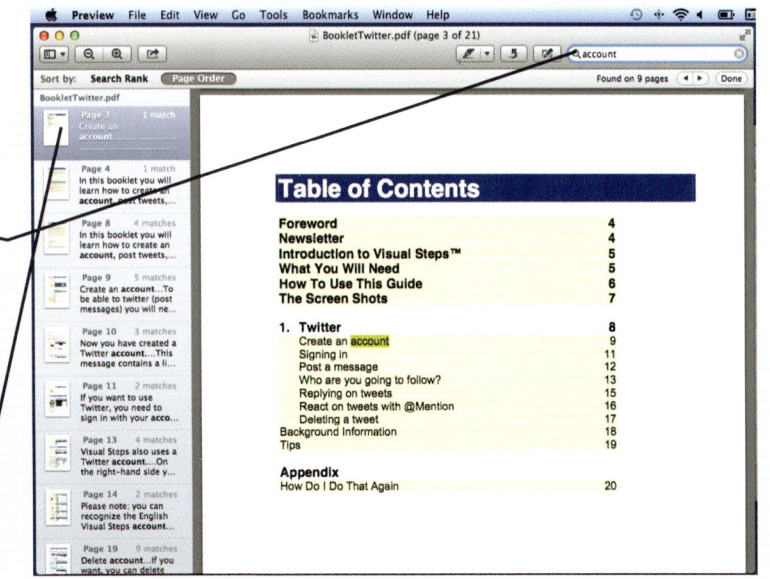

💡 Tip
Take pictures with Photo Booth
If you own a webcam you can use the *Photo Booth* program to take your own picture. If you wish you can use this photo as a profile photo for your accounts, for instance, the photo that is displayed for your user account on the *Mac*.
The *Mac* notebooks have a webcam built into the frame above the computer screen. Other *Mac* computers will require a separate webcam, if you want to use *Photo Booth*.

In the *Dock*:

☞ **Click**

You will see the *Photo Booth* window:

You can take the picture with an added effect, if you want:

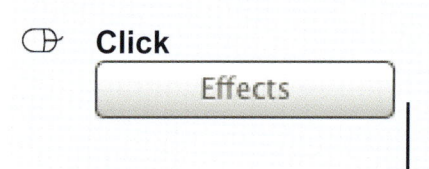

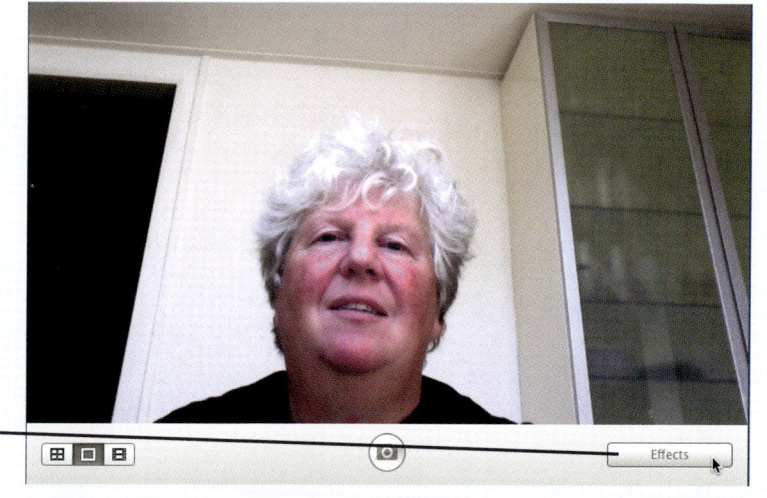

☞ **Click** Effects

You will see the available effects:

By clicking ← or → you will see even more effects.

☞ **For example, click**

- Continue on the next page -

Chapter 1 Working with Photos **67**

You will see the image of your webcam, including the effect you selected:

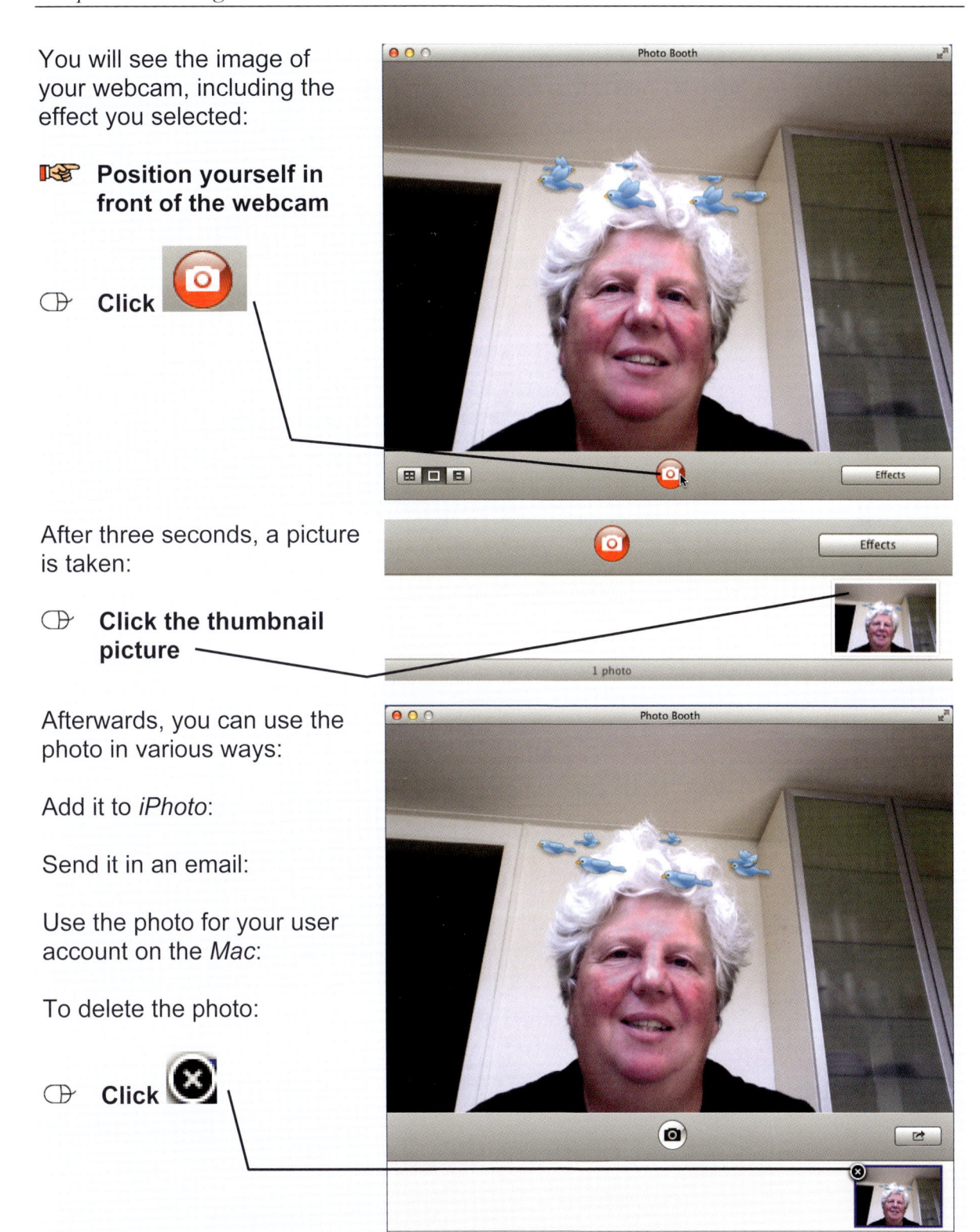

☞ **Position yourself in front of the webcam**

⊕ **Click**

After three seconds, a picture is taken:

⊕ **Click the thumbnail picture**

Afterwards, you can use the photo in various ways:

Add it to *iPhoto*:

Send it in an email:

Use the photo for your user account on the *Mac*:

To delete the photo:

⊕ **Click**

💡 Tip
Facial recognition in iPhoto
In *iPhoto* you can add information about the people represented in the photos. In the library you can add data to the photos, in the *Faces* section:

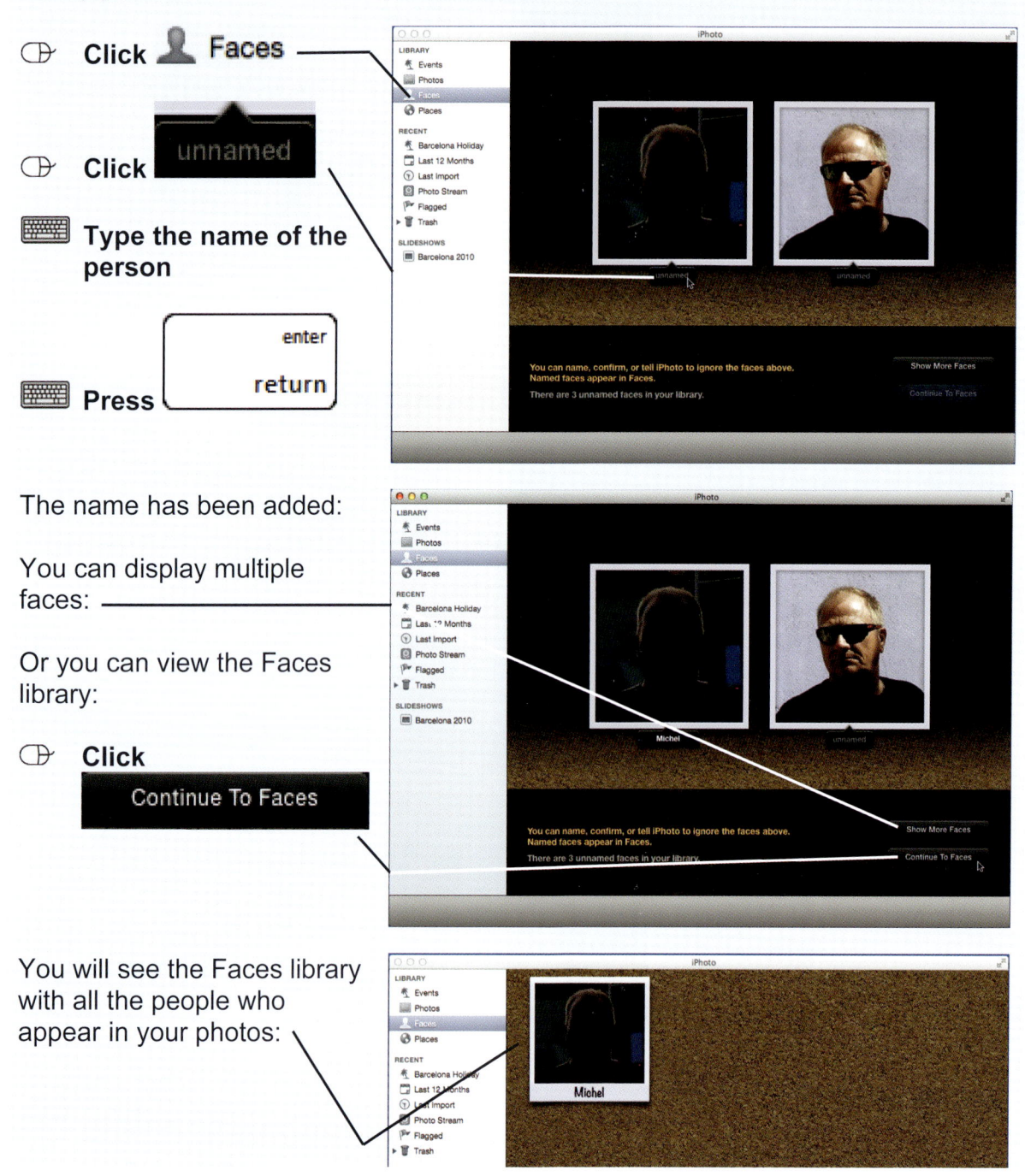

⌖ **Click 👤 Faces**

⌖ **Click** `unnamed`

⌨ **Type the name of the person**

⌨ **Press** `enter return`

The name has been added:

You can display multiple faces:

Or you can view the Faces library:

⌖ **Click** `Continue To Faces`

You will see the Faces library with all the people who appear in your photos:

2. Working with Video

The *Mac* is an ideal computer for working with video. You can view and edit the videos you have recorded yourself. First, you import the videos from your camera and store them on your *Mac*. Next, you can use the video editing program *iMovie* to easily combine various video clips into a video movie, along with some music and special effects.

QuickTime Player is the default program on the *Mac* for playing video files. You can use this program for viewing your homemade videos. You can also use it to watch movies downloaded from the Internet.

With *iDVD* you can burn videos to a DVD that include a homemade menu. You can play such a video DVD (along with other video DVDs) with the *DVD player* program; you can play them on the *Mac* or on the DVD player connected to your television set.

If you want to work with different types of video files, you will need to install the correct *codecs* on your *Mac*. A codec is a software program that ensures that the information in the video files can be correctly read by various other programs. In this chapter you will read how to download and install the right codecs.

In this chapter you will learn how to:

- download and install codecs;
- import video files onto the *Mac*;
- edit video files with *iMovie*;
- play a video with *QuickTime Player*;
- burn a DVD with *iDVD*;
- play a DVD with *DVD player*.

Please note:
If you want to follow the examples in *section 2.2 Importing Video Files from a Camera (with iMovie)* and *2.3 Deactivating and Removing a Camera or SD Card*, you will need to have a digital video camera with some video recordings. If you do not own a digital video camera, you can read through the following sections. Then continue with the steps in *section 2.4 Creating Videos with iMovie*.

➥ Please note:

If you work with a Mac Book Air or a Mac mini, you will not have a CD/DVD player. You will only be able to read through the sections *2.16 Burning a DVD with iDVD* and *2.17 Playing a DVD*, or you will need to carry out the steps by using an external CD/DVD player. If you are thinking of purchasing an external CD/DVD player, make sure to get one that is suitable for use with the *Mac*.

➥ Please note:

For *section 2.16 Burning a DVD with iDVD* you will need to have a writable DVD. If you do not have such a DVD, you can just read through the section.

➥ Please note:

For *section 2.17 Playing a DVD* you will need to use a video DVD that is created with *iDVD* or a video DVD containing a movie or television series. If you do not have such a DVD, you can just read through the section.

2.1 Downloading and Installing Codecs

To make sure that your video files will play correctly on the *Mac*, it is important to have the appropriate codecs installed. Codecs are bits of software that encode and decode the information stored in video files and make it possible for video programs to work with these files. Without the proper codecs, the video programs will not be able to open certain types of video files.

By default, the *Mac* has already been set up to work with various types of video files, such as the *Apple* video file format MOV. For other types of video files, such as the practice files that go with this book, you will need to download and install the proper codecs. *Mac OS X* will help you with this operation.

This is how you can check whether you need to download and install extra codecs:

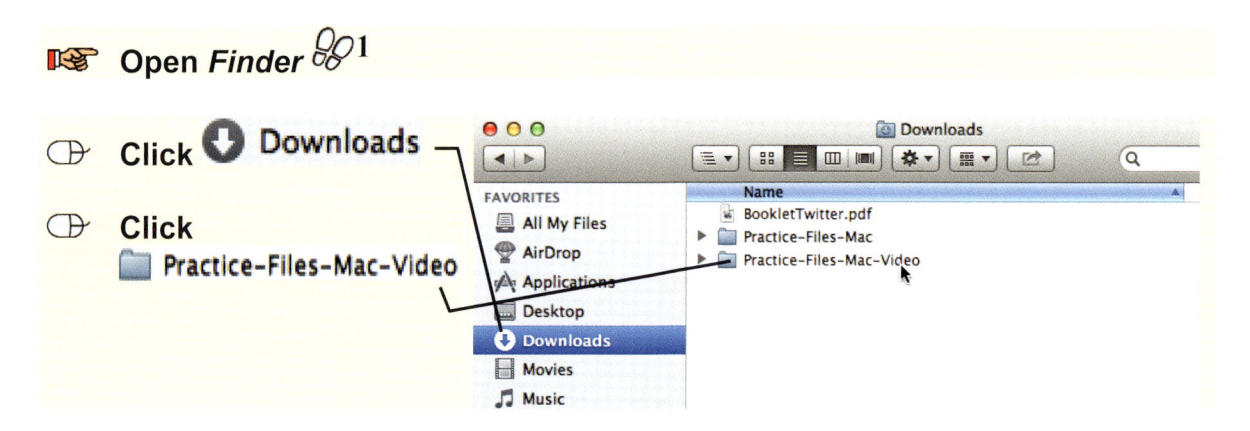

☞ **Open** *Finder* 👣¹

⊕ **Click** ⬇ **Downloads**

⊕ **Click** 📁 **Practice-Files-Mac-Video**

Chapter 2 Working with Video   **71**

You will need to use the Control key:

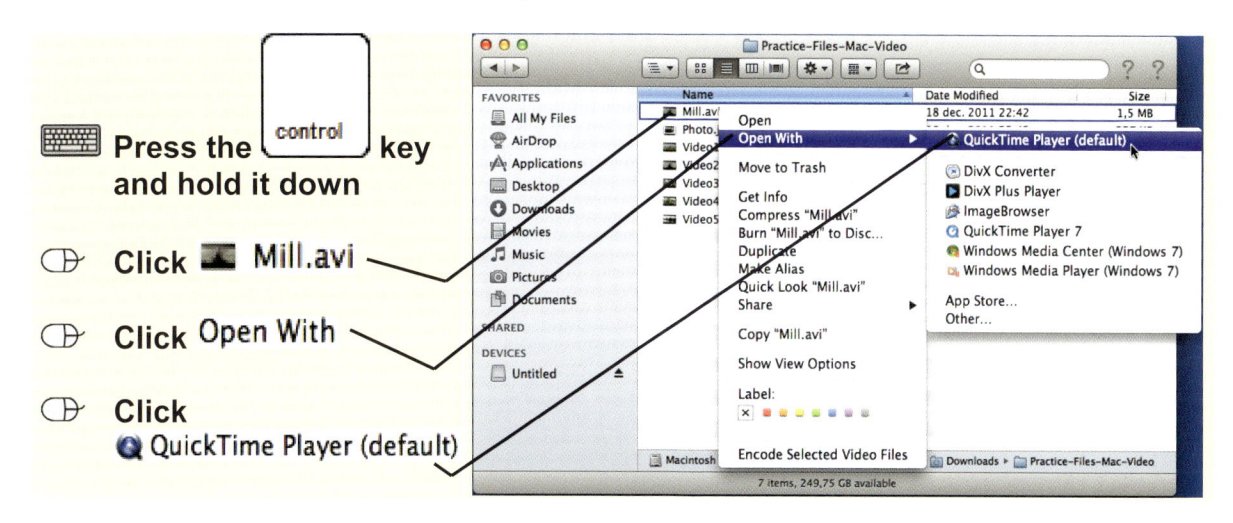

⌨️ **Press the** `control` **key and hold it down**

👆 **Click** 🎬 **Mill.avi**

👆 **Click Open With**

👆 **Click**
   🔵 **QuickTime Player (default)**

If the correct codecs have already been installed, you will see the QuickTime *Player* window below:

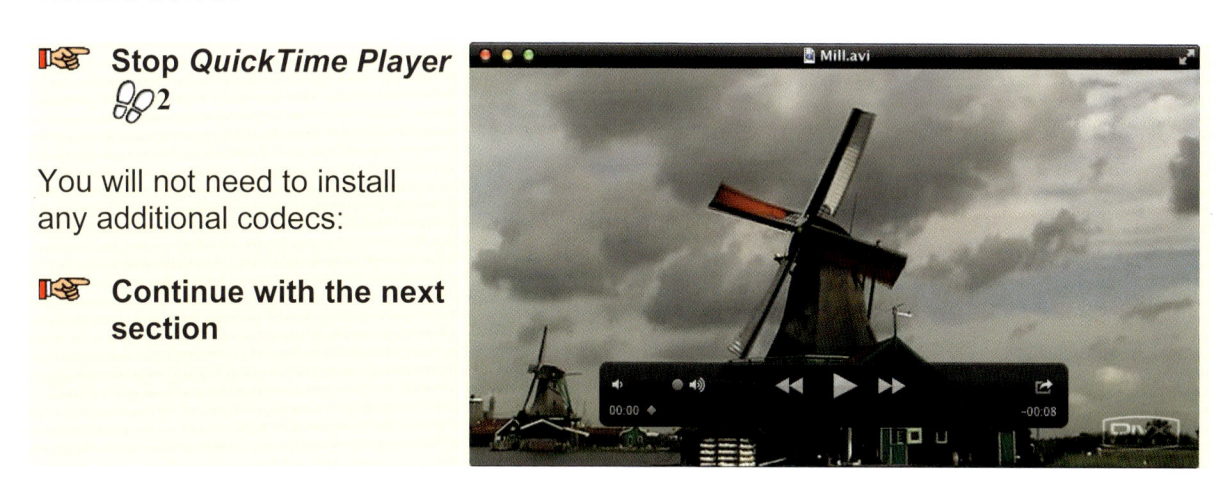

☞ **Stop** *QuickTime Player*
   𝄞2

You will not need to install any additional codecs:

☞ **Continue with the next section**

If the correct codecs have not been installed, you will see a message like the one below. You can download and install the necessary codecs:

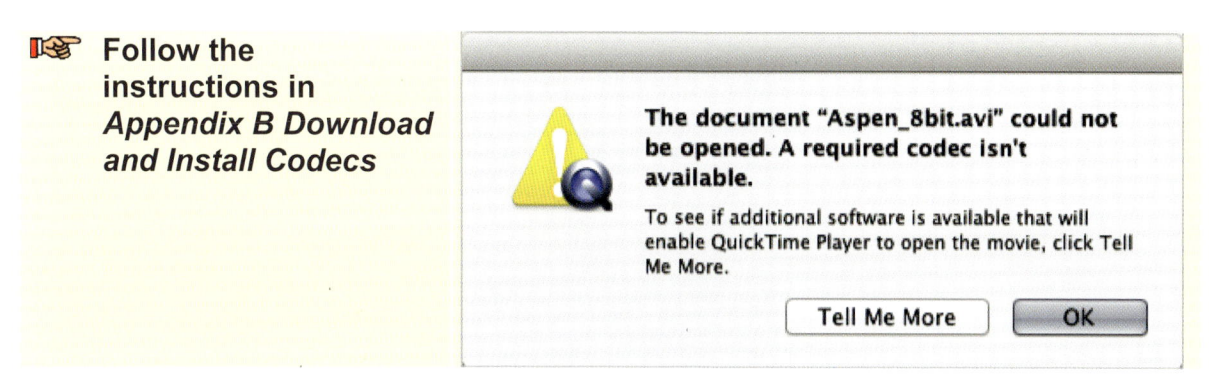

☞ **Follow the instructions in** *Appendix B Download and Install Codecs*

2.2 Importing Video Files from a Camera (with iMovie)

Importing means transferring files from some kind of device to your *Mac*. You can use the video editing program *iMovie* to transfer video files.
If you want to import video files from your digital video camera, you will need to connect the device first. You do this in most cases by using a USB cable:

☞ **Use the cable that comes with your camera to connect the digital video camera to one of your *Mac's* USB ports. Then turn the camera on.**

Usually, you will need to use one of the options on your camera, to indicate that the camera has to make contact with a computer. You can read more about this topic in your camera's manual:

☞ **Select the correct option on your camera for connecting to the computer**

You might need to install the camera software package first, before your camera will be recognized by the program. You can read more about this in your camera's manual:

☞ **If necessary, install the software that goes with the camera**

☞ **If necessary, stop *iPhoto* ⓘ²**

Now you can open *iMovie*:

☞ **Open *Finder* ⓘ¹**

⊕ Click 🅰 **Applications**

⊕ **Double-click** ★ **iMovie**

You will see the *iMovie* window:

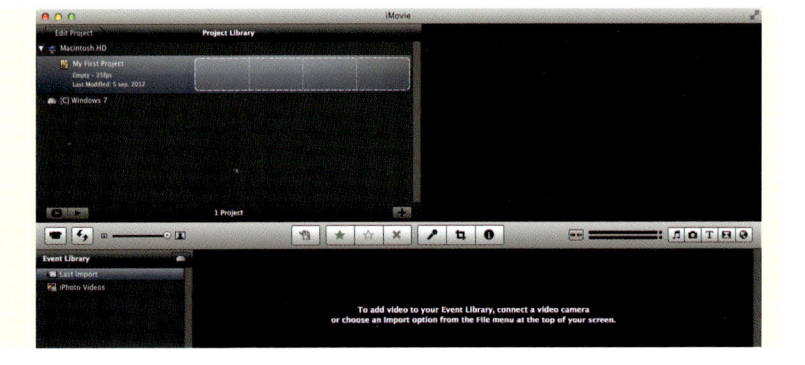

Chapter 2 Working with Video   73

You can use *iMovie* to import the video files from your video camera:

At the top of the window:

- Click **File**

- Click **Import from Camera...**

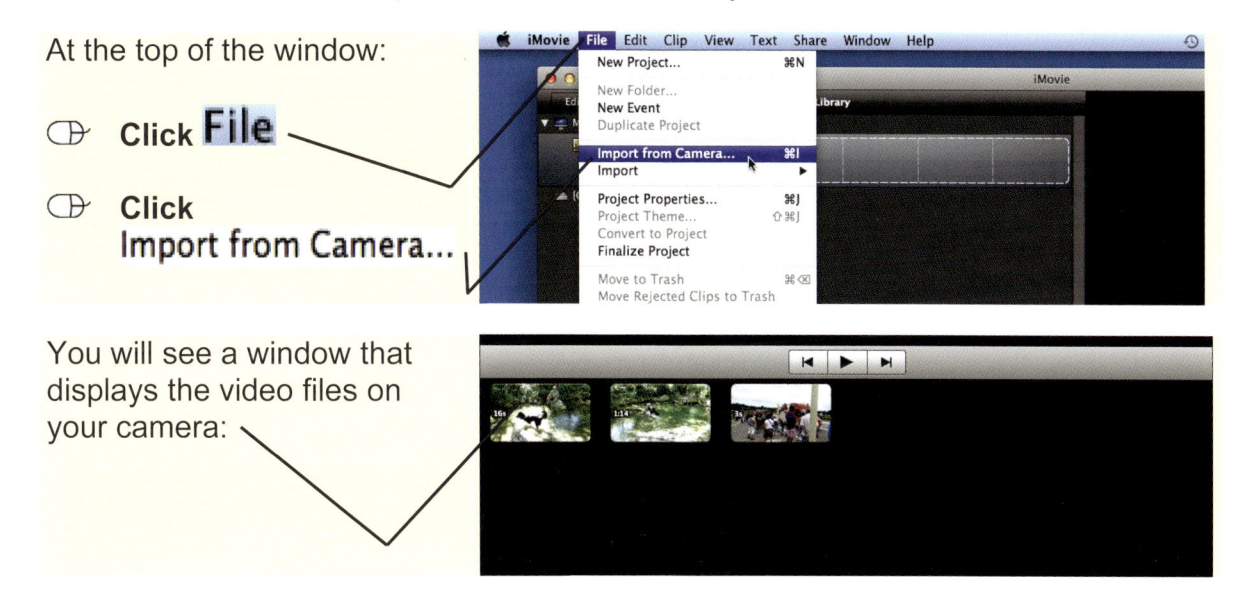

You will see a window that displays the video files on your camera:

⊗ HELP! I cannot see my camera.
It sometimes happens that your camera is not recognized in *iMovie*. This is because *iMovie* does not support all camera types. Here is how to check which types of cameras are supported by *iMovie*:

At the top of the window:

- Click **Help**

- Click **Supported Cameras**

You will be linked to a website that contains more information about the supported cameras:

☞ **Select your brand and type of camera**

- Click **Go**

Now you will see an overview of all supported cameras.

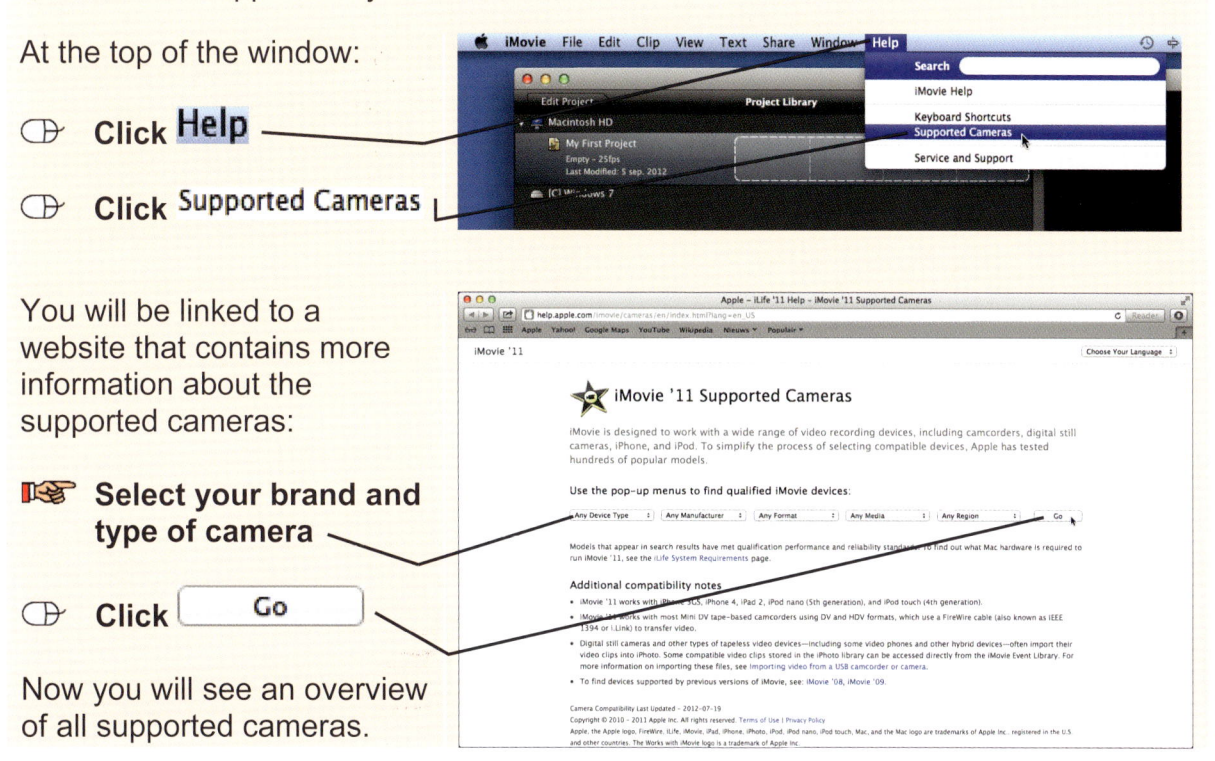

Now you can start importing all the recordings from your camera:

- ☞ **If necessary, drag the slider ◯ to Automatic**

- ☞ **Click** `Import All...`

You can also import just a few selected recordings. Here is how you do that:

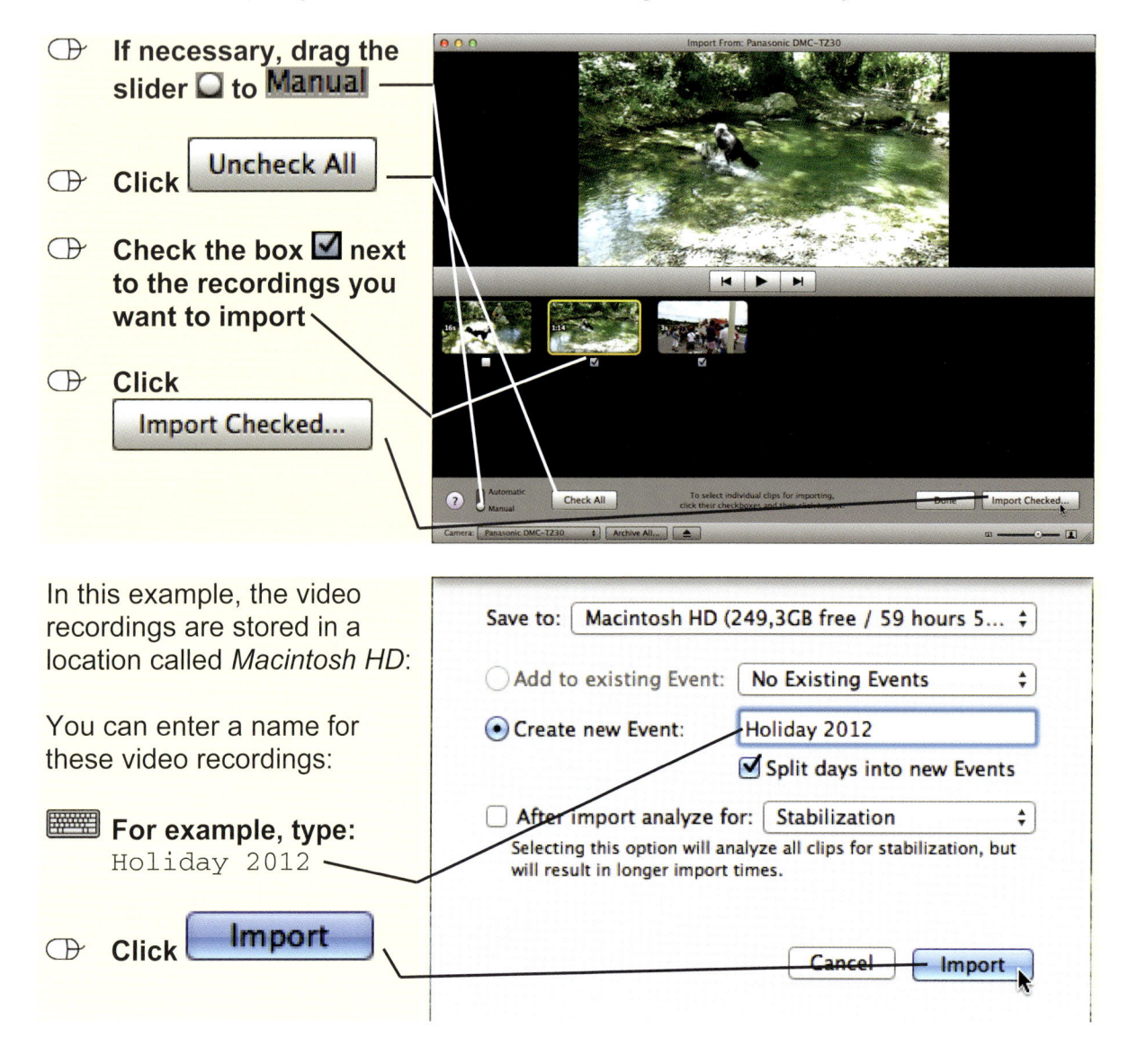

- ☞ **If necessary, drag the slider ◯ to Manual**

- ☞ **Click** `Uncheck All`

- ☞ **Check the box ☑ next to the recordings you want to import**

- ☞ **Click** `Import Checked...`

In this example, the video recordings are stored in a location called *Macintosh HD*:

You can enter a name for these video recordings:

- ⌨ **For example, type:** `Holiday 2012`

- ☞ **Click** `Import`

Chapter 2 Working with Video **75**

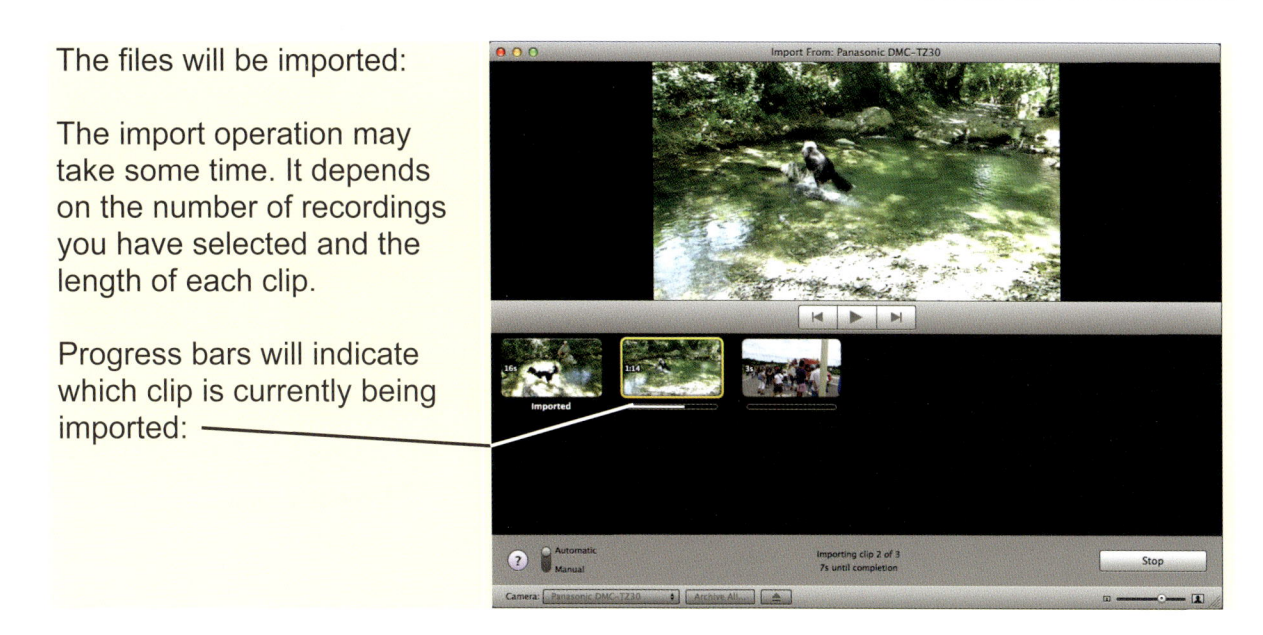

The files will be imported:

The import operation may take some time. It depends on the number of recordings you have selected and the length of each clip.

Progress bars will indicate which clip is currently being imported:

After the import operation has finished you will see this window:

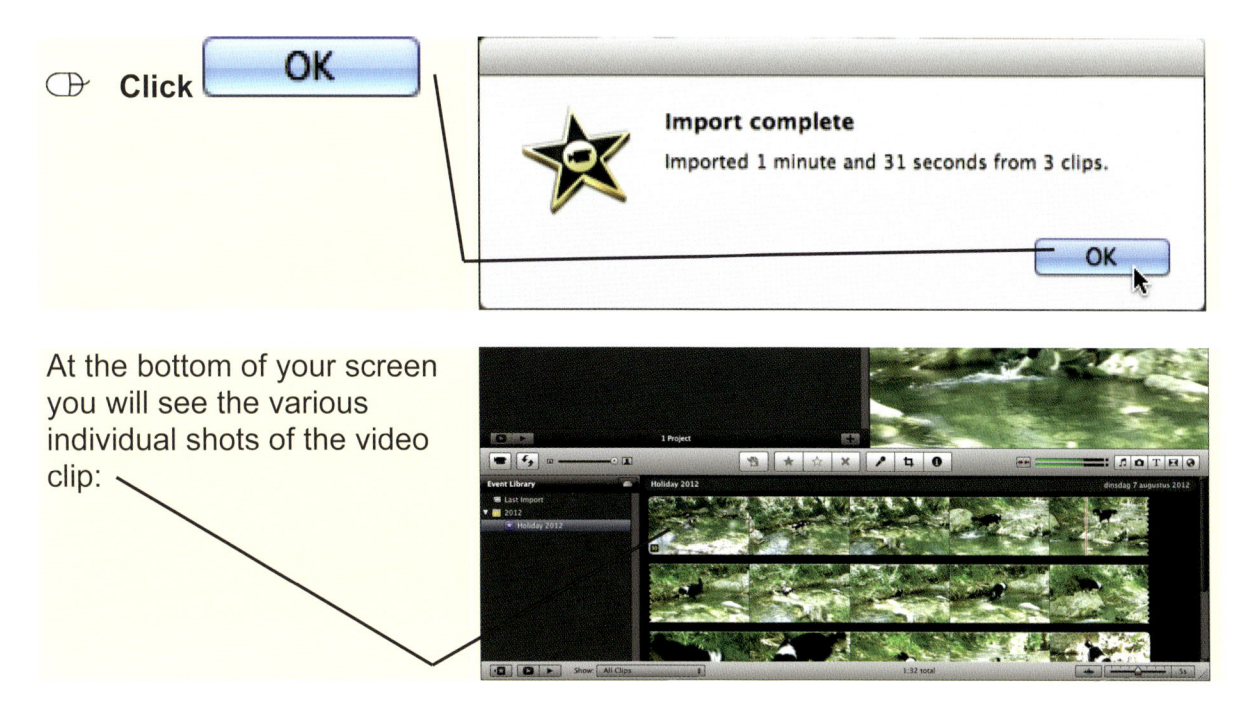

⌘ **Click OK**

At the bottom of your screen you will see the various individual shots of the video clip:

If you are using a *Mac* equipped with a card reader and you own a digital video camera that has an SD memory card, you can also insert the SD card directly into the *Mac's* card reader.

On the iMac, the SD card reader is located on the right-hand side, below the CD/DVD player:

☞ **Carefully insert the SD card into the slot, with the printed side of the card pointing towards you**

On the Mac Book, the card reader is located on the side of the keyboard:

☞ **Carefully insert the SD card into the slot, with the printed side of the card pointing towards you**

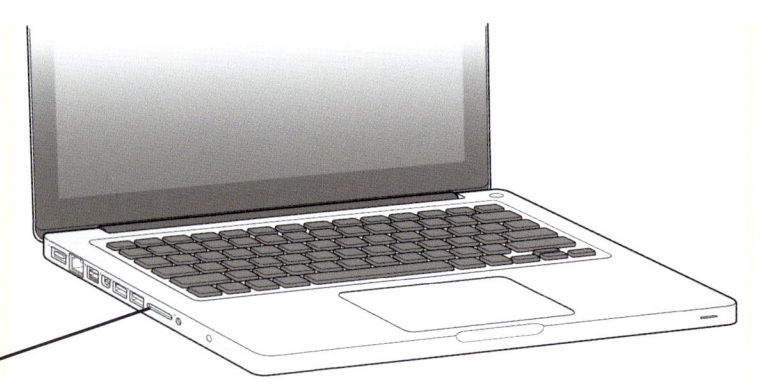

Now you can import the video files from the SD card into *iMovie*, the same way you import video files from a camera.

Chapter 2 Working with Video

2.3 Deactivating and Removing a Camera or SD Card

After you have finished importing the video files, you can deactivate and safely disconnect/remove the digital camera or SD card from your *Mac*, like this:

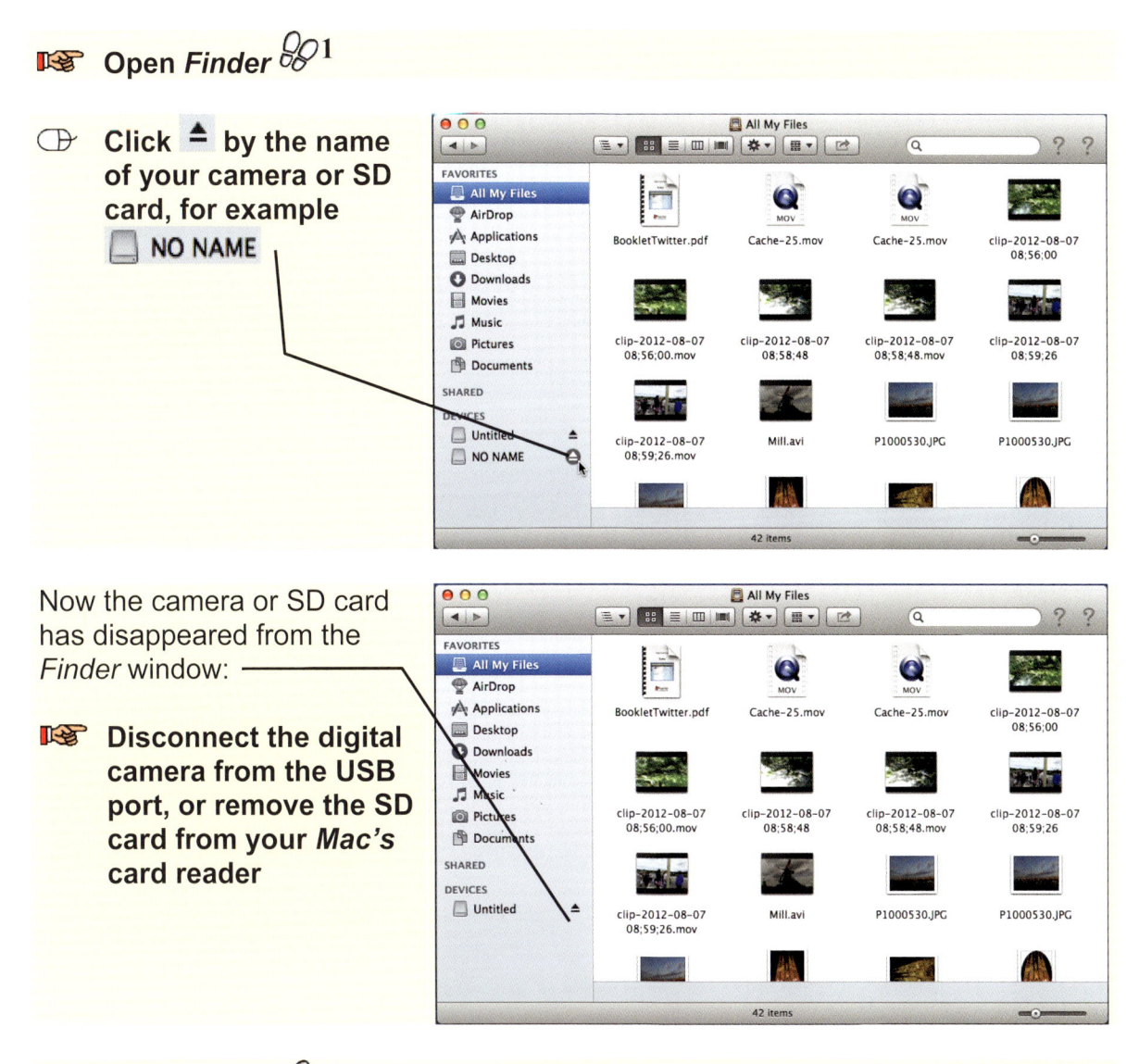

☞ **Open *Finder*** $\mathscr{O}^1$

⌘ **Click ⏏ by the name of your camera or SD card, for example** 🗔 **NO NAME**

Now the camera or SD card has disappeared from the *Finder* window:

☞ **Disconnect the digital camera from the USB port, or remove the SD card from your *Mac's* card reader**

☞ **Close *Finder*** $\mathscr{O}^3$

2.4 Creating Videos with iMovie

You can use *iMovie* not only for importing video clips from your camera, but also to edit your clips and join them together into a real video movie, including music, titles and transitions.

To practice these types of actions you do not need to use the video clips from your own camera. You can use the practice files that go with this chapter instead. In this way, everything you see on your own screen will look exactly the same as the images in this book. You can download these practice files from the website accompanying this book. In *Appendix C Download Practice Files* you can read how to do this.

☞ **If necessary, carry out the actions as described in *Appendix C Download Practice Files***

If the *iMovie* program is not open:

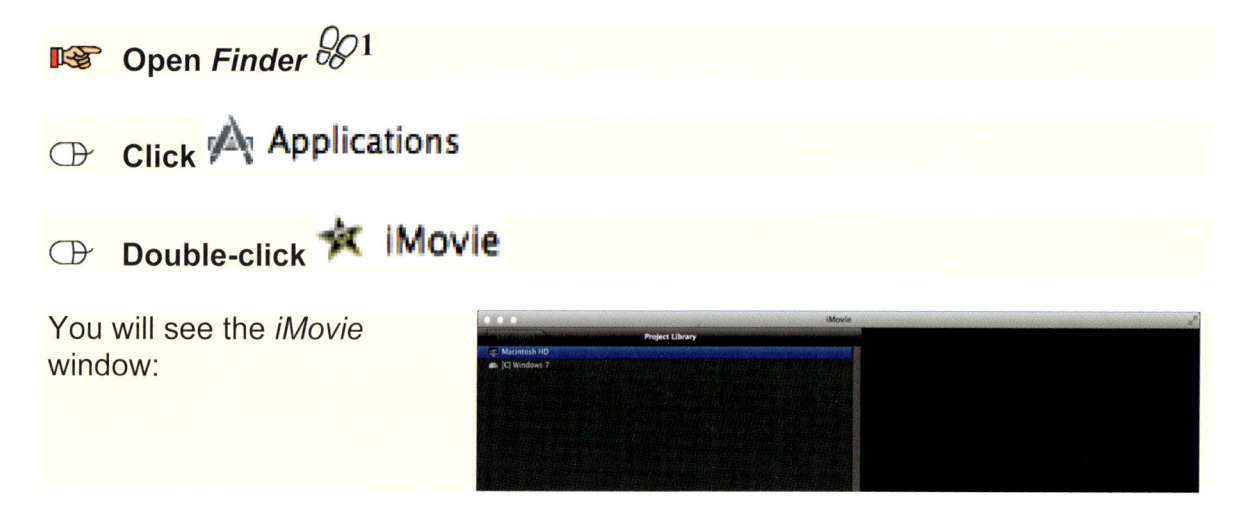

☞ **Open *Finder*** ℘¹

⊕ **Click Applications**

⊕ **Double-click iMovie**

You will see the *iMovie* window:

2.5 Starting a New Project

Before you can start editing your video clips, you will need to create a new video project:

At the top of the window:

⊕ **Click File**

⊕ **Click New Project...**

Chapter 2 Working with Video   **79**

A new project will be opened. You can define various settings for this project right way, for instance, the theme, the aspect ratio and the name of the project.
If you choose a theme, the video clips will be displayed in a certain style, for example, in a frame shaped like a cartoon. This is fun to try out sometime, but for now you will be using a project without a specific theme. You can always add a theme later on.

It is recommended that you start off by entering the correct aspect ratio for your project. The aspect ratio determines whether the video is displayed on a normal screen size (4:3) or a widescreen (16:9). Your camera's manual will contain more information about this topic.

The frame rate indicates how many frames per second are displayed in the video, and which movie format is used. The default rate for the NTSC system (the TV system most in use in America) is 30 frames per second. The default rate for the PAL system (used mostly in Europe) is 25 frames per second.

With the **Automatically add:** option you can set automatic transitions between each video fragment. Usually this is not such a good idea, except when used for a slideshow with photos.

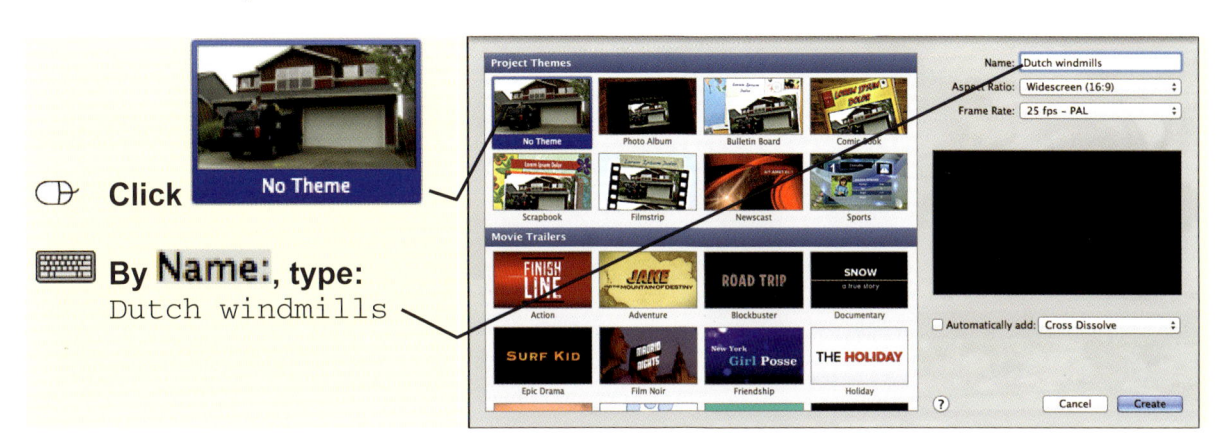

⌁ **Click** No Theme

⌨ **By Name:, type:**
Dutch windmills

💡 **Tip**
Selecting a trailer
A trailer is a short movie that gives a brief impression of a video. A trailer is often used, for example, for advertising purposes, for promoting a movie that is expected to run in your local movie theatre. You can choose to add a trailer at the start of a new project, or you can decide to add it later on, once your video editing is completed.

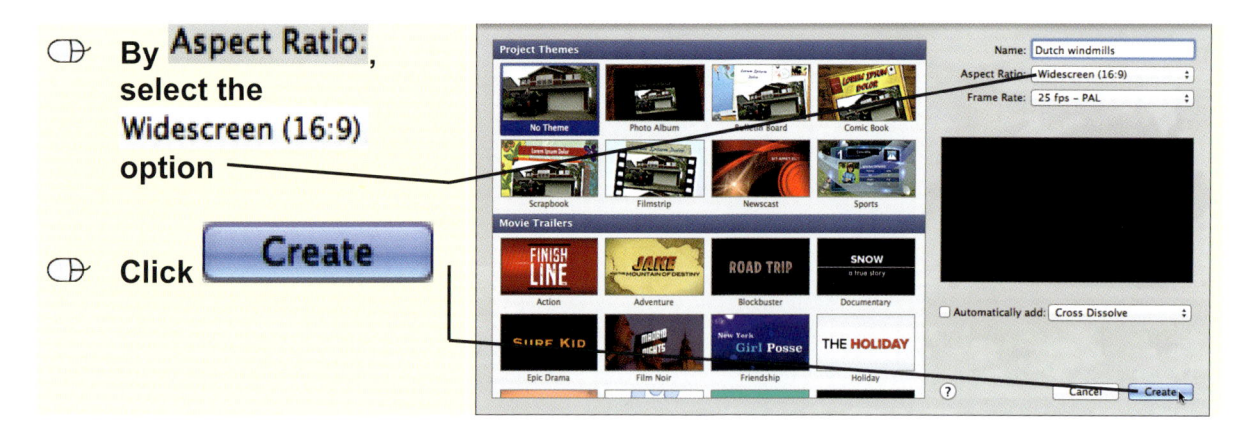

⊕ By **Aspect Ratio:**, select the **Widescreen (16:9)** option

⊕ Click **Create**

Now you have created a new project to which you can add files.

2.6 Importing a Video File Into a Project

Now you can start importing the video clips for your video project. In most cases you will import these files directly from your camera, as described in *section 2.2 Importing Video Files from a Camera (with iMovie)*. But for now, we will be using the practice files that go with this book. Here is how you import the video files:

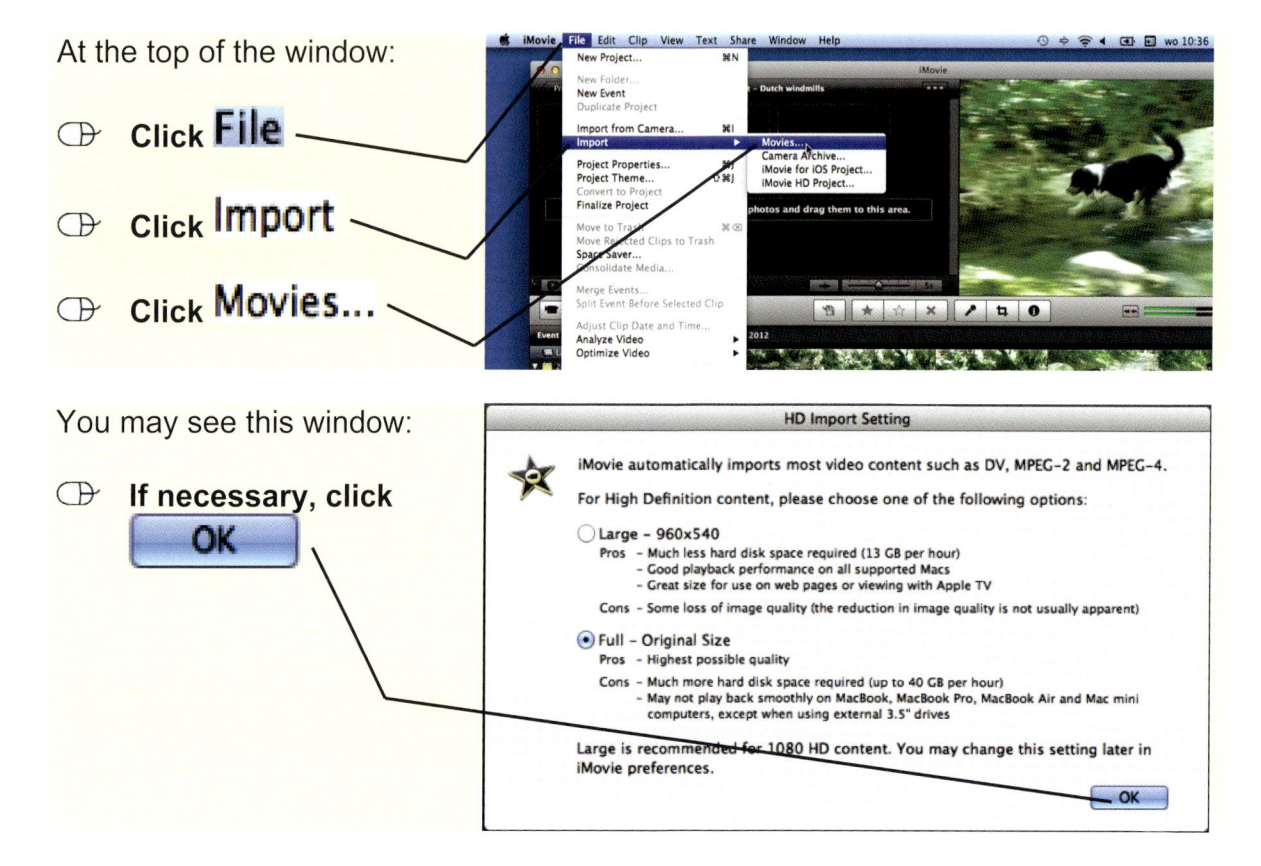

At the top of the window:

⊕ Click **File**

⊕ Click **Import**

⊕ Click **Movies...**

You may see this window:

⊕ If necessary, click **OK**

Chapter 2 Working with Video **81**

Now you will see this window:

Folders and files:

Hard drive for storing the imported files:

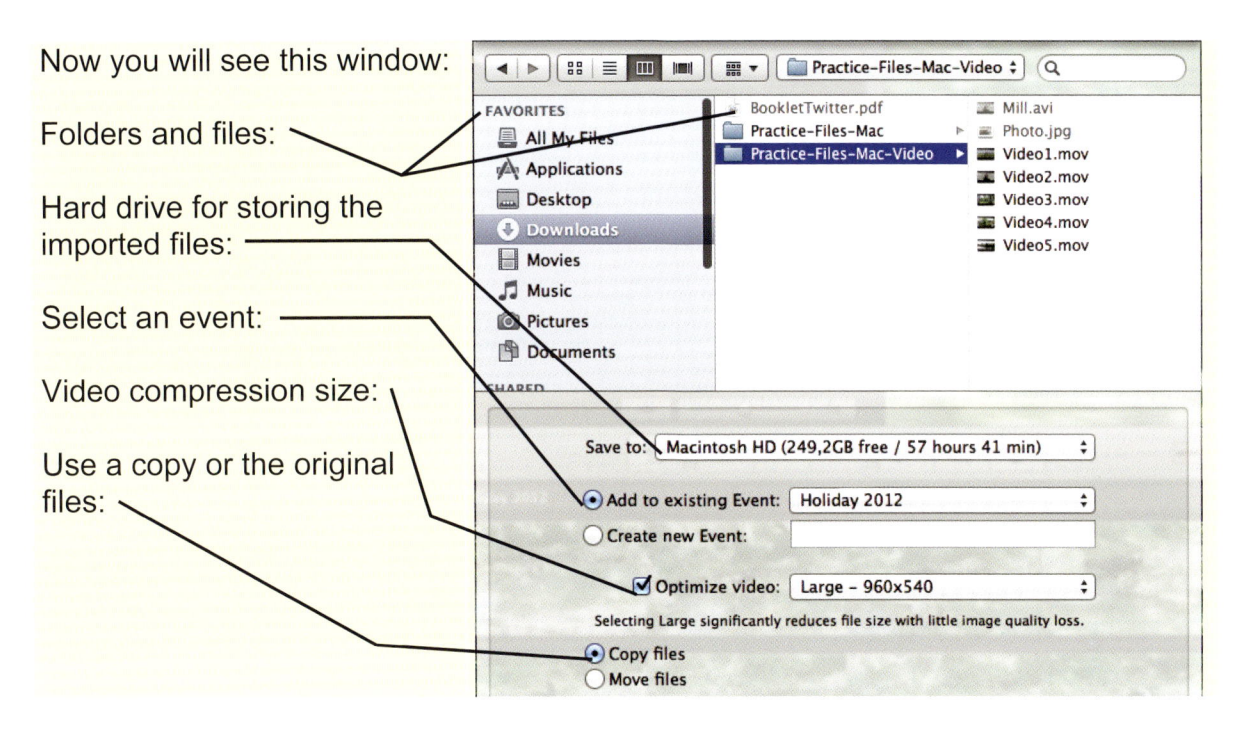

Select an event:

Video compression size:

Use a copy or the original files:

It can be useful to attach a specific event to the video clips you are about to import, in order to link them together. For instance, the location of a recent trip or the name of a special occasion.

You can decide to *compress* a video while importing it. The video file will be reduced in size and will take up less space on the hard drive. But this will result in some loss of quality.

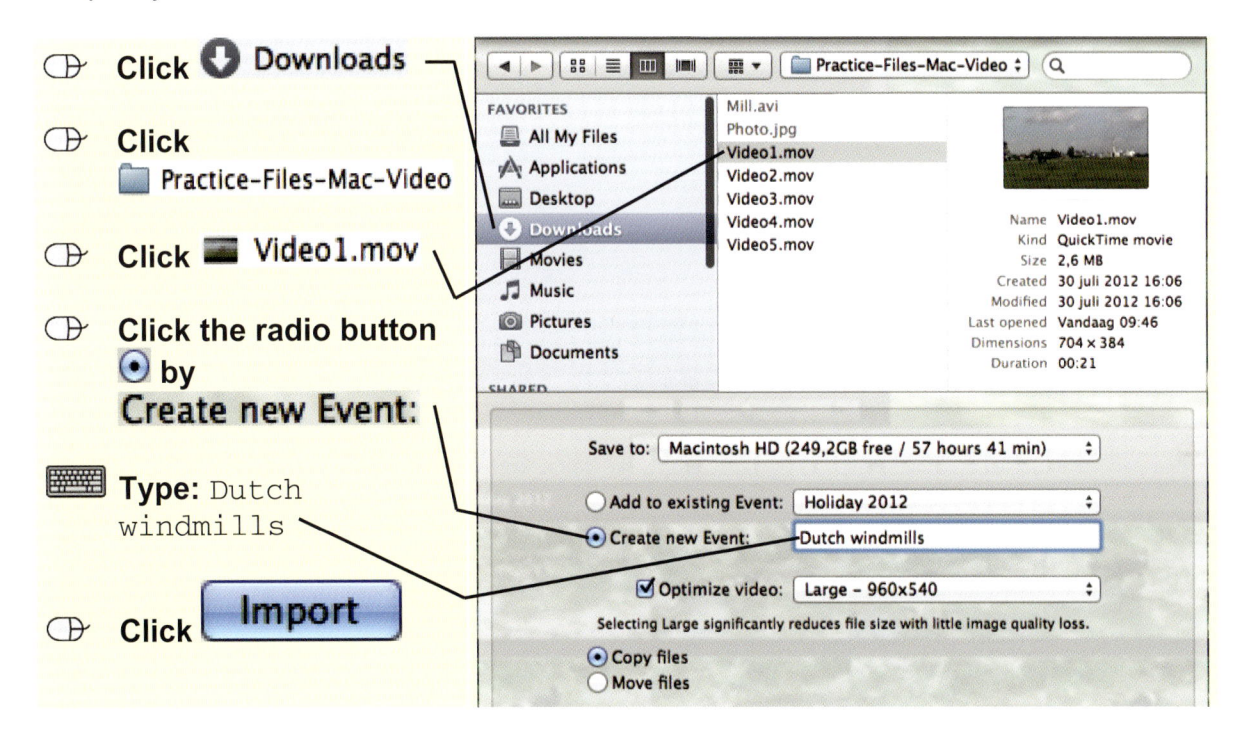

⊕ Click **Downloads**

⊕ Click **Practice-Files-Mac-Video**

⊕ Click **Video1.mov**

⊕ Click the radio button ⦿ by **Create new Event:**

⌨ Type: Dutch windmills

⊕ Click **Import**

💡 Tip
Import videos from an SD card
If you want to transfer your video files from an SD card that has been inserted into your *Mac's* card reader, you can import them in the same way as you would import the files that are stored in a folder on your computer:

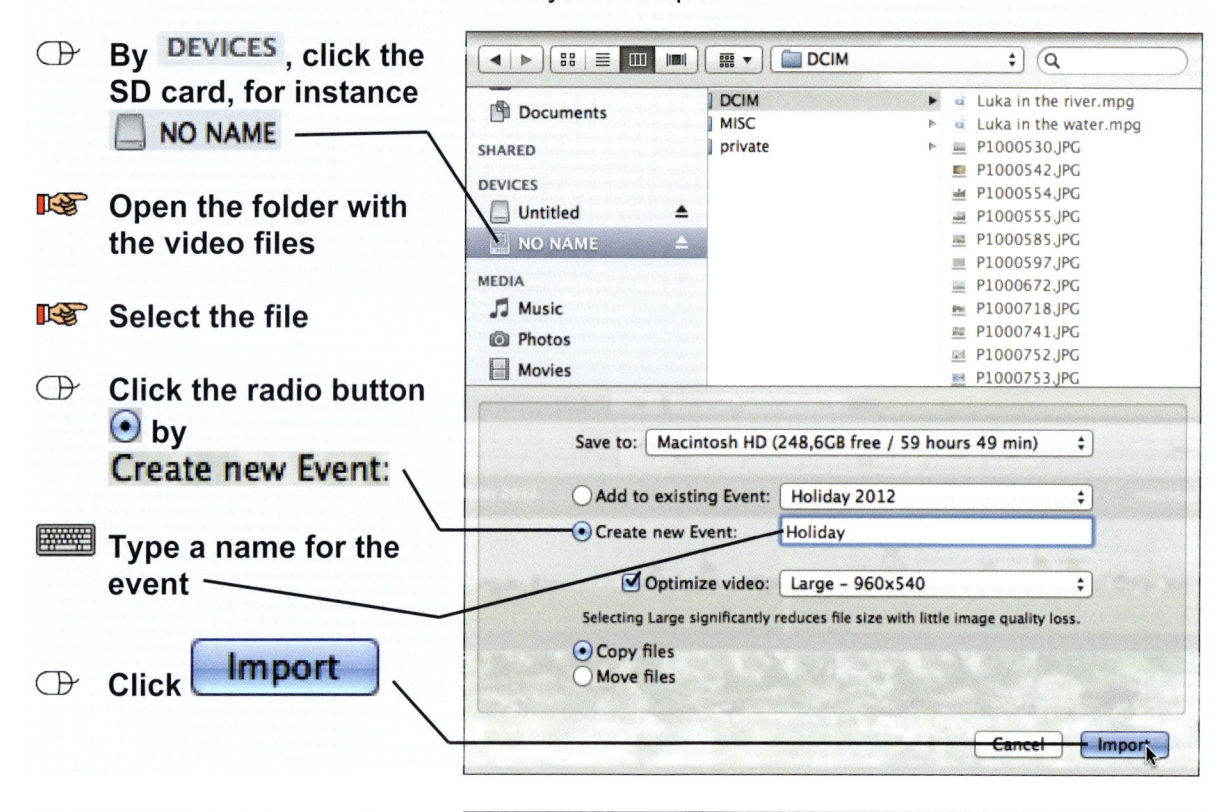

☞ By DEVICES, click the SD card, for instance NO NAME

☞ Open the folder with the video files

☞ Select the file

☞ Click the radio button ⦿ by Create new Event:

☞ Type a name for the event

☞ Click Import

The file has been imported:

The video clips will be divided into various sections.

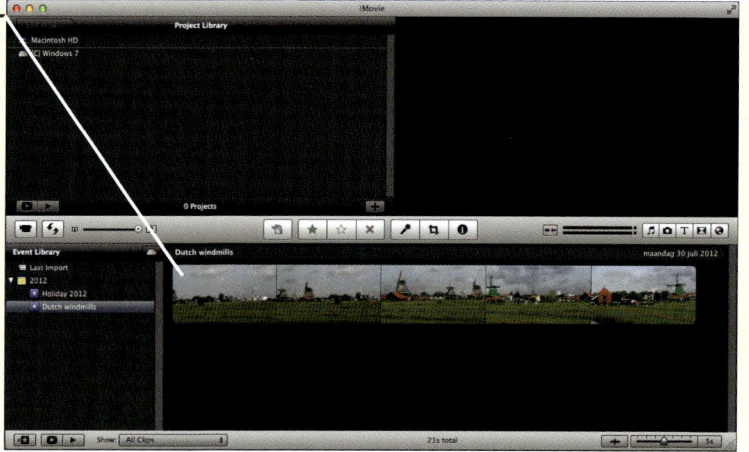

Chapter 2 Working with Video **83**

2.7 Editing a Video Clip

Most video clips will not have the duration you want right away. You will often need to trim the clip, so it that it can be used more effectively in your movie.

It is recommended that you view your clips first. This will help you determine whether the clip needs to be trimmed and in what places.

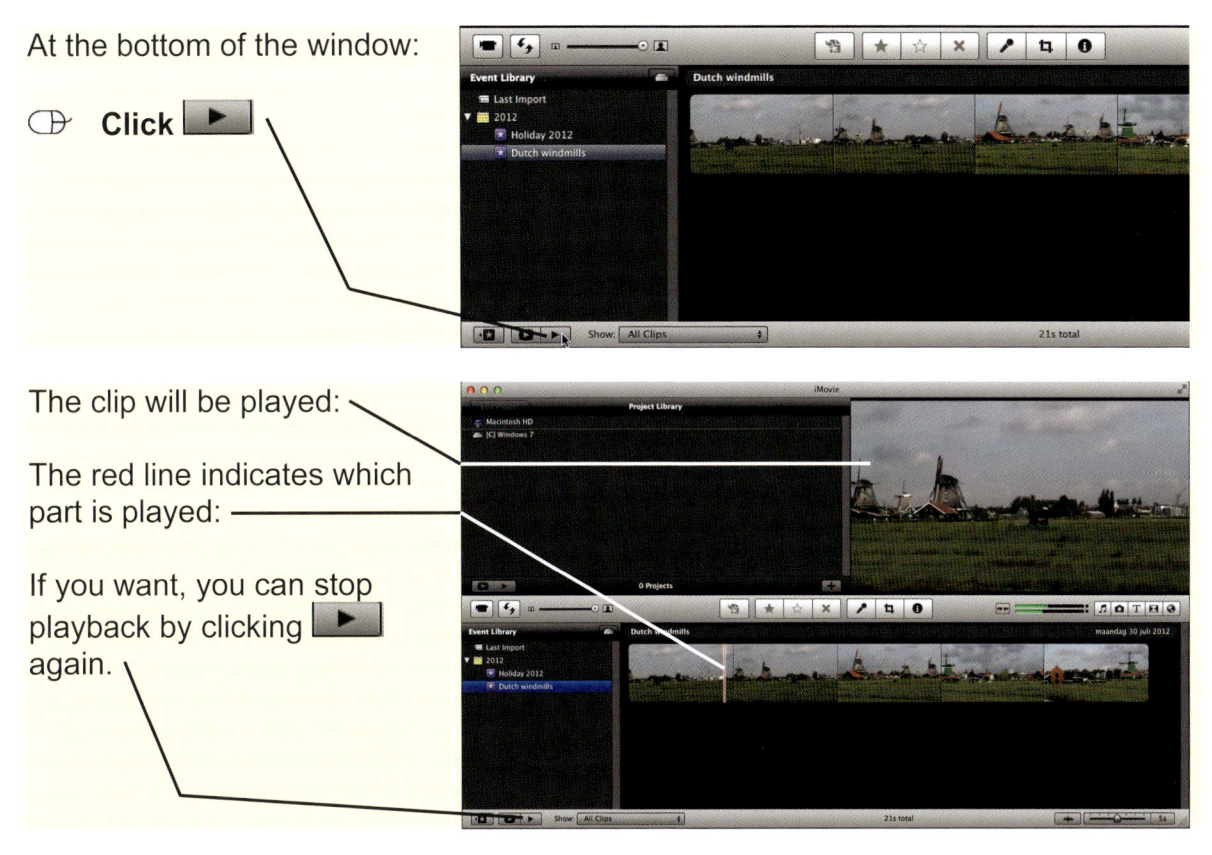

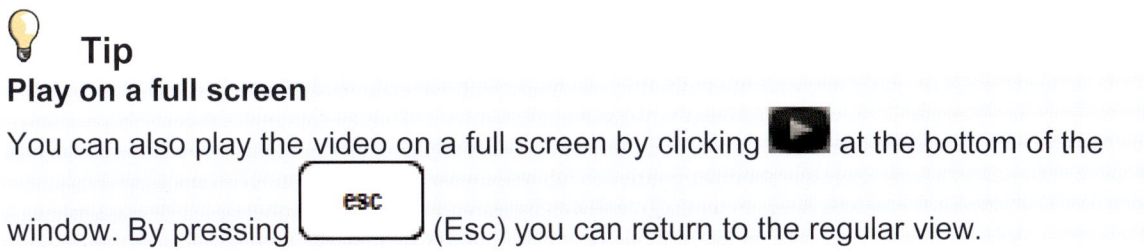

At the bottom of the window:

☞ **Click** ▶

The clip will be played:

The red line indicates which part is played:

If you want, you can stop playback by clicking ▶ again.

💡 Tip
Play on a full screen
You can also play the video on a full screen by clicking ▶ at the bottom of the window. By pressing ⌈esc⌋ (Esc) you can return to the regular view.

First, you need to determine the starting point of the clip. You can do this by dragging the red line in the clip to the desired spot:

☞ **Position the pointer on the red line**

☞ **Drag the red line to the middle of the first frame**

➥ Please note:

You need to make sure that while you drag the red line, the entire clip has not been selected. If the clip has been selected it will have a yellow border. This is how you can undo the selection :

☞ **Click a spot outside of the clip**

☞ **Press the mouse button**

You will see a yellow frame:

☞ **Drag the mouse pointer to the right**

☞ **Keep the mouse button depressed**

☞ **Drag the pointer to the middle of the last frame, or thereabout**

Near the yellow border you will see a timer. This timer indicates the duration of the frame:

☞ **Release the mouse button**

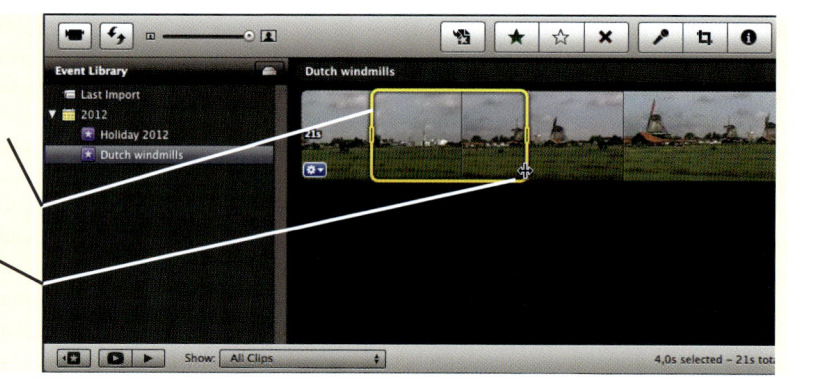

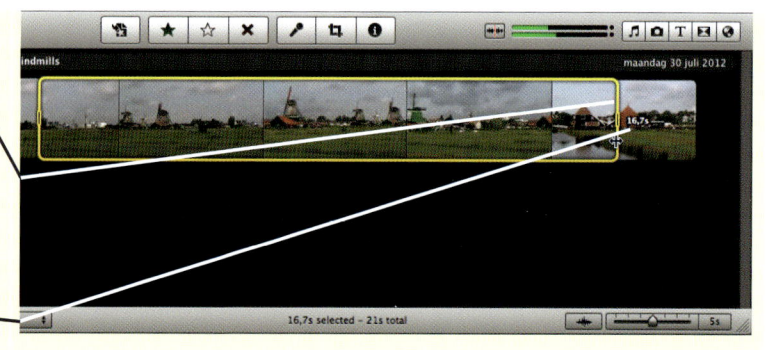

Chapter 2 Working with Video **85**

Now you can check if the selection was successful. You do this by opening a menu with the Control key:

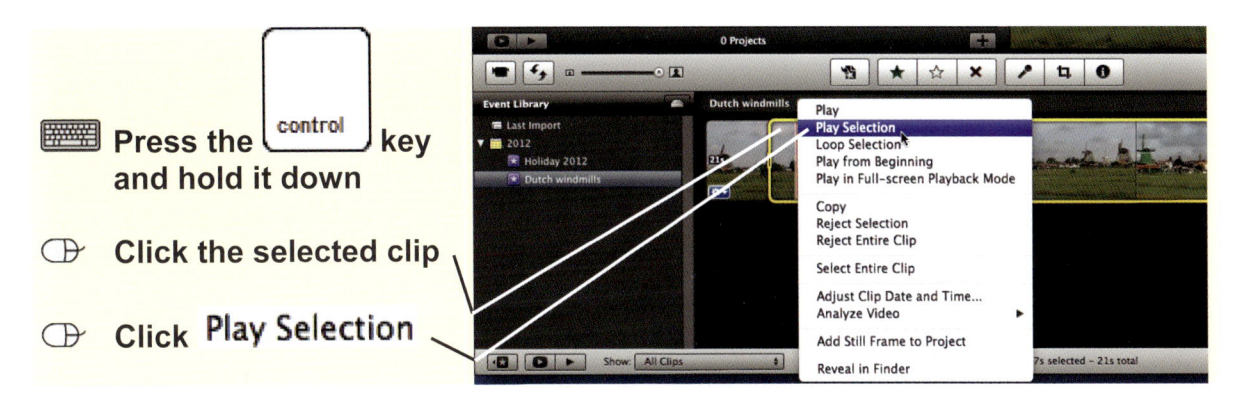

⌨ **Press the** `control` **key and hold it down**

☞ **Click the selected clip**

☞ **Click** Play Selection

Now the selected clip will be played. If you are not yet satisfied with this clip you can adjust it by dragging the borders of the yellow frame:

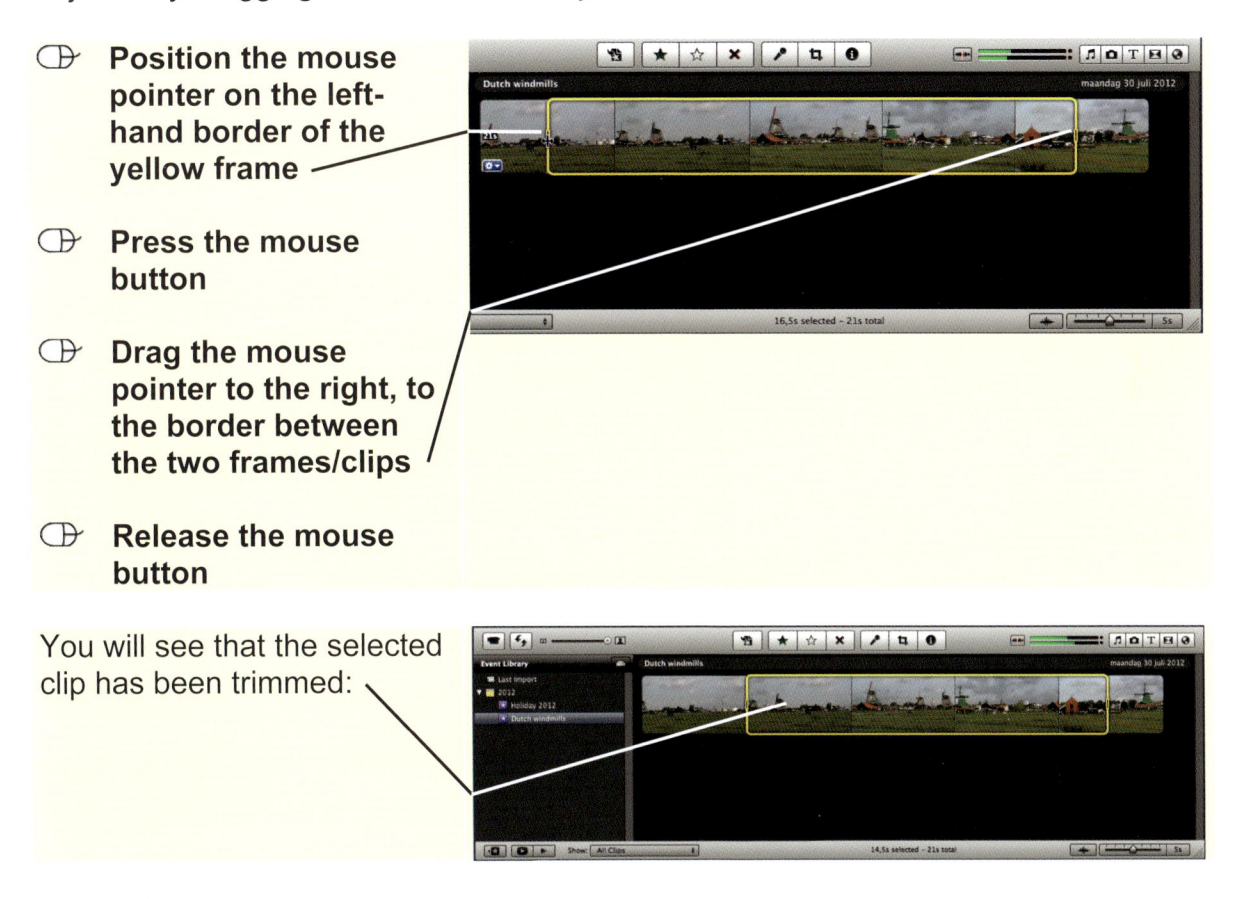

☞ **Position the mouse pointer on the left-hand border of the yellow frame**

☞ **Press the mouse button**

☞ **Drag the mouse pointer to the right, to the border between the two frames/clips**

☞ **Release the mouse button**

You will see that the selected clip has been trimmed:

Now you can add the trimmed clip to your video project:

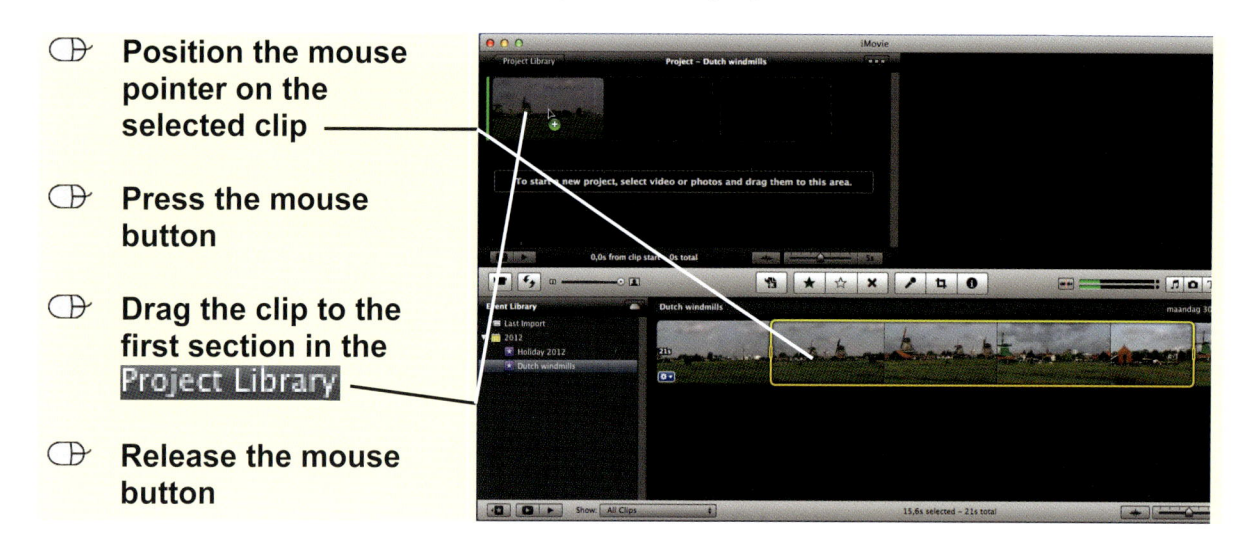

☞ **Position the mouse pointer on the selected clip**

☞ **Press the mouse button**

☞ **Drag the clip to the first section in the Project Library**

☞ **Release the mouse button**

HELP! I see a message concerning the speed of the clip.
You may see a window at this moment containing information about the image speed. You can decide whether you want to adapt the image speed of the project to the new clip you are going to add.

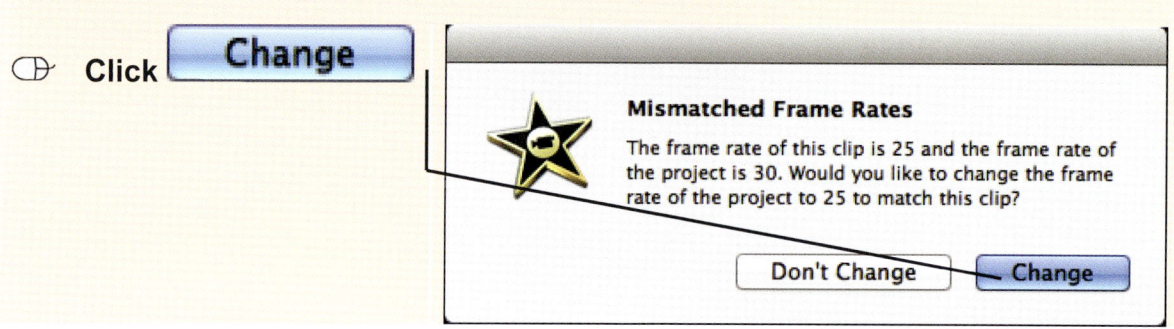

☞ **Click Change**

Mismatched Frame Rates
The frame rate of this clip is 25 and the frame rate of the project is 30. Would you like to change the frame rate of the project to 25 to match this clip?

Don't Change | Change

The selected clip has been added to the project library:

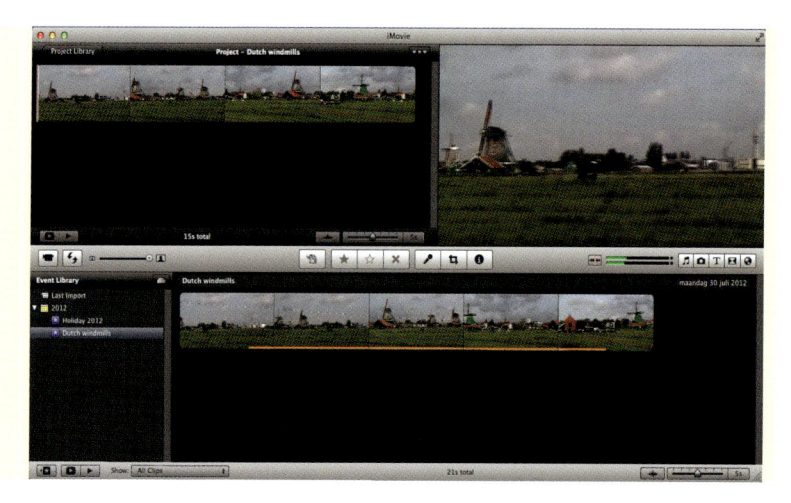

Chapter 2 Working with Video

The clip is now part of your video project. You can remove the original clip from the window. You do this by using the Command key and the Backspace or Delete key:

⌨ Press the [command] key and hold it down

☝ Click the clip in the right-hand section of the window

⌨ Release [command]

⌨ Press [←] (Backspace) or [delete] (Delete)

The selected clip has been removed.

2.8 Adding Multiple Video Files

If you want to quickly add video files to your video, you can import multiple files at once:

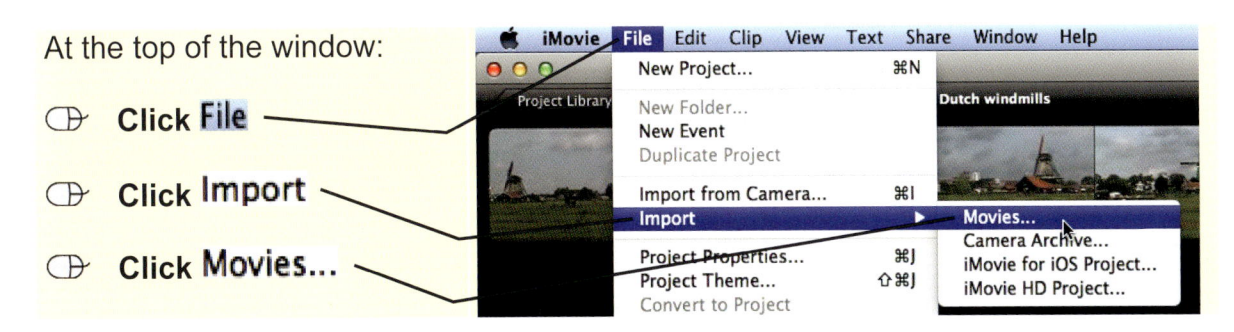

At the top of the window:

☝ Click **File**

☝ Click **Import**

☝ Click **Movies...**

To select multiple videos you need to use the Shift key:

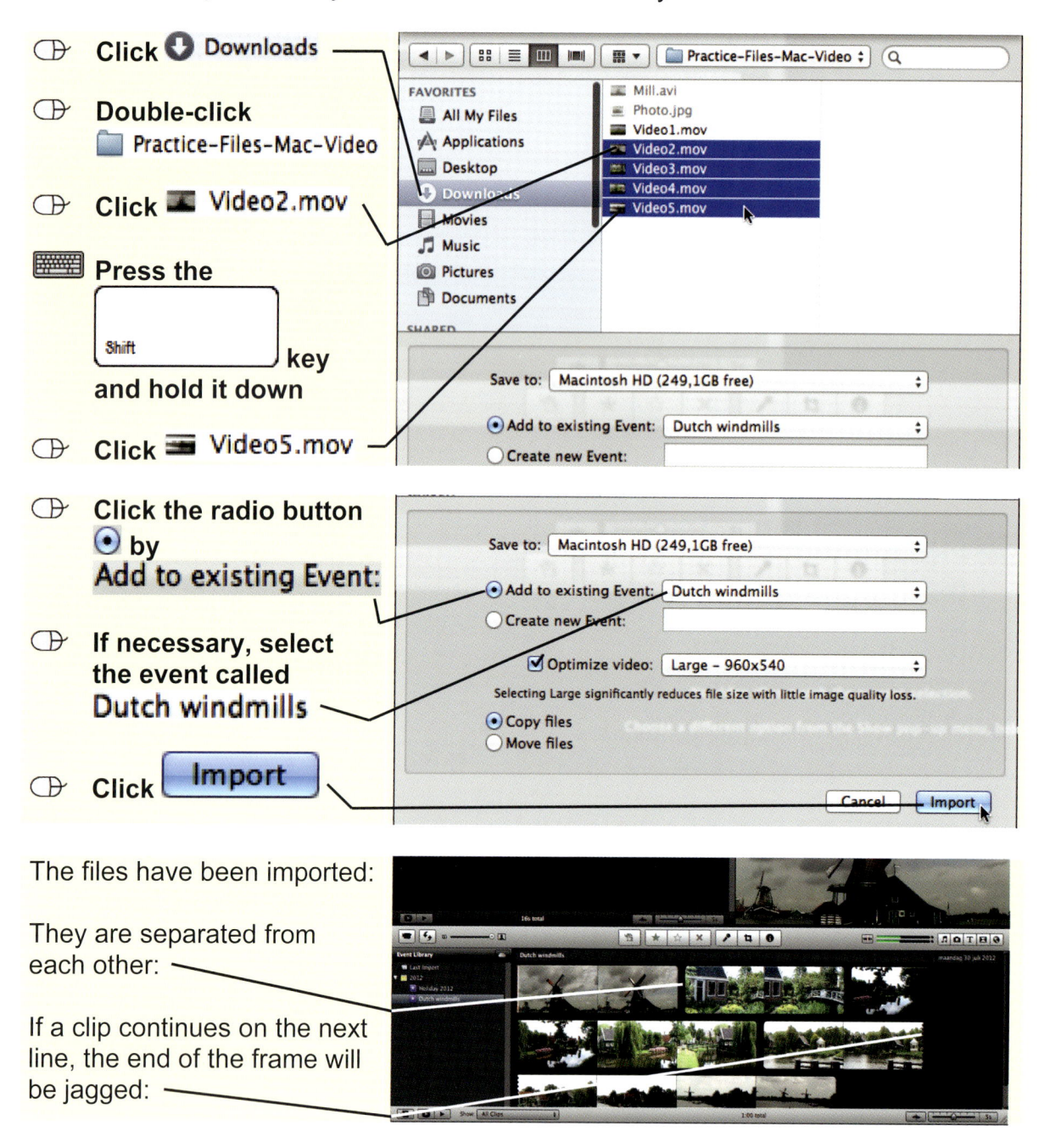

☞ Click ⬇ **Downloads**

☞ **Double-click**
📁 **Practice-Files-Mac-Video**

☞ Click 🎬 **Video2.mov**

⌨ **Press the**
[Shift] **key**
and hold it down

☞ Click 🎬 **Video5.mov**

☞ **Click the radio button**
⦿ **by**
Add to existing Event:

☞ **If necessary, select the event called**
Dutch windmills

☞ Click [**Import**]

The files have been imported:

They are separated from each other:

If a clip continues on the next line, the end of the frame will be jagged:

Chapter 2 Working with Video 89

Now you can trim the clips one by one, and add them to your video project:

☞ **Select a section with a duration of four seconds in the first file, starting at the beginning of the file** ℘14

⊕ **Position the mouse pointer on the selected clip**

⊕ **Press the mouse button**

⊕ **Drag the clip to the spot behind the first clip in the** `Project Library`

⊕ **Release the mouse button**

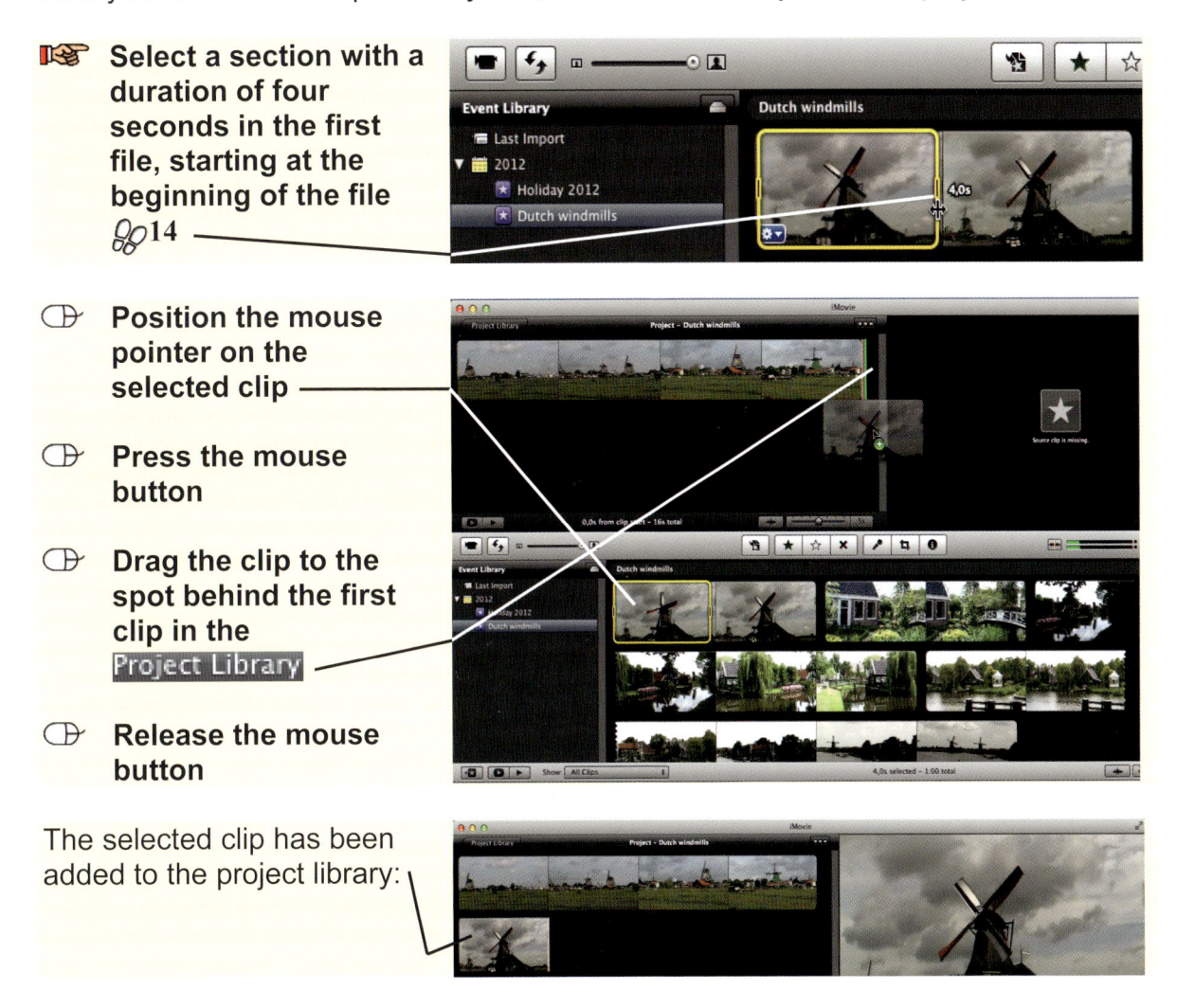

The selected clip has been added to the project library:

You can add the second and third video clips to the video project without having to trim them:

☞ **Add the entire second video clip to the end of the project** ℘7

☞ **Add the entire third video clip to the end of the project** ℘7

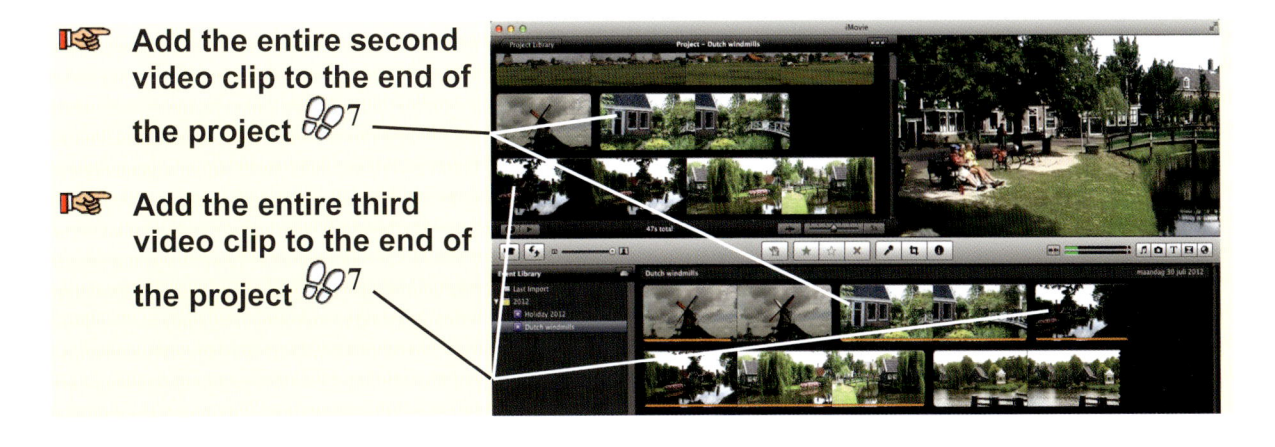

The last video clip needs some trimming:

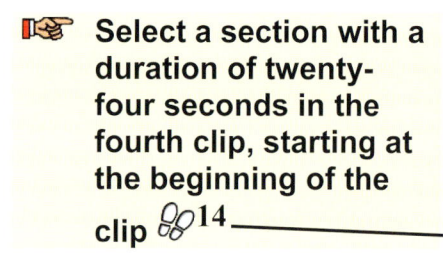

☞ **Select a section with a duration of twenty-four seconds in the fourth clip, starting at the beginning of the clip** ✂¹⁴

☞ **Add the fourth video clip to the end of the project**

Now all clips have been placed in the project library:

💡 Tip
Trim a clip in the project library
You can also trim a clip within the project library. This works in the same way as trimming a clip before moving it to the project library.

Chapter 2 Working with Video   91

2.9 Moving a Video Clip

You have placed the video clips in your project in a certain order. But it is not necessary to keep them in this order. You can rearrange the clips and move them to a different location in the project:

☞ **Click the third clip**

The clip has been selected:

☞ **Drag the clip to a spot between the fourth and fifth clips**

☞ **Release the mouse button**

You will see that the selected clip has been moved:

💡 **Tip**
Delete a clip
You can delete a clip from your video project by selecting it and then pressing ⌫ (Backspace) or delete (Delete).

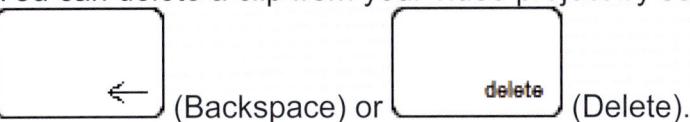

💡 **Tip**
Undo
You can easily undo an operation in *iMovie*. At the top of the window:

☞ **Click Edit, Undo**

You can play the video project when all of the clips are in the correct sequence:

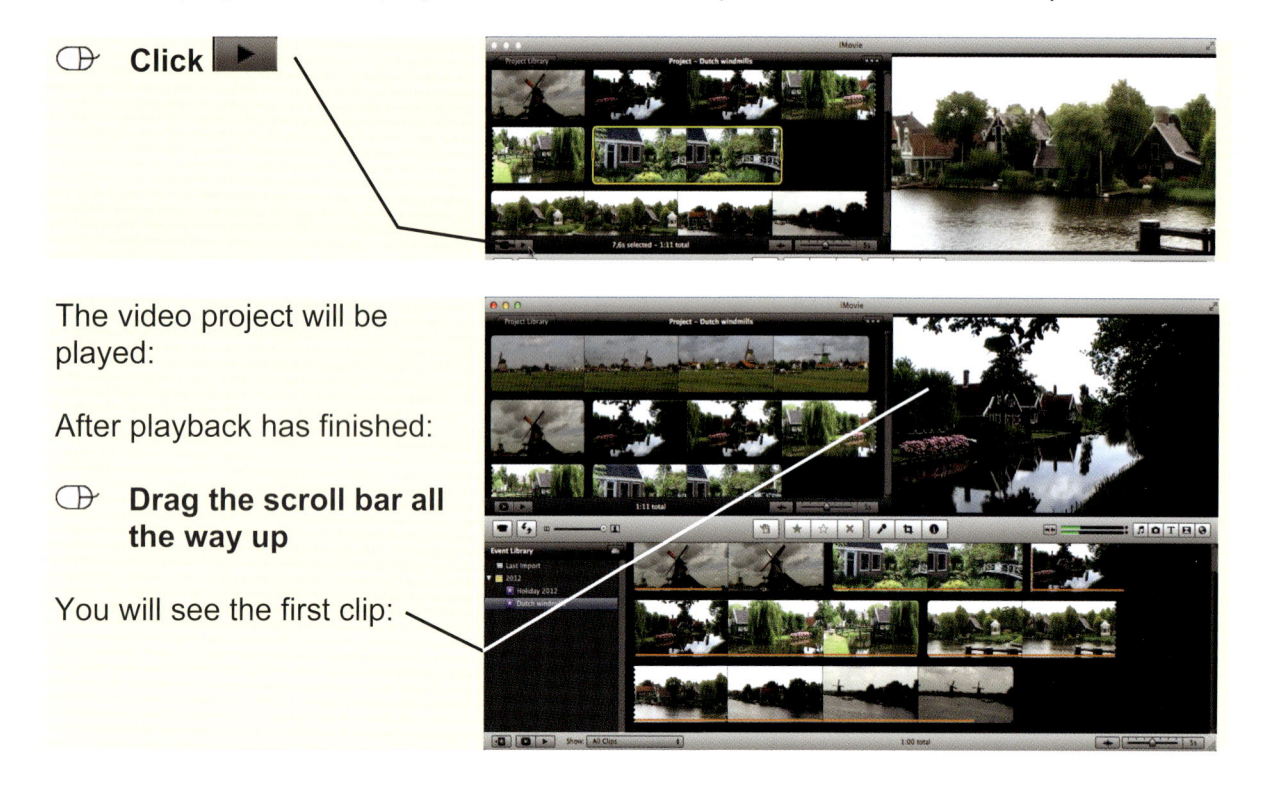

☞ **Click** ▶

The video project will be played:

After playback has finished:

☞ **Drag the scroll bar all the way up**

You will see the first clip:

2.10 Adding a Photo

You can also add photo files to your video project. For example, you can use a photo as a background for the titles at the beginning and end of the video.

This is how you add a photo:

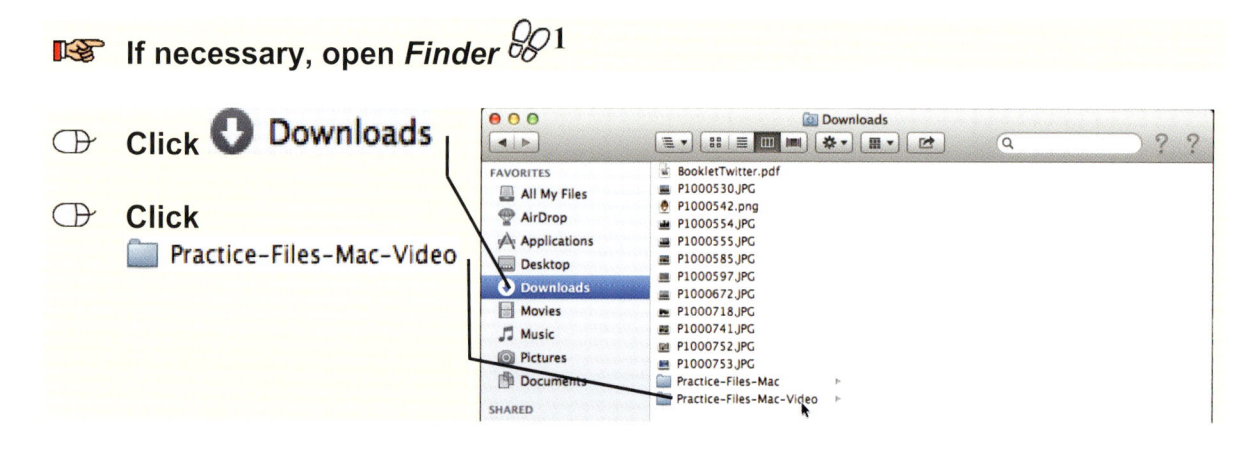

☞ **If necessary, open** *Finder* 👣¹

☞ **Click** ⬇ **Downloads**

☞ **Click** 📁 **Practice-Files-Mac-Video**

Chapter 2 Working with Video

⊕ Click 📷 **Photo.jpg**

⊕ **Drag the file to the *iMovie* window, to the left of the first clip**

⊕ **Release the mouse button**

☞ Close *Finder* ⚶³

You will see that the photo has been added to the beginning of the video project:

Tip
Crop a photo
You can crop a photo, to shorten the playback time. This works the same way as trimming a video clip.

Tip
Add photos from iPhoto
If you have photos stored in *iPhoto*, you can insert the photos from that program into *iMovie*:

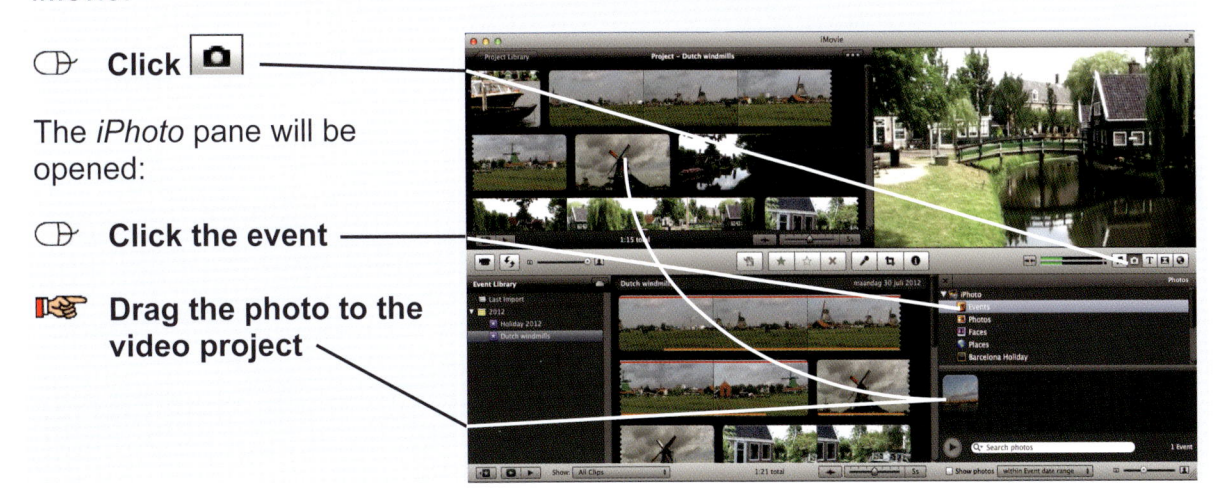

⊕ **Click** 📷

The *iPhoto* pane will be opened:

⊕ **Click the event**

☞ **Drag the photo to the video project**

2.11 Adding Titles

In *iMovie* you can add text to your video project. This means you can add titles and credits to your video.

You can add a title to the photo that is displayed at the start of your video project:

☞ **Click** T

You will see a pane with sample titles. Now you can drag a title to your video project:

☞ **Position the mouse pointer on** Centered

☞ **Press the mouse button**

☞ **Drag the title on to the frame containing the photo**

☞ **Release the mouse button**

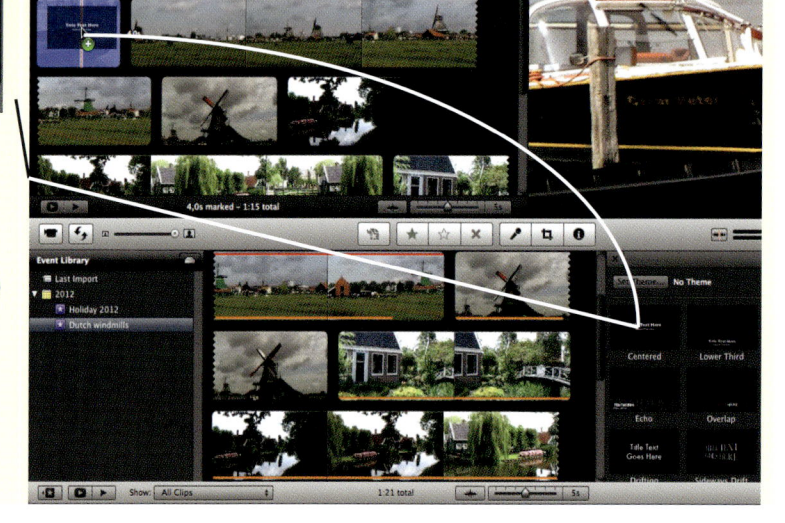

You will see that the title has been added to the photo:

The title is still selected, so you can change the title text right away:

Chapter 2 Working with Video 95

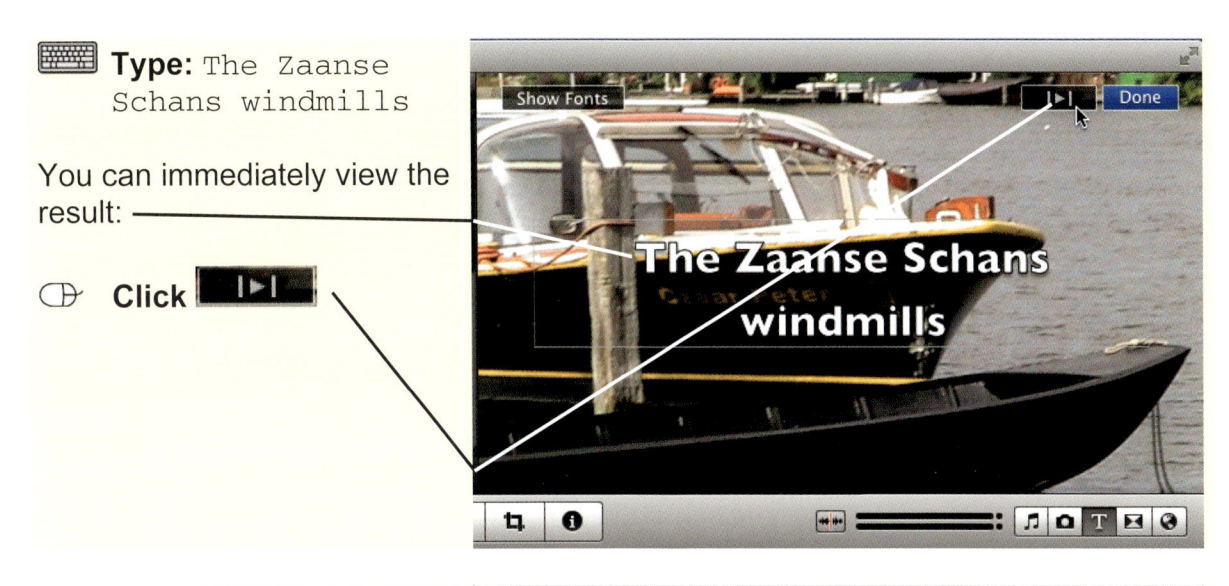

Type: The Zaanse Schans windmills

You can immediately view the result:

☞ **Click** ▶|

The title clip will be played:

In the same way you can add other titles and credits to your project. For now, this title will suffice.

☞ **Click** Done

2.12 Adding a Transition

Besides titles, you can also add transitions to a video project. A transition adds an animation to two separate videos and merges them together fluently.

You can add a transition between the photo at the beginning of your project and the first video clip:

☞ **Click**

You will see a pane containing various transitions.

You can see a preview of a transition by pointing the mouse at that transition:

⊕ **Position the mouse pointer on**

You can drag the transition to your video project:

⊕ **Press the mouse button**

⊕ **Drag the transition to a spot between the photo and the first clip**

⊕ **Release the mouse button**

You will see that the transition has been added to your video project:

You can view your video project, including the title and the transition:

⊕ **Click** ▶

Chapter 2 Working with Video

The video project will be played and you will see the title and the transition:

Tip
Delete a transition
You can remove a transition from the project by clicking the transition and then pressing [⬅] (Backspace) or [delete] (Delete).

2.13 Adding Music

Usually, a video camera records sounds as well as images. Such a soundtrack may be sufficient in itself, but it might be nice to add some music to your video project. By choosing the right music you can make sure that the separate clips form a unified movie. And you can use the music to mask irregularities in the sounds of the various clips.

First, you need to adjust the volume of the sounds you have recorded in the clips:

☞ **Double-click the first clip**

A new window will be opened:

Here you can change the settings for this clip.

☞ **Click Audio**

You will see the audio settings:

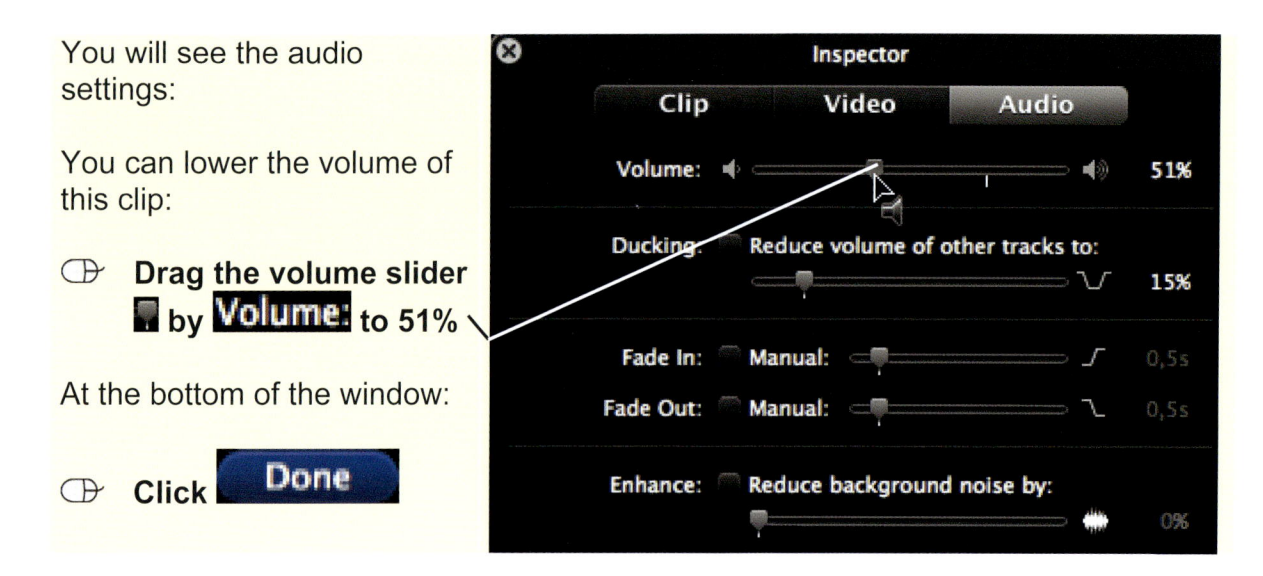

You can lower the volume of this clip:

☞ **Drag the volume slider ▮ by Volume: to 51%**

At the bottom of the window:

☞ **Click Done**

You can listen to the changes you have made:

☞ **Play the video** ⚘⁸

In the same way, you can change the volume of the other clips:

☞ **Change the volume of the other four clips to 51%** ⚘⁹

Now you can add some background music:

☞ **Make sure you can see the last clip**

☞ **Click 🎵**

You will see a pane with all sorts of programs that have to do with audio. You can use one of these programs to add an audio clip or a music track.

💡 **Tip**
Music programs on the Mac
The *Mac* contains several music programs. Normally, these programs are used to add sounds to a video project. You can read more about these programs in *Chapter 3 Working with Music*.

Chapter 2 Working with Video 99

You can add a music file from the *iLife* program. This is a software suite developed by *Apple*. With the various programs in this suite you can edit and save audio files, photos and videos.

☞ **Click**
   iLife Sound Effects

You will see the audio files in *iLife* and you can listen to a file:

☞ **Double-click**
   Acoustic Sunrise.caf

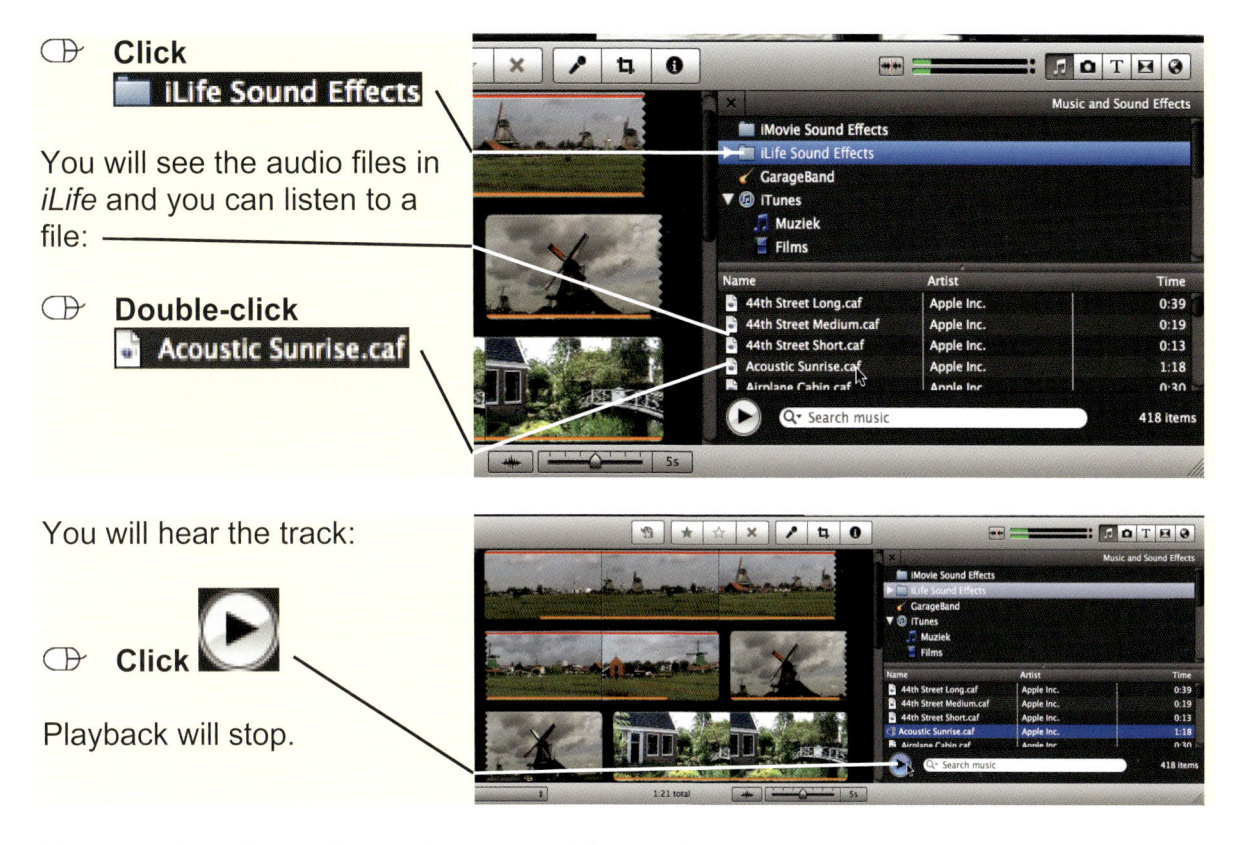

You will hear the track:

☞ **Click**

Playback will stop.

You can drag the audio track to your video project:

☞ **Position the mouse pointer on**
   Acoustic Sunrise.caf

☞ **Press the mouse button**

☞ **Drag**
   Acoustic Sunrise.caf
   to the end of the last clip

Now the pane will turn green:

☞ **Release the mouse button**

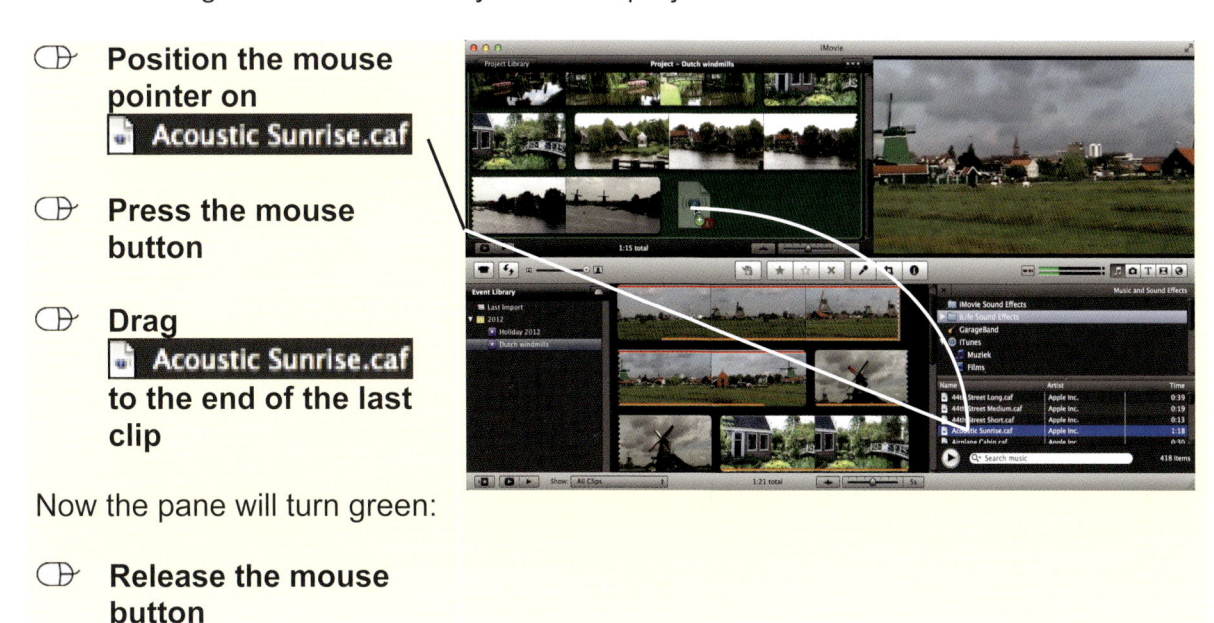

The green background indicates that the music file has been added to your video project as background music:

Now you can play your video project, including the background music:

☞ **Click** ▶

The video project will be played:

The music will automatically stop playing at the end of the video.

💡 Tip
Delete music
This is how you delete the background music again:

☞ **Click the green background**

The background will be selected. You can delete the selection with the Control key:

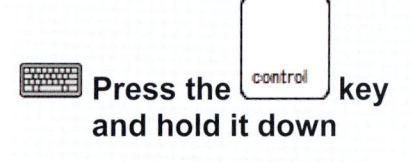

⌨ **Press the** `control` **key and hold it down**

☞ **Click the green background**

☞ **Click** Delete Selection

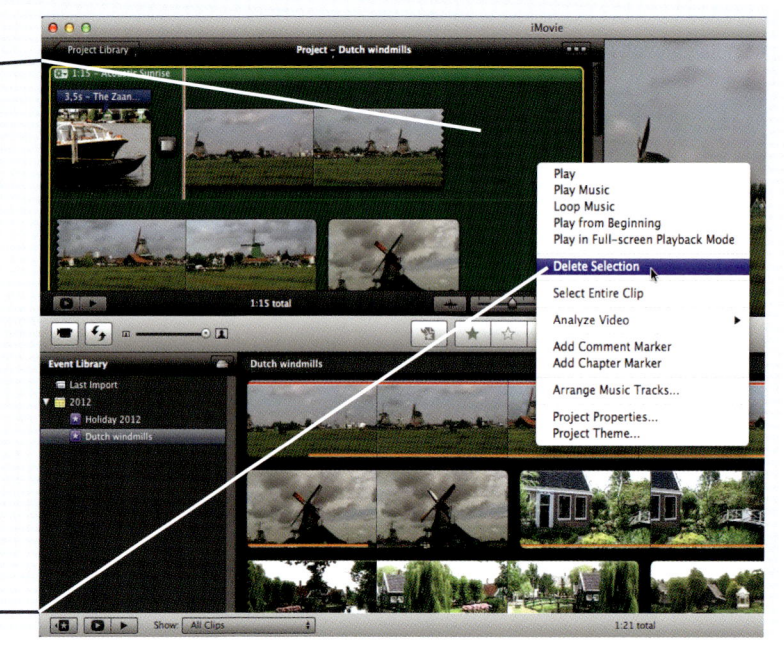

Chapter 2 Working with Video **101**

💡 Tip
Add other music
You will usually import music files in *iMovie* from programs such as *iTunes* and *iLife*. But you can also use music files that are not being used by one of the *Mac's* programs. Although you need to keep in mind that certain file types cannot be played in *iMovie*. You can import MP3 files, though:

☞ **Open *Finder* 👣¹**

☞ **Open the folder containing the music file**

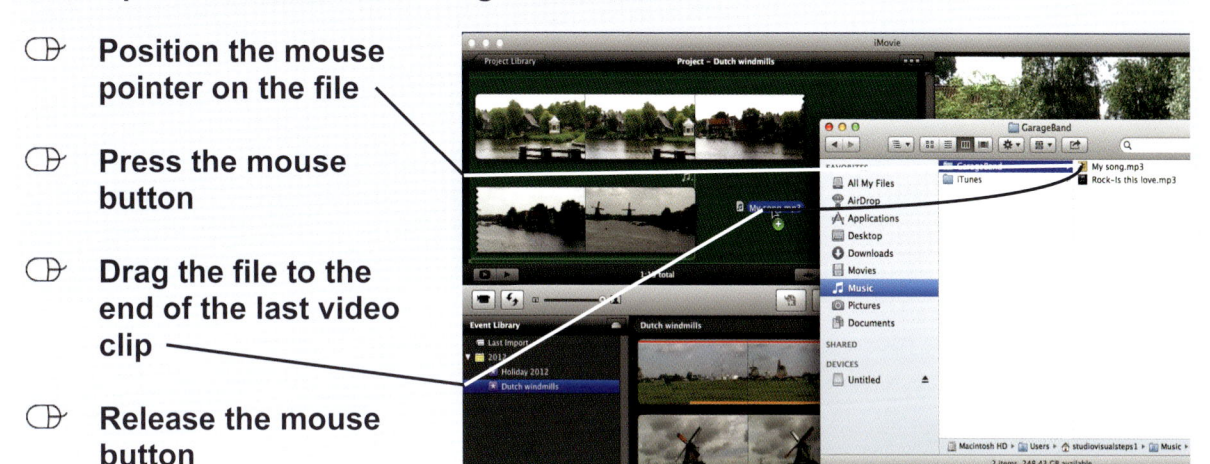

⊖ **Position the mouse pointer on the file**

⊖ **Press the mouse button**

⊖ **Drag the file to the end of the last video clip**

⊖ **Release the mouse button**

2.14 Creating a Video File

You will often need to save projects yourself, if you want to use them later on. In *iMovie* the video projects are automatically saved.
After you have finished editing the video project, you can *finalize* or export it. This means that you can turn your video project into a video file that can be played on a video player. You can play this video file on your computer as well as other video players, such as a media player. You can also share your video file with others.

This is how you export a video project:

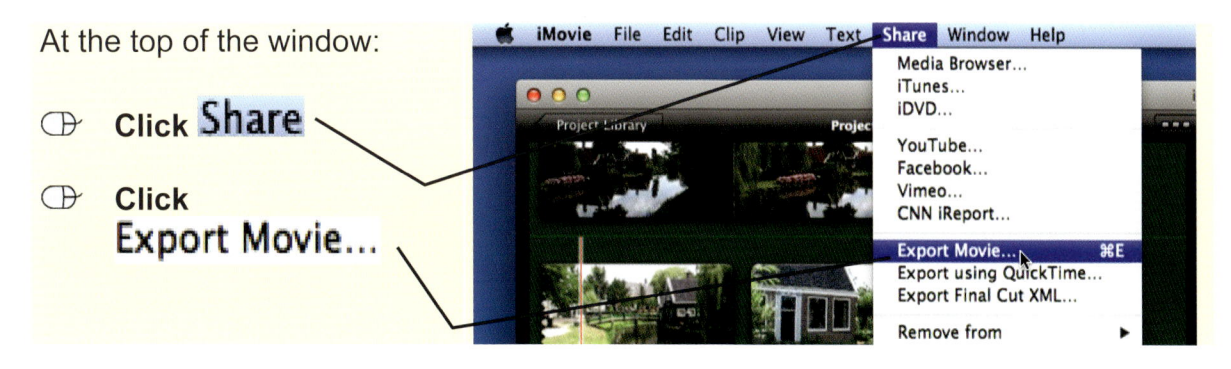

At the top of the window:

⊖ **Click Share**

⊖ **Click Export Movie...**

Now you will see a window with options for creating various types of video files:

File name:

Folder name for this file:

Type of player:

File size:

Screen resolution:

The choice of file type will depend on what you want to do with the video. You can choose a higher or smaller *resolution* based on the type of device the video will be played on. A low resolution file can be played on mobile equipment such as an iPhone or iPad, but is not suitable for use on a television. A high resolution file is not necessary for mobile devices with small screens, but it will look great on televisions and computers. The higher the resolution, the larger the file will be.

Please note:
When you export a video project, all parts will be merged into a single file. If your video project is large and you have selected a higher resolution file type, the time needed for the export process will increase. This also depends on the speed of your computer.

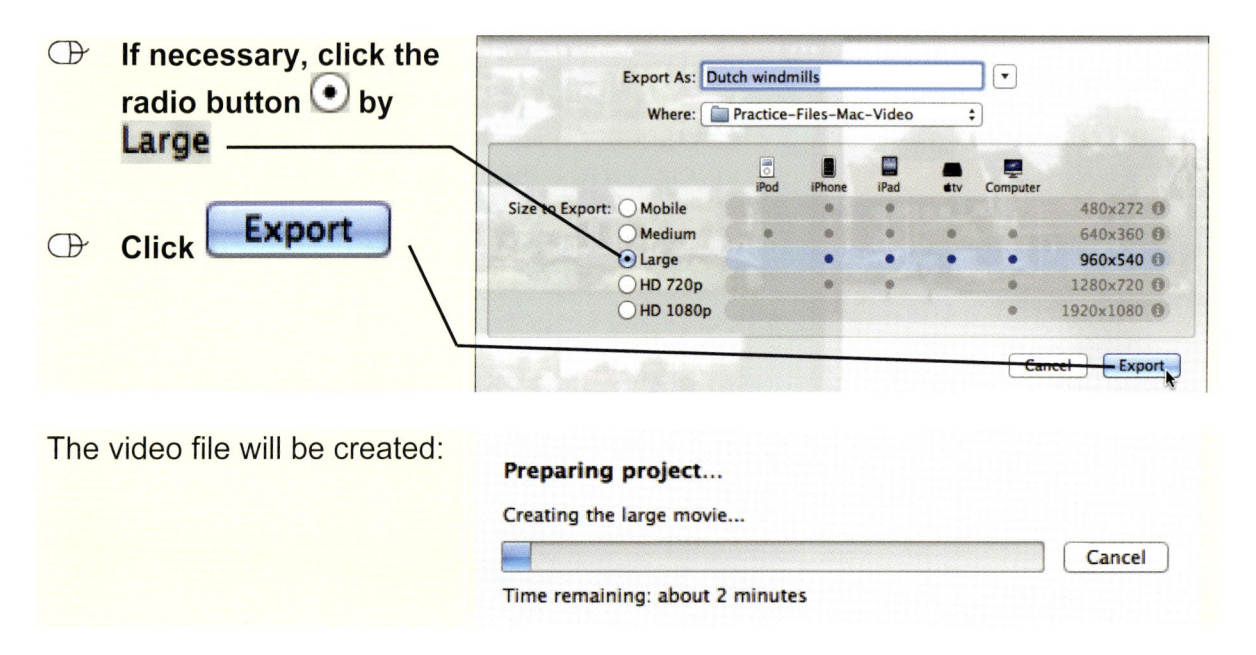

☞ **If necessary, click the radio button ⦿ by Large**

☞ **Click Export**

The video file will be created:

Chapter 2 Working with Video   **103**

When the export process has finished you can view the video file you have created:

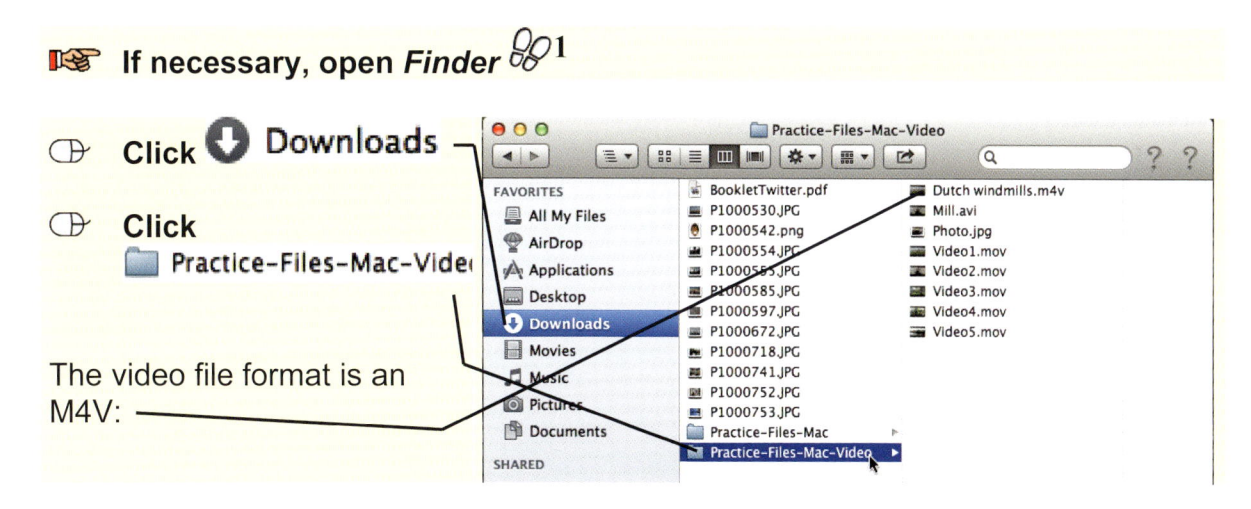

☞ **If necessary, open *Finder* ⚙️¹**

⊕ **Click 🔽 Downloads**

⊕ **Click**
   Practice-Files-Mac-Video

The video file format is an M4V:

M4V is a file type developed by *Apple* for use in the *iTunes* program, among others. In *section 2.15 Playing a Video with QuickTime Player* you will be playing the video in the *QuickTime Player*.

💡 **Tip**
Finalize a video project
Another option available for you video project is to use the *finalize* option. If you use this option the video project will be exported to multiple video files. This will result in a number of video files with different extensions (and thus various resolutions):

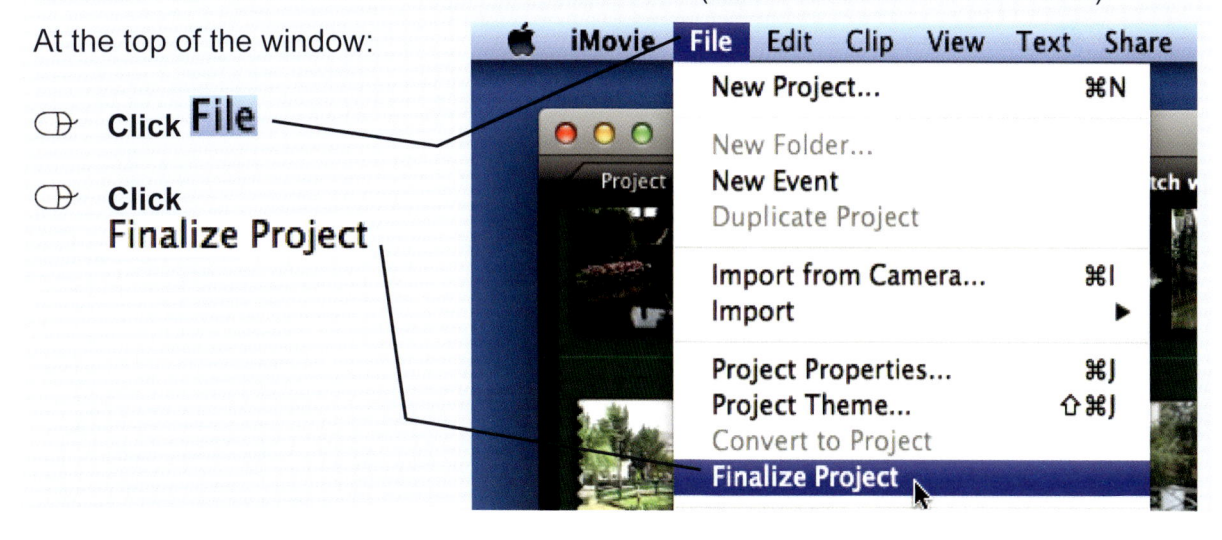

At the top of the window:

⊕ **Click File**

⊕ **Click**
   Finalize Project

☞ **Close *iMovie* and *Finder* ⚙️³**

2.15 Playing a Video with QuickTime Player

The *QuickTime Player* program is the default program for viewing video files on the Mac. In this example we will use the video file you have previously made in *iMovie*. Here is how to play a video file with *QuickTime Player*:

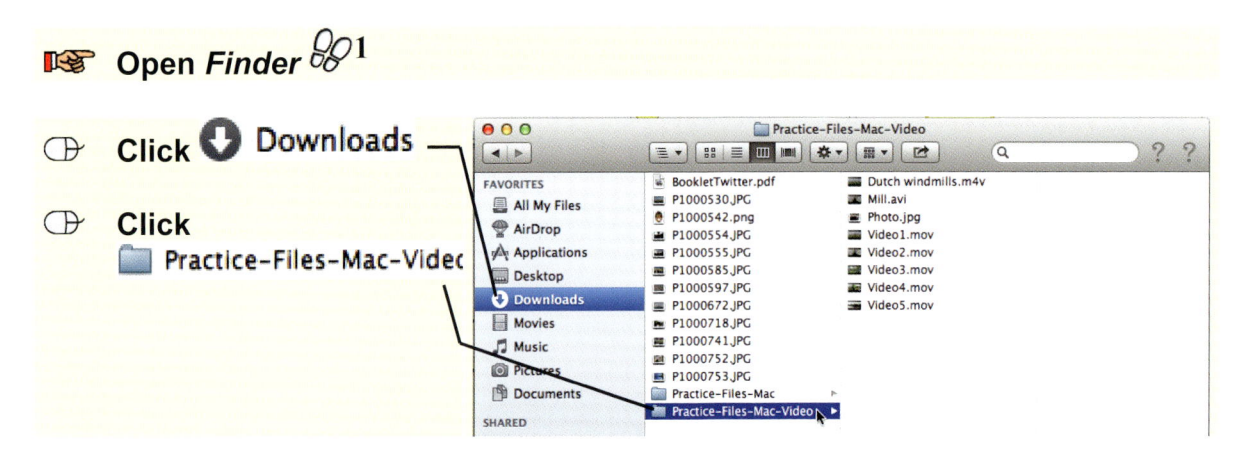

☞ **Open** *Finder* ⓔ¹

◯ **Click** ⬇ **Downloads**

◯ **Click** 📁 **Practice-Files-Mac-Video**

You use Control key to open the file:

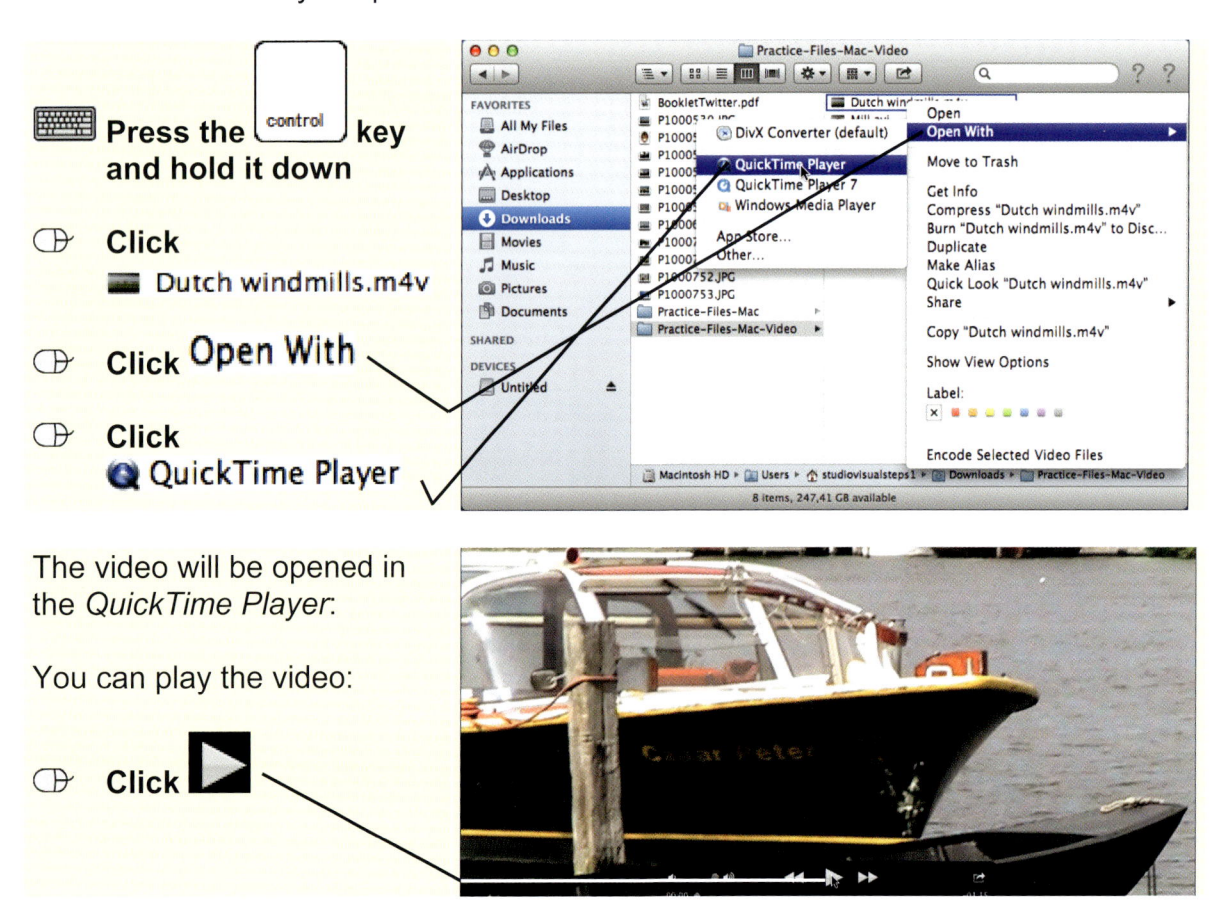

⌨ **Press the** [control] **key and hold it down**

◯ **Click** 🎬 **Dutch windmills.m4v**

◯ **Click Open With**

◯ **Click** 🔵 **QuickTime Player**

The video will be opened in the *QuickTime Player*.

You can play the video:

◯ **Click** ▶

Chapter 2 Working with Video **105**

Click ◀◀ to rewind or ▶▶ to fast forward: _____

Click 🔊 for volume control: —

You can also play the video on a full screen:

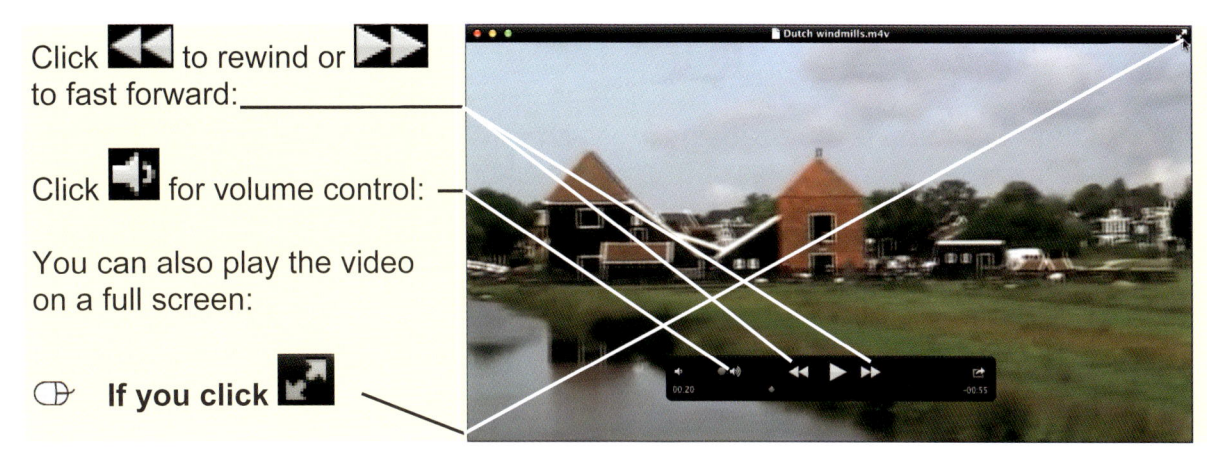

⊕ **If you click** ⤢

You can watch the video in full screen mode:

You can use the Esc key to return to the previous view:

⌨ **Press** `esc`

Now the video is displayed in a smaller window again.

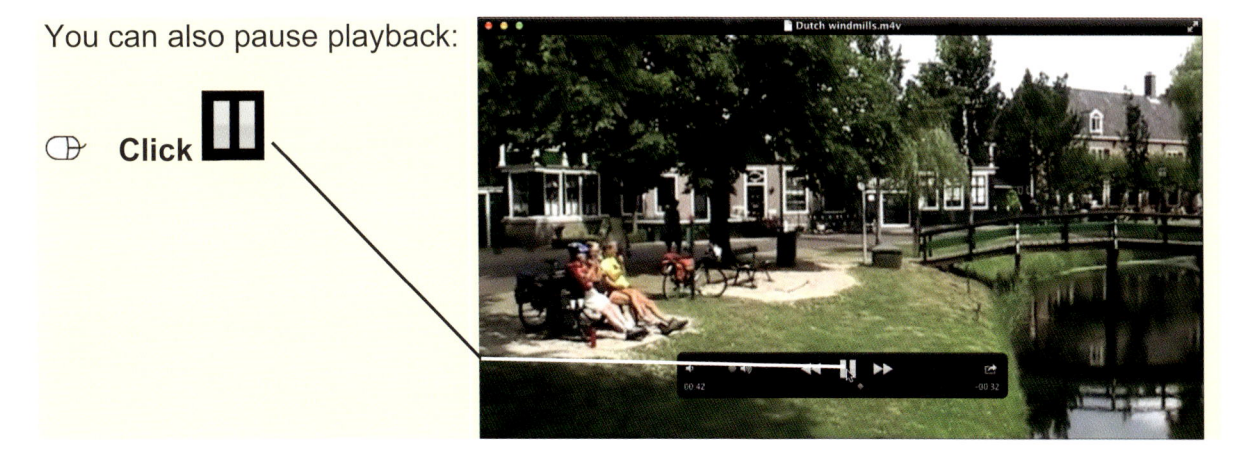

You can also pause playback:

⊕ **Click** ⏸

☞ **Stop** *QuickTime Player* 👣²

2.16 Burning a DVD with iDVD

Although they are not as popular as a few years back, DVDs are still used for storing files. These may be backup copies of ordinary files, but you can also use a DVD to burn a video to it and play it on a regular DVD player. If you have a DVD available, you can practice doing this by burning the video you created in *iMovie*. You do this with the *iDVD* program.

➥ Please note:
If the *iDVD* program is not installed on your computer, ask your local computer retailer about it, or try to find a similar program. If you are going to use a different program, you may find it works in the same way as *iDVD*.

➥ Please note:
If you are using a MacBook Air or a Mac mini, you will not have a CD/DVD player. In that case you can just read through this section for future use. However, you can continue with the following steps if you have an external CD/DVD player that is connected to your Mac.
Please note: the external CD/DVD player needs to be suitable for use with a *Mac*.

➥ Please note:
For burning a DVD you will need to use a blank, writable DVD. If you do not have a DVD of this type available, you can just read through this section.

First you open *iDVD*:

☞ **If necessary, open *Finder*** 🐾[1]

⊕ **Click** 🅰 **Applications**

⊕ **Double-click** 🔵 **iDVD**

Chapter 2 Working with Video **107**

You will see the *iDVD* window:

Work with a DVD project:

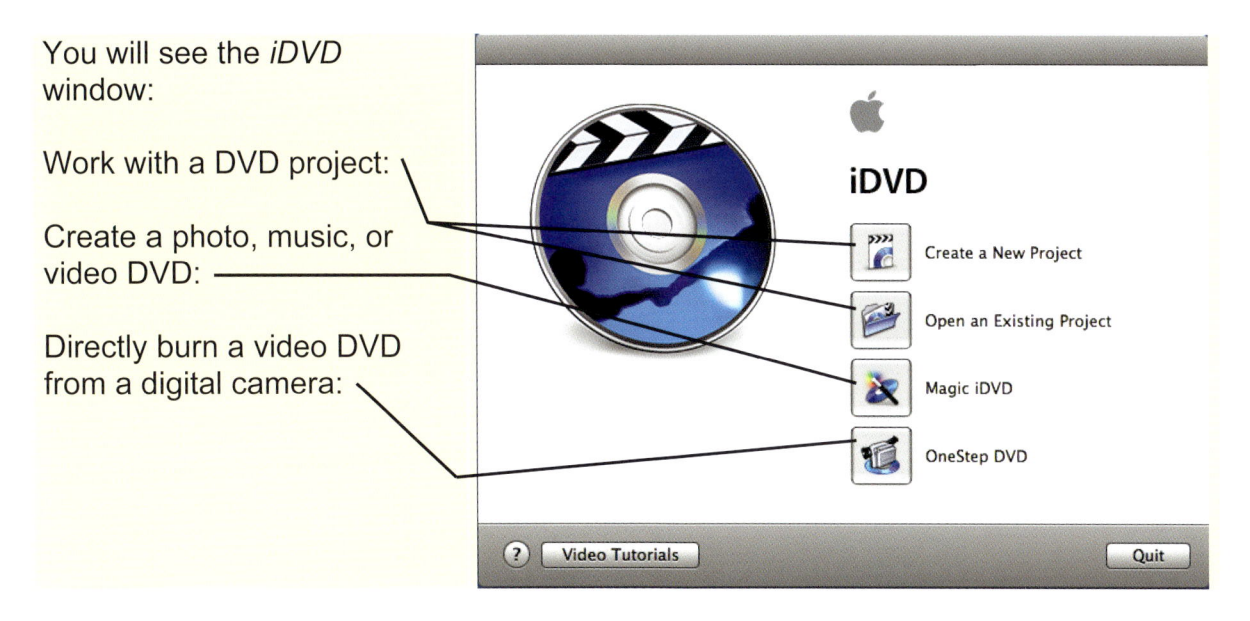

Create a photo, music, or video DVD:

Directly burn a video DVD from a digital camera:

You can easily create a video DVD with *iDVD*. You do this by using *Magic iDVD*:

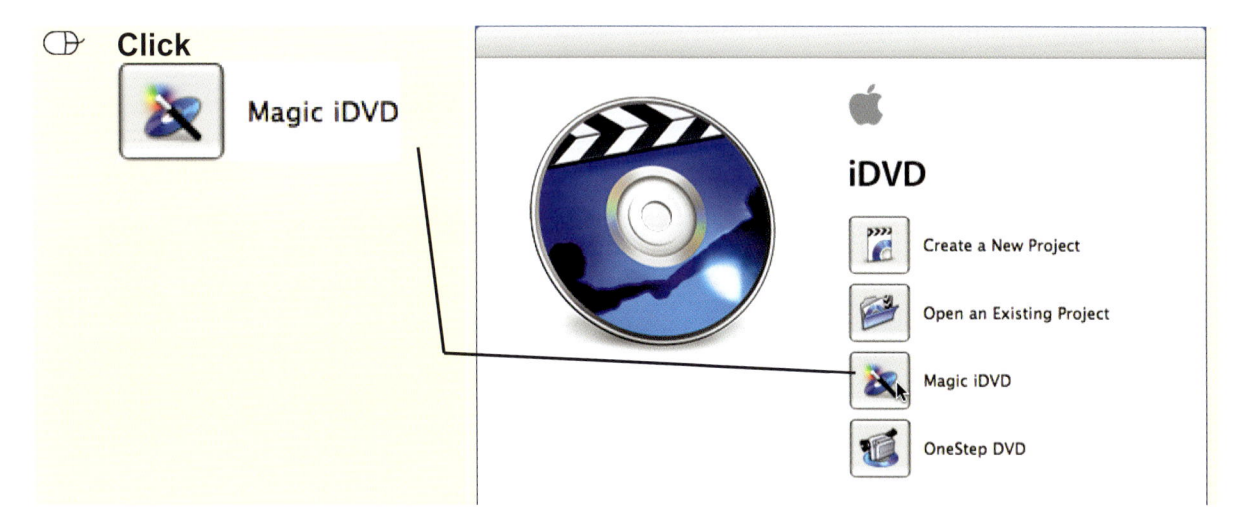

⊕ **Click** Magic iDVD

You will see the *Magic iDVD* window:

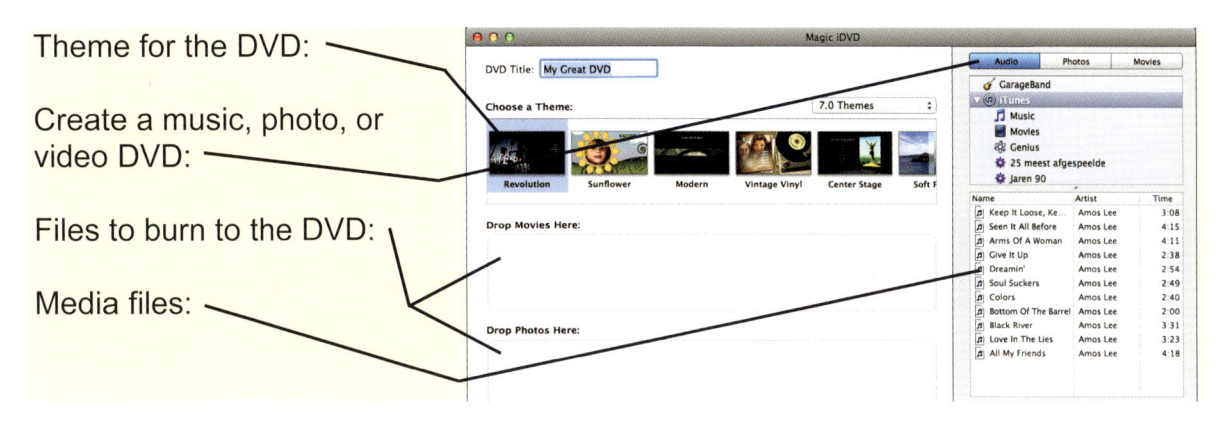

Theme for the DVD:

Create a music, photo, or video DVD:

Files to burn to the DVD:

Media files:

First you type the title of the DVD, and then you select the theme. You will see the theme again in the DVD menu, among several others:

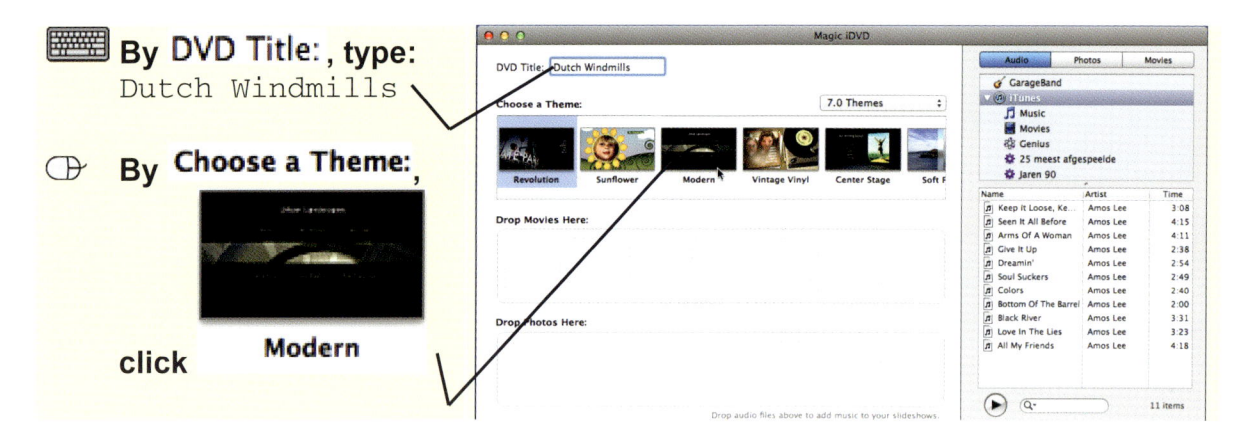

⌨ By **DVD Title:**, type: `Dutch Windmills`

☞ By **Choose a Theme:**, click **Modern**

Now you can add a single file or multiple video files to the project:

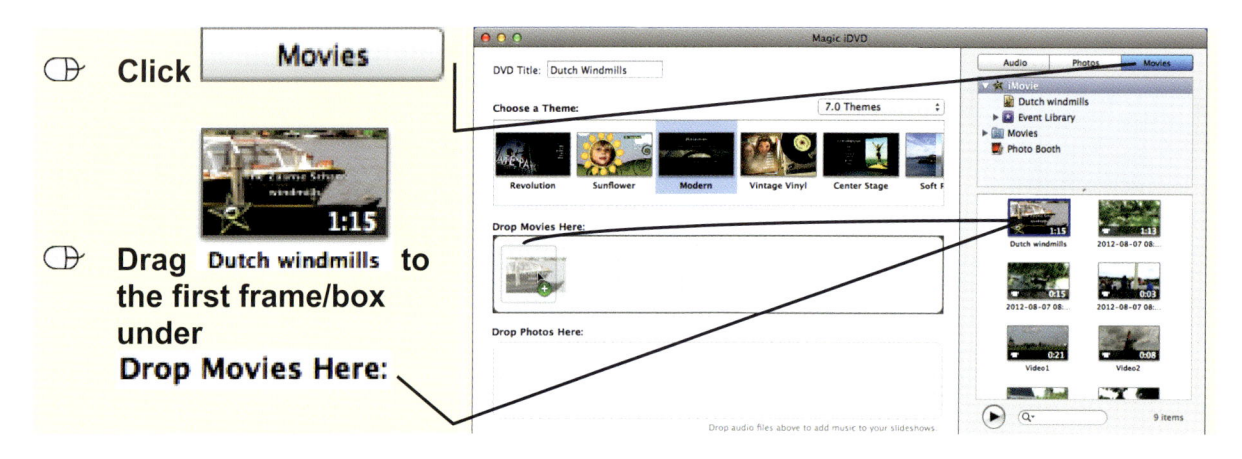

☞ Click **Movies**

☞ Drag **Dutch windmills** to the first frame/box under **Drop Movies Here:**

The video file has been added:

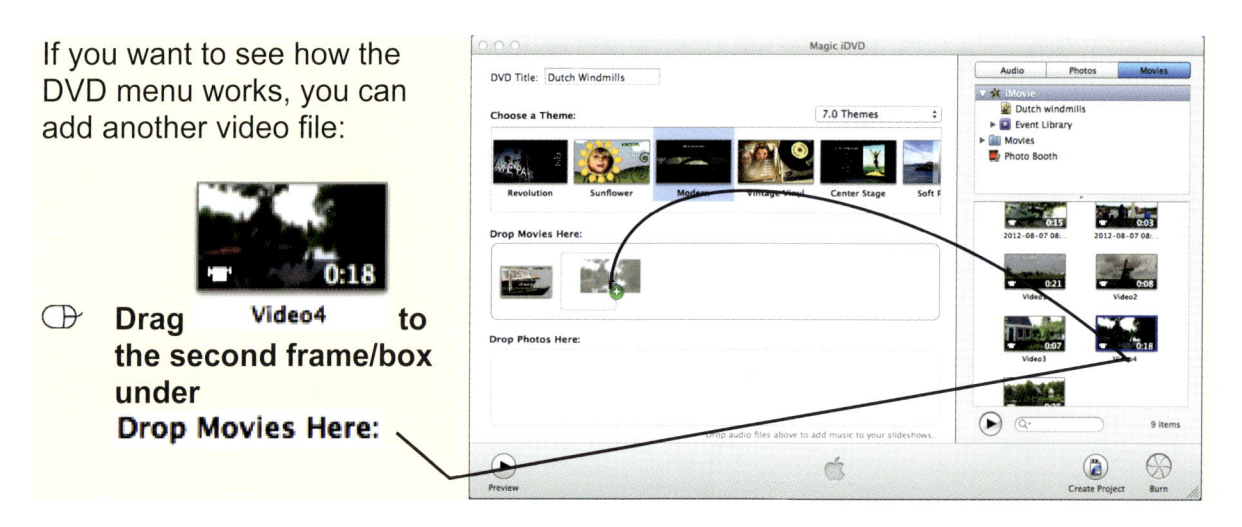

If you want to see how the DVD menu works, you can add another video file:

☞ Drag **Video4** to the second frame/box under **Drop Movies Here:**

Chapter 2 Working with Video   **109**

The video file has been added:

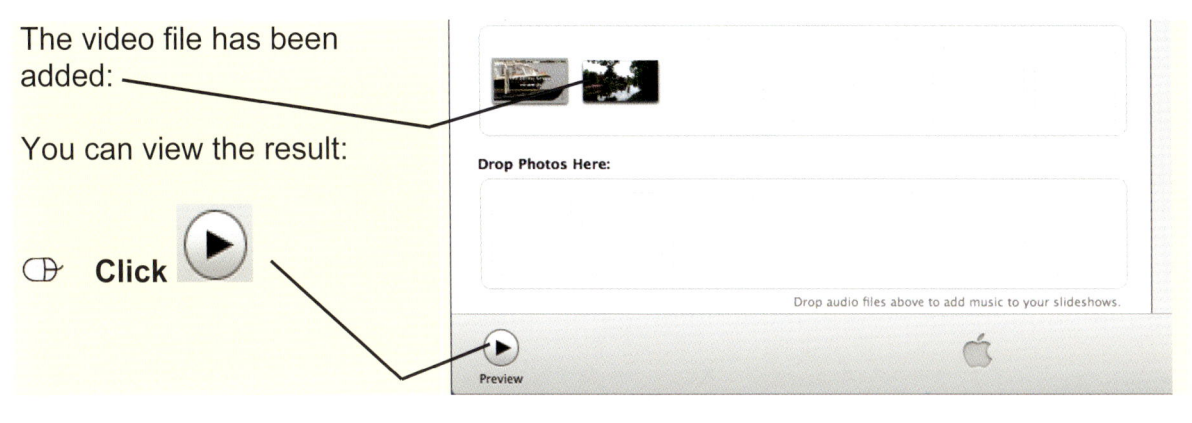

You can view the result:

☞ **Click** ▶

You will see the DVD menu:

If you want, you can find out how the DVD menu works.

In this case this will not be necessary:

☞ **Click**

Now you can burn the project to the DVD. You can use the built-in CD/DVD player in the *Mac* or use an external CD/DVD player, if you work with a MacBook Air or a Mac mini.

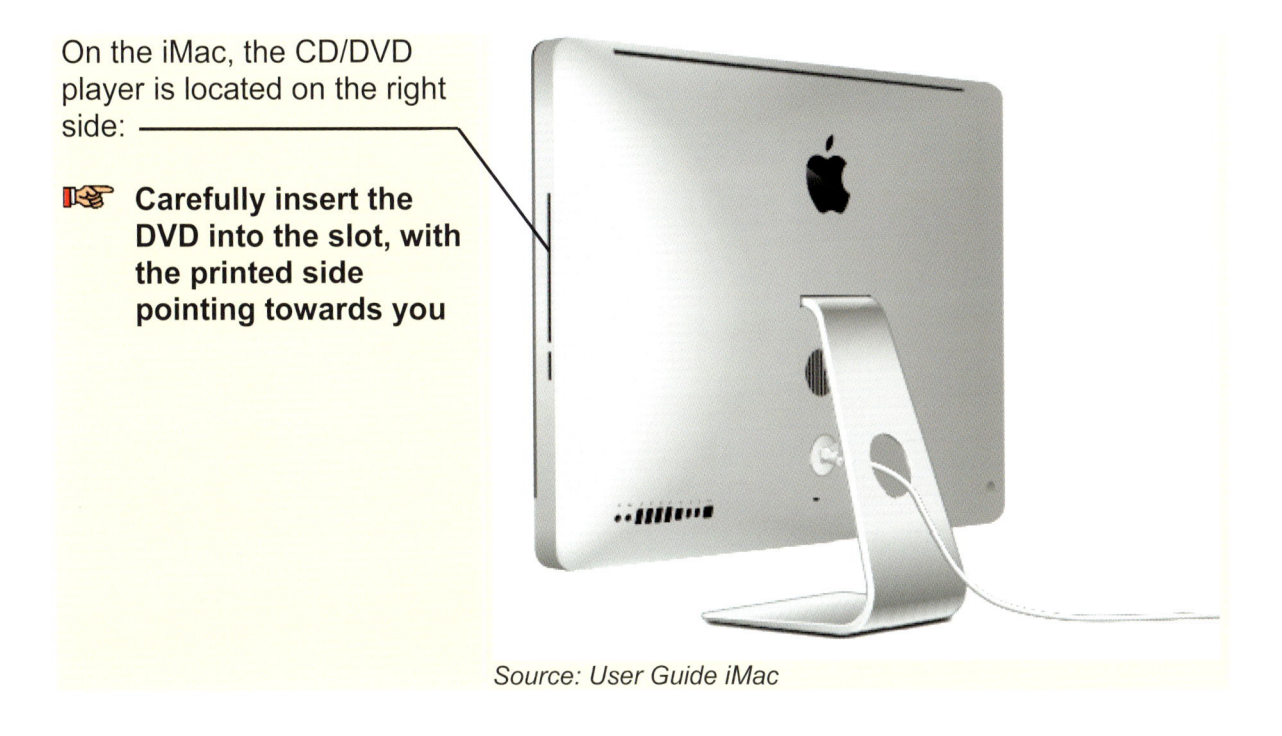

On the iMac, the CD/DVD player is located on the right side:

☞ **Carefully insert the DVD into the slot, with the printed side pointing towards you**

Source: User Guide iMac

On the MacBook Pro, the CD/DVD player is located on the side:

☞ **Carefully insert the DVD into the slot, with the printed side facing upwards**

Source: User Guide MacBook Pro

You will see this window:

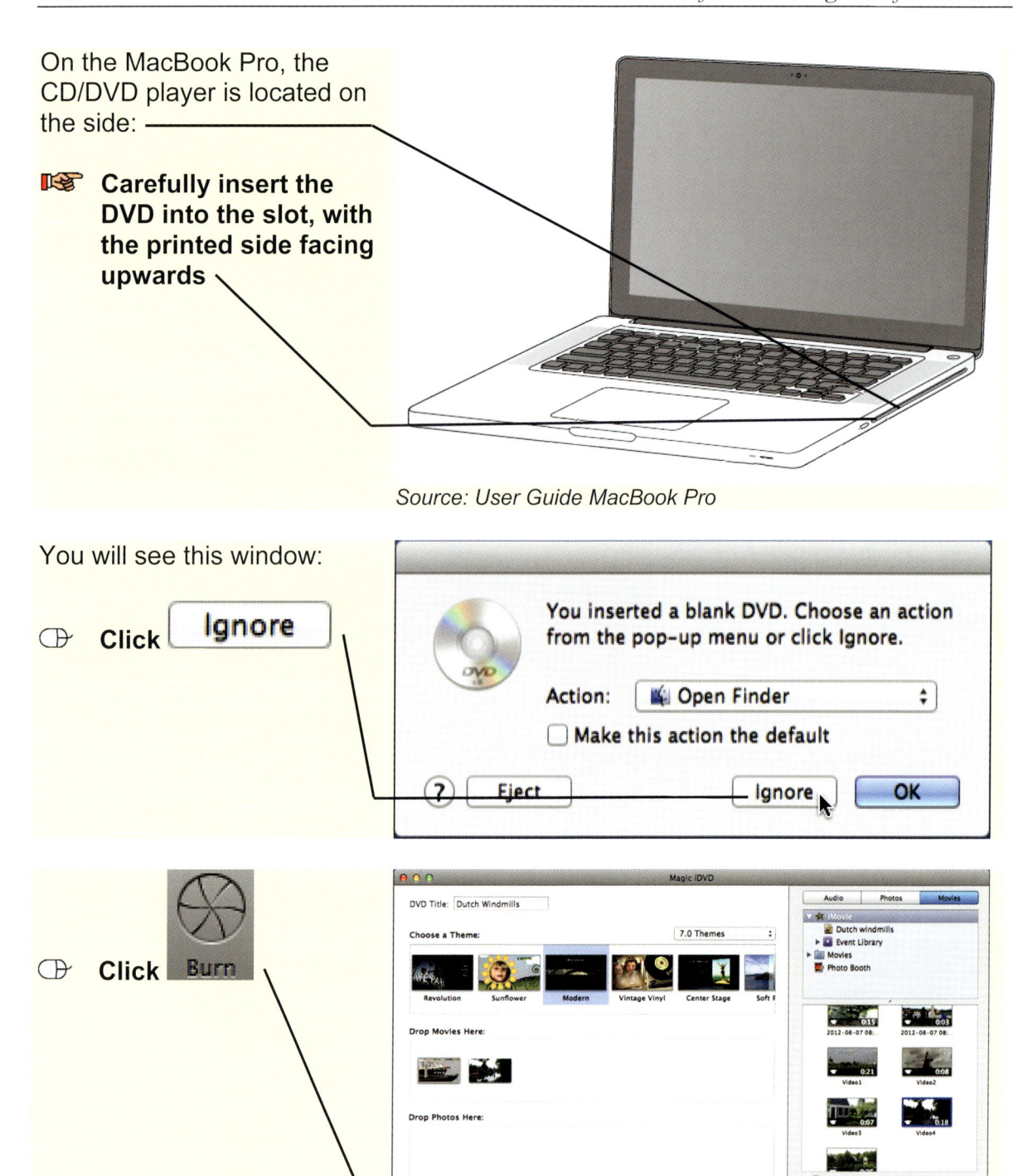

⊕ **Click** Ignore

⊕ **Click** Burn

Chapter 2 Working with Video   111

The DVD will be burned:

This may take a few minutes, depending on the speed of the burner.

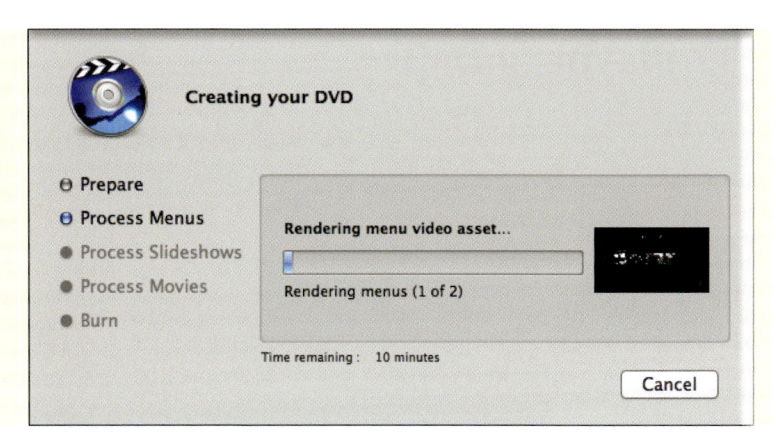

After the disk has been burned, it will be ejected and the menu will be played in *iDVD*:

You can close the program:

⊕ **Click** 🔴

Now the DVD is suitable for playback on a DVD player. You can close *iDVD*:

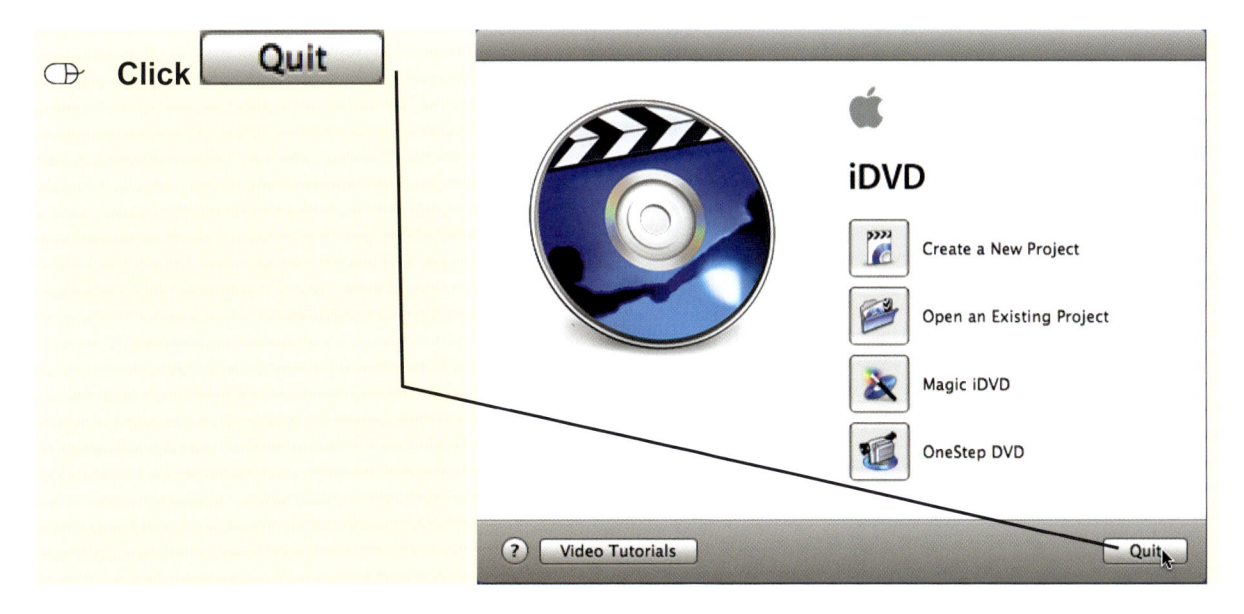

⊕ **Click** [Quit]

☞ **Close** *Finder* ⱷ³

2.17 Playing a DVD

In *Mac* you can easily play a DVD with the *DVD Player* program. In this program we will use a DVD from a TV series.

➥ Please note:
If you are using a MacBook Air or a Mac mini, you will not have a CD/DVD player. In that case you can just read through this section for future use. You can continue with the following steps if you have an external CD/DVD player connected to your *Mac*. **Please note:** the external CD/DVD player needs to be suitable for use with a *Mac*.

➥ Please note:
To continue with the following steps, you will need to use a DVD. In this example we will be using a DVD from a TV series, but you can also use a DVD you created yourself with *iDVD*. If you do not have a DVD available, you can just read through this section.

☞ **Insert a DVD into your computer's CD/DVD player**

The *DVD Player* program should open automatically. If this is the very first time you are using this program, you will see this window:

You will need to select the region code for your DVD player. The code for the US is 1, the European code is 2:

⊕ **If necessary, click 1 by Change drive region to:**

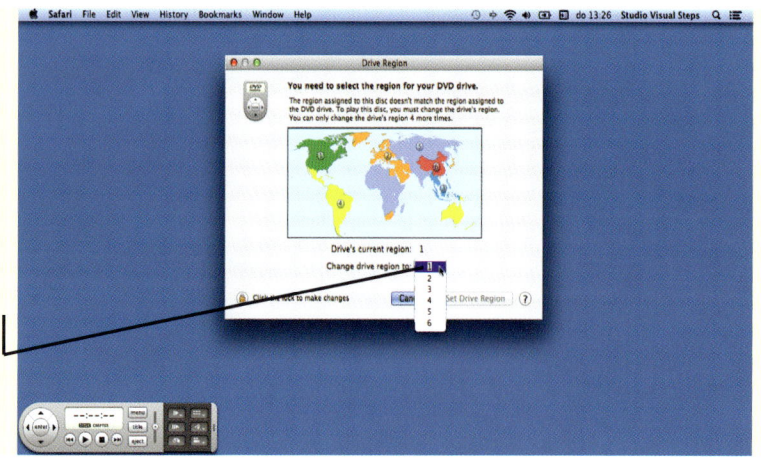

Chapter 2 Working with Video 113

At the bottom of the window:

⌨ **Click** (**Set Drive Region**)

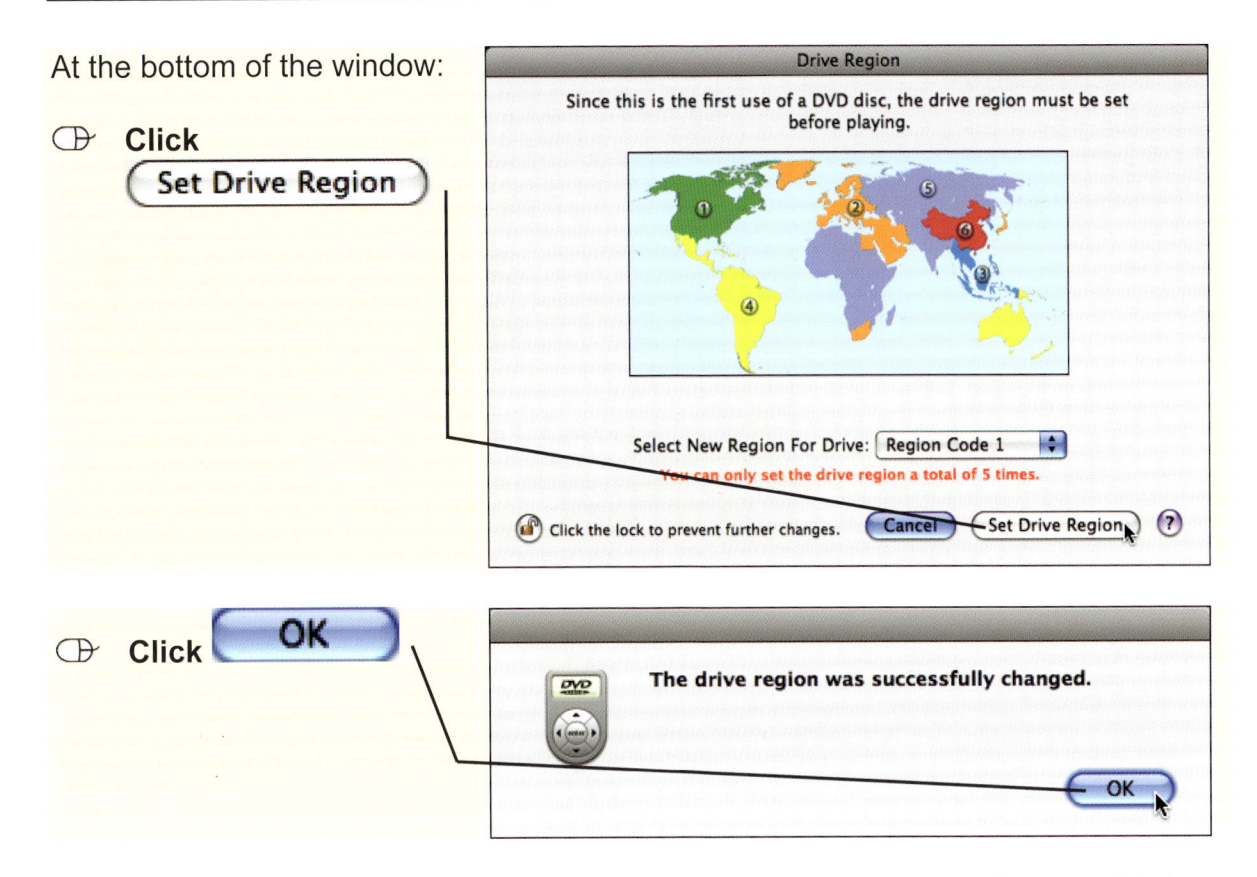

⌨ **Click** `OK`

The *DVD Player* program will open and you will see the first scenes from the DVD. Almost every DVD comes with a built-in menu, where you can choose the settings for the language, subtitles and various other playback options. In this menu you can also select which part of the DVD you want to watch. The DVD we are using in this example automatically displays the main menu, right after the copyright messages:

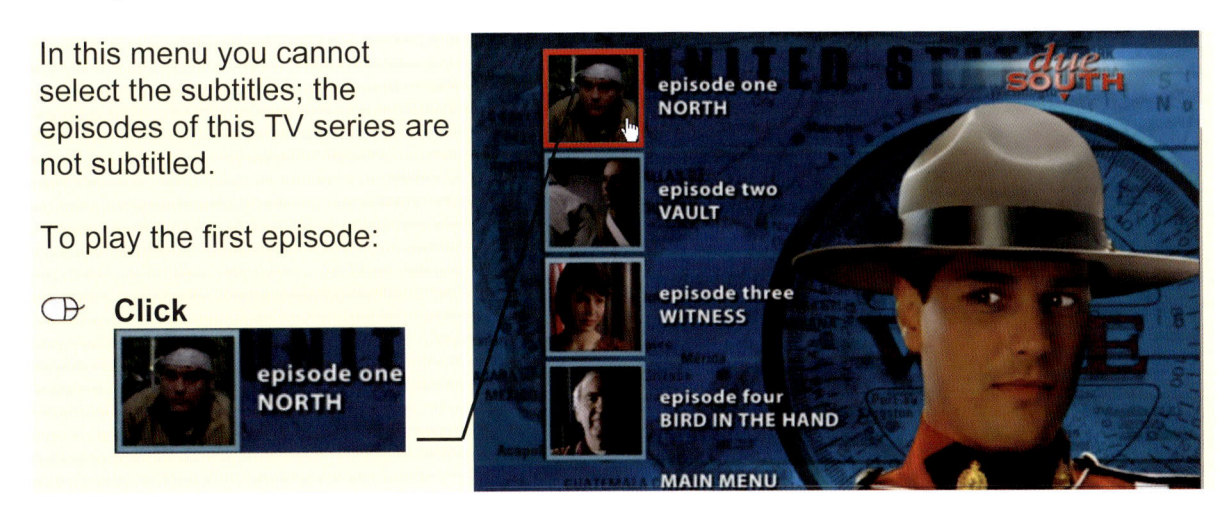

In this menu you cannot select the subtitles; the episodes of this TV series are not subtitled.

To play the first episode:

⌨ **Click** *episode one NORTH*

↳ Please note:

The structure of the main menu can be different for each DVD. You may need to select several menu options on your own DVD, before you reach the main menu or the subtitle menu.

The first episode will be played without any subtitles:

When the video is played in full screen mode, you will see a control bar at the bottom of the screen, every time you move the mouse pointer:

Here is an explanation of the buttons on the control bar:

Arrow keys to scroll through the menu.
Use the button in the middle of the arrows to select a marked menu option.

Open the main or title menu during playback.

Volume slider.

Pause playback.

Stop playback.

Go to the previous or next chapter.

Rewind or fast forward.

Enable subtitles and captions for speech and sound.

Quit full screen view.

Chapter 2 Working with Video **115**

You can now disable the full screen view:

- **Click**

Tip
Another shortcut to quit the full screen view
You can quit the full screen view also by pressing the Esc key.

- **Press** esc

When the *DVD Player* window is minimized, you will see a smaller version of the *DVD Player's* control panel with similar buttons. You can stop the video like this:

- **Click**

HELP! I do not see the control panel.
If the control panel is hidden you can open it through the *Dock*:

- **Click**

Now you can eject the DVD:

- **Click** eject

☞ **Stop** *DVD Player* ℘2

In this chapter you have learned how to create a movie from your own video files with *iMovie* and how to play a DVD with *QuickTime Player*.

2.18 Background Information

Dictionary

Aspect ratio	The aspect ratio determines whether the video is displayed in the regular format of 4:3 or in the widescreen mode of the 16:9 format (also called HD). The aspect ratio of an image is the proportional relationship between its width and its height.
Codecs	A type of software that encodes (compresses) and decodes the information in video files, so that video programs can work with this information. Without the proper codecs, certain types of video files cannot be opened by various video programs.
Compress	A video file is shrunk by compressing it, so it will take up less space. This may result in some loss of quality.
DVD Player	A program you can use to play DVDs.
Event	In the *iMovie* program you can organize your video clips per event. An event may contain the video clips you have made in a certain period of time, for instance during a wedding or a recent vacation.
Finalize	An option that allows you to export a video project to multiple video files with different extensions and various resolutions. The video can then be played on a variety of devices of different size.
Frame rate	The frame rate indicates how many frames per second the video is displayed and which video format will be used. The default rate in PAL is 25 frames per second. In the NTSC format, it is approximately 30 frames per second (fps).
iDVD	A program you can use to burn music, photo or video DVDs.
iMovie	A program you can use for importing and editing video files.

- Continue on the next page -

Import	Transferring video files from your digital camera to your computer or other device.
iPhoto	A program you can use to save, organize and edit digital photos.
PAL	PAL is a video format used on television in most European countries. In the US, the NTSF format is used.
QuickTime Player	A platform developed by *Apple* for creating, sharing, distributing and playing multimedia content on the *Mac*. There is also a version for computers running *Windows*.
Resolution	Allows you to set a particular screen size. You can choose a higher or smaller setting based on the type of device your video will be played on. A low resolution file can be played on mobile devices such as an iPhone or iPad, but will not be suitable for use on a television. A high resolution file is not necessary for the smaller screens of a mobile device but will look great on a television or a larger computer screen. Bear in mind, that the higher the resolution, the larger the file will be.
SD card	Short for *Secure Digital*. A card, approximately the size of a stamp, used by digital cameras, tablets and mobile phones for storing data.
Trailer	A short clip that gives a brief impression of a video or a movie. A trailer is often used for promoting a forthcoming movie.
Transition	A transition inserts an animation between video frames, so that they gradually merge with one another.
Video editing	Editing video images from a camera or other sources with a video editing program. With this type of program you can trim video clips and merge them into a single movie. You can also add titles, transitions and music.
Writable DVD	A DVD to which you can burn files by using a DVD burning program.

Source: Apple Dictionary, www.apple.com, Wikipedia

2.19 Tips

💡 Tip
Burn a DVD through Finder
You can easily burn a DVD with *iDVD* but if you prefer you can also use *Finder* to burn a DVD. Not a video DVD but a regular DVD containing data. You can use this type of DVD to burn data from your hard drive. You will not be able to play this type of DVD on an external DVD player connected to your television set, but you can play it on a *Mac* or on a *Windows* computer.

This is how you burn a data DVD with *Finder*:

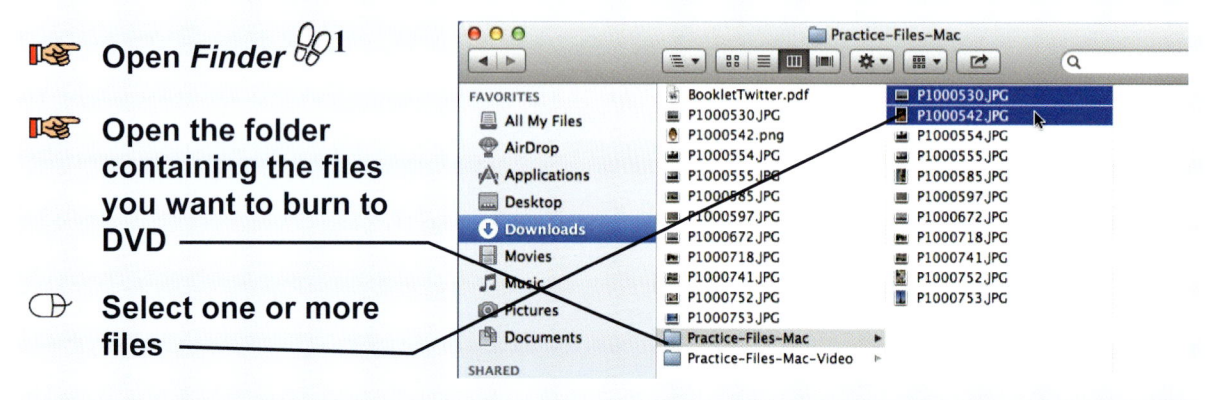

☞ Open *Finder* 🐾¹

☞ Open the folder containing the files you want to burn to DVD

☞ Select one or more files

Use the Control key to open an additional menu:

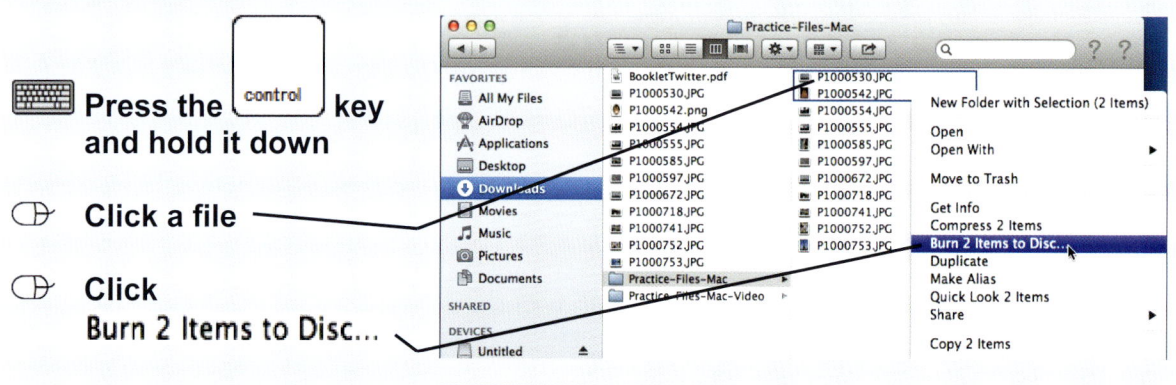

☞ Press the `control` key and hold it down

☞ Click a file

☞ Click **Burn 2 Items to Disc...**

Now you will see this window:

☞ Insert a blank, writable DVD into the DVD burner

- Continue on the next page -

Chapter 2 Working with Video **119**

⌨ **If you want, type a name for the DVD by** Disc Name:

💿 **Click** Burn

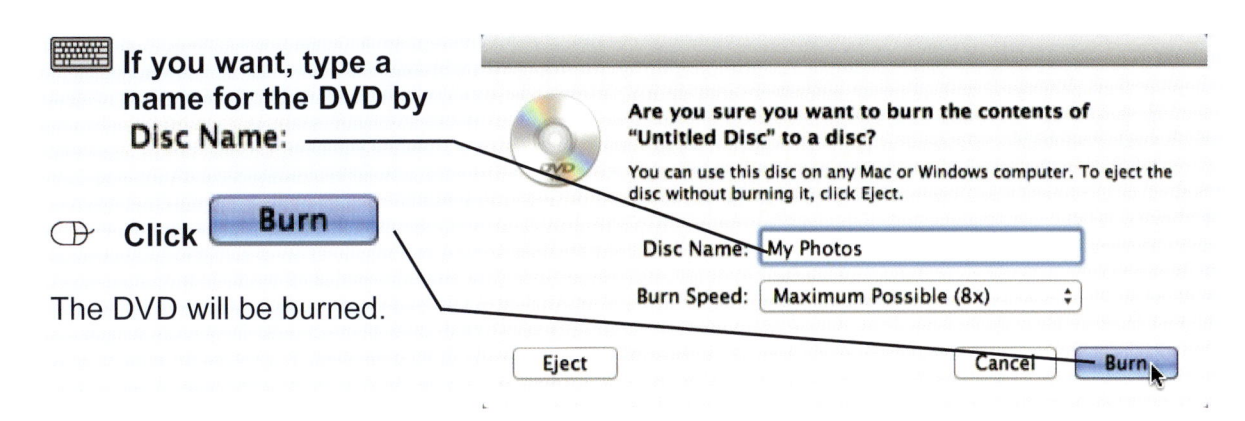

The DVD will be burned.

💡 **Tip**
Share a movie through YouTube
When you have finished editing your movie you can share it with others. For example, you can publish the movie on *YouTube*. Here is how you do that:

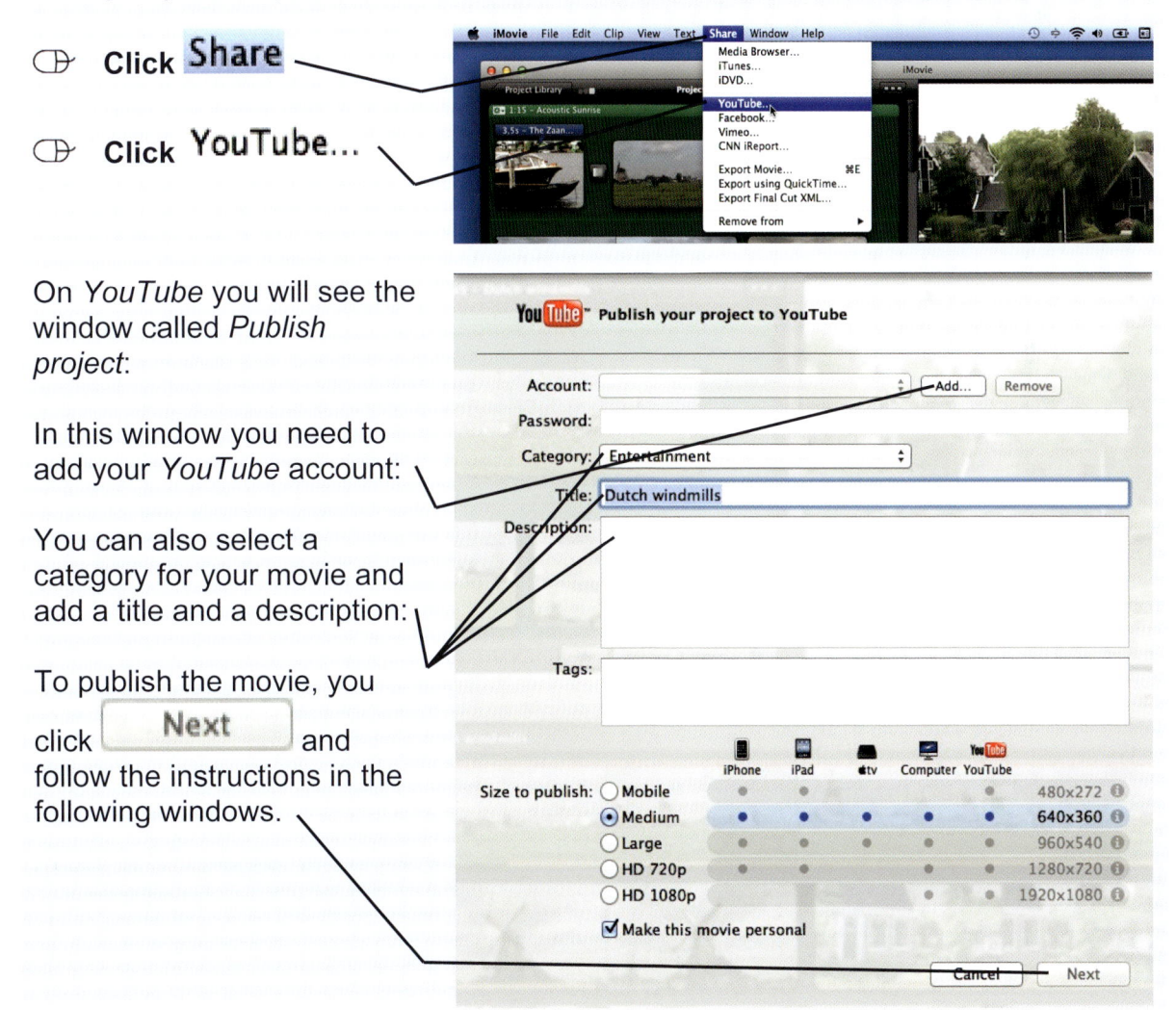

💿 **Click** Share

💿 **Click** YouTube...

On *YouTube* you will see the window called *Publish project*:

In this window you need to add your *YouTube* account:

You can also select a category for your movie and add a title and a description:

To publish the movie, you click Next and follow the instructions in the following windows.

Notes

Write your notes down here.

3. Working with Music

iTunes is a user-friendly program for playing, creating and managing your music collection.

You can use *iTunes* to copy the tracks from a music CD and convert them to music files that can be played on a computer, iPad, iPhone or other device. This is called ripping or importing a CD. You can also create your own playlists with tracks from the *Library*. In this way, you can create a list composed of songs you like to listen to while doing particular activities like administrative work, daily chores or even while exercising at the local gym.

In the *iTunes Library* you can store a variety of information about your music tracks. You can add this information manually to any particular track as desired. You can also rate the tracks by using stars. You can use the star rating later on to create a *smart playlist*.

Another nice feature in *iTunes* is the ability to listen to a wide variety of internet radio broadcasts. *iTunes* even helps you find radio stations for a specific type of music.

In this chapter you will learn how to:

- work with *iTunes*;
- import a CD in *iTunes*;
- play music in *iTunes*;
- manage music in *iTunes*;
- rate tracks in *iTunes*;
- search for tracks in *iTunes*;
- work with playlists in *iTunes*;
- listen to the radio with *iTunes*.

Please note:
You will need a music CD on hand, so that you can carry out each of the steps described in this chapter yourself. The tracks on this CD will be used to explain the various functions in *iTunes*.

Please note:

If you are using a MacBook Air or a Mac mini, you will not have a CD/DVD player. This means you will not be able to import a CD in *iTunes*. But if you have an external CD/DVD player you *will* be able to do this. If you are thinking about purchasing an external player, make sure the player is suitable for use with a *Mac*.

3.1 Opening iTunes

There are several ways to import music files into *iTunes*. One of the methods is to transfer music from a CD (importing). When you have done this, you will be able to listen to the music on your computer whenever you want and without the CD.

☞ **Open** *Finder* [1]

⊕ **Click** **Applications**

⊕ **Double-click** **iTunes**

If this is the very first time you use *iTunes*, you will need to confirm that you agree with the software licensing conditions:

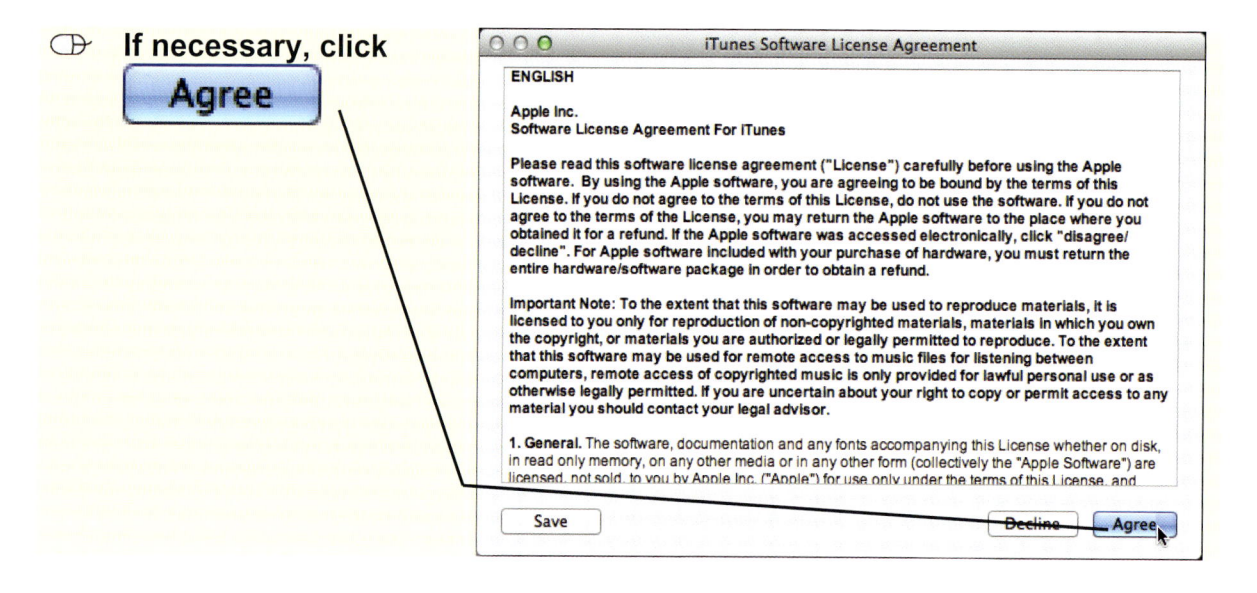

⊕ **If necessary, click** **Agree**

Chapter 3 Working with Music   **123**

You will see the *iTunes* window:

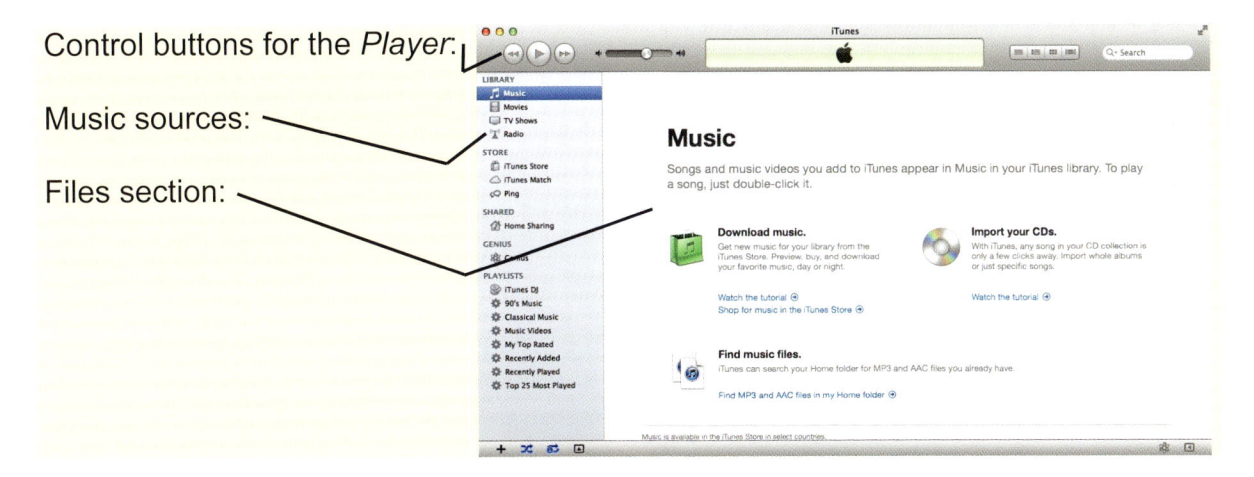

Control buttons for the *Player*:

Music sources:

Files section:

Currently, the *iTunes Library* is probably empty. You may see the *iTunes Videos* window. You can close this window.

☞ If necessary, close the *iTunes Videos* window ℰ³

3.2 Importing a CD

In *iTunes* you can copy the tracks from a music CD and convert them into files that can be used on a computer and many other external devices. In *iTunes* this is called importing a CD. In other music programs this process is called 'ripping'.

☞ Insert a CD into your computer's CD/DVD player

If your computer is connected to the Internet, a search will be performed regarding information about the CD. The titles of the songs on the CD (called *tracks*) will automatically be downloaded.

Here you see the titles of the tracks on the CD:

On the left-hand side you will see the DEVICES heading with the title of the CD below:

Right away, *iTunes* will ask you if you want to import the CD. You can go ahead and import the CD to the computer:

☞ Click **Yes**

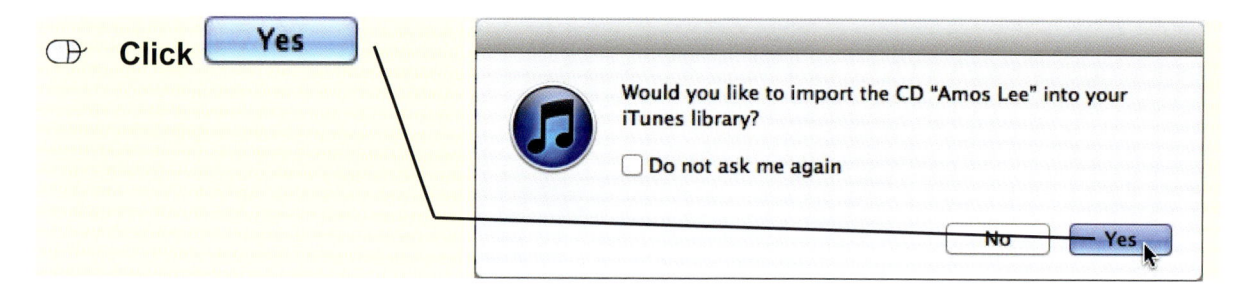

In the *iTunes* window, a progress bar indicates the amount of time left remaining in the import process:

The track that is currently imported is indicated by this icon 🟠:

In the information pane on the right, you can see which track is being imported and how much time remains for the operation to be completed:

By default, all the tracks are checked, so they will all be imported:

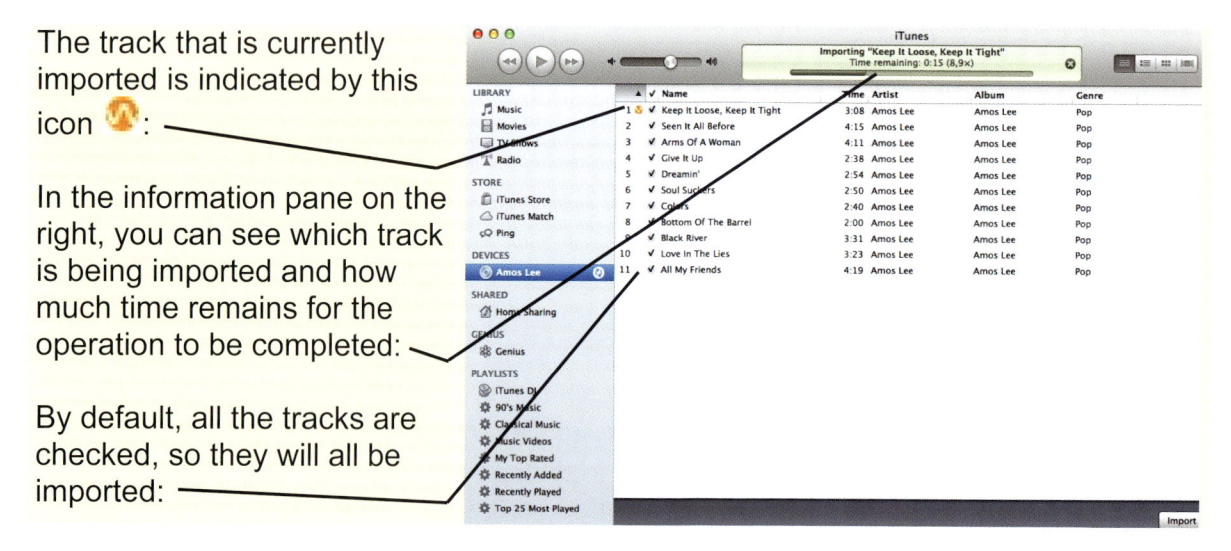

The tracks will be imported one by one.

➥ Please note:
The import operation may take a little while.

After the CD has been imported you will hear a sound signal.

Now all tracks will be marked by ✅:

This means the import operation has been successful.

Chapter 3 Working with Music

Now you can remove the CD from the CD/DVD player. You do that like this:

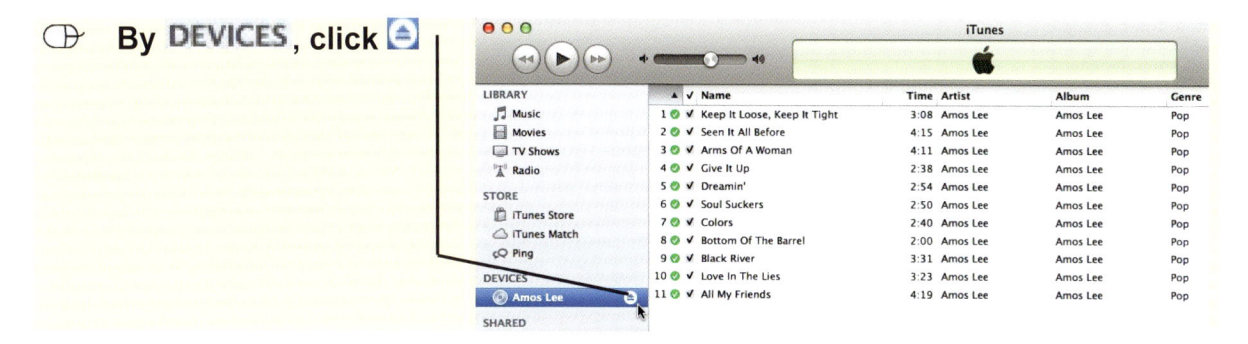

☞ By `DEVICES`, click ⏏

The CD will be ejected from the CD/DVD player.

The CD you have just imported will be displayed in the list by `Music`:

This CD displays the title and the artist:

3.3 Playing Music in iTunes

You can also play music in *iTunes*. You can do this with the music files you just imported:

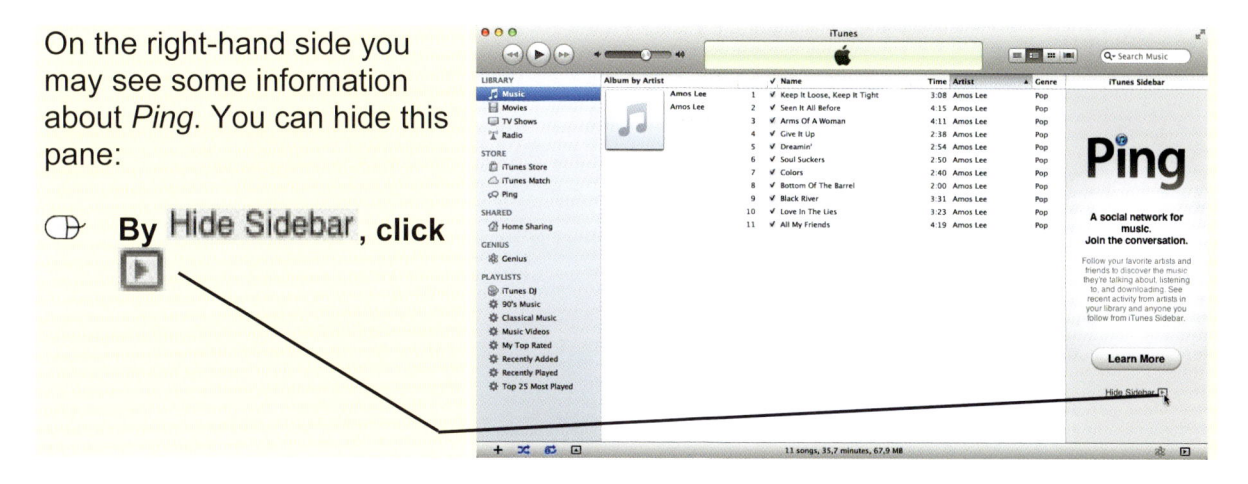

On the right-hand side you may see some information about *Ping*. You can hide this pane:

☞ By `Hide Sidebar`, click

You can now play the first track of the CD you just imported:

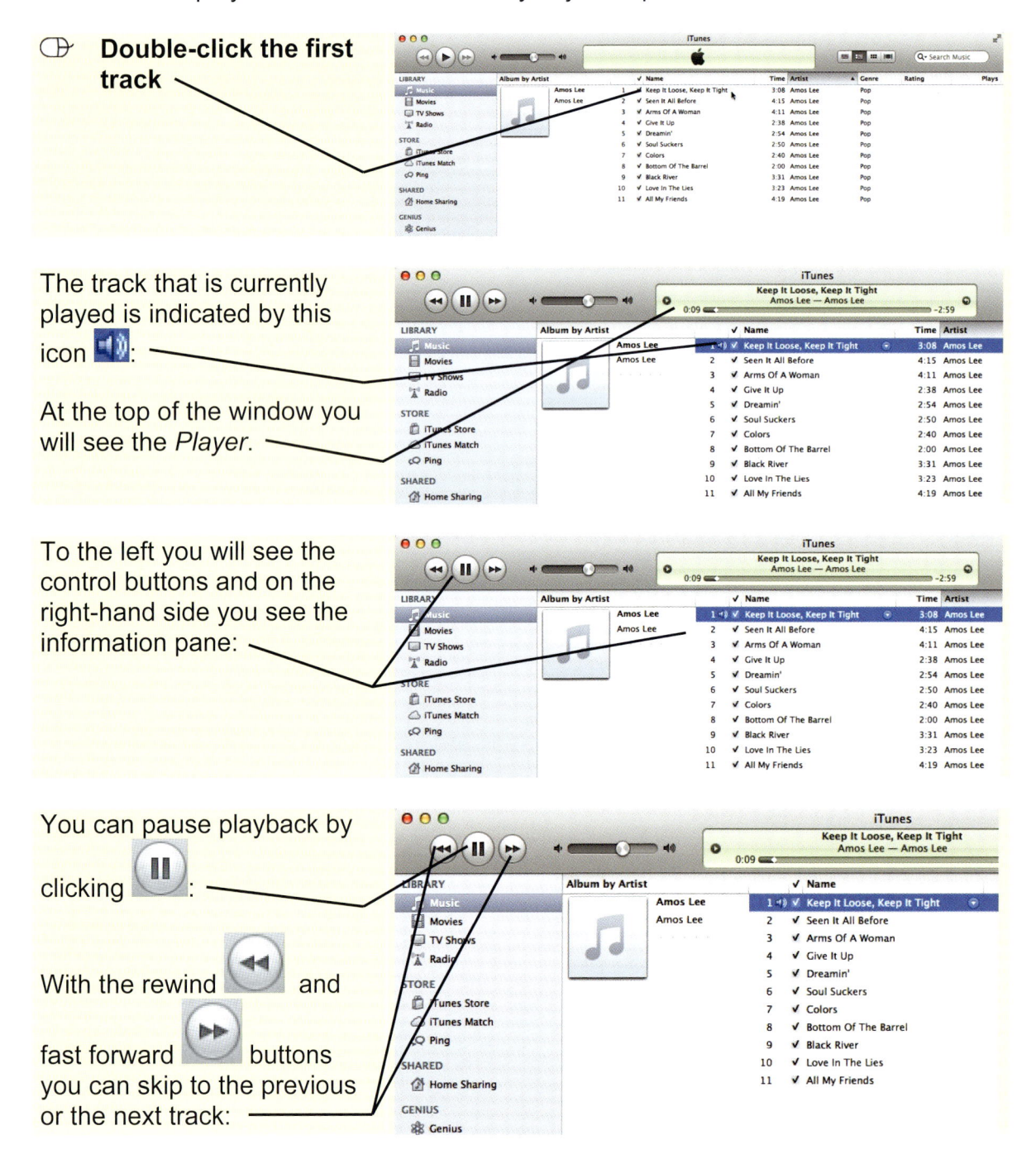

☞ **Double-click the first track**

The track that is currently played is indicated by this icon 🔊:

At the top of the window you will see the *Player*.

To the left you will see the control buttons and on the right-hand side you see the information pane:

You can pause playback by clicking ⏸:

With the rewind ⏪ and fast forward ⏩ buttons you can skip to the previous or the next track:

Chapter 3 Working with Music **127**

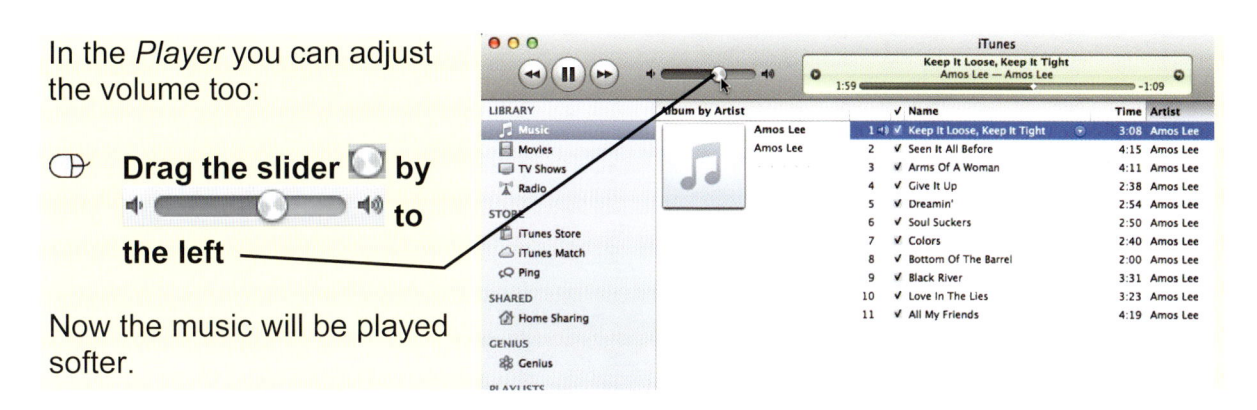

In the *Player* you can adjust the volume too:

☞ **Drag the slider by to the left**

Now the music will be played softer.

iTunes has a function called *shuffle* for playing the tracks in random order. You may already be familiar with this feature since many regular CD players have this as well. This is how you use it in *iTunes*:

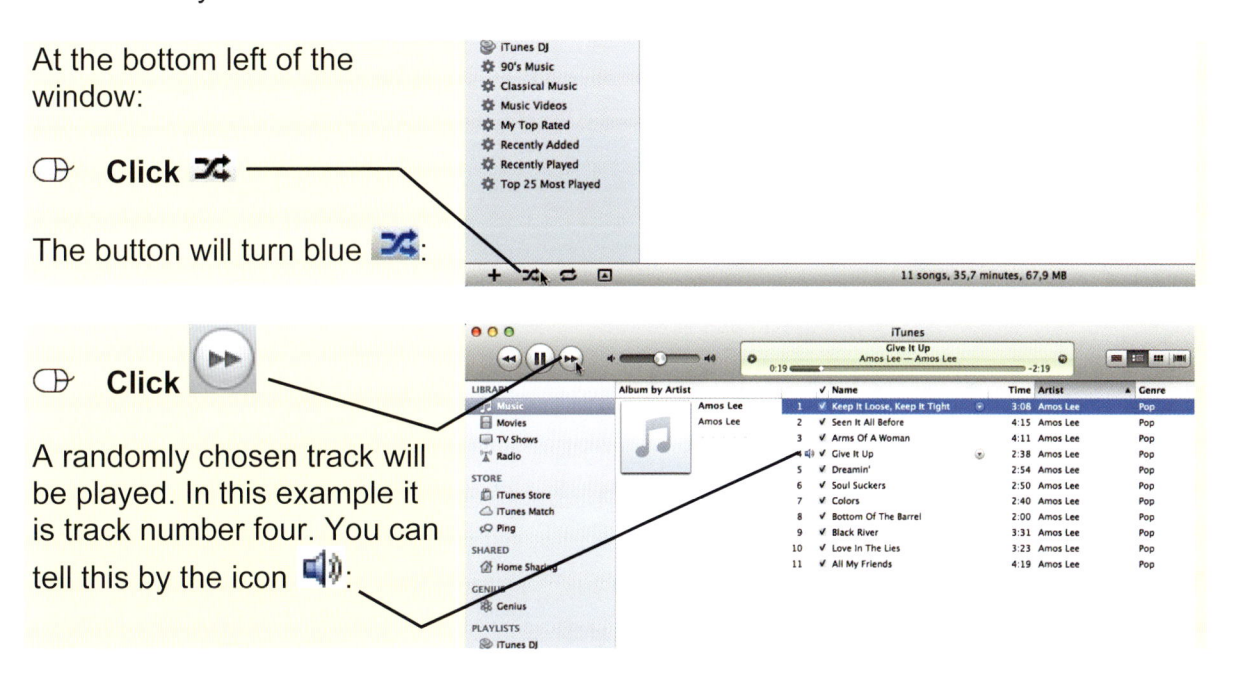

At the bottom left of the window:

☞ **Click**

The button will turn blue:

☞ **Click**

A randomly chosen track will be played. In this example it is track number four. You can tell this by the icon:

You can repeat the playback of the tracks:

At the bottom left of the window:

☞ **Click**

The button will turn blue:

After the CD has finished playing, playback will resume. You can also repeat playback of just a single track:

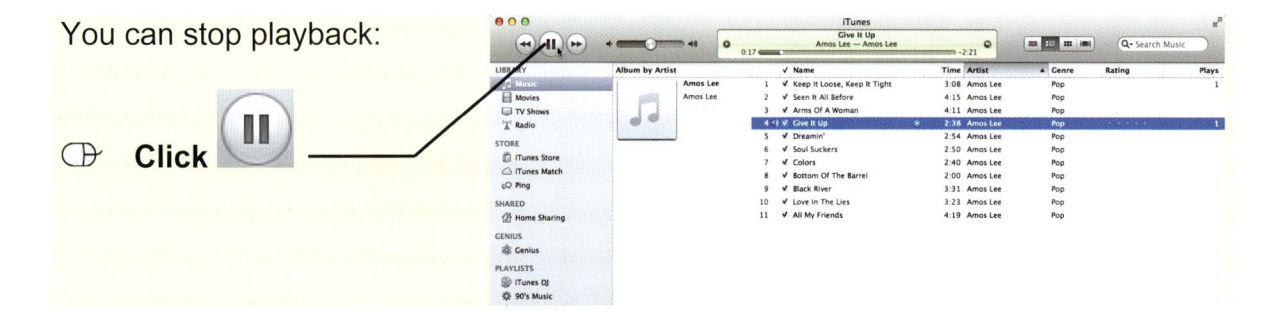

⌦ **Click** 🔁

The button turns into 🔂:
After the track that is currently playing has finished, it will start playing again.

You can stop playback:

⌦ **Click** ⏸

3.4 Viewing Information in the Library

Information about each track can be stored in the *iTunes Library.* You can view the properties of each track. You can do this by using the Control key:

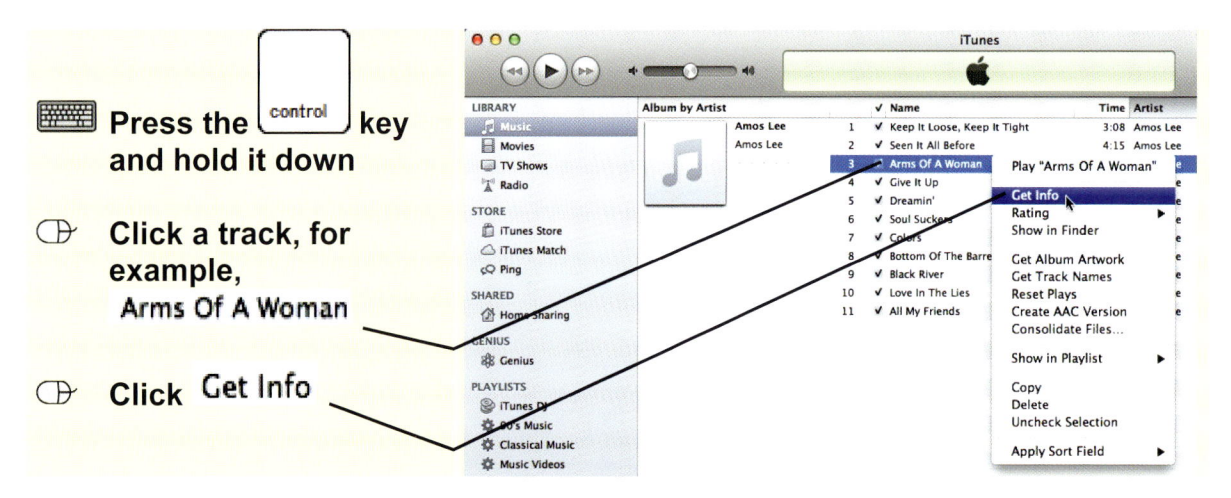

⌨ **Press the** `control` **key and hold it down**

⌦ **Click a track, for example,** *Arms Of A Woman*

⌦ **Click** *Get Info*

Chapter 3 Working with Music 129

A window will be opened with the same name as the title of the track:

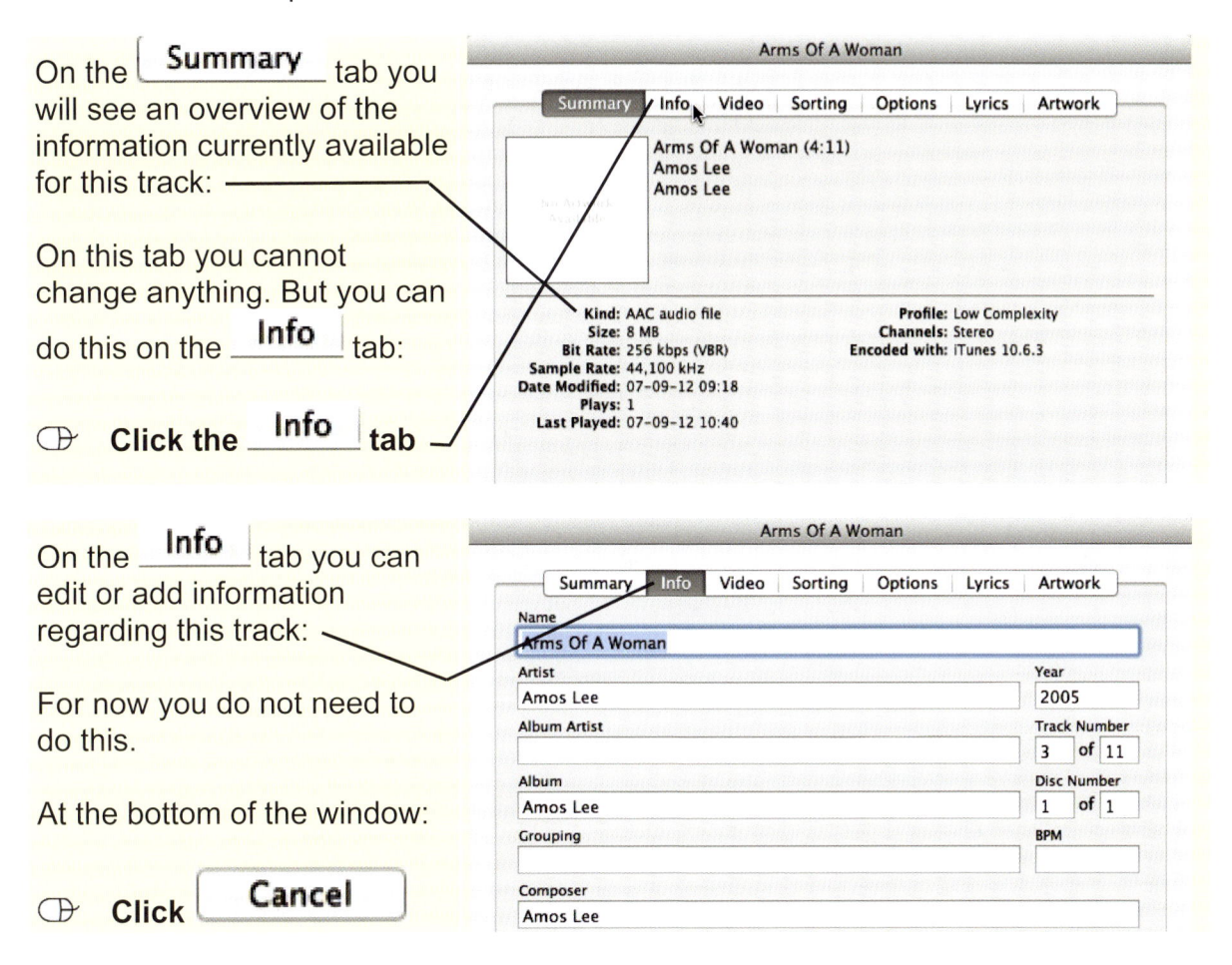

On the [Summary] tab you will see an overview of the information currently available for this track:

On this tab you cannot change anything. But you can do this on the [Info] tab:

☞ Click the [Info] tab

On the [Info] tab you can edit or add information regarding this track:

For now you do not need to do this.

At the bottom of the window:

☞ Click [Cancel]

3.5 Modifying the Information on a Track

You can modify the shared properties for a number of tracks all at once. First, you need to select the relevant tracks. This is how to use the Shift key for selecting all the tracks on the CD you previously imported:

⌨ Press [Shift] and hold it down

☞ Click the first track

☞ Click the last track

Now all tracks on the CD have been selected. You can also view the information about these tracks by using the Control key:

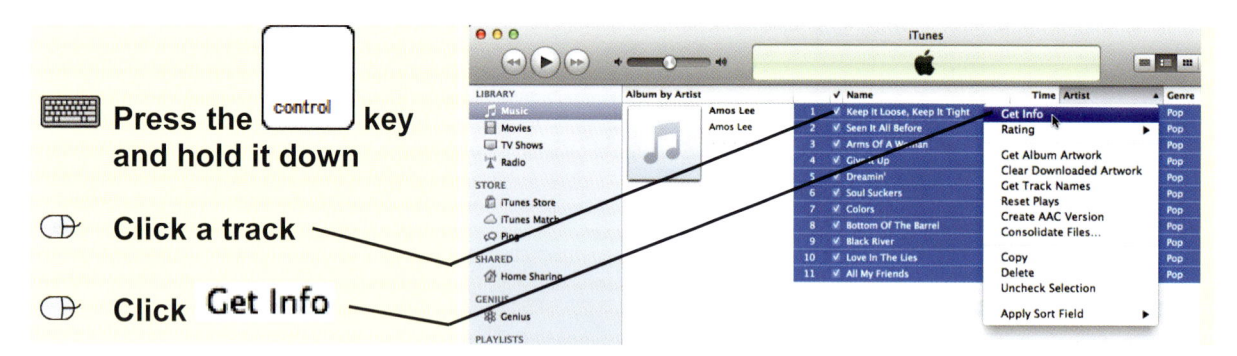

⌨ **Press the** `control` **key and hold it down**

☞ **Click a track**

☞ **Click** Get Info

You will see a question:

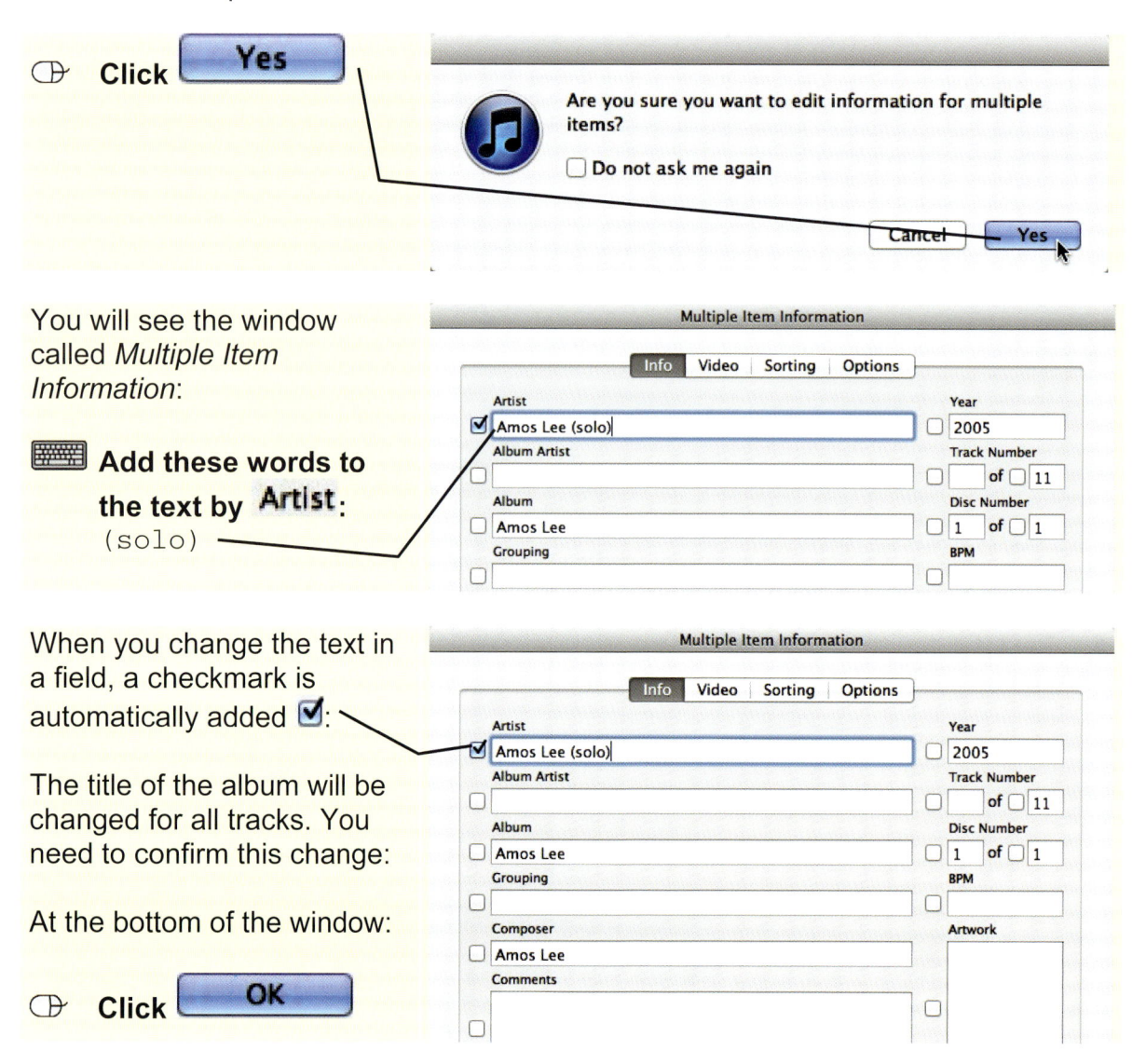

☞ **Click** Yes

You will see the window called *Multiple Item Information*:

⌨ **Add these words to the text by** Artist:
`(solo)`

When you change the text in a field, a checkmark is automatically added ☑:

The title of the album will be changed for all tracks. You need to confirm this change:

At the bottom of the window:

☞ **Click** OK

Chapter 3 Working with Music 131

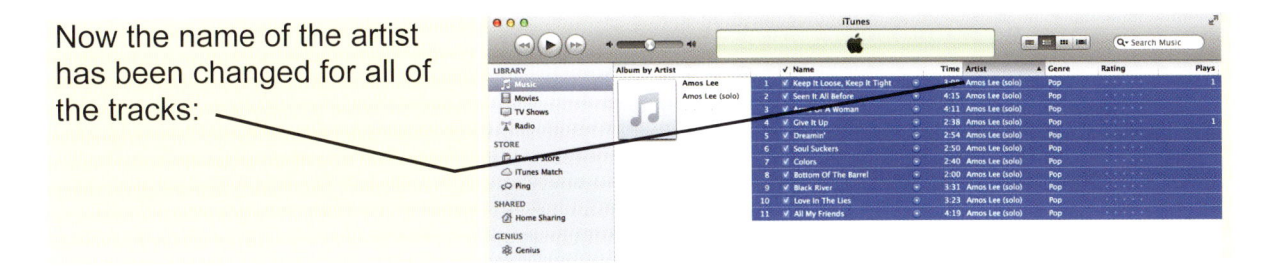

Now the name of the artist has been changed for all of the tracks:

3.6 Rating Tracks

You can rate songs in the *Library*, by using stars. The highest rating for a song (or track) is five stars; the lowest rating is zero stars. In this way you can make a selection of your favorite songs and play them at a later stage.
This is how you rate the tracks by adding stars:

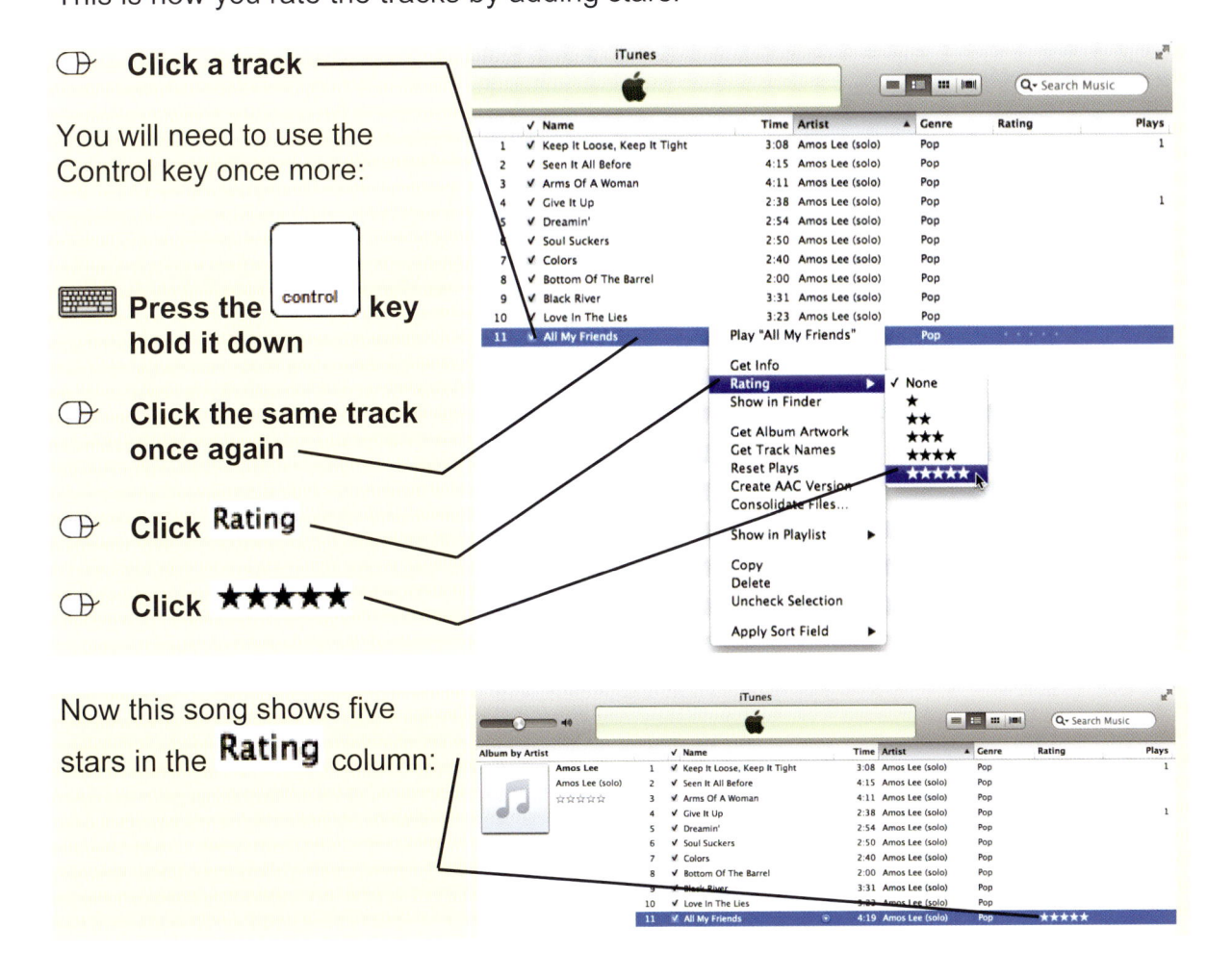

☞ **Click a track**

You will need to use the Control key once more:

⌨ **Press the** `control` **key hold it down**

☞ **Click the same track once again**

☞ **Click** Rating

☞ **Click** ★★★★★

Now this song shows five stars in the **Rating** column:

You can also rate a number of songs simultaneously. You do this by using the Command key:

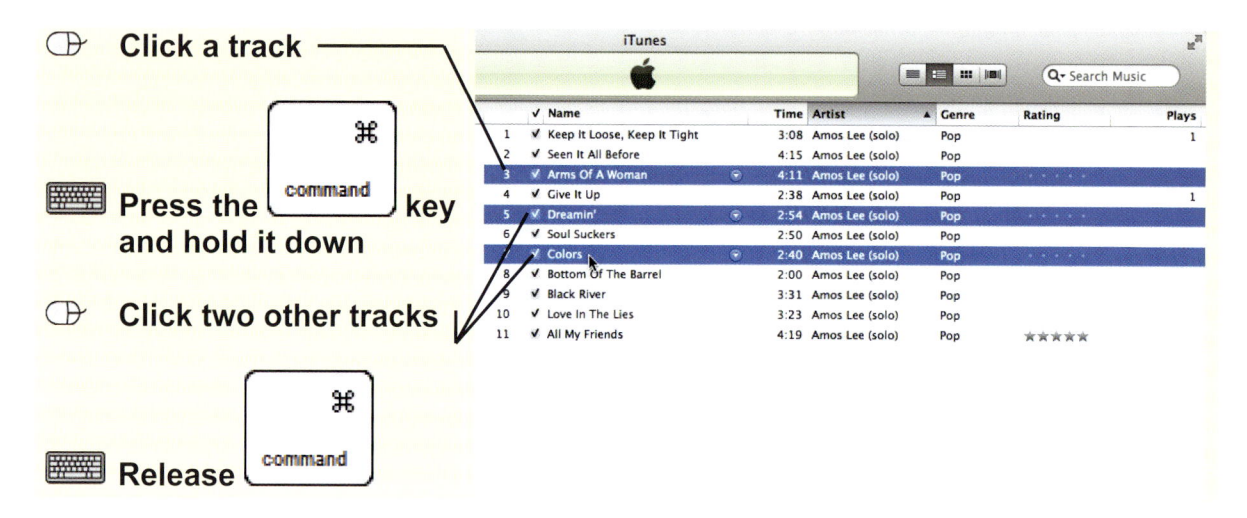

☞ **Click a track**

⌨ **Press the** ⌘ **key and hold it down**

☞ **Click two other tracks**

⌨ **Release** ⌘

Now three tracks have been selected. You can rate these tracks with three stars:

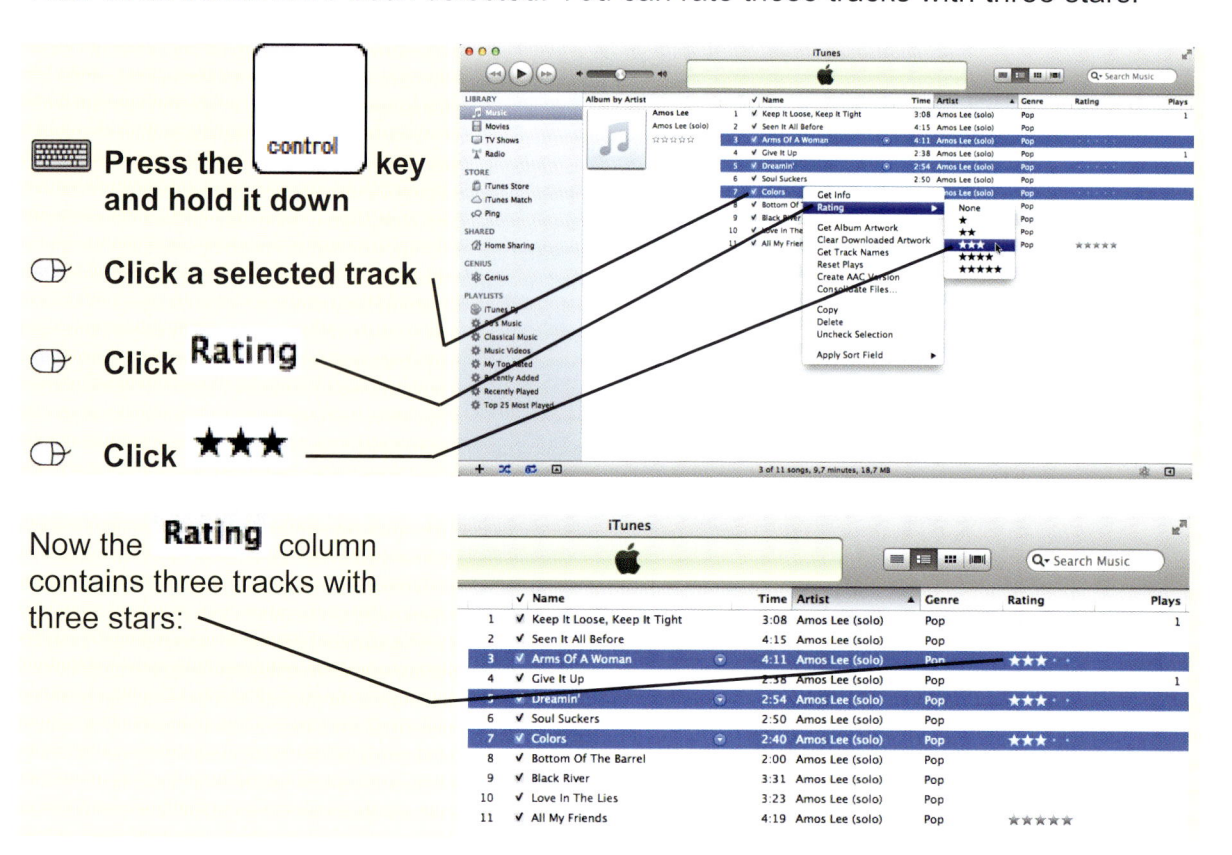

⌨ **Press the** control **key and hold it down**

☞ **Click a selected track**

☞ **Click** Rating

☞ **Click** ★★★

Now the Rating column contains three tracks with three stars:

Chapter 3 *Working with Music* **133**

You can also rate songs by clicking the appropriate number of stars in the *Rating* column:

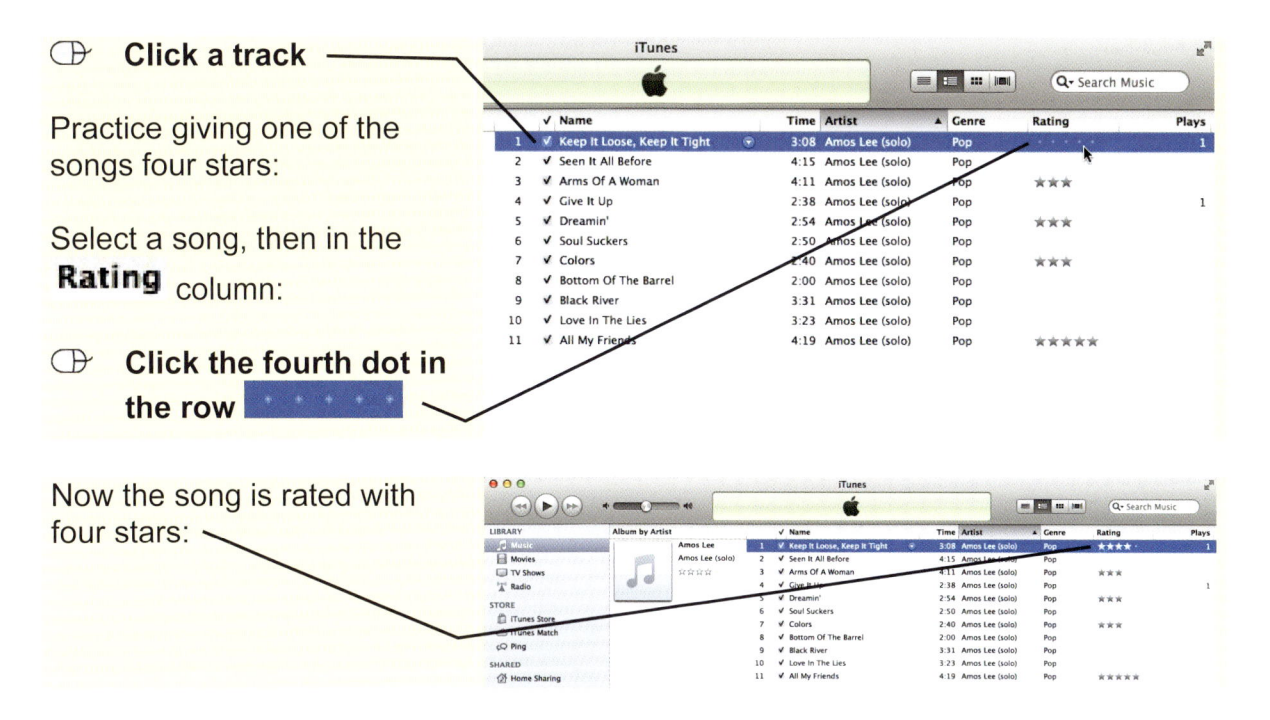

☞ **Click a track**

Practice giving one of the songs four stars:

Select a song, then in the **Rating** column:

☞ **Click the fourth dot in the row**

Now the song is rated with four stars:

💡 **Tip**
Smart playlist
In *section 3.14 Using Smart Playlists* you can read how to create a smart playlist on the basis of the ratings you have assigned to the songs in your *Library*.

3.7 Searching for Songs

The *iTunes Library* contains its own search engine. This is a very useful feature if you have a lot of music stored on your computer.

☞ **Click the** *Search Music* **search box**

Now you can enter a keyword. This may be part of a song title or an artist's name:

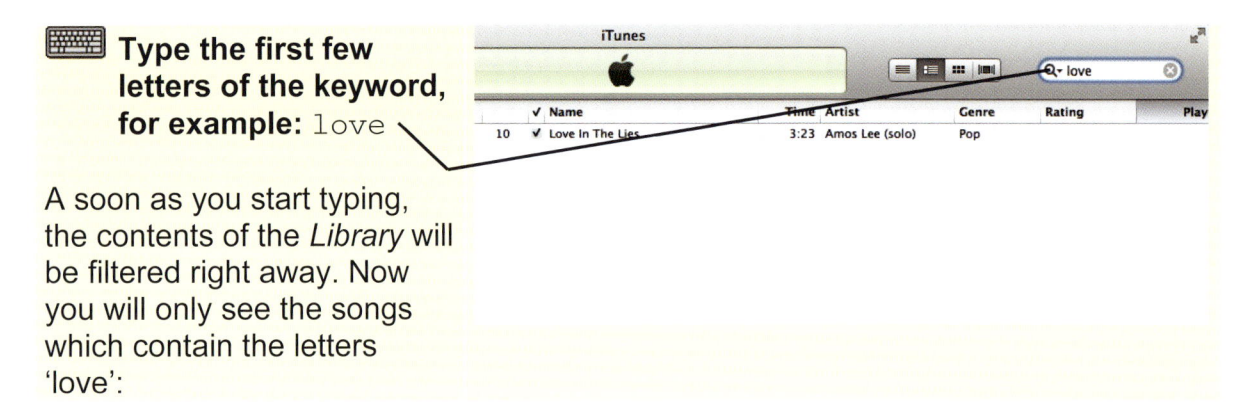

⌨ **Type the first few letters of the keyword, for example:** love

A soon as you start typing, the contents of the *Library* will be filtered right away. Now you will only see the songs which contain the letters 'love':

💡 **Tip**
Search for parts of names and titles
You can also search for parts of names and titles, instead of for the initial letters. For example, if you type the letters 'To', not only will the songs by Toto be found, but also the songs that contain the letters 'to' in their title.

This is how you delete the search results and return to the full track list in the *Library*:

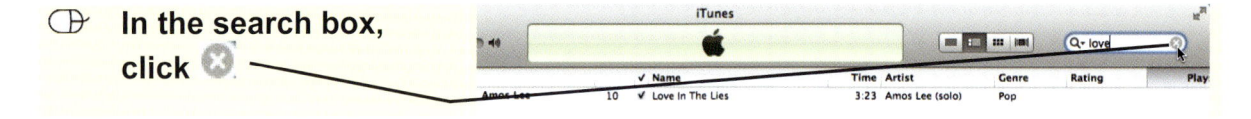

☞ **In the search box, click** ⊗

Now all tracks are displayed once more.

💡 **Tip**
Specific search
If you are sure you are looking for the name of an artist or an album, you can restrict your search operation to these specific columns:

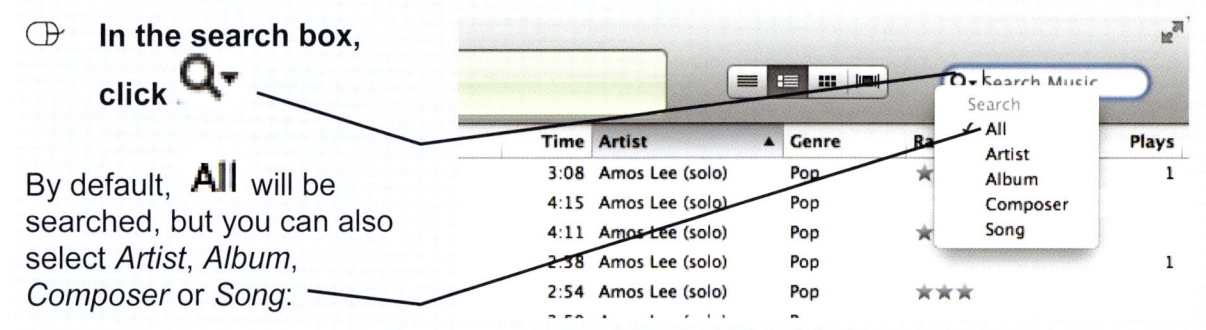

☞ **In the search box, click** 🔍▾

By default, **All** will be searched, but you can also select *Artist*, *Album*, *Composer* or *Song*:

After you have made your choice, you can start searching in the same way as you did before.

3.8 Creating a Playlist

One of the most popular and useful functions in *iTunes* is the ability to create playlists. In a playlist you can gather your favorite songs and arrange them in the order you want. Afterwards, you can play this list over and over again. This way, you will not need to search for your favorite songs each time you want to listen to them.

You can use the songs that are currently displayed in the *Library* to create a new playlist. Here is how you open a new, blank playlist:

At the top of the window:

☞ Click **File**

☞ Click **New Playlist**

The new playlist will be added and you can enter a name for it:

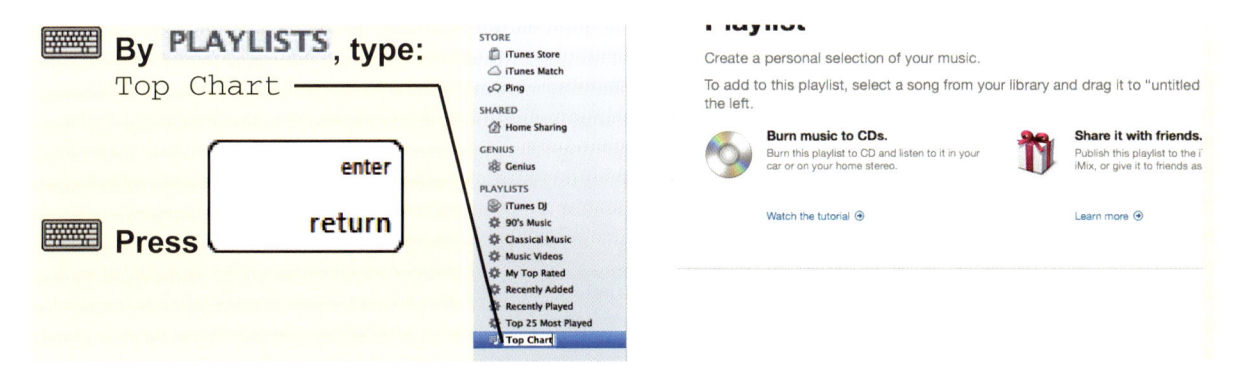

⌨ By **PLAYLISTS**, type: Top Chart

⌨ Press **enter** / **return**

3.9 Adding Songs to a Playlist

You can choose the songs you want to add to the playlist. First, you need to display the tracks in the *Library*:

☞ Click **Music**

You will see all the tracks in the *Library* again:

There are two ways of adding tracks to a playlist. The first method is to drag a track to the playlist:

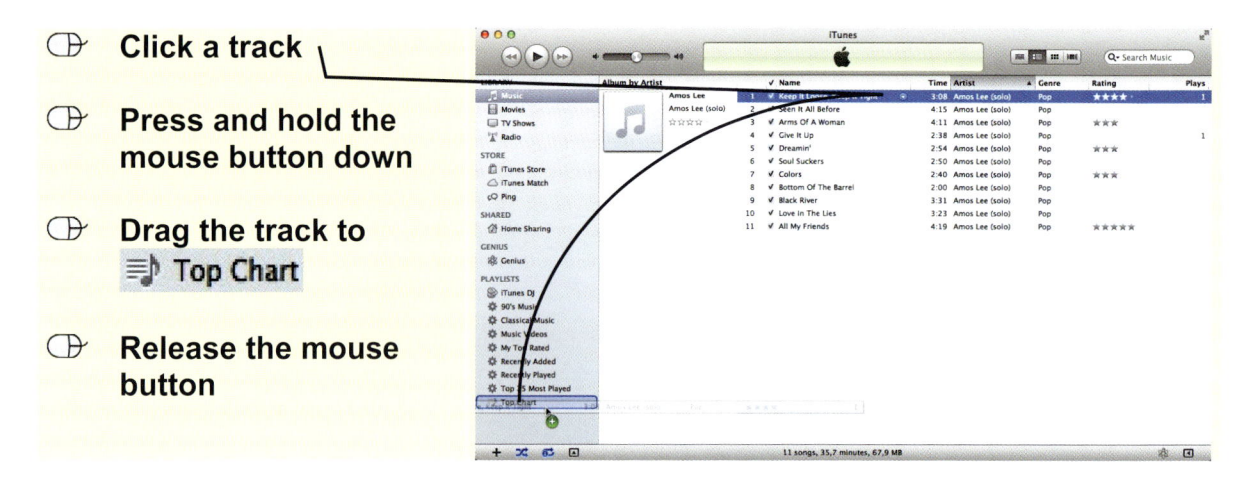

- ☞ **Click a track**

- ☞ **Press and hold the mouse button down**

- ☞ **Drag the track to Top Chart**

- ☞ **Release the mouse button**

The track has been added to the playlist called *Top Chart*. You can check to make sure:

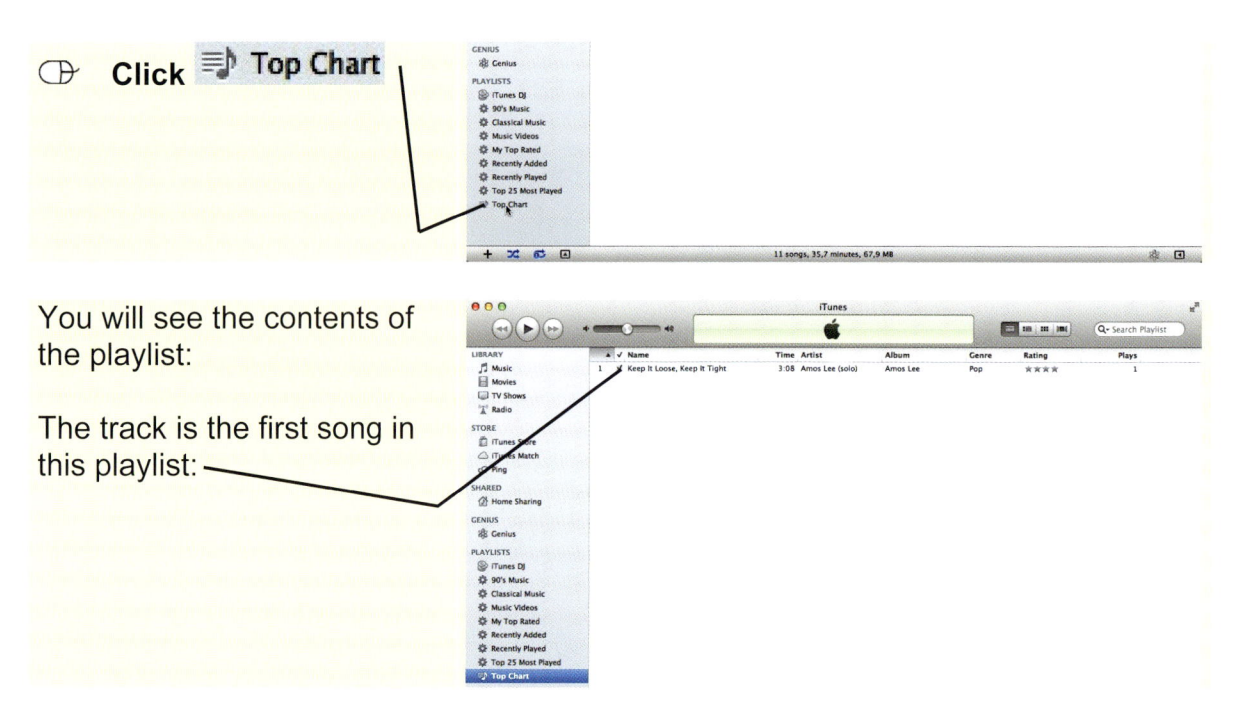

- ☞ **Click Top Chart**

You will see the contents of the playlist:

The track is the first song in this playlist:

You can also use a quick start menu to add tracks to the playlist. This is how you do that:

- ☞ **By LIBRARY, click Music**

Chapter 3 Working with Music 137

Open the contextual menu with the Control key:

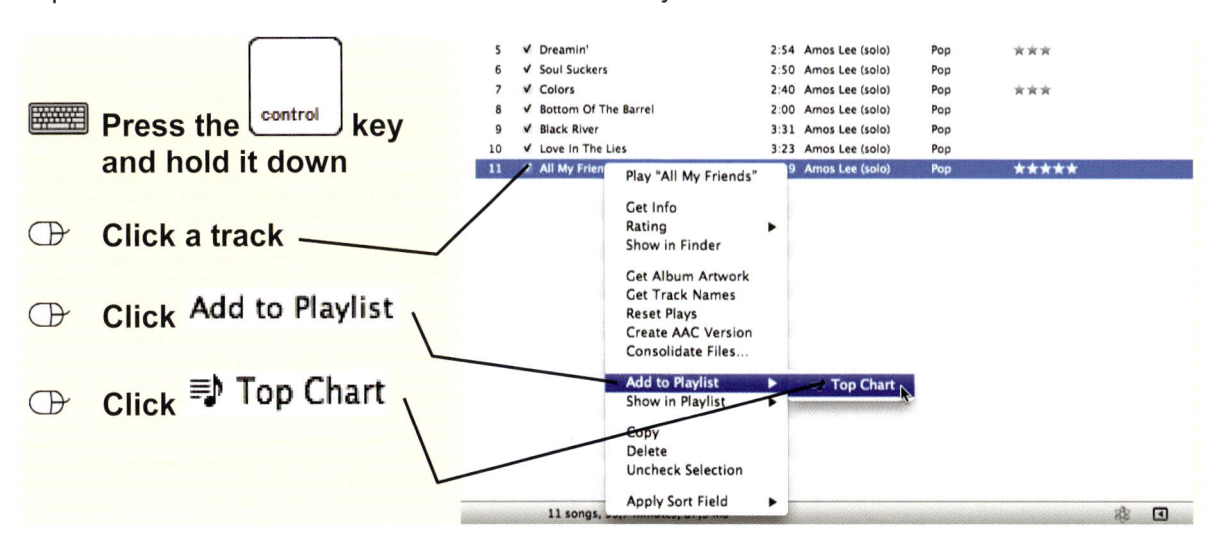

⌨ **Press the** `control` **key and hold it down**

☞ **Click a track**

☞ **Click Add to Playlist**

☞ **Click 🎵 Top Chart**

Now you can check to see if the track has actually been added to the playlist:

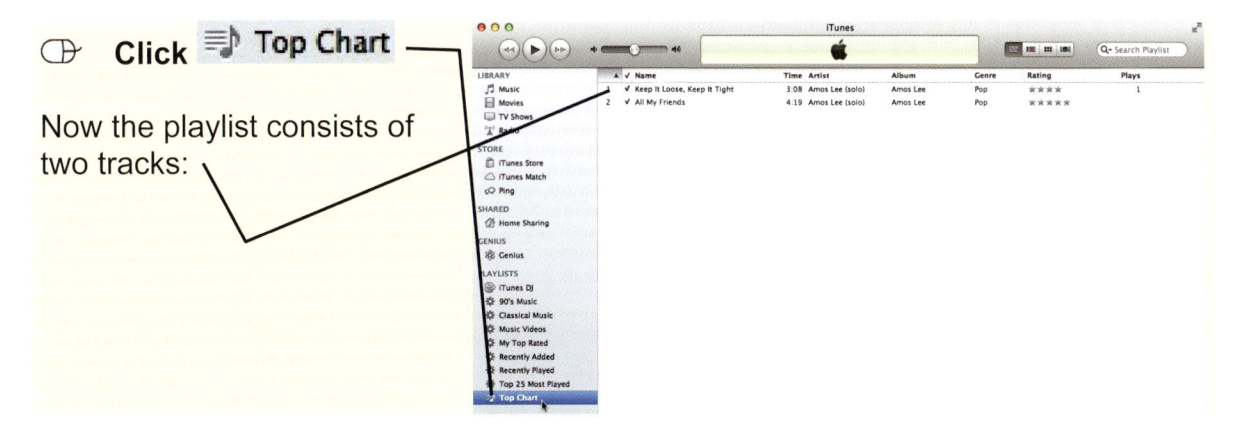

☞ **Click 🎵 Top Chart**

Now the playlist consists of two tracks:

3.10 Adding Multiple Tracks At Once

If you want to work a bit quicker, you can also add multiple tracks at once to the playlist. You do this by making smart selections with the Command key:

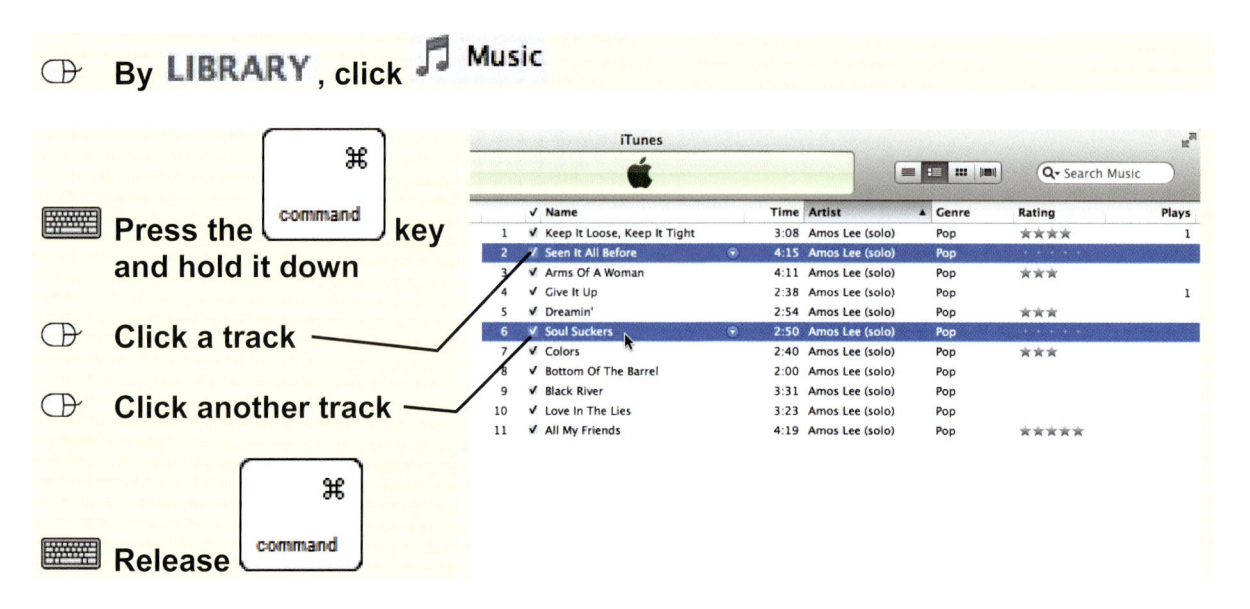

☞ By **LIBRARY**, click ♪ **Music**

⌨ Press the ⌘ **command** key and hold it down

☞ Click a track

☞ Click another track

⌨ Release ⌘ **command**

You can add the selected tracks to the playlist:

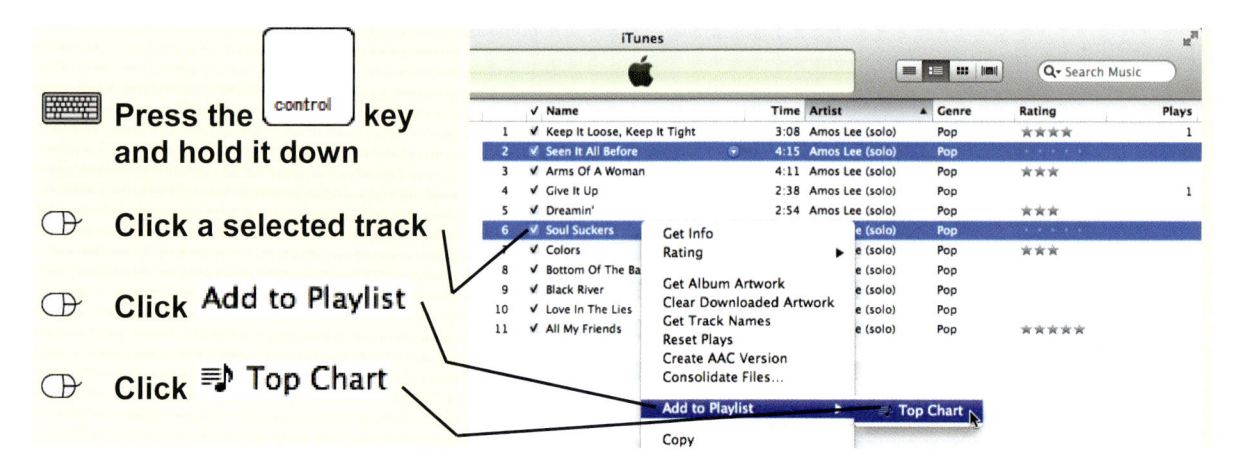

⌨ Press the **control** key and hold it down

☞ Click a selected track

☞ Click **Add to Playlist**

☞ Click ♪ **Top Chart**

Chapter 3 Working with Music

⊕ Click 🎵 **Top Chart**

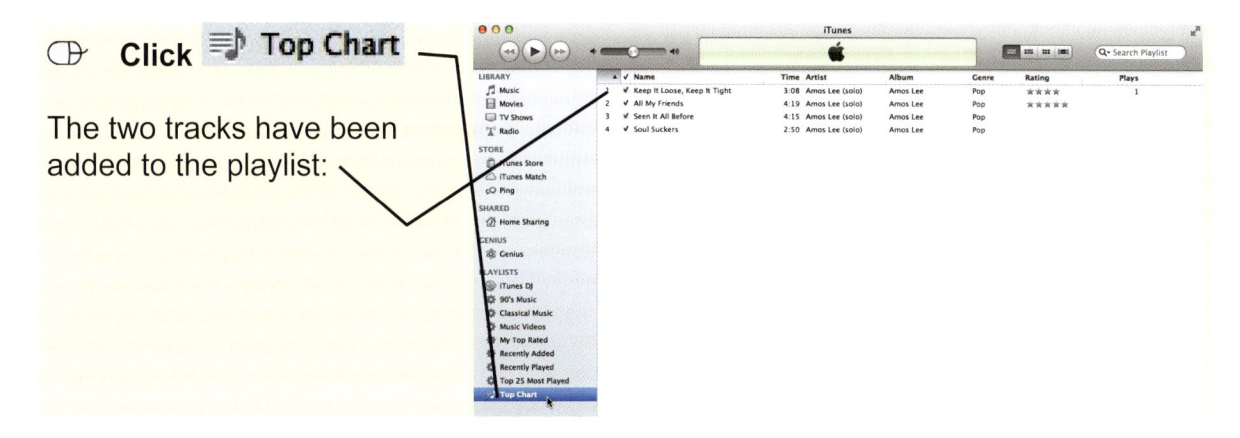

The two tracks have been added to the playlist:

➥ **Please note:**
By adding tracks to the playlist you will not influence the location of where the tracks are stored in the *Library* or on your computer. The *Library* and the playlist only contain shortcuts to these tracks and not the actual tracks themselves.

💡 **Tip**
Add an album to a playlist
It is possible to add an entire album to a playlist. You do that like this:

⊕ Click 🎵 **Music**

Select the *Grid* view:

⊕ Click ▦

You will see an overview of the albums in *iTunes*:

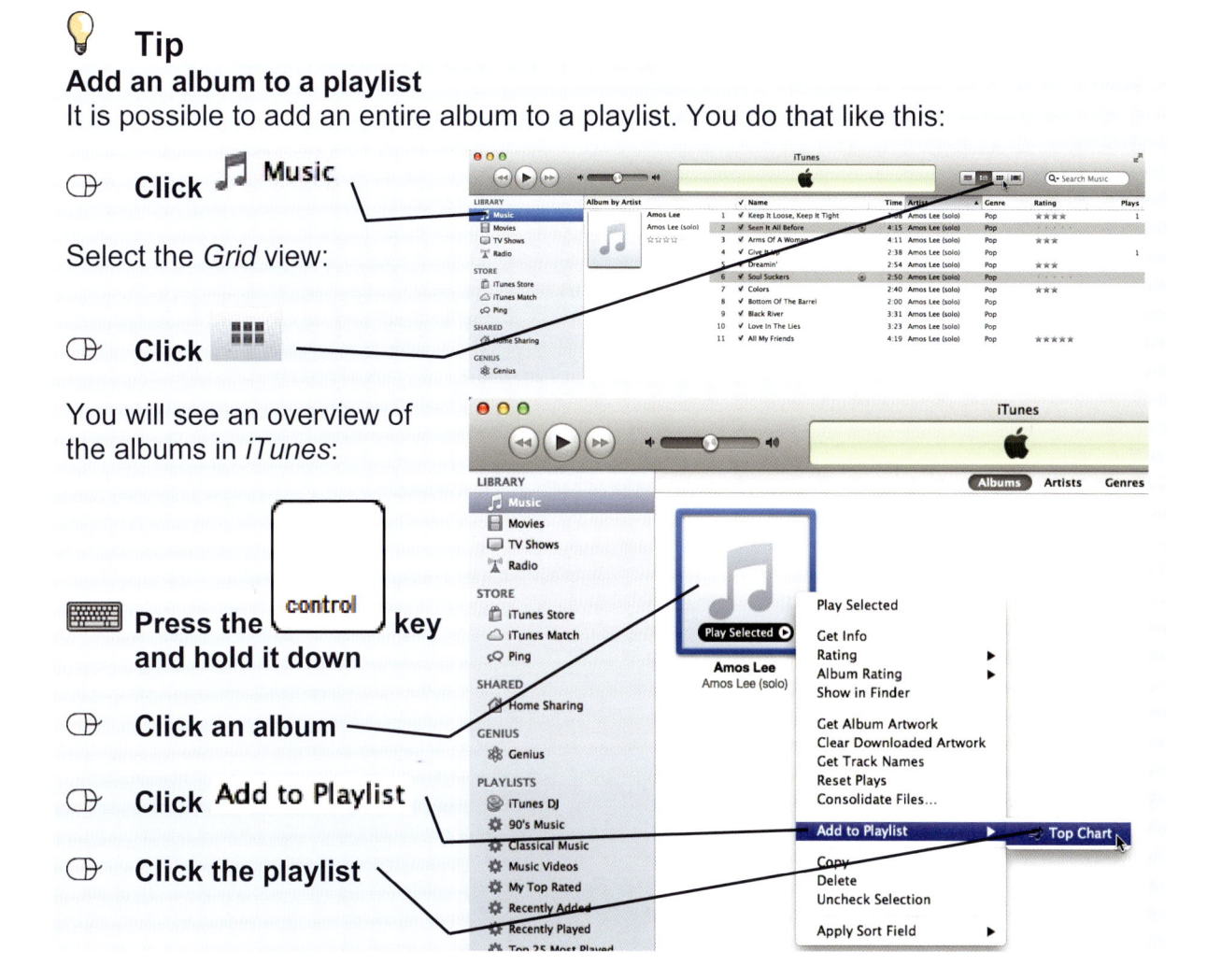

⌨ Press the `control` key and hold it down

⊕ Click an album

⊕ Click **Add to Playlist**

⊕ Click the playlist

3.11 Changing the Order of the Playlist

The order of the tracks in the playlist is determined by the order in which you have added the tracks. You can change this order. You do this by dragging the tracks to a different place. Just give it a try. Move a track between the first and second tracks of the playlist:

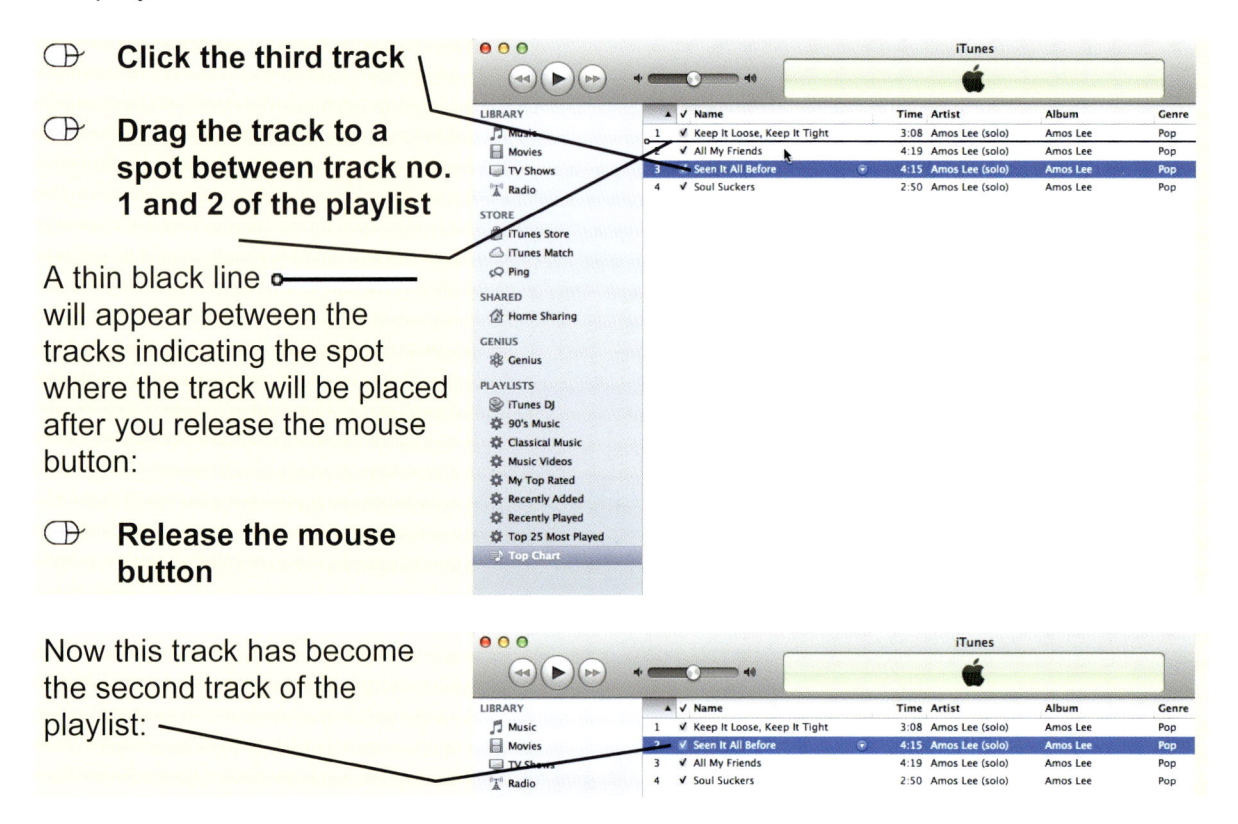

☞ **Click the third track**

☞ **Drag the track to a spot between track no. 1 and 2 of the playlist**

A thin black line will appear between the tracks indicating the spot where the track will be placed after you release the mouse button:

☞ **Release the mouse button**

Now this track has become the second track of the playlist:

3.12 Removing a Track From the Playlist

If you decide you no longer want a particular track in the playlist, you can remove it:

☞ **Click the last track**

⌨ **Press** *delete* **(Delete) or** ⌫ **(Backspace)**

Chapter 3 Working with Music **141**

Before permanently removing an item, *iTunes* will ask for confirmation:

☞ Click **Remove**

The track has been removed from the playlist:

3.13 Playing a Playlist

You can play all the tracks in the playlist:

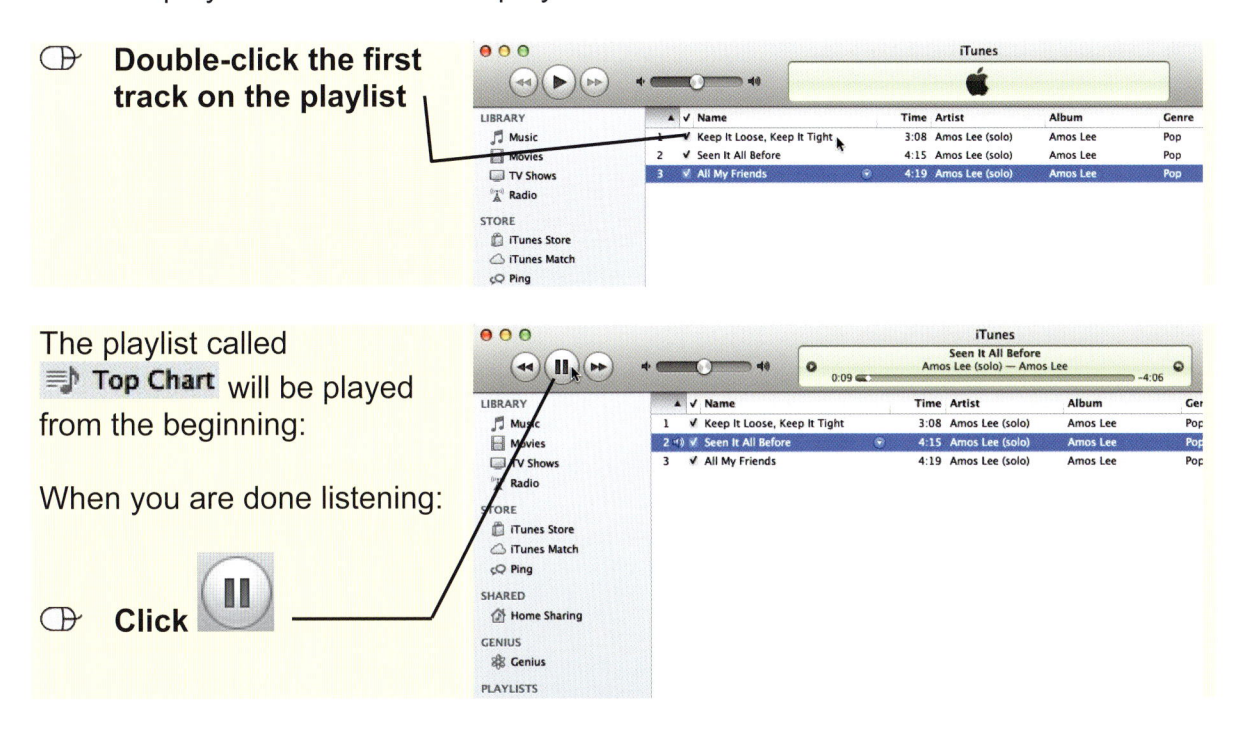

☞ **Double-click the first track on the playlist**

The playlist called **Top Chart** will be played from the beginning:

When you are done listening:

☞ Click ⏸

3.14 Using Smart Playlists

If you have a large number of tracks stored in the *Library* it is a good idea to use the *smart playlists*. These playlists are created by *iTunes* and filled with tracks from the *Library*.

By default, *iTunes* contains a number of smart playlists. You can recognize them by the ⚙ icon on the left side of the name of the playlist, for example ⚙ **Recently Played**:

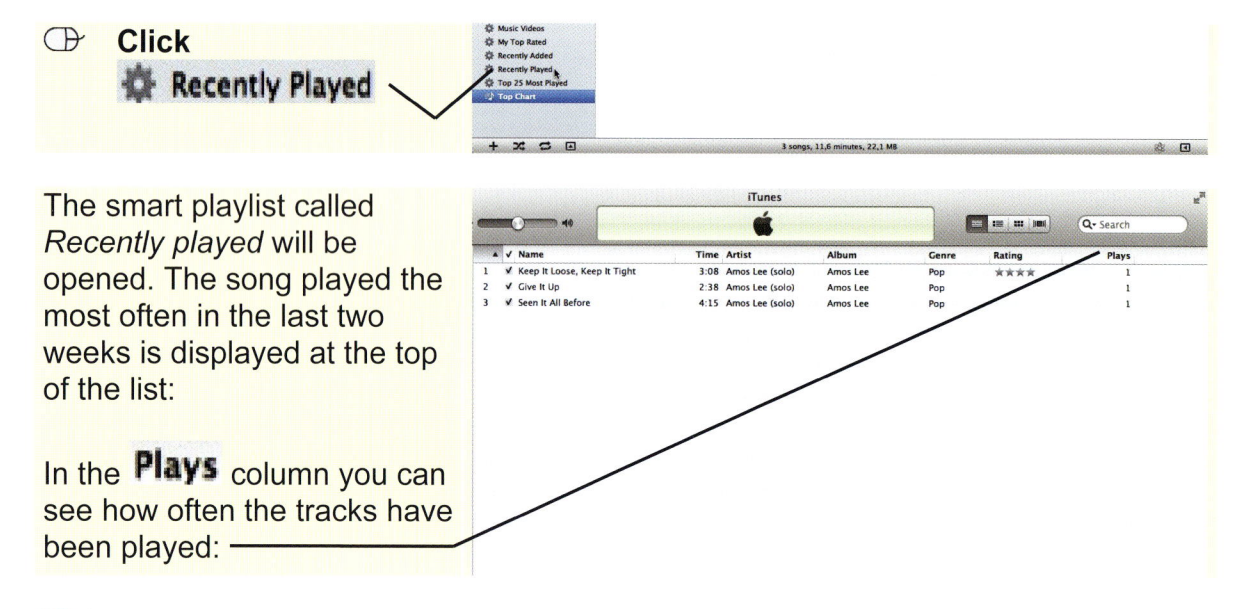

☞ **Click** ⚙ **Recently Played**

The smart playlist called *Recently played* will be opened. The song played the most often in the last two weeks is displayed at the top of the list:

In the **Plays** column you can see how often the tracks have been played:

Please note:
If you open the same smart playlist a few days later, the number and the order of the tracks may have changed. This can be caused by the addition or removal of songs from the same artist, or you may have played certain other songs repeatedly. Each time you open a smart playlist, the list is dynamically re-created based on the information currently stored in the *Library*.

Tip
Other standard smart playlists

⚙ **Top 25 Most Played**: this list contains the 25 tracks you have played most often.

⚙ **90's Music**: this list contains all tracks from 1990 up to 1999.

⚙ **My Top Rated**: this list consists of the tracks you have rated with more than three stars.

⚙ **Recently Added**: this list contains the tracks you have added in the past two weeks.

Chapter 3 Working with Music   **143**

3.15 Creating Your Own Smart Playlist

iTunes also gives you the ability to create your own smart playlist. You can select the tracks according to a few simple rules you determine yourself.

At the top of the window:

☞ **Click File**

☞ **Click New Smart Playlist...**

In the *Smart playlist* window you can select the criteria for the new smart playlist. You can let *iTunes* search in the basic information listed for the songs. For instance, you can create a playlist containing all the songs from a single artist with a five star rating:

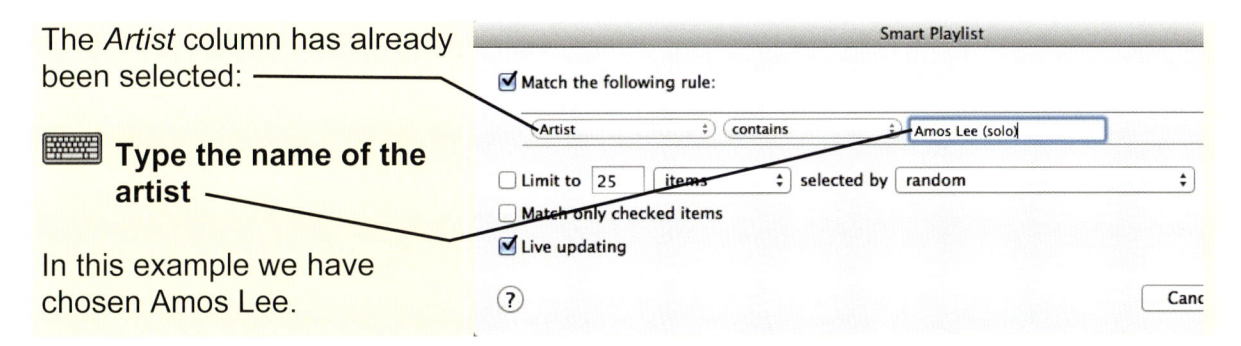

The *Artist* column has already been selected:

⌨ **Type the name of the artist**

In this example we have chosen Amos Lee.

You can easily add a second rule:

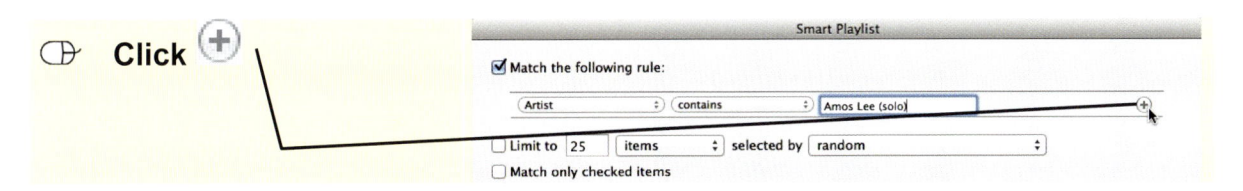

☞ **Click +**

Now you can select the basic data you want to use for this rule:

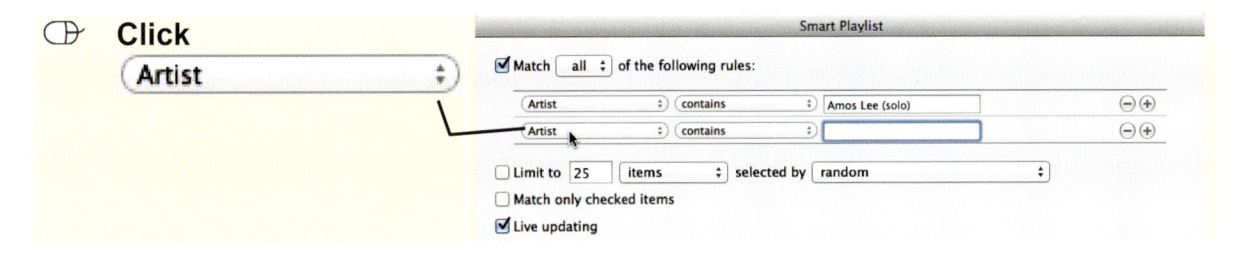

☞ **Click Artist**

To make a selection based on a song's rating:

☞ Click **Rating**

By default, a five star rating is selected:

☞ Click **OK**

The new smart playlist is added. Now you will see the songs listed in this smart playlist:

On your own computer you will see different songs.

iTunes suggests to name this playlist after the artist:

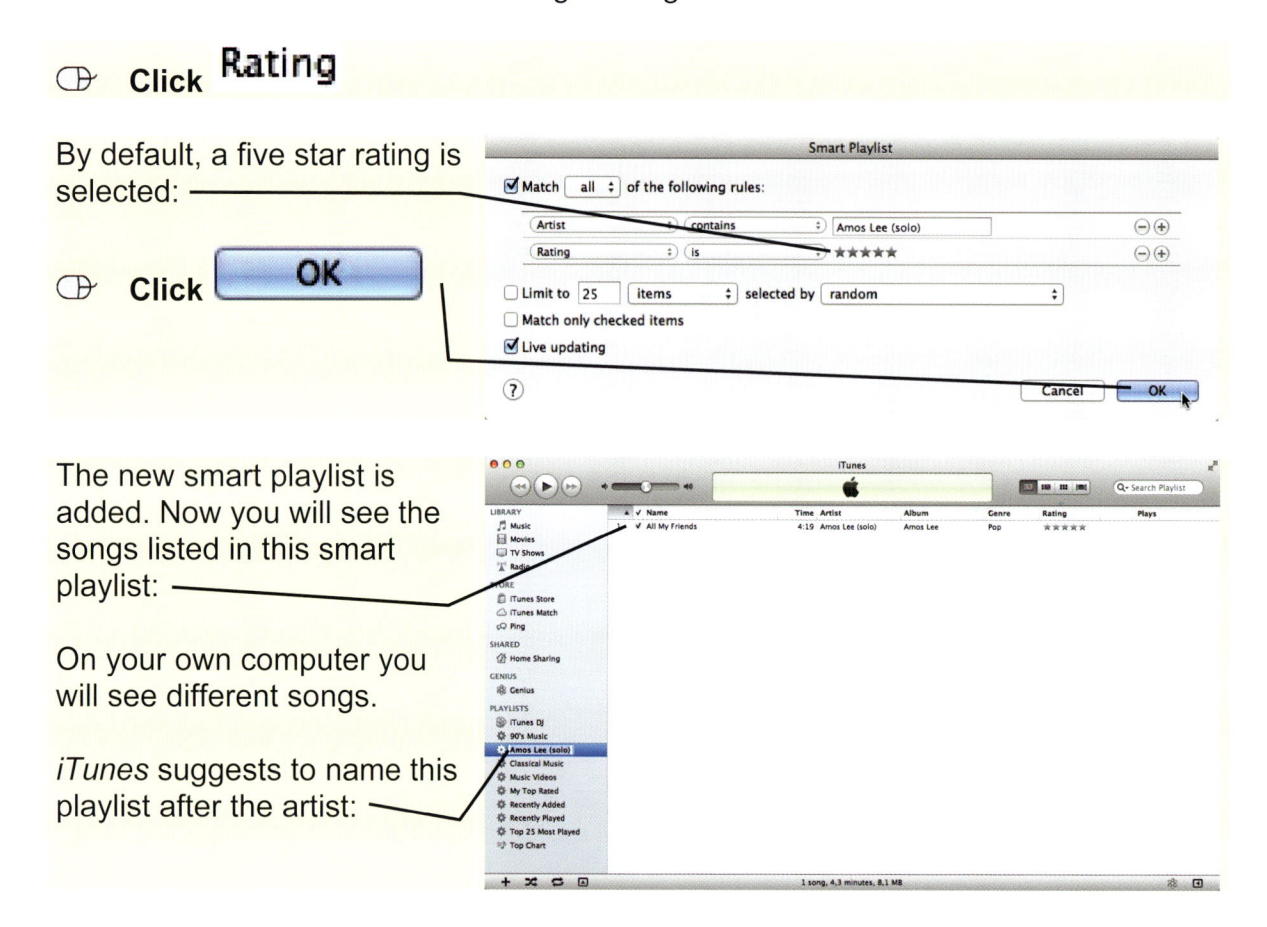

But you can also enter a different name:

⌨ **For example, type:**
Amos Lee first album

⌨ **Press** *enter/return*

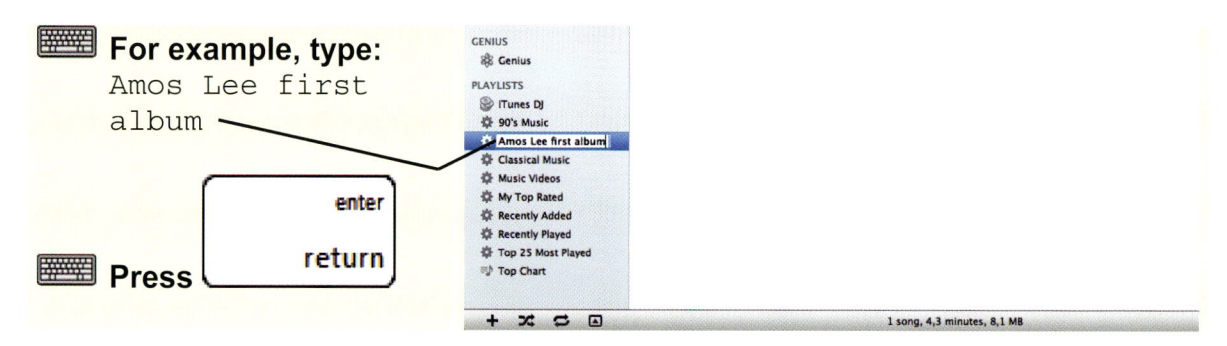

Now you have created your own smart playlist.

Chapter 3 Working with Music **145**

3.16 Deleting a Playlist

The playlists you have created can always be deleted from the *Library*. You can delete the smart playlists, and the playlists you have created track by track too. This is how you delete the smart playlist you created in the previous section:

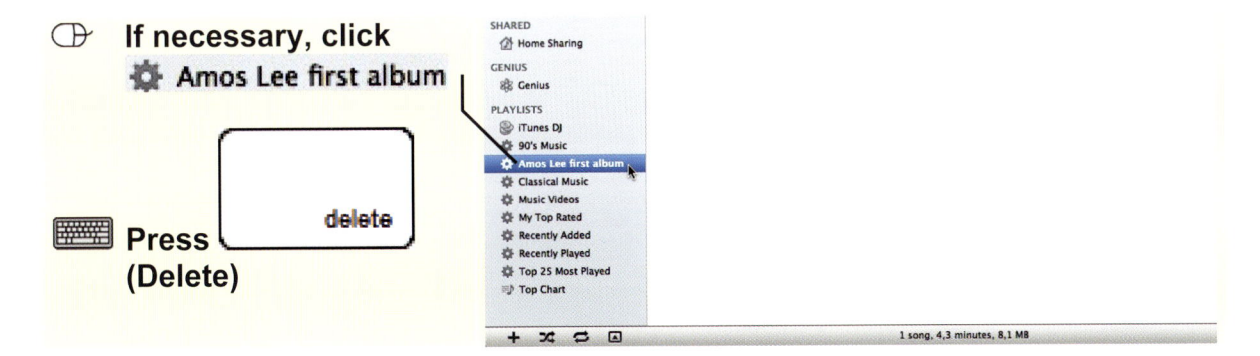

☞ **If necessary, click** ⚙ **Amos Lee first album**

⌨ **Press** `delete` **(Delete)**

Before permanently deleting a playlist, *iTunes* will ask for confirmation:

☞ **Click** `Delete`

The playlist has been deleted. But the songs in the playlist have not been deleted from your *Mac*; only the shortcuts to them.

3.17 Adding Tracks To an iPod

You can also transfer music to your iPod with the *iTunes* program. Here is how you do that:

☞ **Connect the iPod**

➥ **Please note:**
In the following examples, we will be using an iPod. You can also transfer music to your iPad or iPhone in the same manner.

This is how you connect the iPod classic, iPod nano and iPod:

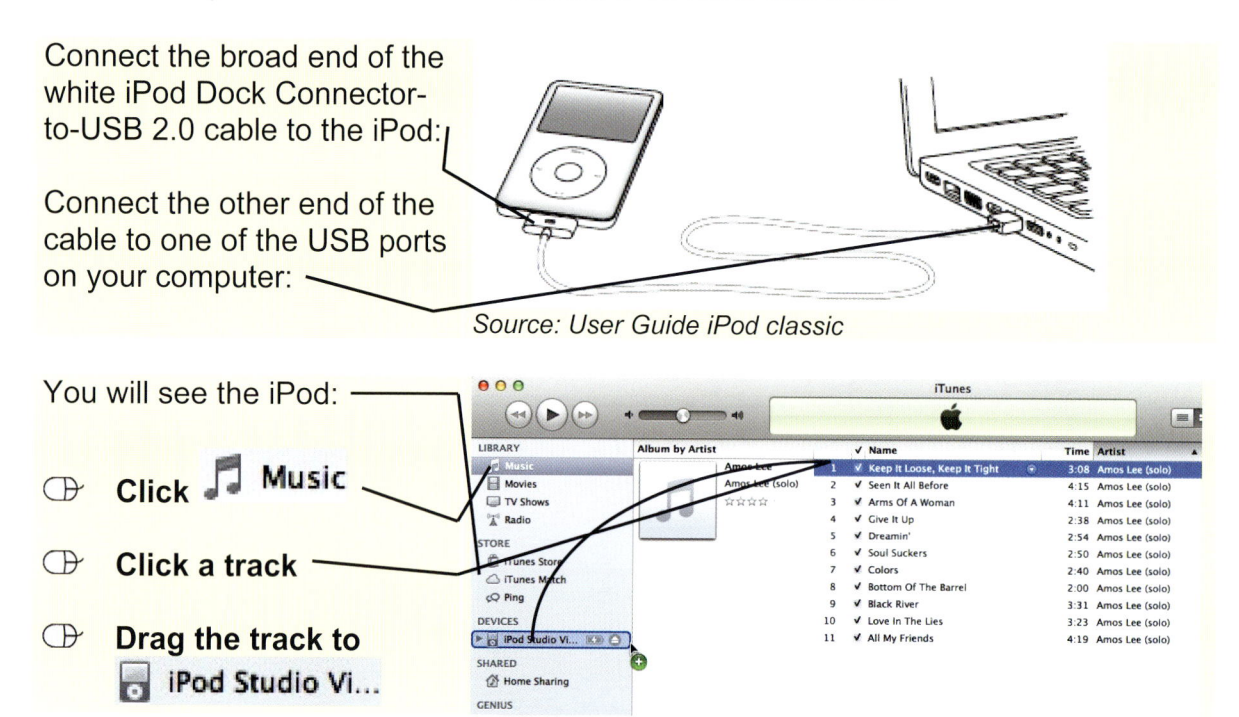

Connect the broad end of the white iPod Dock Connector-to-USB 2.0 cable to the iPod;

Connect the other end of the cable to one of the USB ports on your computer:

Source: User Guide iPod classic

You will see the iPod:

☞ **Click 🎵 Music**

☞ **Click a track**

☞ **Drag the track to 📱 iPod Studio Vi...**

The track will be copied to the iPod. You can also copy multiple tracks to an iPod. In the *Tips* at the end of this chapter you can read how to do this.

You are going to check the contents of the iPod:

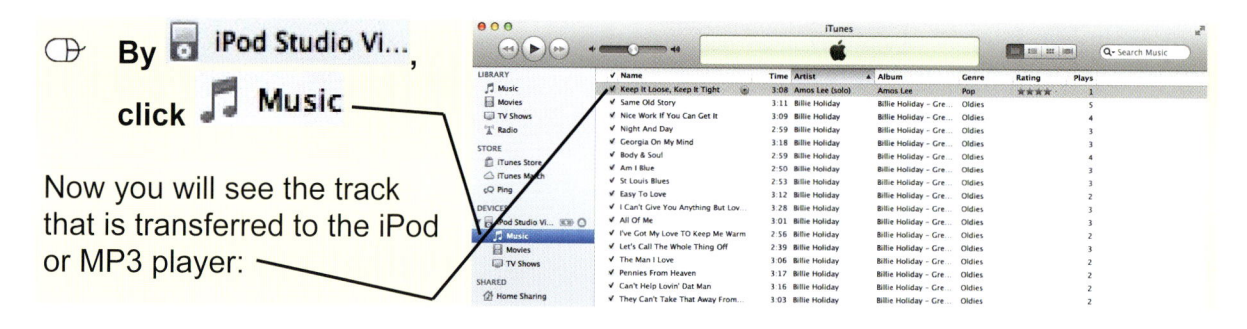

☞ **By 📱 iPod Studio Vi..., click 🎵 Music**

Now you will see the track that is transferred to the iPod or MP3 player:

In the *Tips* at the end of this chapter you can read how to delete a track from the iPod. Now you can safely disconnect the iPod from the computer:

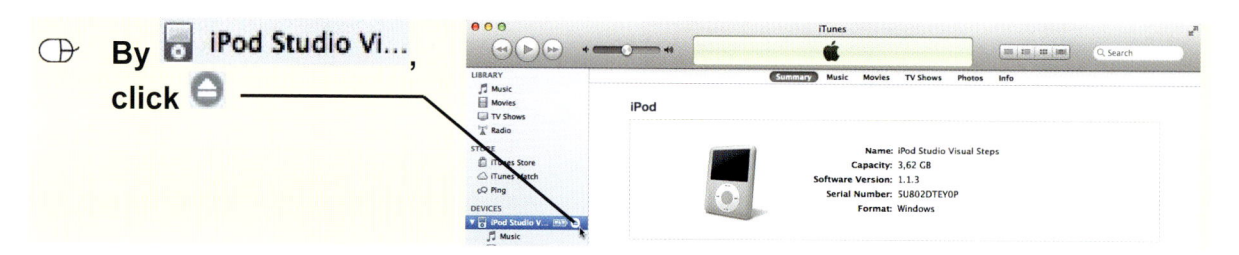

☞ **By 📱 iPod Studio Vi..., click ⏏**

Chapter 3 Working with Music

The *iPod* has disappeared from the *iTunes* window:

You can remove the cable connected to the *iPod*.

3.18 Listening To the Radio

Listening to Internet radio or web radio on the computer has become very popular. You can chose between thousands of Internet radio stations from all over the world. *iTunes* has a built-in feature for listening to Internet radio on the *Mac*:

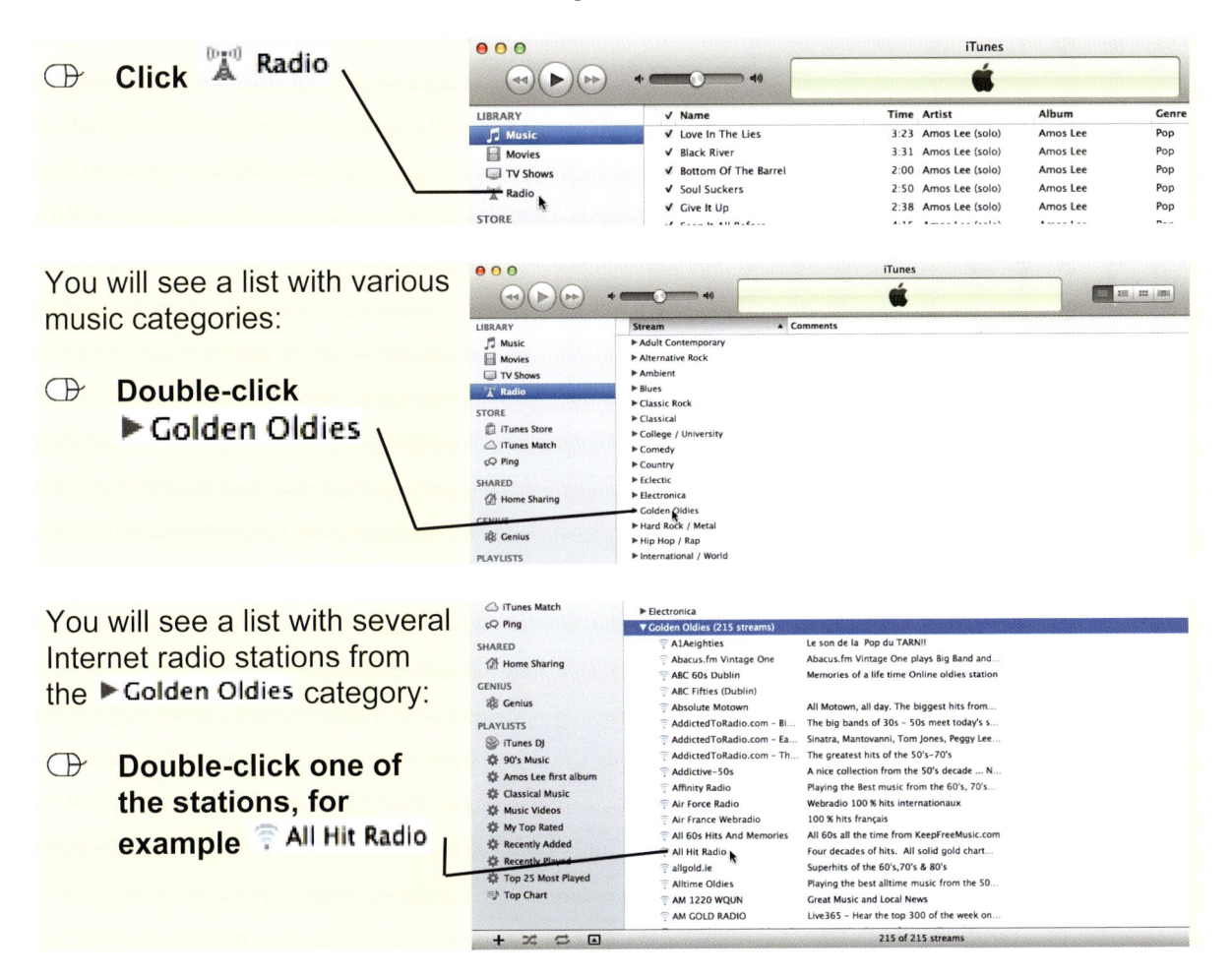

☞ Click 📡 Radio

You will see a list with various music categories:

☞ Double-click ▶ Golden Oldies

You will see a list with several Internet radio stations from the ▶ Golden Oldies category:

☞ Double-click one of the stations, for example 📶 All Hit Radio

The connection will be made and after a few seconds you will be able to hear the Internet radio station:

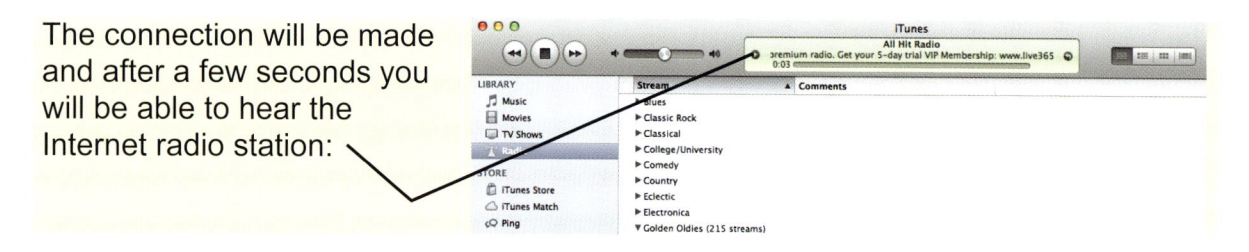

You can pause playback, just like you do while listening to a regular music file:

☞ **Click** ■

You can also resume playback of the Internet radio station:

☞ **Click** ▶

In a short while, the music will continue:

Since the broadcast of the music has continued in the meantime, you might be hearing a different song.

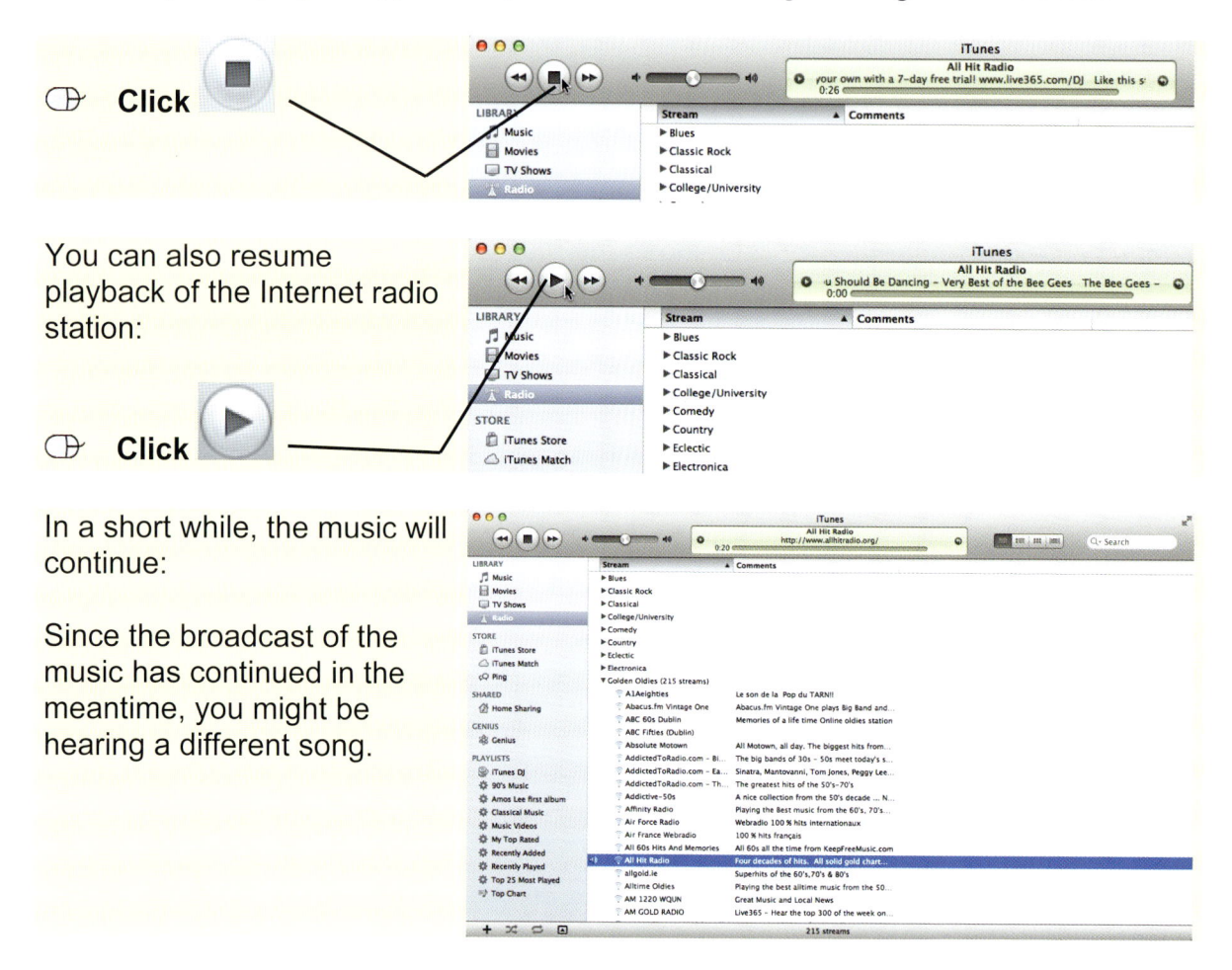

To listen to one of the other Internet radio stations you just need to select that station from the list.

💡 **Tip**
Go to a previous or next radio station

You can return to a previous Internet radio station with the ⏮ button. With the ⏭ button you skip to the next radio station in the list.

Chapter 3 Working with Music **149**

You can close the Internet radio:

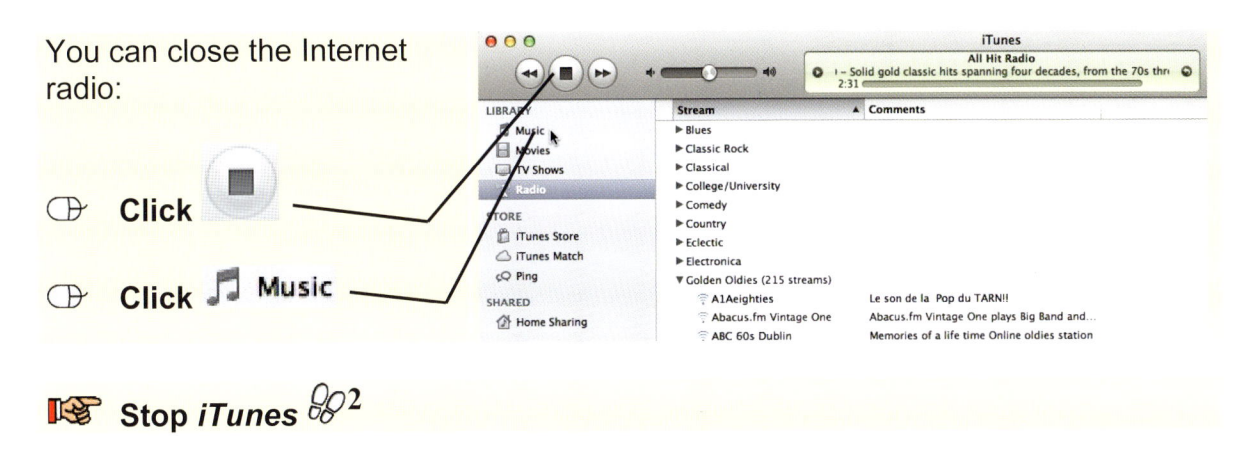

☞ **Click** ⬛

☞ **Click** 🎵 **Music**

👉 **Stop** *iTunes* 👣²

In this chapter you have learned to work with the *iTunes* program. In the next chapter you will be learning to use some of the utility programs on the *Mac*.

3.19 Background Information

Dictionary

Internet radio	A Radio broadcast that is transmitted by radio stations through the Internet.
iTunes	A program with which you can play digital music and video files. You can also use the program to download digital music, games, software, audio books, podcasts and movies, through an Internet connection with the *iTunes Store*. The program can also import music from a CD.
Library	All the music tracks stored in *iTunes*.
Playlist	A collection of songs, arranged in a certain order.
QuickTime	A platform developed by *Apple* for creating, distributing, playing, and sharing multimedia, for *Windows* as well as for *Mac* computers.
Rip	A term used for importing tracks from a CD.
Shuffle	Playing songs on a CD or a playlist in random order.
Smart playlist	A playlist for which you can define your own specific rules (criteria). When you add a track to the *Library* that matches the rules, it will be added to the smart playlist automatically.
Track	Another name for a song on a CD.

Source: Apple Dictionary, www.apple.com, iTunes Help

Chapter 3 Working with Music   **151**

3.20 Tips

💡 **Tip**
Enable sound check in iTunes
If your playlist consists of tracks taken from different imported CDs, the volume level of these tracks may vary. You may need to turn up the volume for a certain song, and turn it down again for the next song. *iTunes* has a *Sound Check* option that makes sure all the tracks are played at the same volume level. Here is how to enable that option:

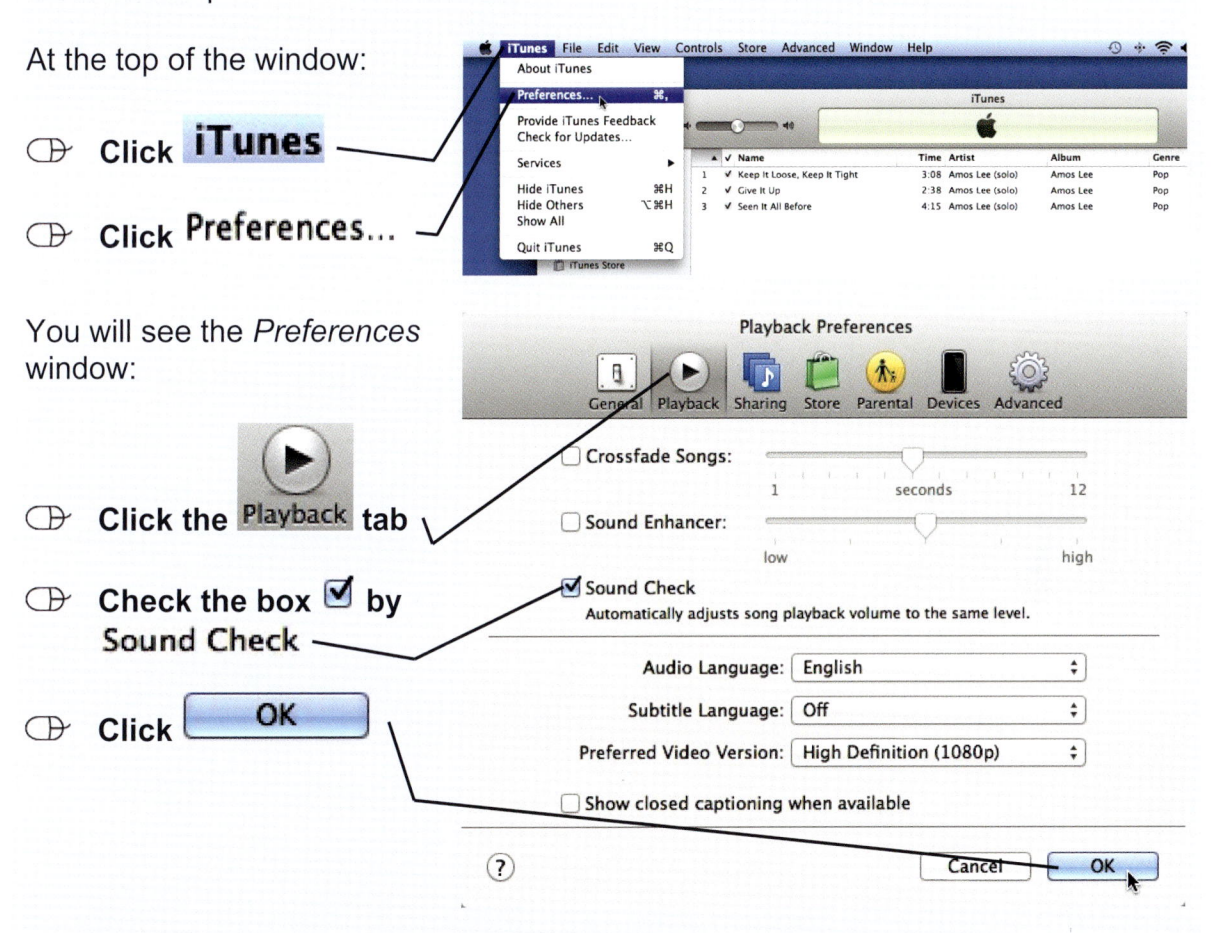

At the top of the window:

☞ Click **iTunes**

☞ Click **Preferences...**

You will see the *Preferences* window:

☞ Click the **Playback** tab

☞ **Check the box ☑ by Sound Check**

☞ Click **OK**

iTunes will analyze the sound levels of all the tracks in the *Library* and synchronize them. You cannot see this happen, but from now on you will not notice as much difference in the sound levels whenever you play songs in *iTunes*.

💡 Tip
Copy multiple files to the iPod
You can also copy multiple tracks to the iPod at once. First, you need to select the desired tracks:
To select all tracks on a CD:

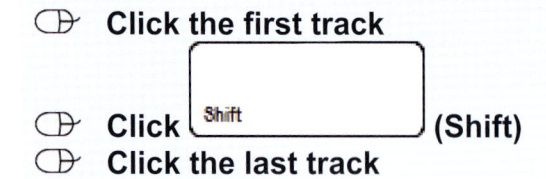

- **Click the first track**

- **Click** `Shift` **(Shift)**
- **Click the last track**

To select specific tracks:
- **Click a track**

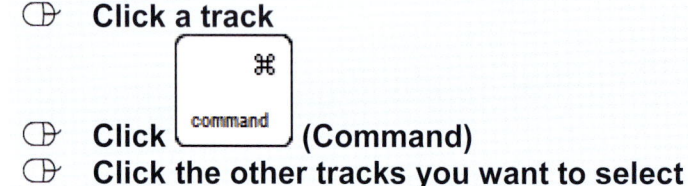

- **Click** `command` **(Command)**
- **Click the other tracks you want to select**

After the tracks have been selected you can drag the tracks to the iPod.

💡 Tip
Delete tracks from the iPod
You can manually delete the tracks you no longer want to save on your iPod. Here is how you do that:

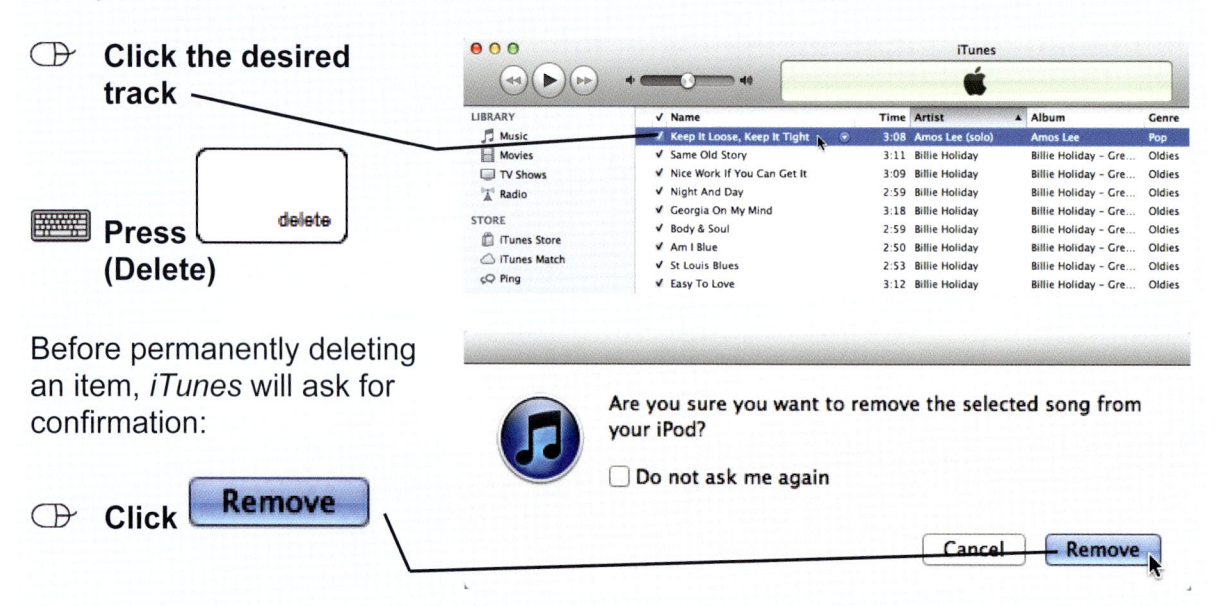

- **Click the desired track**

- **Press** `delete` **(Delete)**

Before permanently deleting an item, *iTunes* will ask for confirmation:

- **Click** `Remove`

Now the track is no longer stored on the iPod.

4. Practical Applications on the Mac

Along with the built-in programs the *Mac* offers for carrying out popular activities such as editing photos or listening to music, the *Mac* also contains a number of auxiliary programs that help to make the *Mac* a bit easier to use.

For instance, you can use *Launchpad* to open programs (apps) from a single point. You can add your favorite apps to *Launchpad* yourself and you can use it to find apps easier by placing them into folders.

Disk Utility is specifically intended to help you manage your hard drive. You can use it to look up information about your hard drive as well as get help when you have a recurring problem.

Do you need help trying to find a specific file? The *Mac* has a powerful searching tool to help you accomplish this task. It is called *Spotlight*.

In this chapter you will also learn how to download, install and remove a program.

Finally and perhaps most importantly, is taking care of a task that you should be performing on a regular basis: the creation of a backup. The *Mac* has another great tool to help you do this, the *Time Machine* program.

In this chapter you will learn how to:

- open apps with *Launchpad*;
- work with the *Disk Utility* program;
- search with *Spotlight*;
- download, install and remove apps;
- create a backup with *Time Machine*.

Please note:
If you are using a Mac Book Air or a Mac mini you will not have a CD/DVD player. This means you will not be able to create a backup on an external disk. If you have a CD/DVD player you will be able to do this. If you are thinking about purchasing an external CD/DVD player, make sure the player is suitable for use with a *Mac*.

4.1 Removing and Adding Apps in Launchpad

On the *Mac* there is a button located on the *Dock* with which you can open the *Launchpad* app. *Launchpad* is a new feature that allows you to quickly open (or launch) any of the applications (apps) installed on your *Mac*.

Apps that have been downloaded and installed from the *App Store* will automatically be added to *Launchpad*. The *App Store* is an online store where you can download all sorts of apps for your *Mac*. But you can also manually add and remove apps yourself using *Launchpad*.

First we will show you how to remove an app from *Launchpad*.

➥ Please note:
You can only remove apps from *Launchpad* if they were installed from the *App Store*. If you have not yet downloaded any apps, you can just read through this section.

➥ Please note:
If you remove an app from *Launchpad* it will also be removed from your computer. You can always install it again from the *App Store*, for free. If you do not want to remove an app from your computer, you can just read through this section for future use.

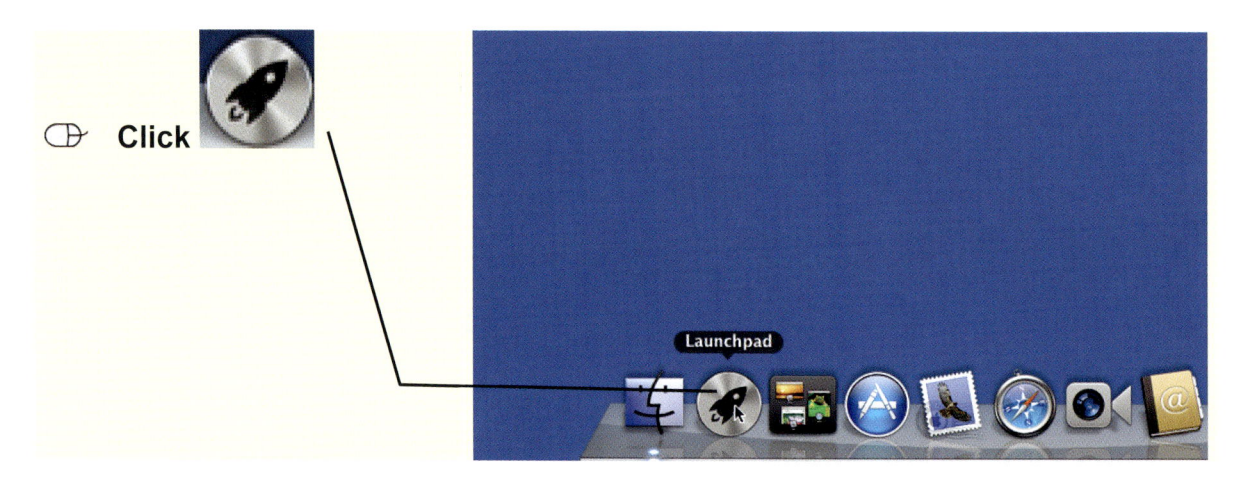

☞ **Click**

Chapter 4 Practical Applications on the Mac **155**

Launchpad will be opened:

You will see all sorts of icons for the apps (programs) already installed on your *Mac*:

You may see some different icons on your own *Mac*, a few less or a few more.

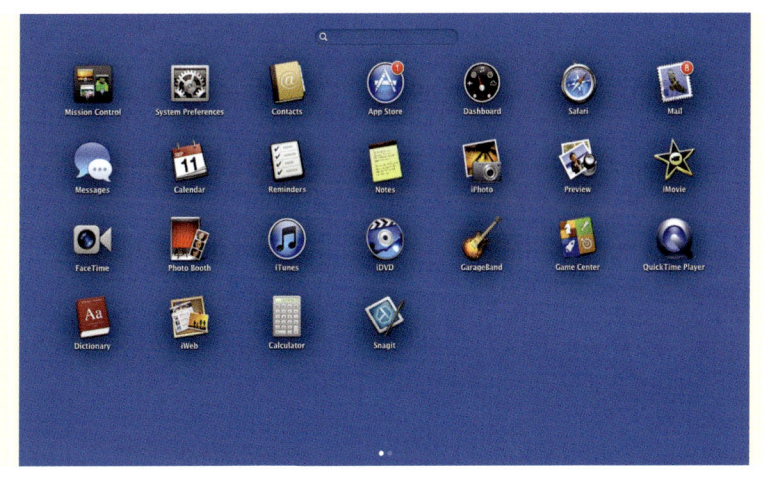

⊕ **Click one of the icons,  for example** Preview **Press and hold the mouse button down**

The icons will start to jiggle:

If any of these apps can be removed, a small ⊗ will be displayed on top of the icon.

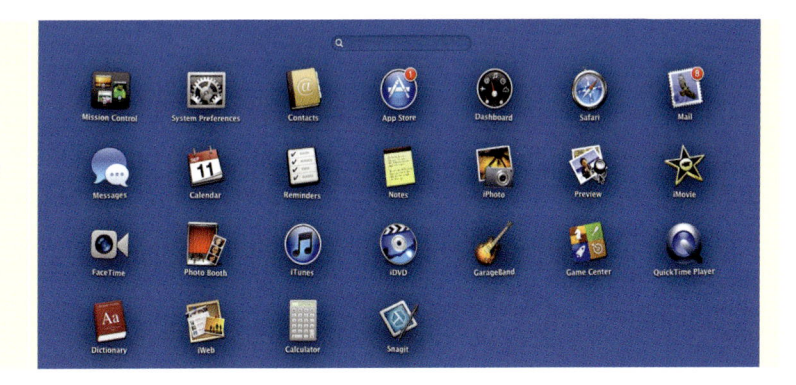

If you do not see any ⊗'s:

- **At the bottom of the *Launchpad* screen, click the blurred dot next to the white dot** ⊙

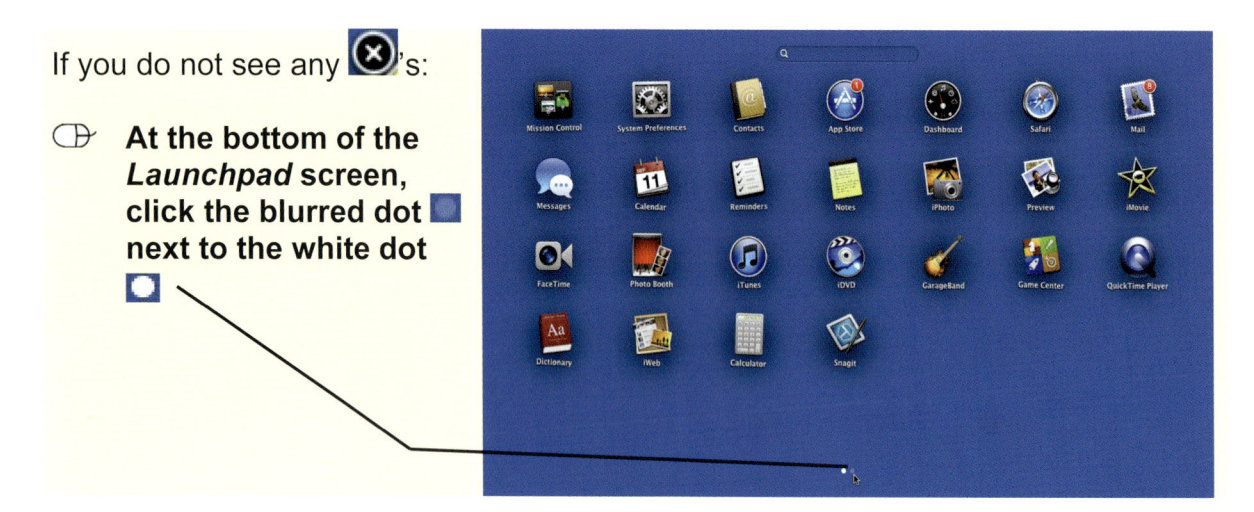

You will see a second page with icons:
You may see other icons on your own *Mac*.

The icons are still jiggling:

If this page contains any apps that can be removed, a small ⊗ will be displayed on top of the icon.

- **Click** ⊗

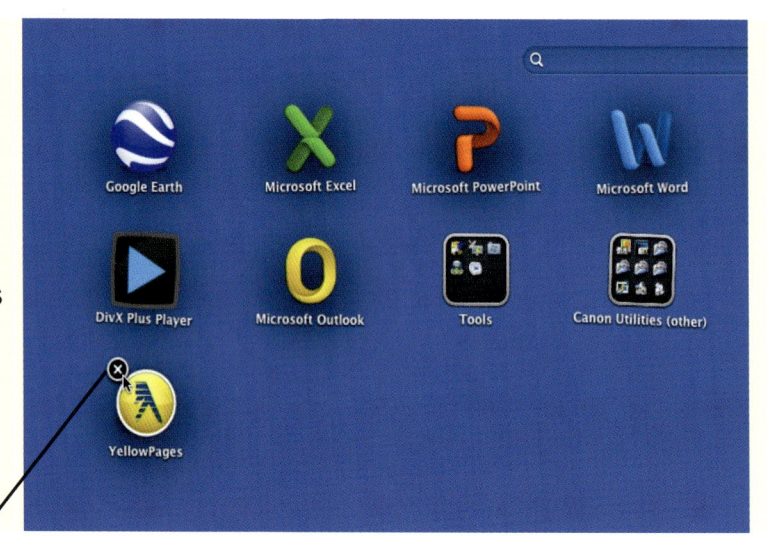

🩹 HELP! I do not see an ⊗

If you do not see an ⊗ on top of any icon, it means that there is not a single app that can be remove from *Launchpad*. You can simply read this section for future use.

Now you will see this window:

- **Click** `Delete`

The app will now be removed from *Launchpad* and from your computer as well:

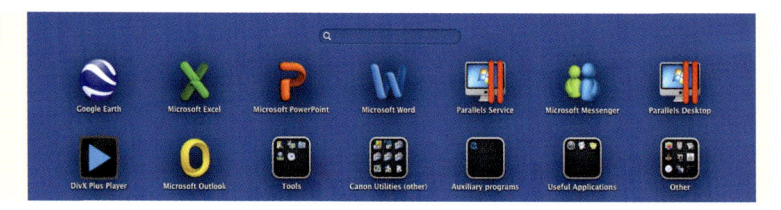

Chapter 4 Practical Applications on the Mac   **157**

You can also add apps (programs) to *Launchpad*.

👉 Please note:
If you do not wish to add an app to *Launchpad*, just read through this section.

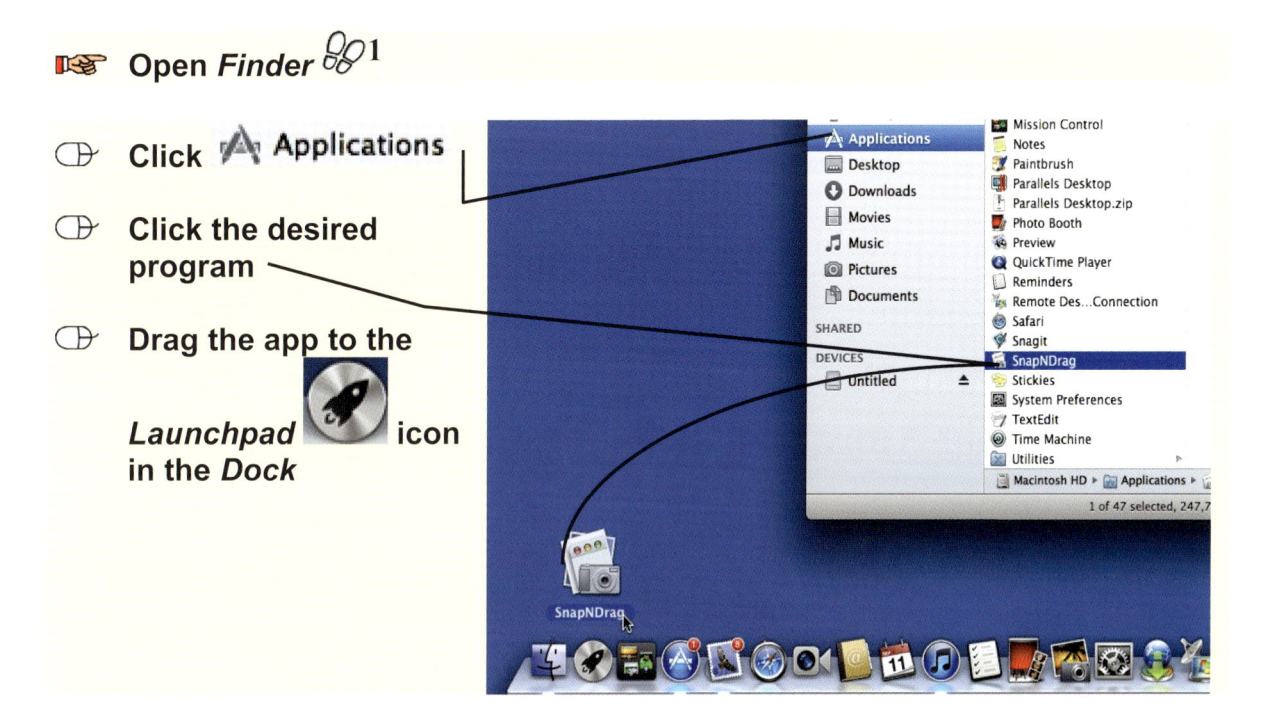

☞ **Open *Finder*** 👣¹

⊕ **Click Applications**

⊕ **Click the desired program**

⊕ **Drag the app to the *Launchpad* icon in the *Dock***

Now the app has been added to *Launchpad*:

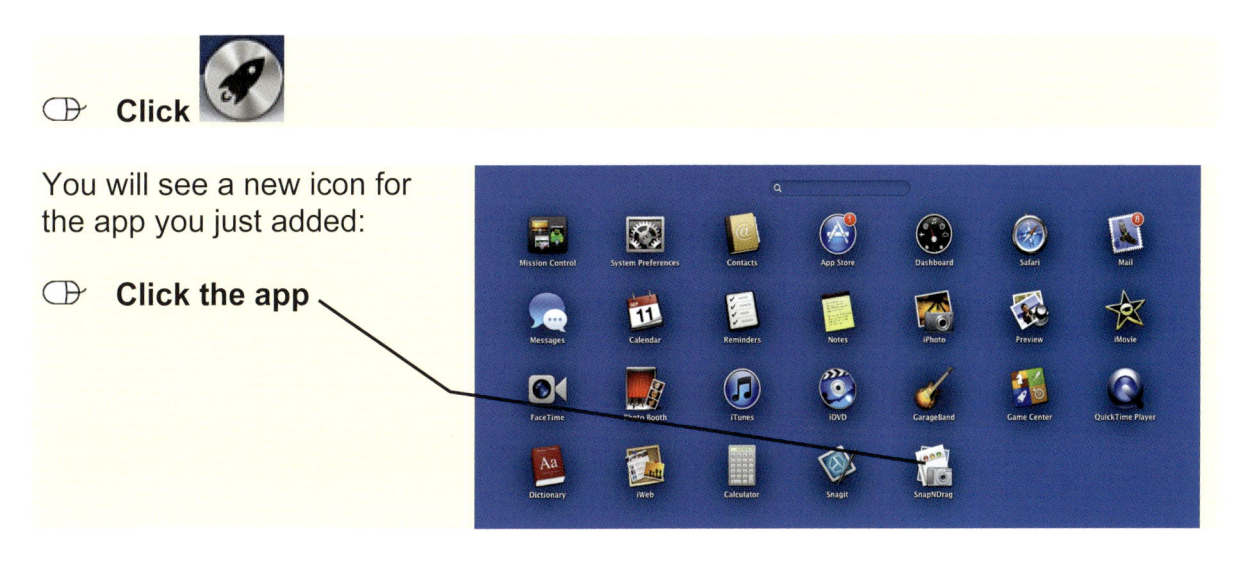

⊕ **Click**

You will see a new icon for the app you just added:

⊕ **Click the app**

The program will be opened:

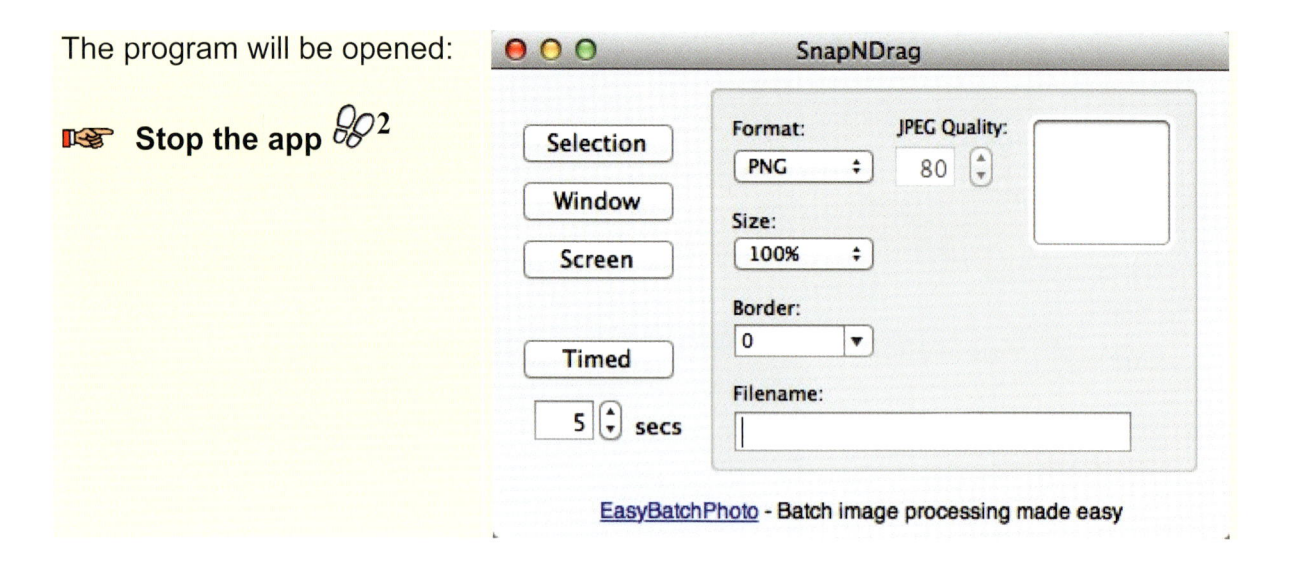

☞ **Stop the app** 👣²

4.2 Combining Apps into Folders in Launchpad

If *Launchpad* contains a lot of apps it may be harder to find one of them. You can create folders containing your favorite or most often used apps so that they are easier to access.

↪ **Please note:**
As an exercise, you can use two other apps than the ones we use in this section.

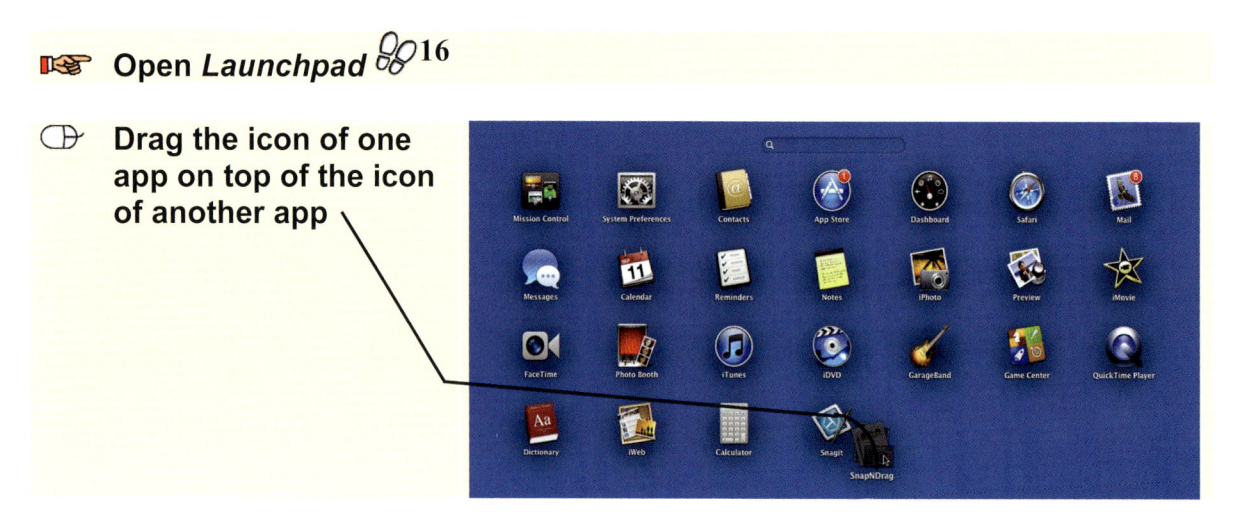

☞ **Open** *Launchpad* 👣16

⌘ **Drag the icon of one app on top of the icon of another app**

Chapter 4 Practical Applications on the Mac **159**

The apps are now gathered together into a single folder:

You can enter a name for this new folder:

☞ **Click Untitled**

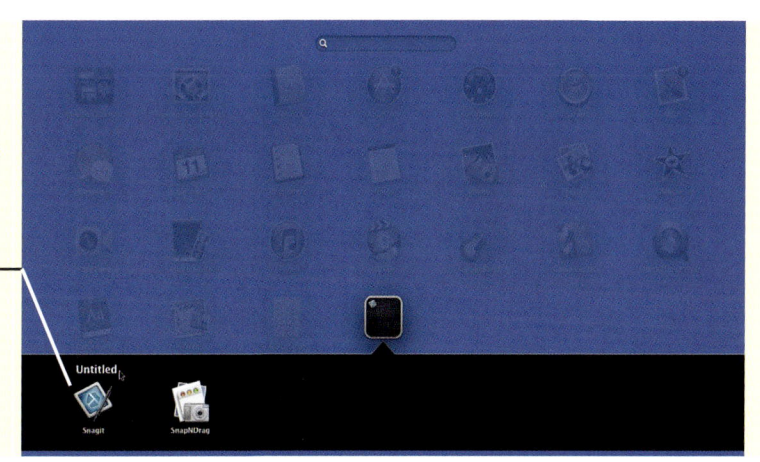

⌨ **Type the name you want to use**

☞ **Click next to the folder**

Now you will see the folder containing the two apps:

You can add other apps to this folder by dragging them to the folder's icon.

This is how you open an app within the folder:

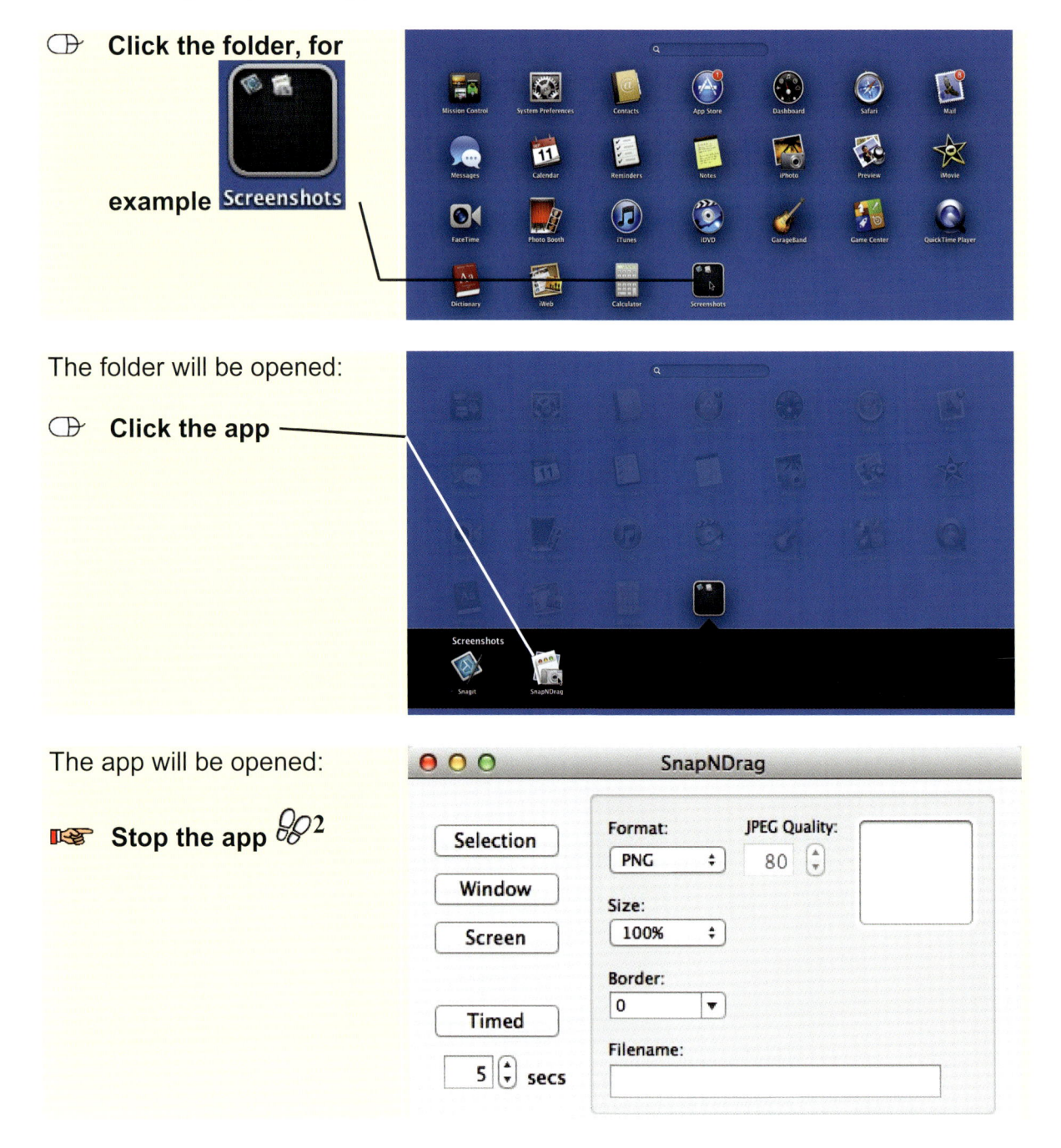

☞ **Click the folder, for example** Screenshots

The folder will be opened:

☞ **Click the app**

The app will be opened:

☞ **Stop the app** ₆₆²

You can also delete an app from the folder and place back to where it was in *Launchpad* with its own individual icon:

☞ **If necessary, open** *Launchpad* ₆₆¹⁶

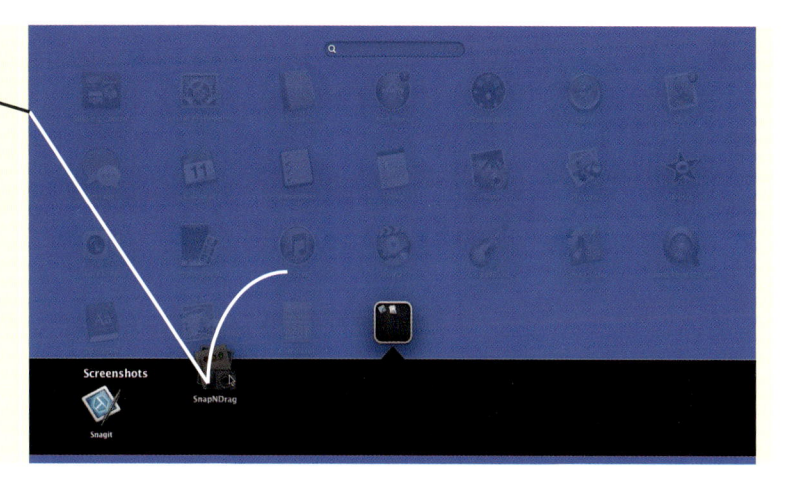

Chapter 4 Practical Applications on the Mac **161**

⊕ **Drag the desired app out of the folder**

Now you will see the regular *Launchpad* view again:

If the folder contained only two apps, both of the apps will be placed in *Launchpad* with their two separate icons:

The folder will also be deleted.

You can close *Launchpad*:

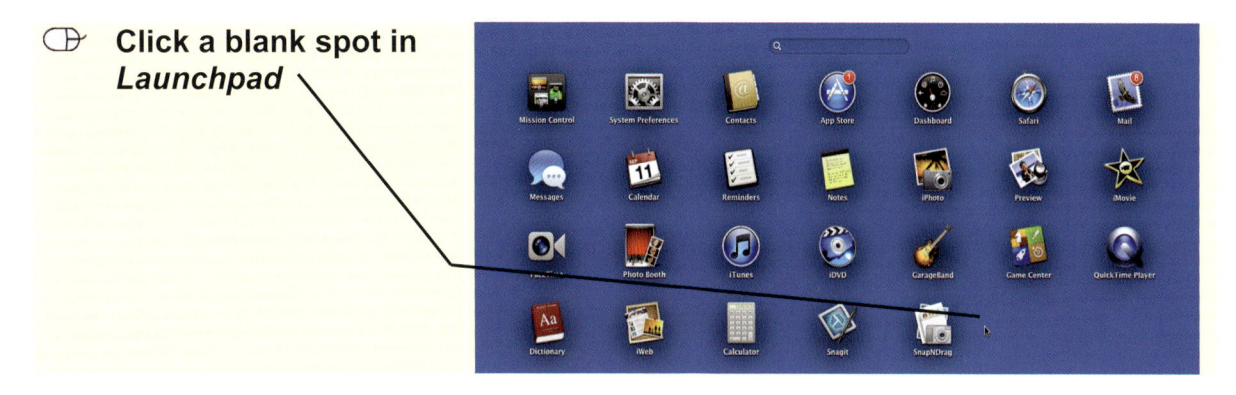

⊕ **Click a blank spot in Launchpad**

☞ **If necessary, close Finder** 𝄞³

4.3 Working with Disk Utility

The *Disk Utility* tool is used for managing the hard drive on your computer. For instance, you can use this program to look up information about your hard drive and attempt repair of any problems found:

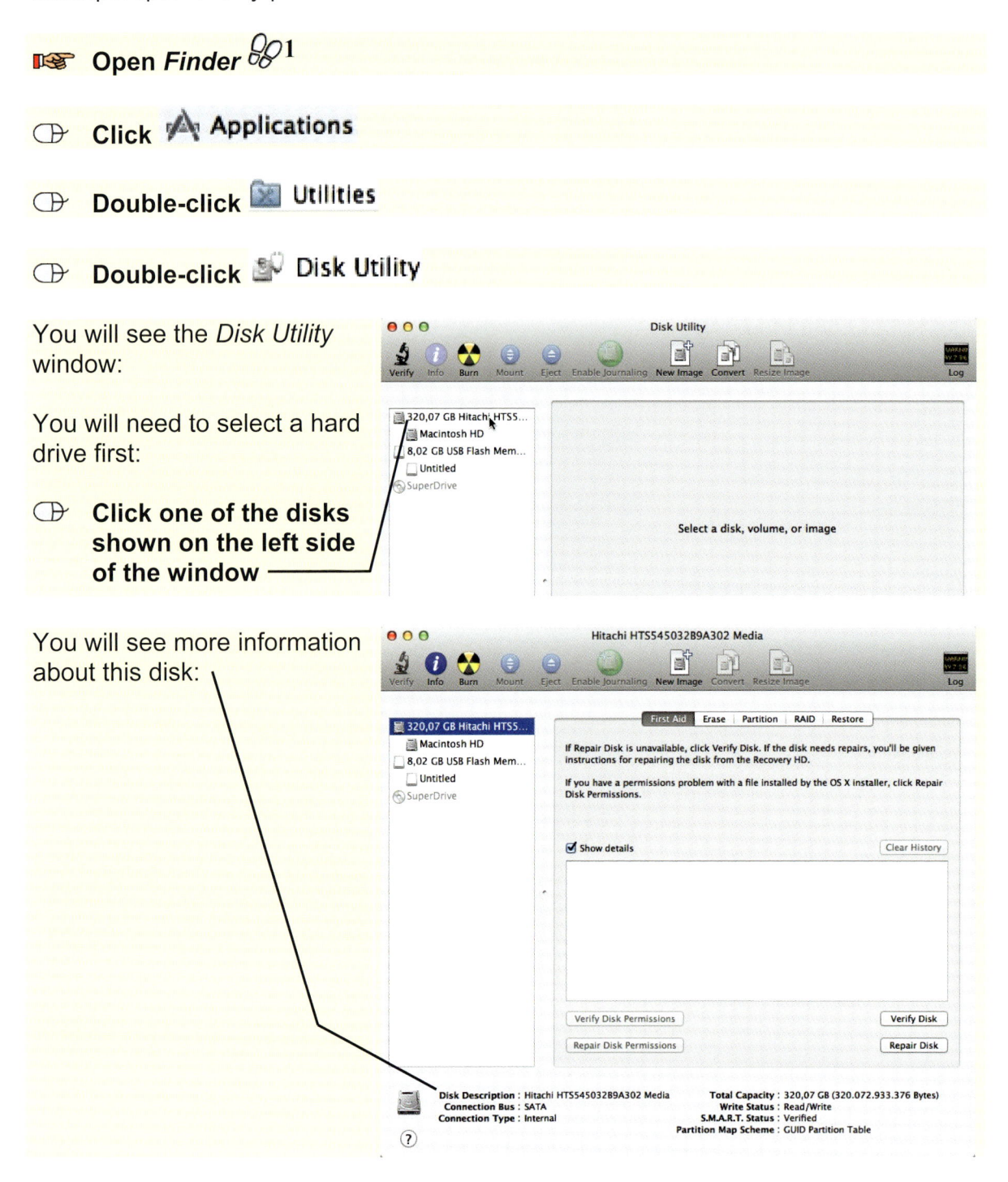

☞ **Open** *Finder* ⚘¹

◯ **Click** 🅰 **Applications**

◯ **Double-click** 📁 **Utilities**

◯ **Double-click** 💿 **Disk Utility**

You will see the *Disk Utility* window:

You will need to select a hard drive first:

◯ **Click one of the disks shown on the left side of the window**

You will see more information about this disk:

Chapter 4 Practical Applications on the Mac 163

In this window you can perform various tasks for the selected hard disk. The window contains several tabs:

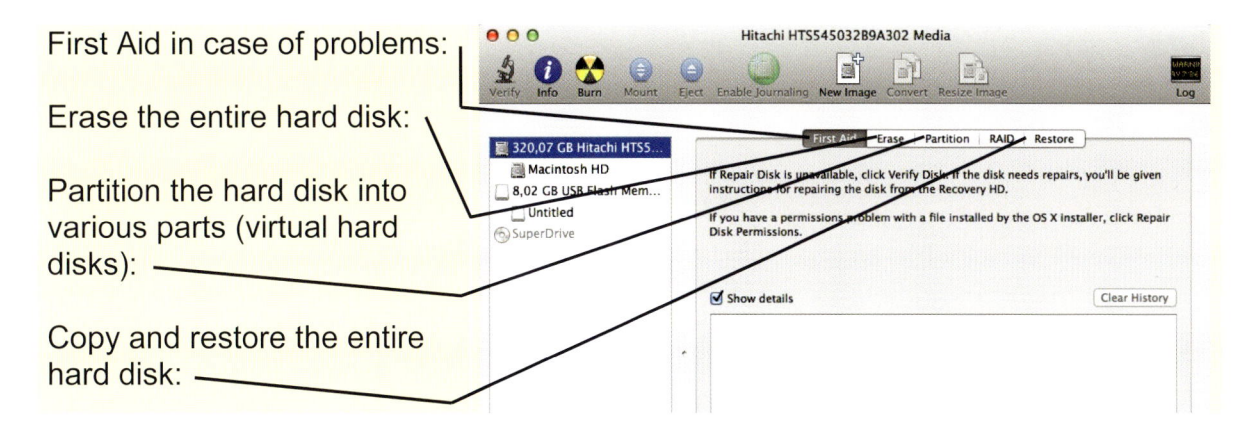

First Aid in case of problems:

Erase the entire hard disk:

Partition the hard disk into various parts (virtual hard disks):

Copy and restore the entire hard disk:

Most of these tasks are advanced operations. Use them only if you know exactly what you are doing.

If you want, you can let the program verify (check) your hard disk. This is something you can do when you notice a problem with your hard disk. For example, if you cannot access certain files, or if it takes a very long time to read and write files.

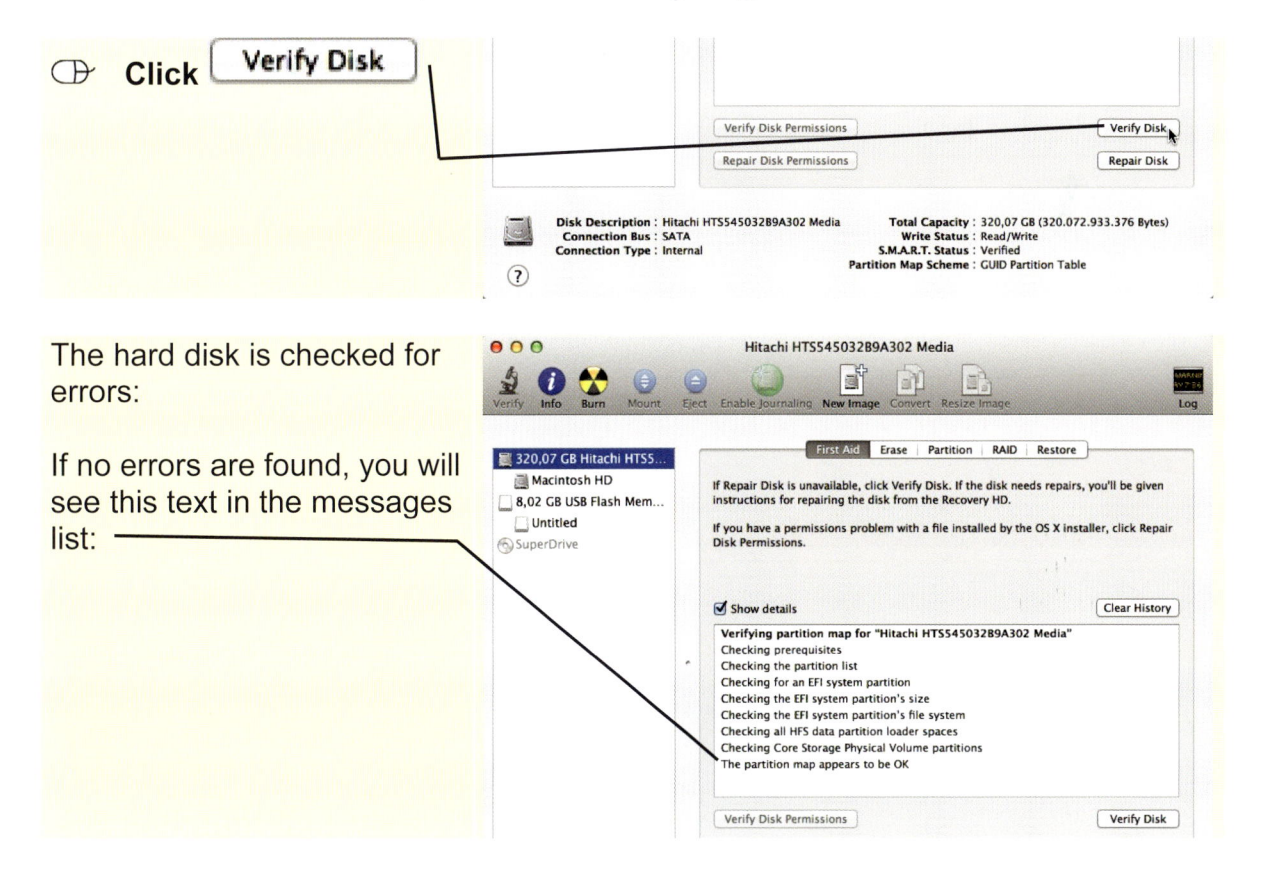

☞ **Click** `Verify Disk`

The hard disk is checked for errors:

If no errors are found, you will see this text in the messages list:

If any errors are found, you can use this information to contact a service desk or your local computer retailer. This window may also display suggestions to help you resolve a particular problem. If that is the case, you can follow the instructions as shown.

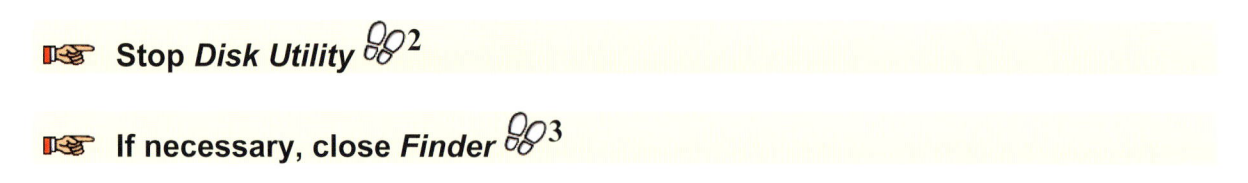

☞ **Stop *Disk Utility*** ℘2

☞ **If necessary, close *Finder*** ℘3

Now you have learned how to check if there are any problems with your hard disk.

4.4 Searching with Spotlight

In *Finder* you can search for files by using the search box. But the *Mac* is also equipped with a much more powerful search engine called *Spotlight*. With *Spotlight*, not only can you search regular files, but you can also search the contents of email messages within the *Mail* program.

You do not need to open *Finder* in order to use *Spotlight*. You can use *Spotlight* for searches right from your desktop:

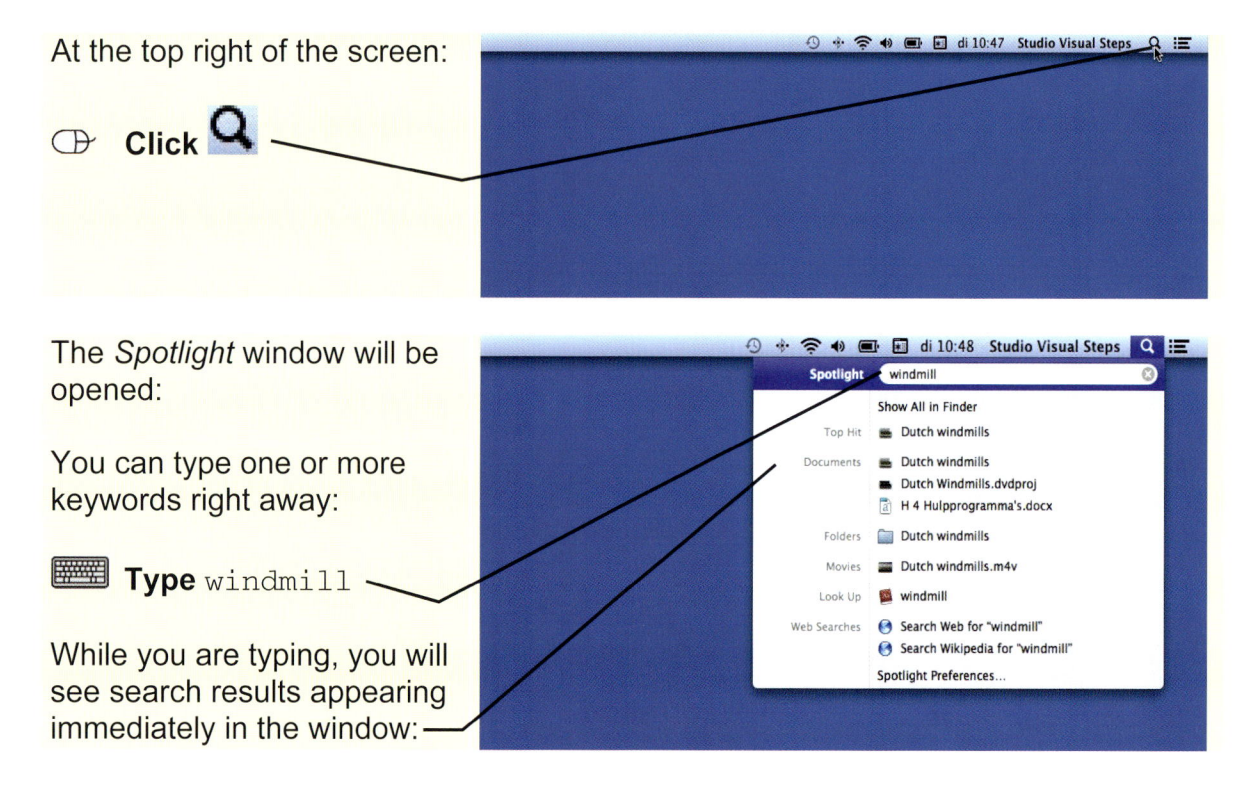

At the top right of the screen:

⌕ **Click** 🔍

The *Spotlight* window will be opened:

You can type one or more keywords right away:

⌨ **Type** `windmill`

While you are typing, you will see search results appearing immediately in the window:

Chapter 4 Practical Applications on the Mac

Spotlight allows you to preview any of the files found:

☞ **Position the mouse pointer on** ▬ **Dutch windmills.m4v**

You will see the contents of the file:

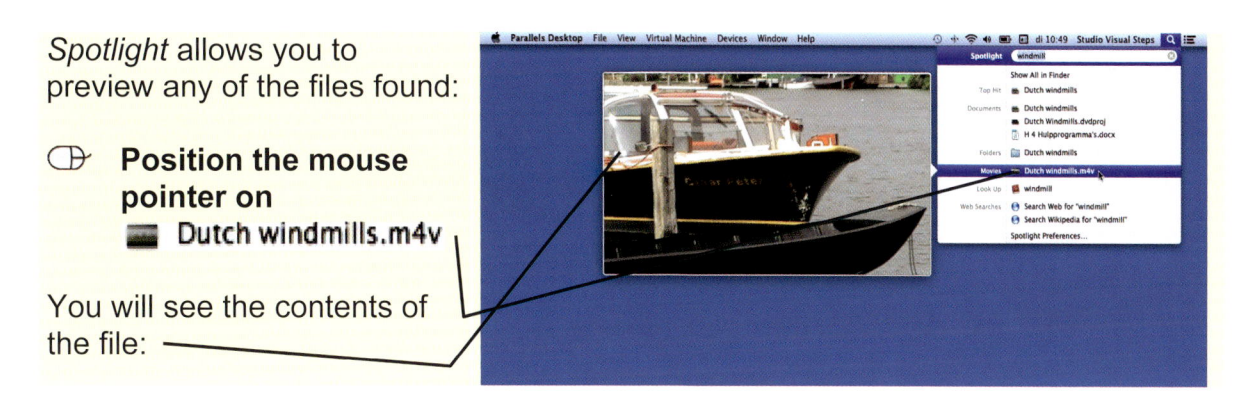

In *Spotlight* you can also easily open a file with its corresponding program (app):

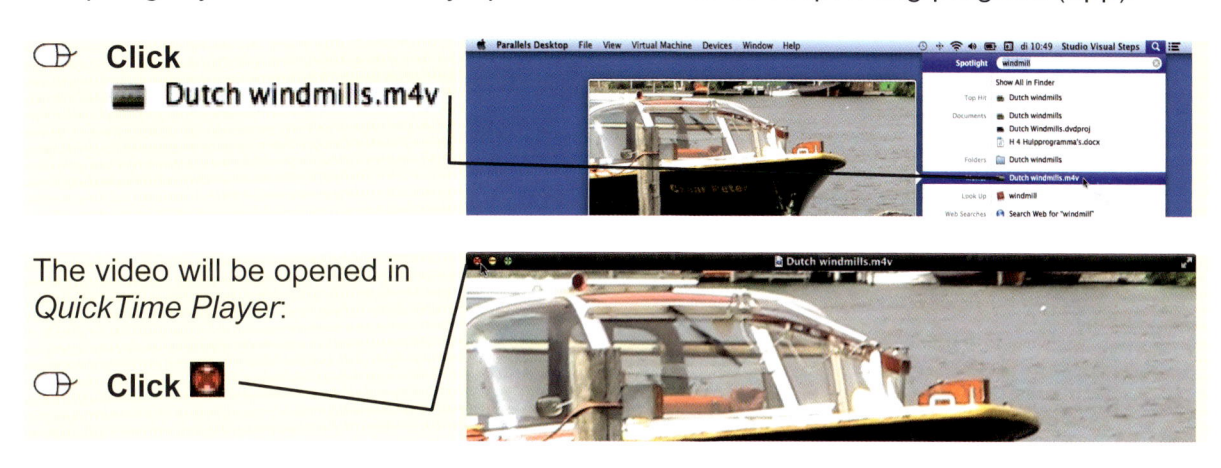

☞ **Click** ▬ **Dutch windmills.m4v**

The video will be opened in *QuickTime Player*:

☞ **Click** 🟥

HELP! The video is opened in a different program

If the file is opened in a different program, this may be due to the fact that a different program has been assigned to open M4V files. This is how you select *QuickTime Player* as your default program. You will need to use the Control key:

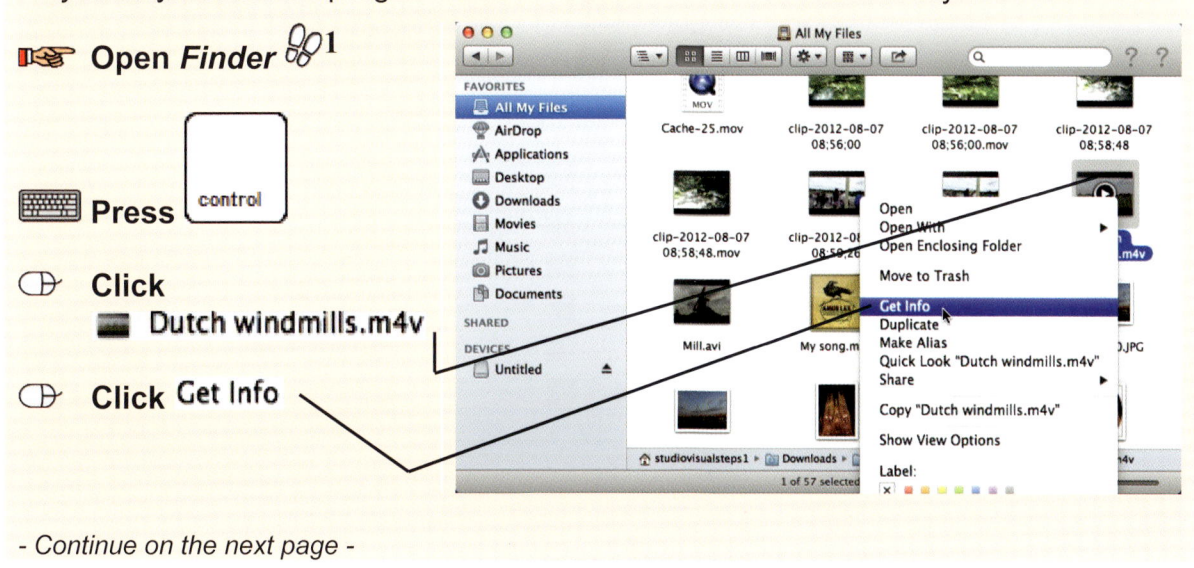

☞ **Open** *Finder* 👣¹

⌨ **Press** `control`

☞ **Click** ▬ **Dutch windmills.m4v**

☞ **Click Get Info**

- Continue on the next page -

- By *Open with:*, click ▶

By the program:

- Click ⇵

- Click
  QuickTime Player

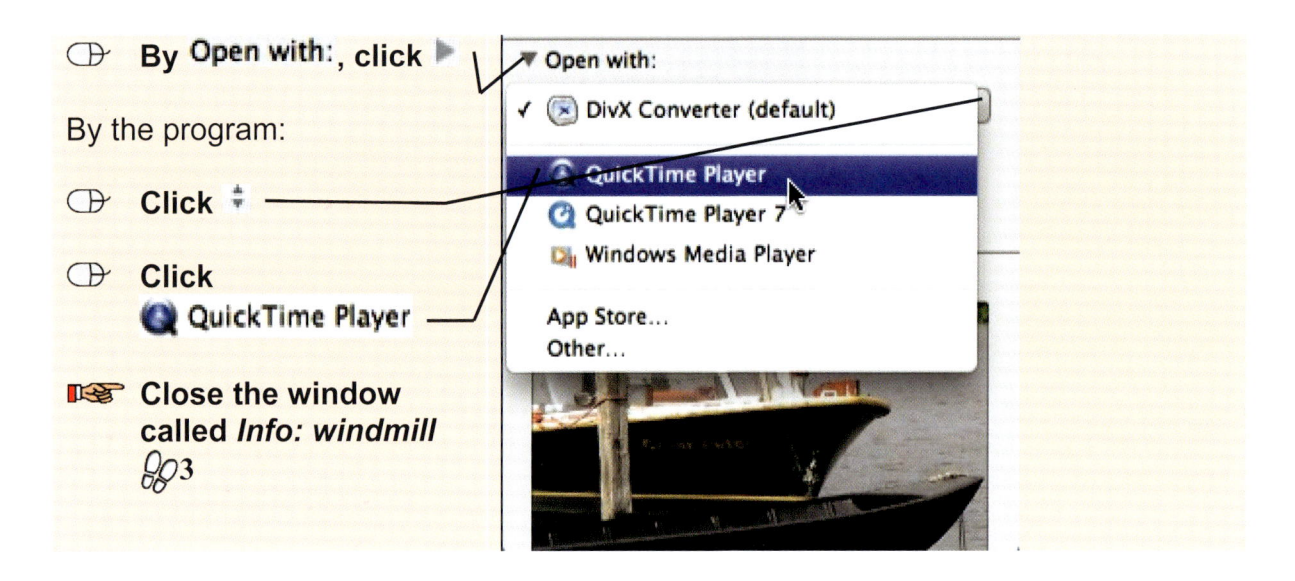

☞ Close the window called *Info: windmill* ℘3

4.5 Downloading and Installing an App

Your *Mac* already contains lots of standard programs (apps). But you can also download an app yourself and install it to your *Mac*. In this example you are going to download the *Adobe Reader* program from the *Adobe* website and install it. You can use a similar method for other apps.

☞ Open the web page www.adobe.com ℘10

- Click **Downloads**

- Click **Get ADOBE READER**

Chapter 4 Practical Applications on the Mac **167**

⊕ **Click**

[⬇ Download now]

The program will be downloaded:

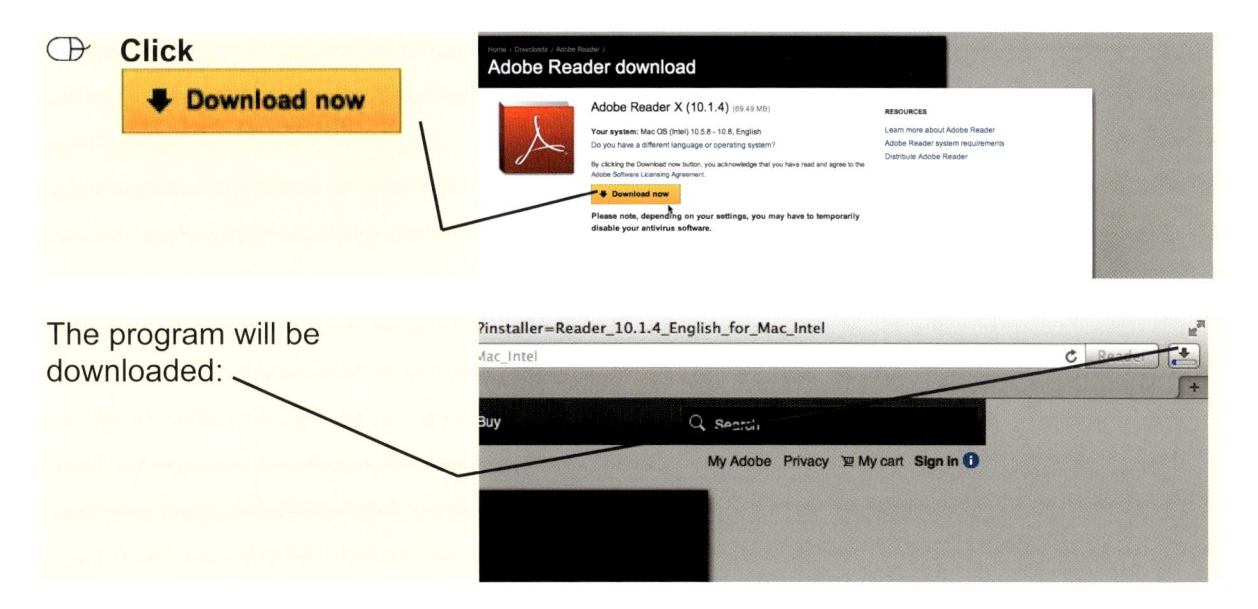

Once the download has finished:

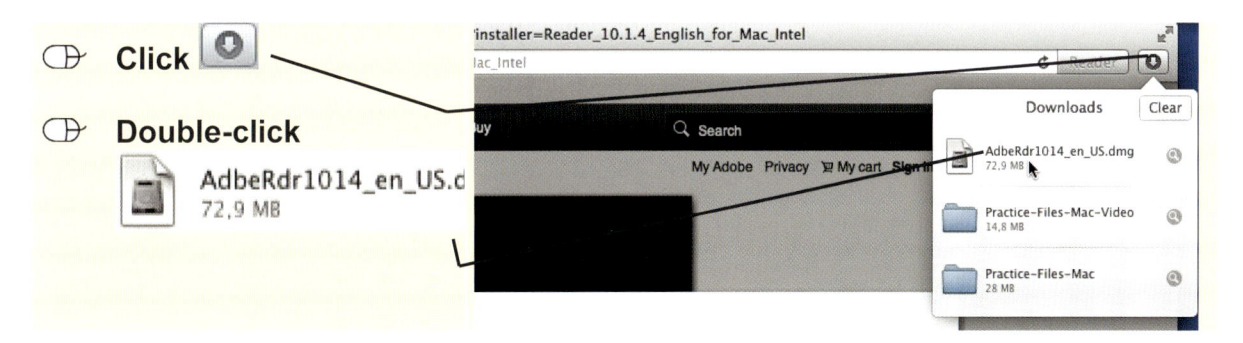

⊕ **Click**

⊕ **Double-click**

AdbeRdr1014_en_US.d
72,9 MB

The window may be hidden behind the *Safari* window:

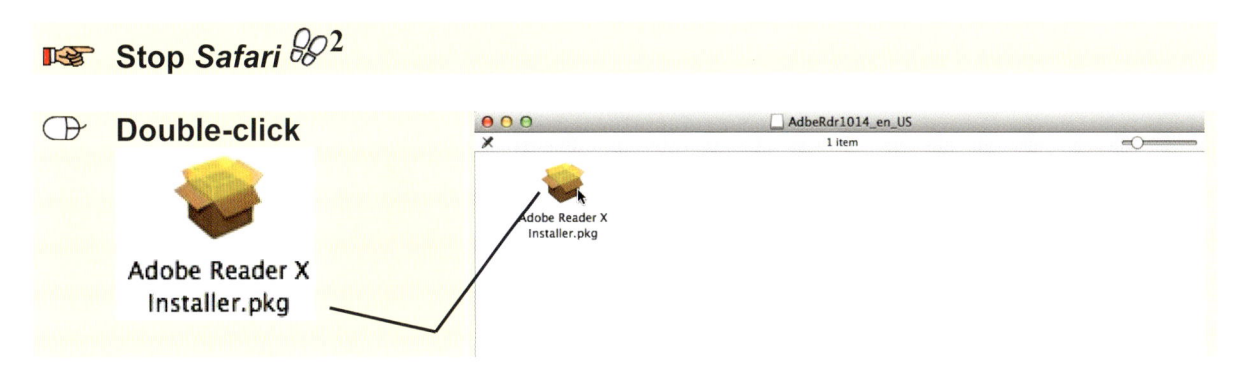

☞ **Stop** *Safari* ℘²

⊕ **Double-click**

Adobe Reader X
Installer.pkg

At the bottom of the window:

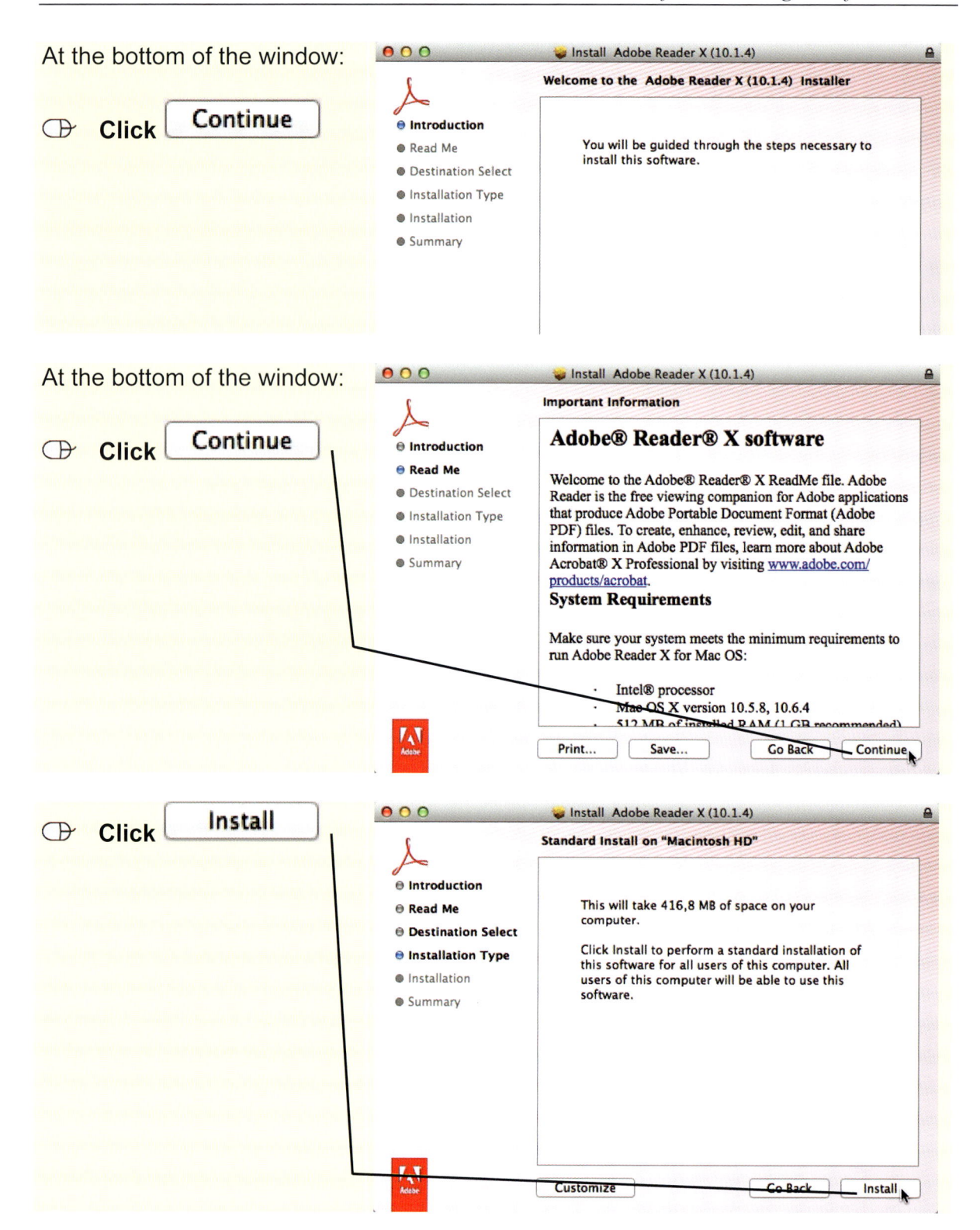

☞ **Click** Continue

At the bottom of the window:

☞ **Click** Continue

☞ **Click** Install

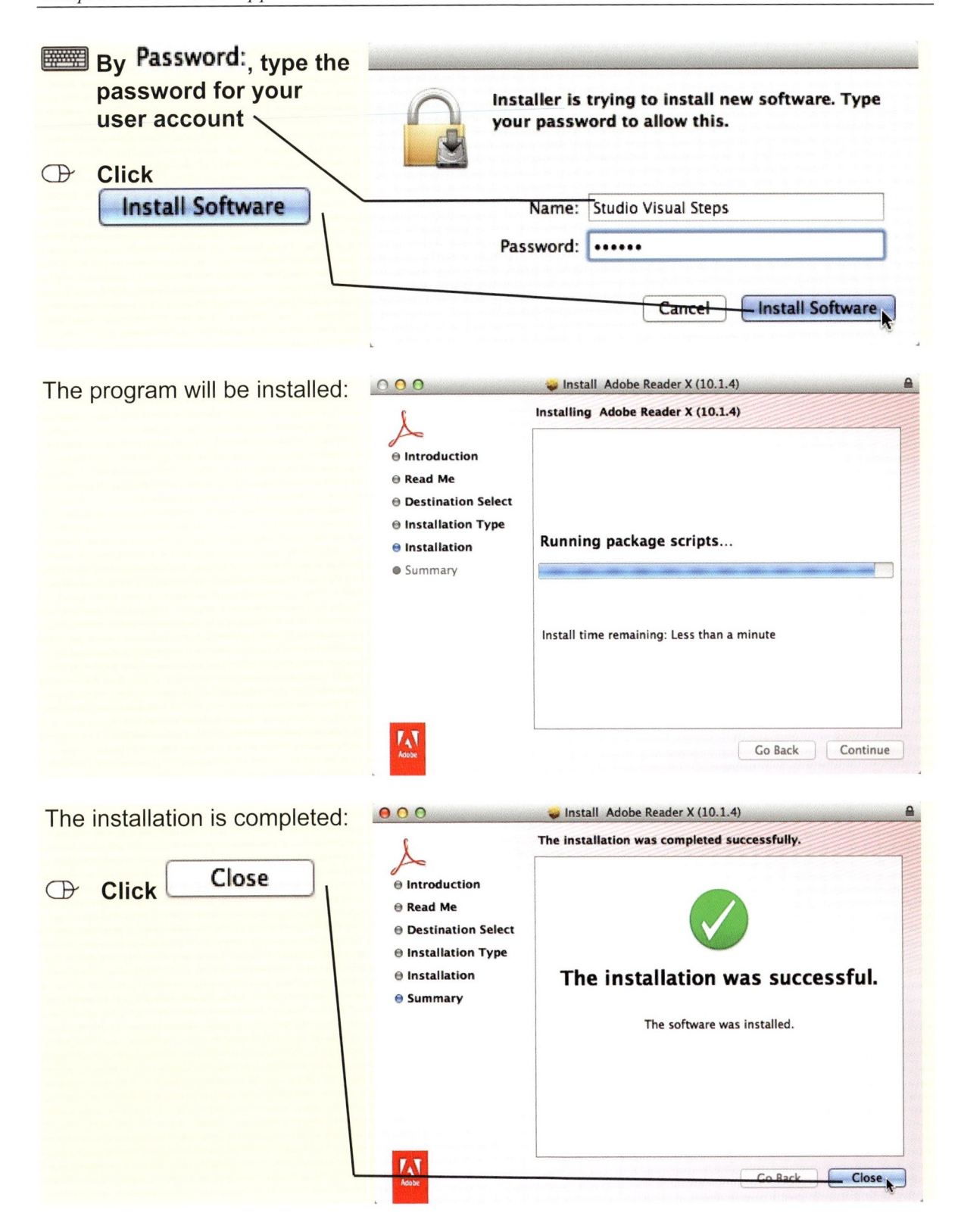

Chapter 4 Practical Applications on the Mac **169**

⌨ **By** Password:**, type the password for your user account**

☞ **Click** `Install Software`

The program will be installed:

The installation is completed:

☞ **Click** `Close`

Now the program will be listed in *Finder*. You can take a look to make sure:

☞ **Close the *Adobe* window** ⚘³

☞ **Open *Finder*** ⚘¹

⌖ **If necessary, click Applications**

You will see Adobe Reader and its new icon in the list:
You can open the program by double-clicking it.

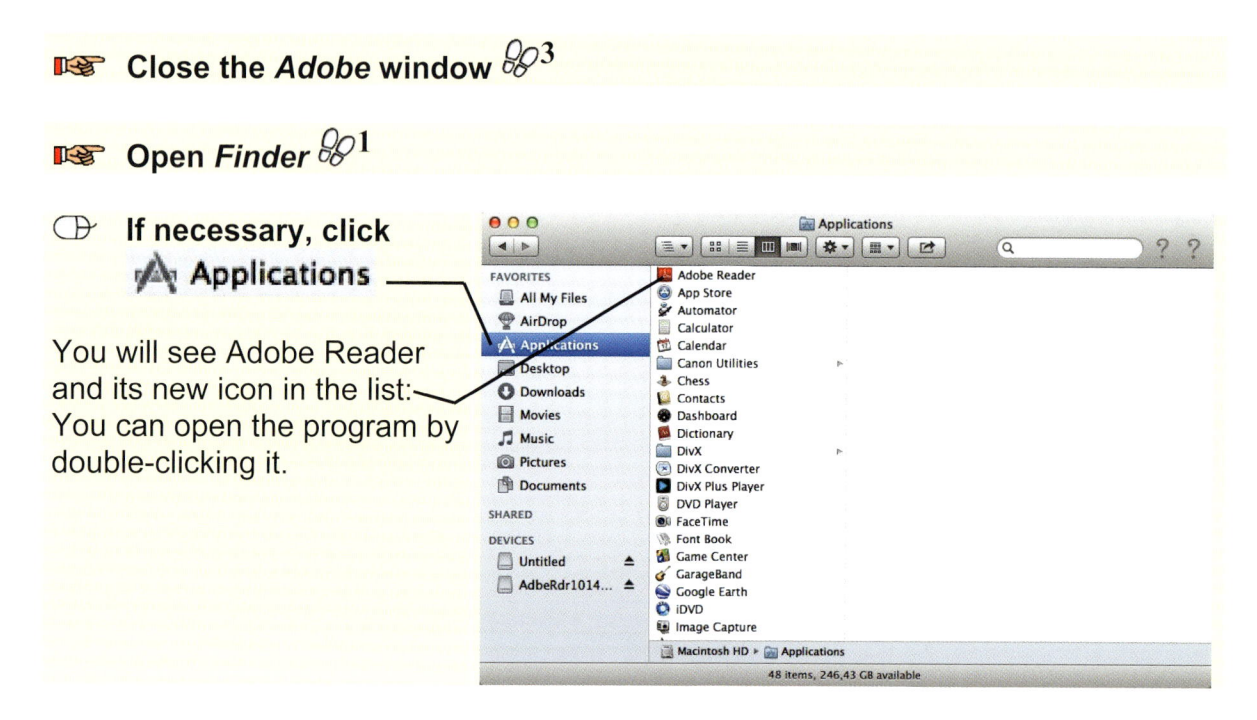

4.6 Removing an App from the Mac

If you no longer want to use a particular app you have installed yourself you can delete it from the *Applications* folder in the following way. You will need to use the Control key:

⌨ **Press** control

⌖ **Click Adobe Reader**

⌖ **Click Move to Trash**

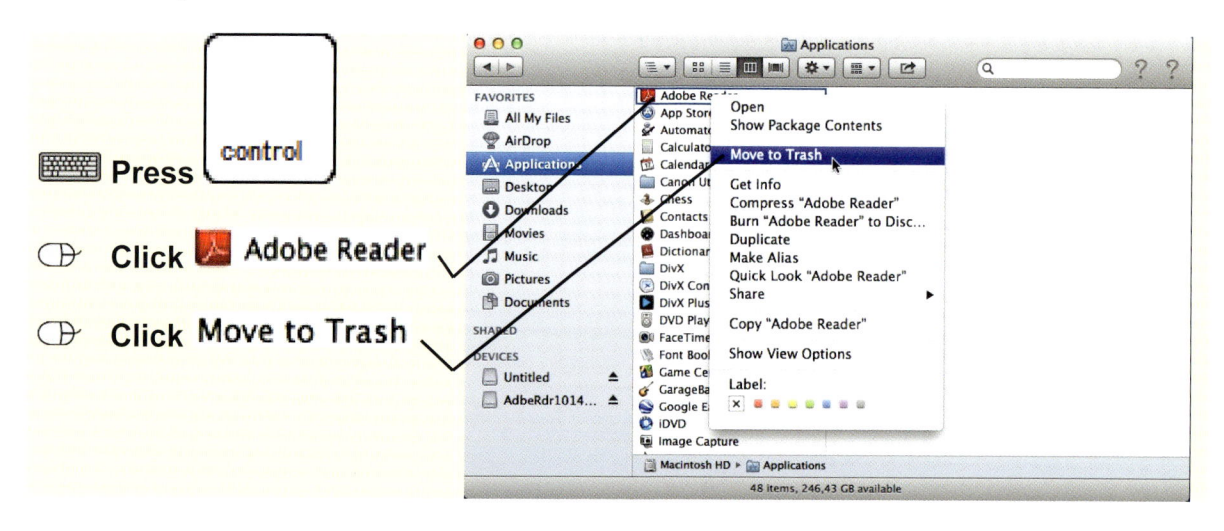

The program will be moved to the *Trash*.

Chapter 4 Practical Applications on the Mac **171**

4.7 Creating a Backup with Time Machine

Sometimes, a problem on your computer can lead to an accidental loss of one or more files. That is why it is important to make regular backups of all your files. By using a backup you can restore a lost file. You can create a backup copy on an external hard drive. If you are considering the purchase of an external hard drive, make sure it will be suitable for use with your *Mac*.

You can create a backup on the *Mac* with the *Time Machine* app:

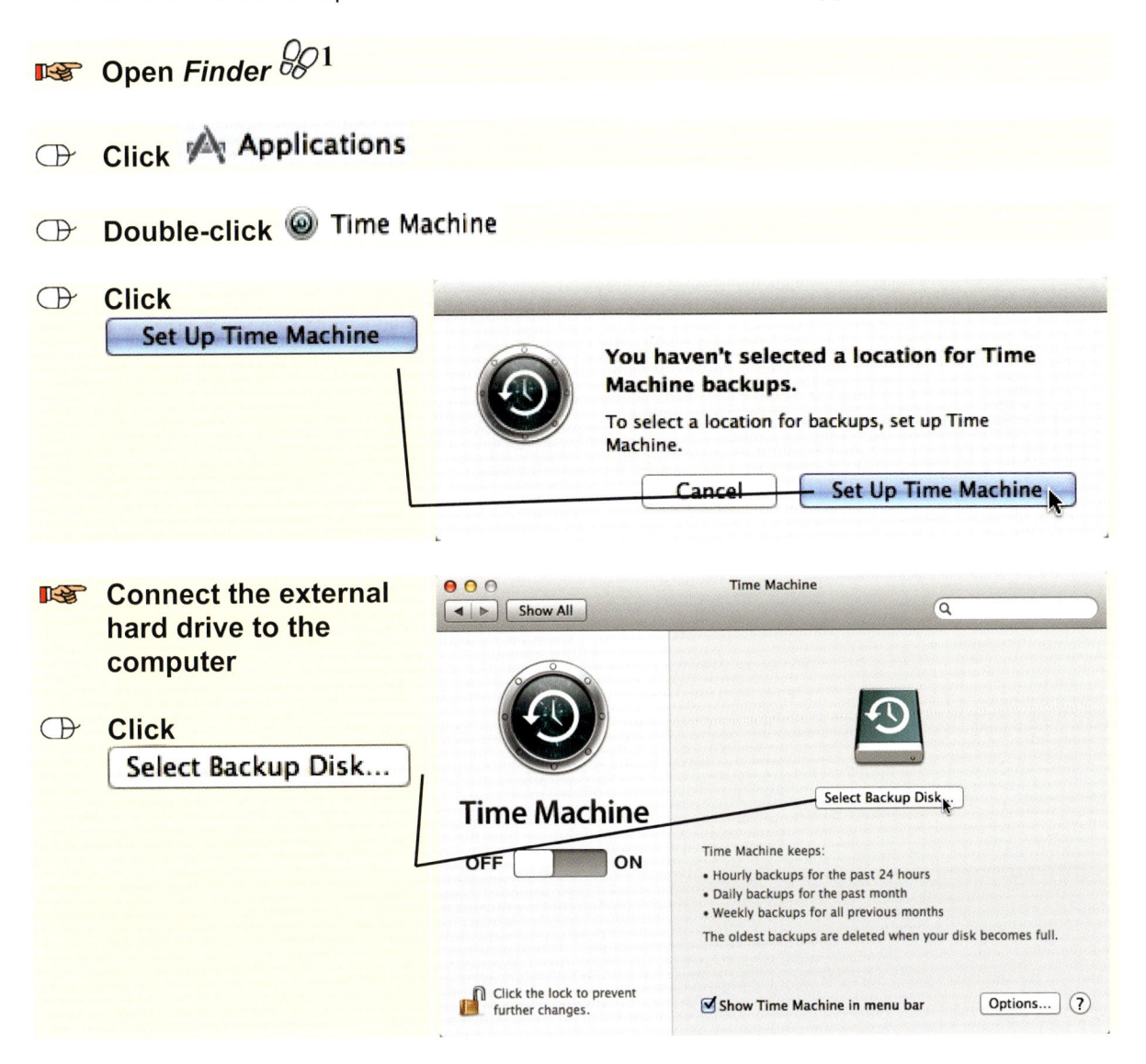

☞ **Open** *Finder* 🐾¹

⊕ **Click** 🅰 **Applications**

⊕ **Double-click** ⓦ **Time Machine**

⊕ **Click** [Set Up Time Machine]

You haven't selected a location for Time Machine backups.
To select a location for backups, set up Time Machine.

[Cancel] [**Set Up Time Machine**]

☞ **Connect the external hard drive to the computer**

⊕ **Click** [Select Backup Disk...]

Time Machine

OFF [ ] ON

Time Machine keeps:
• Hourly backups for the past 24 hours
• Daily backups for the past month
• Weekly backups for all previous months
The oldest backups are deleted when your disk becomes full.

🔒 Click the lock to prevent further changes.

☑ Show Time Machine in menu bar   [Options...] ⓘ

⌐ **Click the external hard drive**

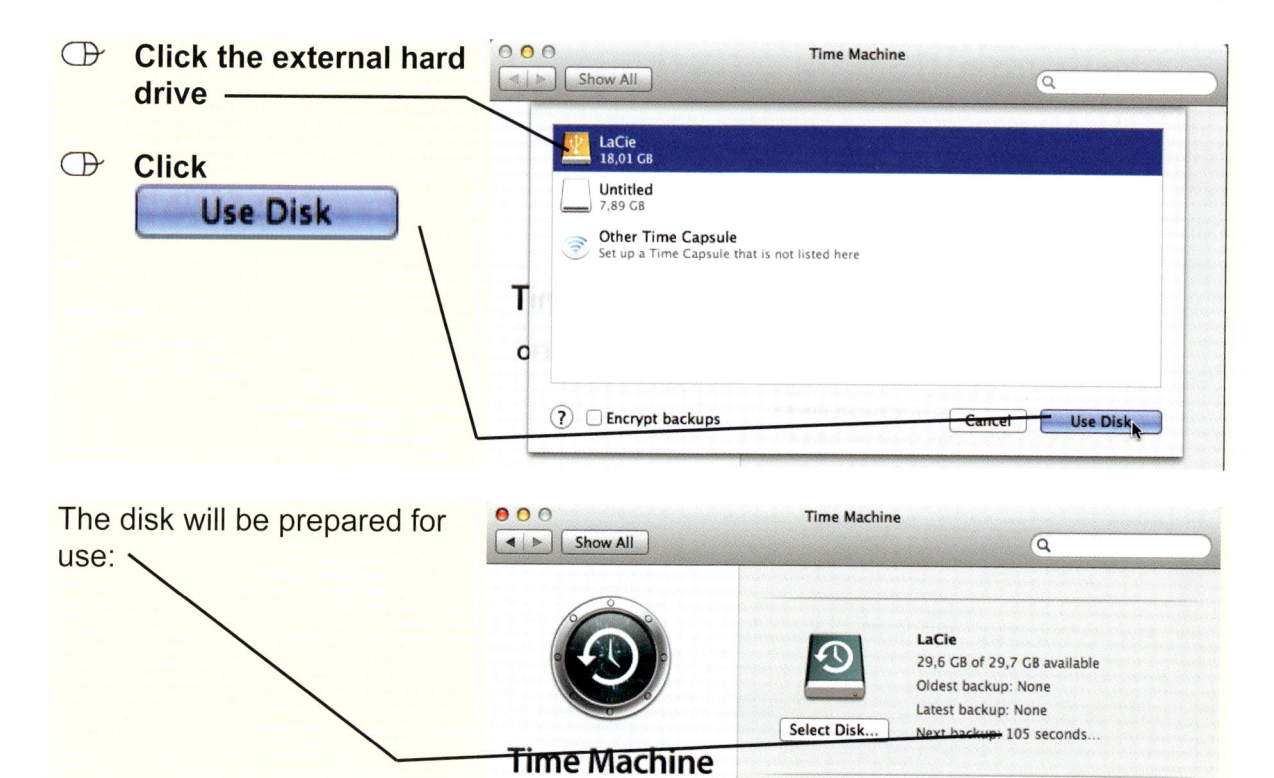

⌐ **Click** **Use Disk**

The disk will be prepared for use:

Next you will see this small window:

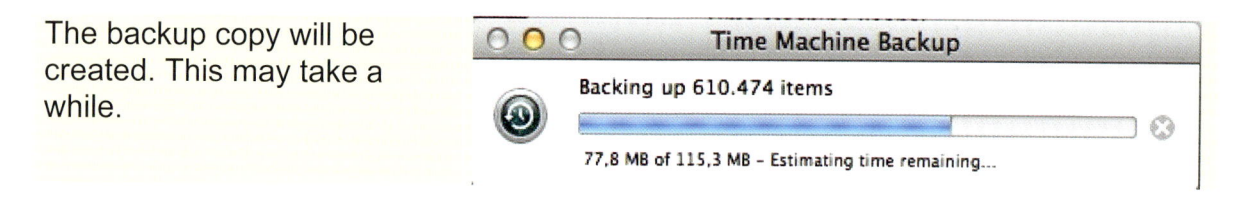

The backup copy will be created. This may take a while.

After the backup copy has been created, you can close *Time Machine*:

☞ **Stop** *Time Machine* ℘²

In the *Tips* at the end of this chapter you can read how to restore a file from a backup copy.

In this chapter you have learned how to add and remove apps in *Launchpad*. You have also learned how to use *Disk Utility* to check your hard disk for any problems and how to create a backup. Furthermore, you have learned how to download and install an app and how to delete it as needed.

4.8 Background Information

Dictionary

App	Short for application. These are programs that can be downloaded from the Internet for use on the *Mac*. The type of program may vary, from games to useful tools and utilities.
Backup	A backup copy of one or more files on your hard drive. This could also be a copy created on an external hard drive.
Disk Utility	One of the built-in programs on the *Mac.* It is used for executing all kinds of tasks regarding your hard disks, internal or external. With *Disk Utility* you can copy and activate disks, delete disks, re-format, partition, burn and repair disks.
External hard drive	A hard drive that is not built-in to a computer but connected to it with a cable. The disk has its own casing and power supply.
Launchpad	A program (app) that is used to open (or launch) other programs.
Spotlight	A built-in search technology found on *Mac* computers. *Spotlight* builds a database containing information about the files stored on the computer. When you enter a keyword in the *Spotlight* search box, the database will search for files matching the keyword and display a list of search results.
Time Machine	One of the built-in programs on the *Mac. Time Machine* regularly creates backups of all the files on the computer, such as data files, software programs and operating system files, so you can easily retrieve and restore the correct version of these files.

Source: Apple Dictionary, www.apple.com

4.9 Tips

💡 Tip
Restoring a file from a backup copy
You can use *Time Machine* to restore a file or a certain version of a file to the *Mac* when necessary. To do this, the external hard drive containing the backup copy needs to be connected to the *Mac*.

☞ **Connect the external hard drive to the *Mac***

☞ **Open *Finder* 👣¹**

⊕ **Click 🅰 Applications**

⊕ **Double-click 🕰 Time Machine**

You will see the *Time Machine* windows:

With the time bar you can jump to a specific date and time:

Click the file you want to restore. Then click **Restore**:

5. Sending Emails and Surfing the Internet Made Easier

The built-in application for sending and receiving email messages on the *Mac* is called *Mail*. Along with common features found in many email programs, *Mail* offers a number of additional options that make it easier for you to use email.

You can use various folders (*mailboxes*) to sort your email messages thereby separating for example, your personal email from your work-related messages. The search function allows you to quickly look up and retrieve email messages. And you can also add extra items to email messages, such as notes and a signature.

Safari is the built-in browser application used to surf the Internet. This program makes it very easy to create a *bookmark*. A bookmark can be any web address you like. By using bookmarks, you can quickly jump from one web page to another. You can also arrange your bookmarks in various ways to make them even easier to find. You may want to gather bookmarks of a similar content and put them on the *bookmarks toolbar* or the *bookmarks menu*. *Safari* also has a function called *Top Sites* which arranges your favorite websites all by itself.

Safari now has a *Reading List* feature that lets you save specific web pages to read later. With the offline feature, you can catch up on your reading even when you do not have an Internet connection.

In this chapter you will learn how to:

- create mailboxes in *Mail*;
- display conversations in *Mail*;
- add a signature to an email message;
- search for emails;
- delete an email message;
- arrange bookmarks in *Safari*;
- create a bookmark menu in *Safari*;
- work with *Top Sites*;
- create a *Reading List* in *Safari*.

5.1 Creating Mailboxes in Mail

If you have used *Mail* to send and receive your email messages for a long enough time, you may begin to notice that you have built up a considerable amount of email messages. It is probably a good idea to arrange these emails in order to have a better overview of your stored messages. For example, you can separate your personal messages from your work-related messages. In the following examples, we will be using an email address that has been added to *Mail*. But you can also perform the same actions with a webmail address, such as a *Hotmail* or *Gmail* web address, which has been added to *Mail*.

The next few steps will show you how to use mailboxes to arrange your email correspondence. First, you will need to create a few new mailboxes:

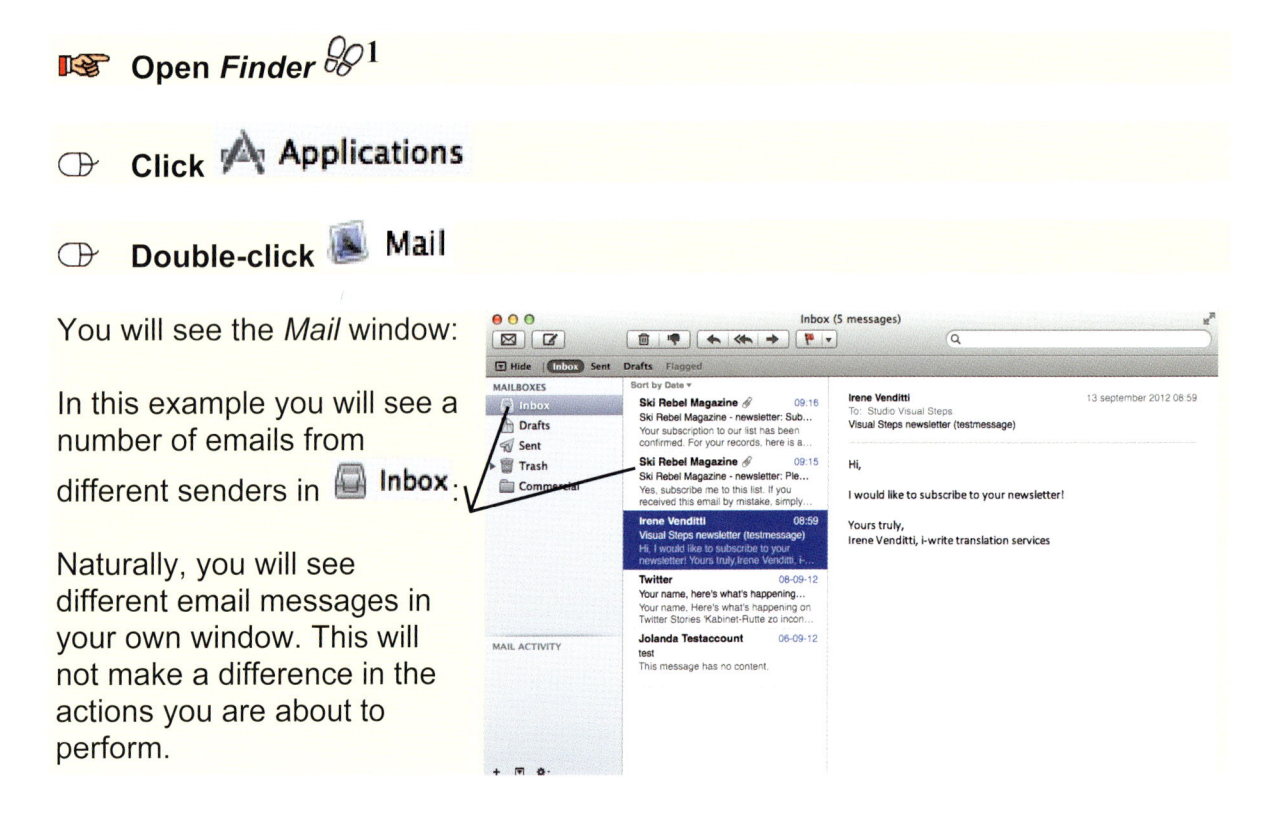

☞ **Open *Finder*** ⚘¹

⊕ **Click** 🅰 **Applications**

⊕ **Double-click** 📧 **Mail**

You will see the *Mail* window:

In this example you will see a number of emails from different senders in 📥 **Inbox**:

Naturally, you will see different email messages in your own window. This will not make a difference in the actions you are about to perform.

Chapter 5 Sending E-mails and Surfing the Internet Made Easier **177**

You can sort your email messages into various folders (mailboxes). You do this by using the Control key. In this case a new mailbox will be created for all the messages you have received from businesses and other organizations. Here is how to create a new mailbox:

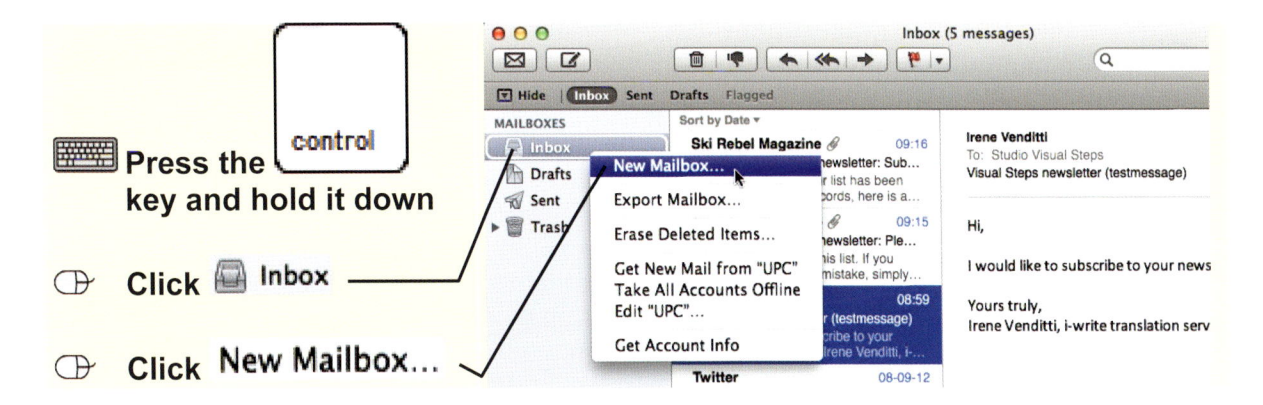

⌨ **Press the** `control` **key and hold it down**

🖱 **Click** 📥 **Inbox**

🖱 **Click New Mailbox...**

You can enter a name for the mailbox:

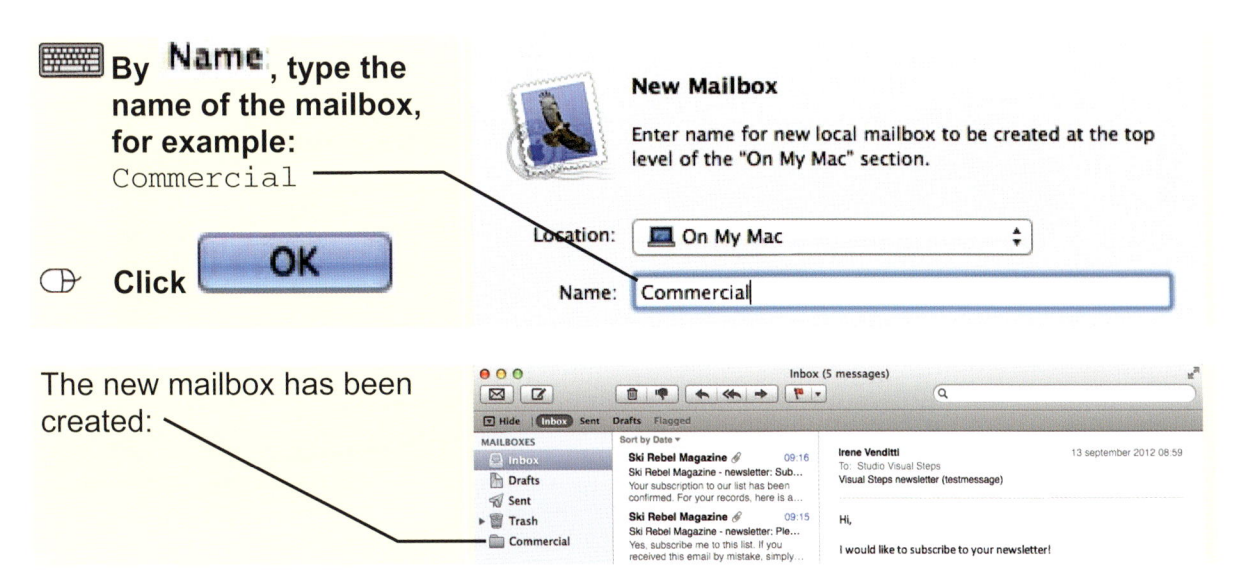

⌨ **By Name, type the name of the mailbox, for example:**
`Commercial`

🖱 **Click OK**

The new mailbox has been created:

You can move an email message by dragging it to the mailbox:

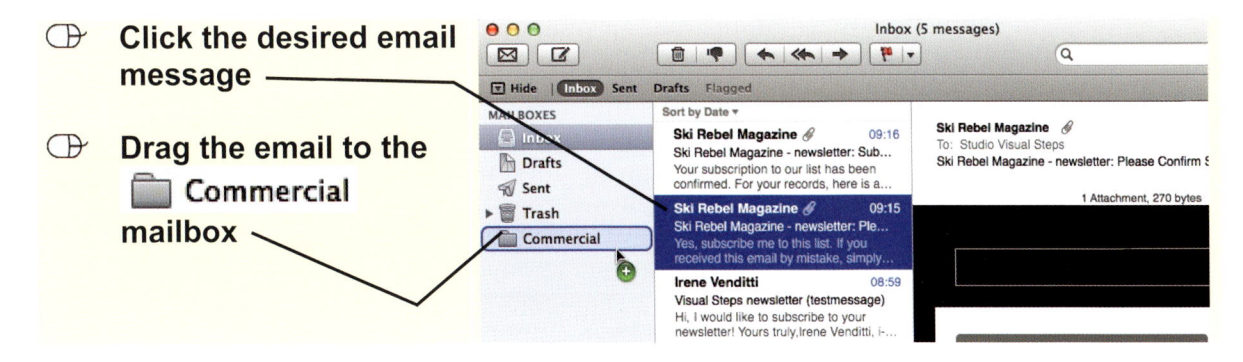

🖱 **Click the desired email message**

🖱 **Drag the email to the** 📁 **Commercial mailbox**

The email will be moved to 📁 **Commercial**.

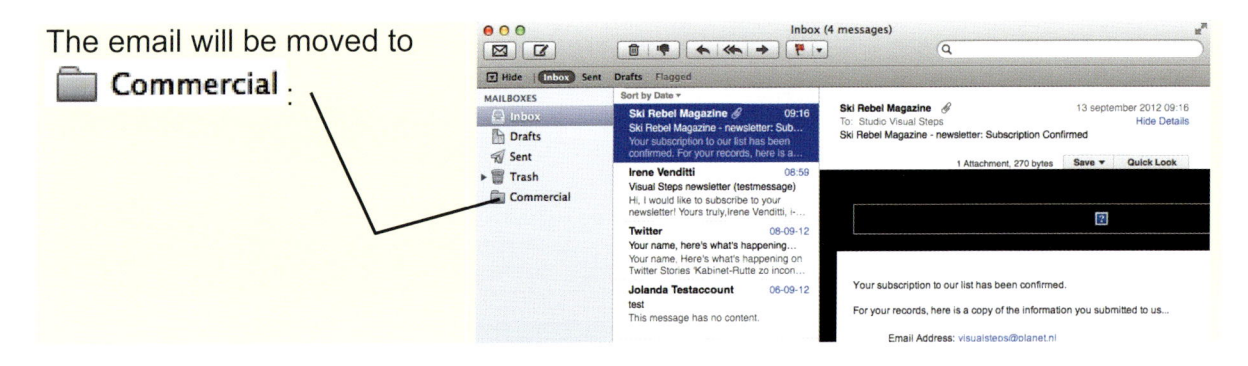

By using the Shift key you can move multiple messages to a mailbox at once:

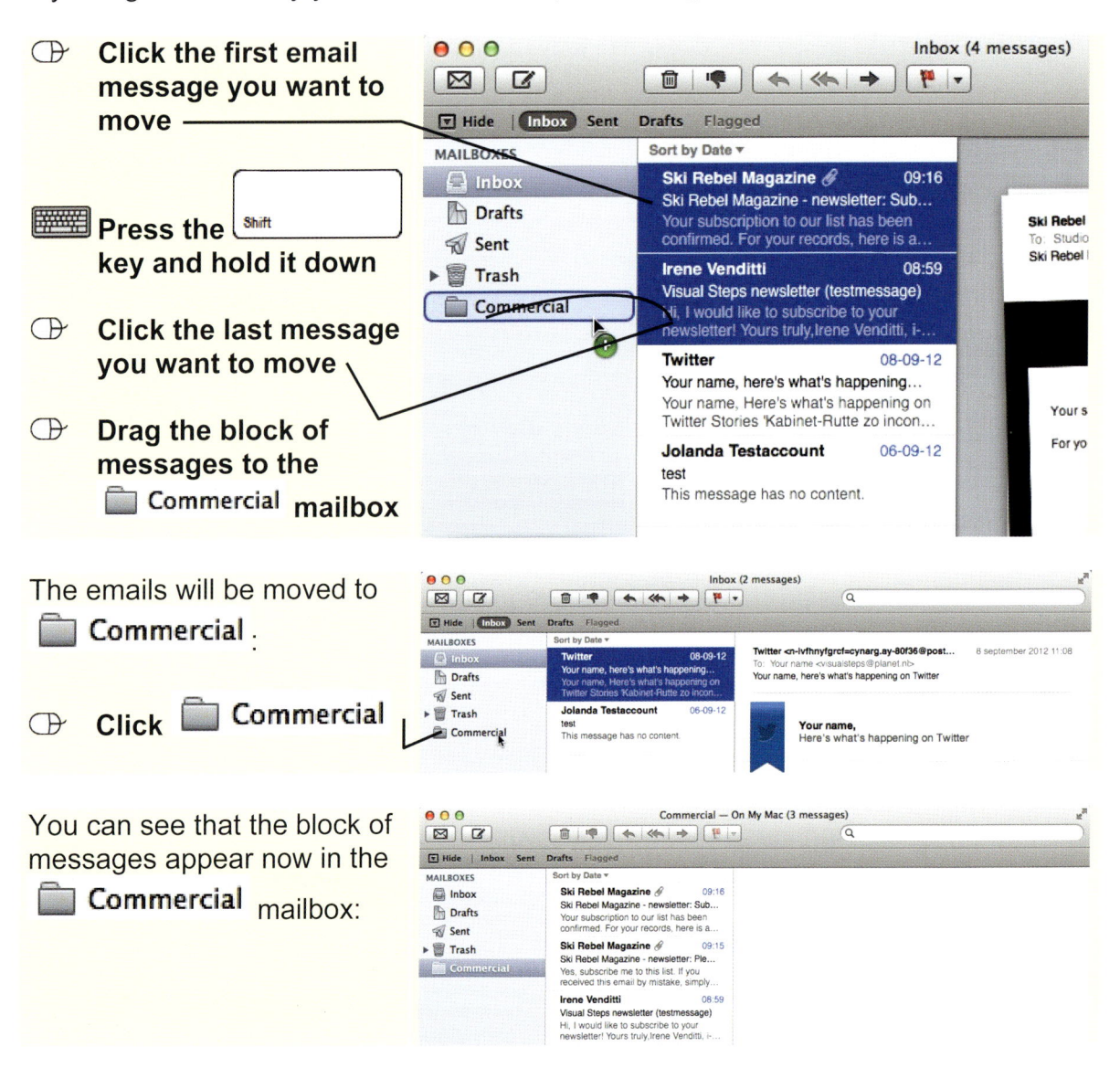

- 🖱 **Click the first email message you want to move**

- ⌨ **Press the** [Shift] **key and hold it down**

- 🖱 **Click the last message you want to move**

- 🖱 **Drag the block of messages to the** 📁 **Commercial mailbox**

The emails will be moved to 📁 **Commercial**.

- 🖱 **Click** 📁 **Commercial**

You can see that the block of messages appear now in the 📁 **Commercial** mailbox:

Chapter 5 Sending E-mails and Surfing the Internet Made Easier **179**

In this way you can create mailboxes for different purposes and move your email messages to them accordingly.

💡 Tip
Move to the standard mailboxes
You can always move an email message from a mailbox you have created yourself back to the standard mailboxes, such as 📥 Inbox, ✈ Sent and 🗑 Trash.

💡 Tip
Select multiple email messages
You can select multiple email messages that are not ordered consecutively. You do this by pressing the Command ⌘ key and holding it down as you select the desired messages.

💡 Tip
A mailbox within a mailbox
In a mailbox, you can also create other new mailboxes. It is much the same as folders and subfolders. This way you can arrange and sort your emails even further. You need to use the Control key to do this:

⌨ **Press the** `control` **key and hold it down**

⊙ **Click the mailbox**

⊙ **Click New Mailbox...**

💡 Tip
Delete the mailboxes you have created
If you no longer need a mailbox you have created, you can delete it.
Please note: this action will delete the emails in this mailbox too. You use the Control key to do this:

⌨️ Press the `control` key and hold it down

👆 Click the mailbox

👆 Click `Delete Mailbox...`

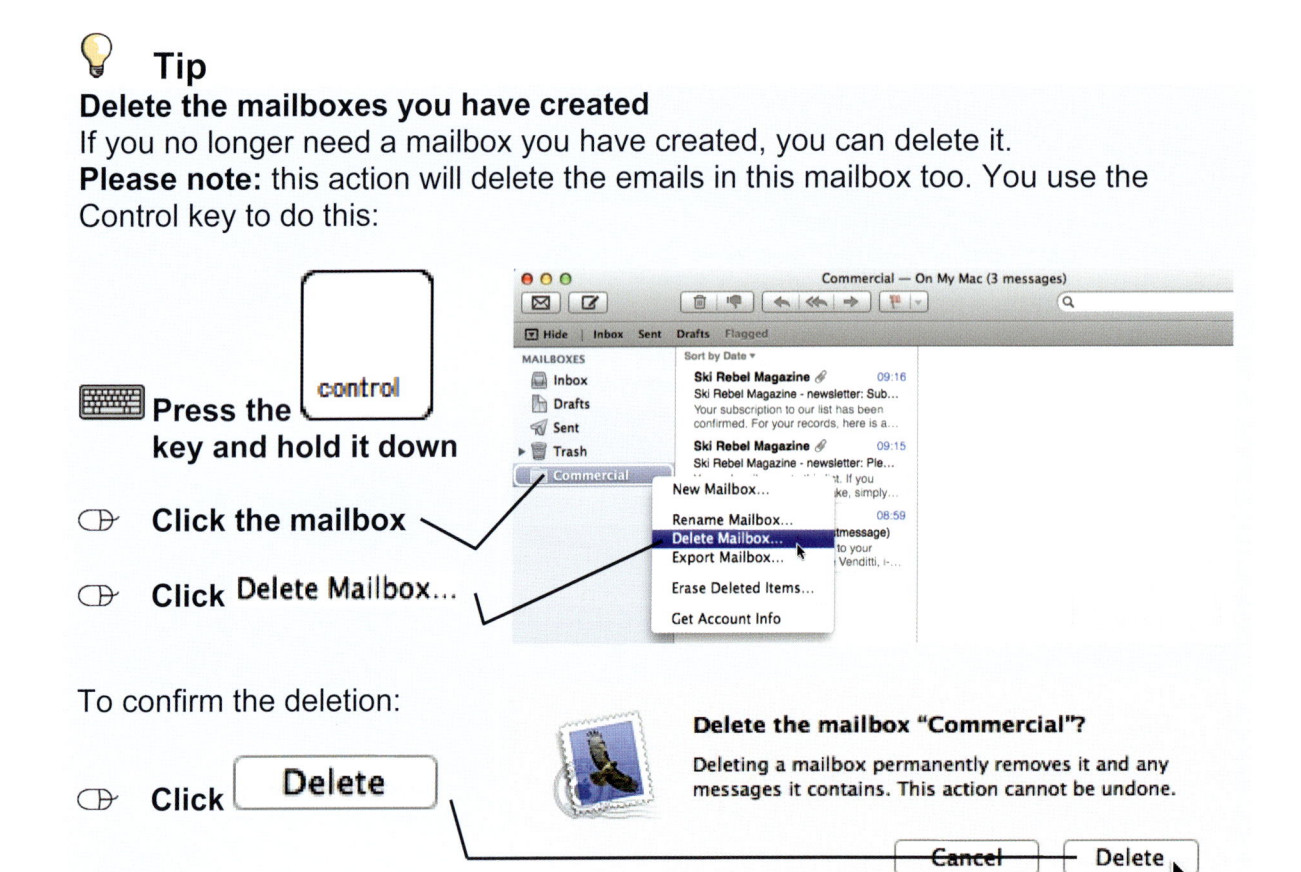

To confirm the deletion:

👆 Click `Delete`

5.2 Displaying Conversations

You probably have noticed that multiple email messages regarding the same subject are sent back and forth. In *Mail* this is called a conversation:

👆 Click `Inbox`

In this example you will see a conversation. This is indicated by a grey or white number ② appearing in the message:

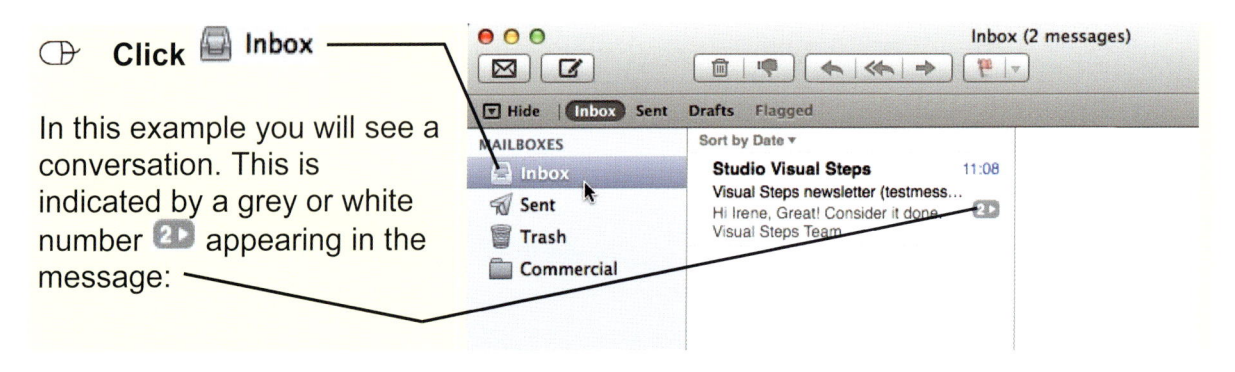

The number indicates the number of messages contained in this conversation. For example, if four email messages have been sent back and forth, the number that appears in the message is four.

Chapter 5 Sending E-mails and Surfing the Internet Made Easier **181**

By default, only the last message in a conversation will be displayed. You can read the previous email messages by opening the conversation:

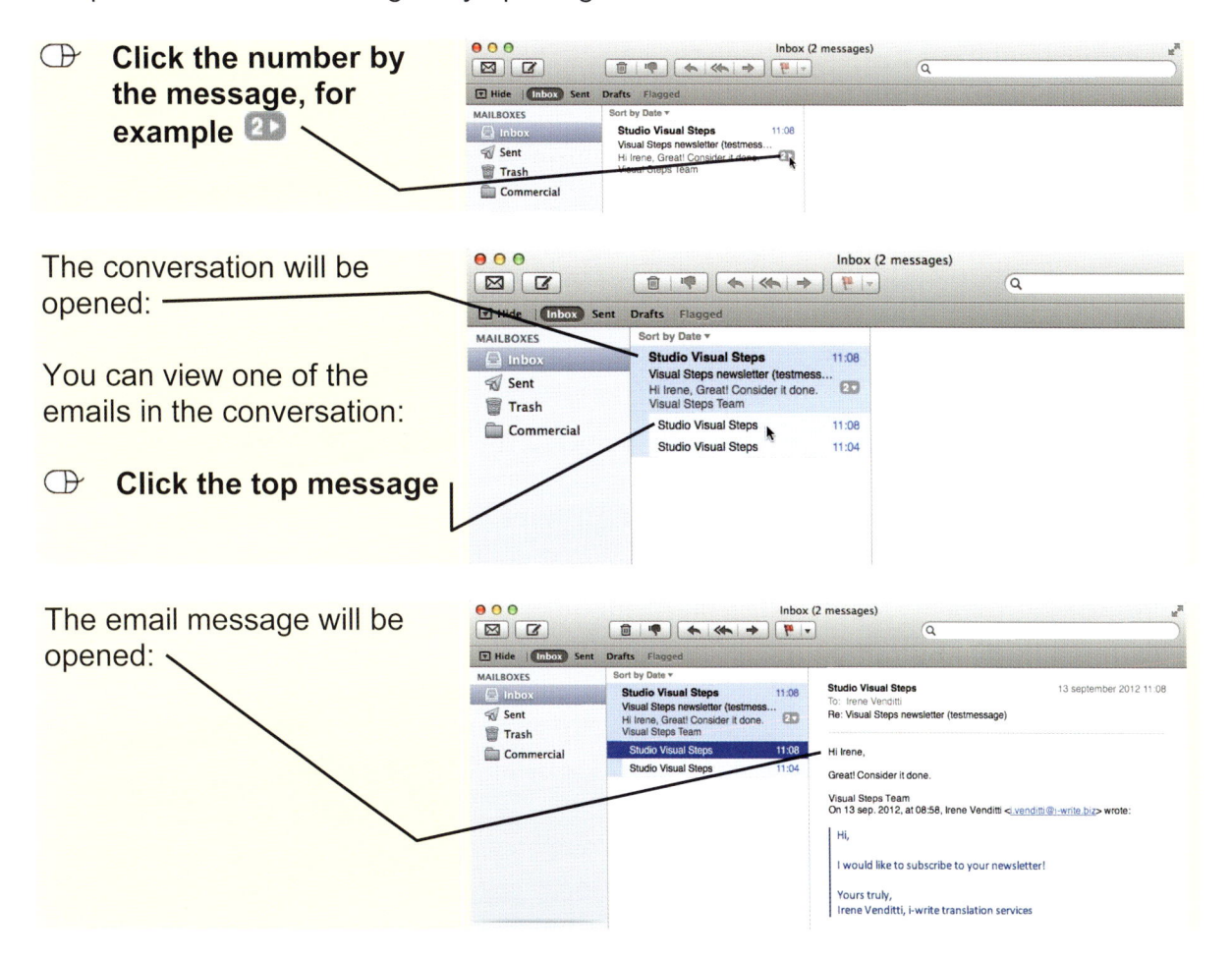

⊕ **Click the number by the message, for example** 2▷

The conversation will be opened:

You can view one of the emails in the conversation:

⊕ **Click the top message**

The email message will be opened:

If you want to keep a clear overview of the *Mail* window you can close this conversation again:

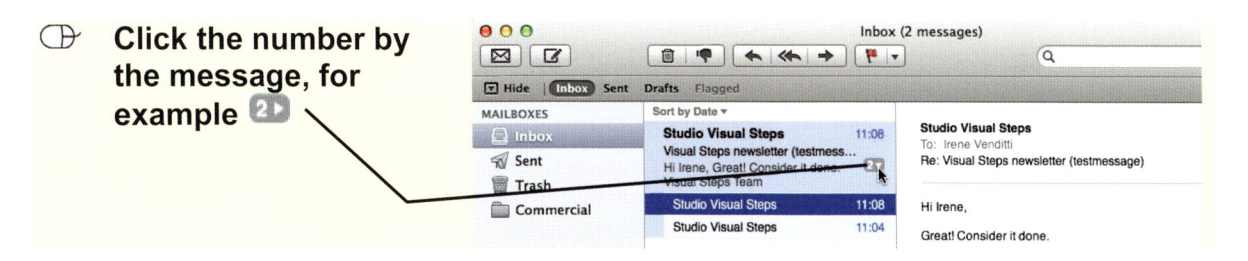

⊕ **Click the number by the message, for example** 2▷

The conversation has been closed:

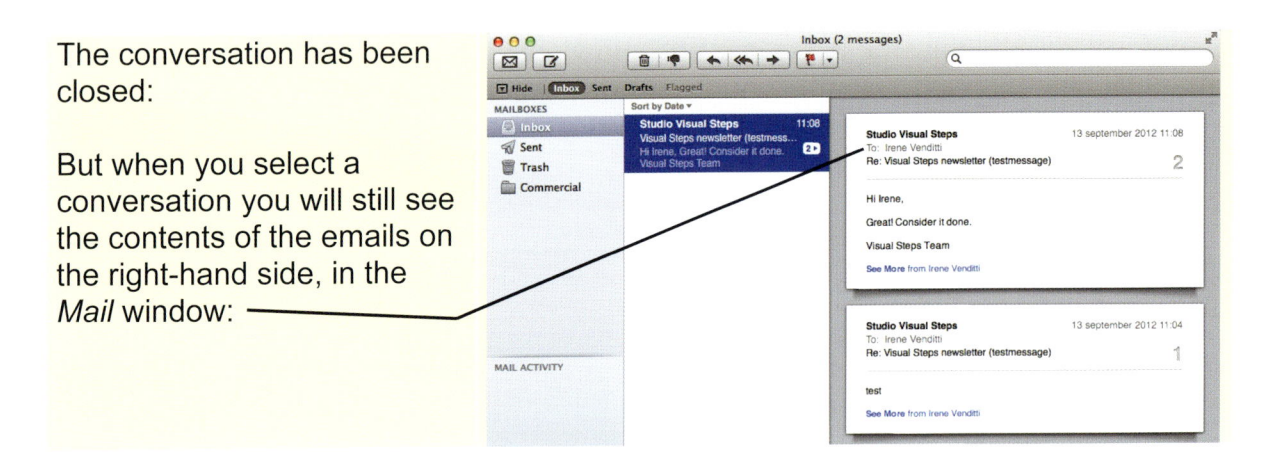

But when you select a conversation you will still see the contents of the emails on the right-hand side, in the *Mail* window:

5.3 Adding a Signature To an Email Message

A signature within an email message is not quite the same thing as a signature on paper. In an email message; a signature is a text containing your name and address. A signature is often used in business correspondence, for quickly and easily adding address information to an email message. If you use a signature you will not need to enter this information over and over again. This is how you create a signature:

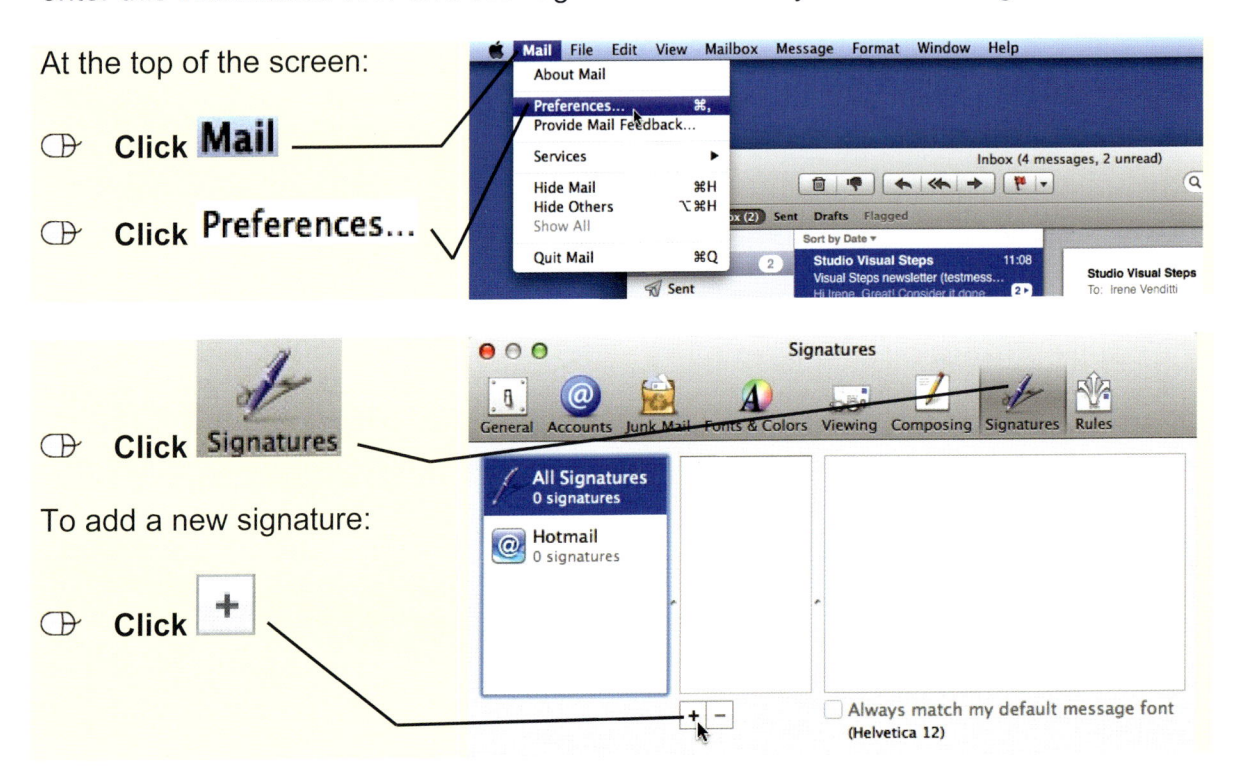

At the top of the screen:

☞ Click **Mail**

☞ Click **Preferences...**

☞ Click **Signatures**

To add a new signature:

☞ Click **+**

Chapter 5 Sending E-mails and Surfing the Internet Made Easier   183

By default, the name and email address of your email account will be entered in the signature:

You can add extra information:

⌒₊ **Click the right-hand side of your name, shown in the text box**

⌨ **Press** `enter return`

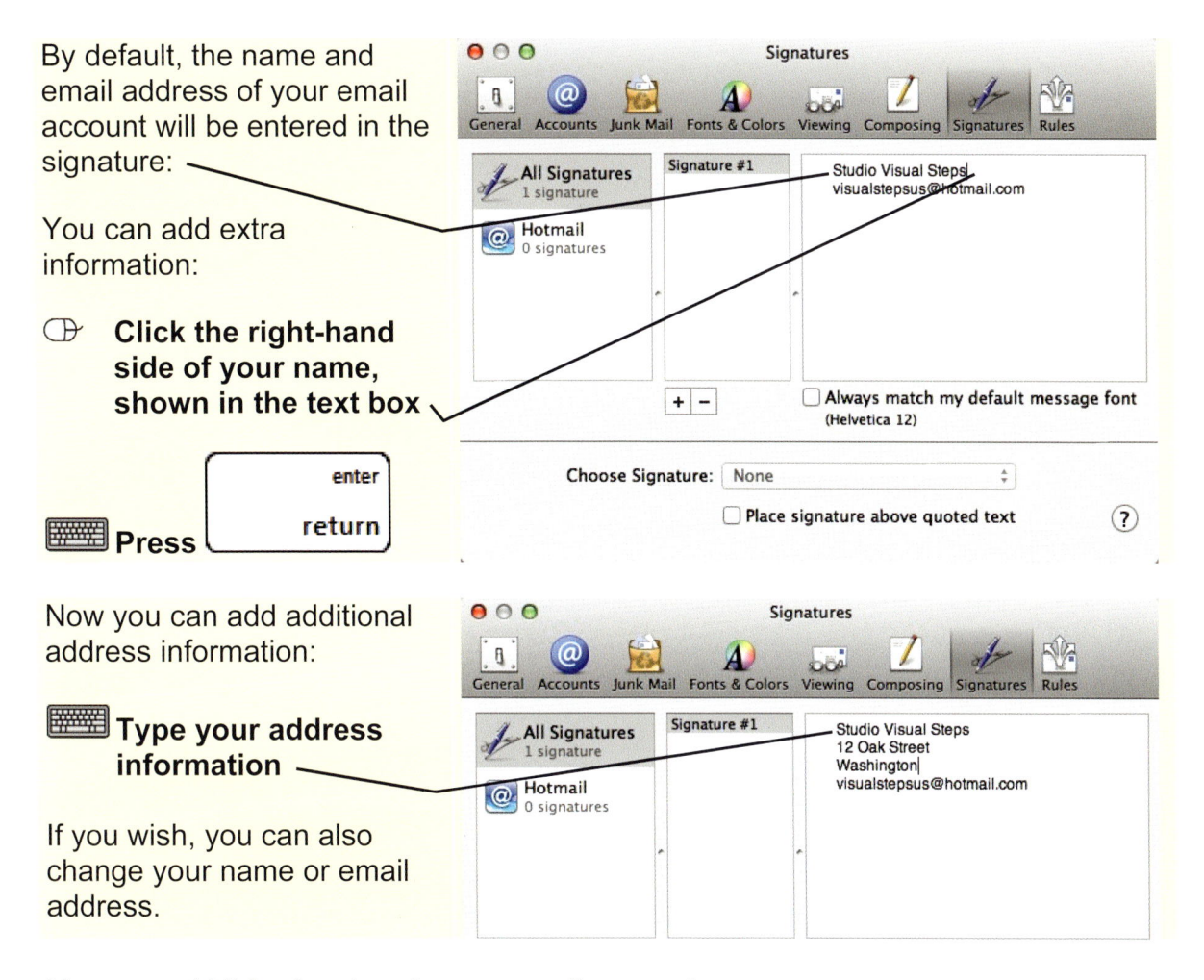

Now you can add additional address information:

⌨ **Type your address information**

If you wish, you can also change your name or email address.

You can add this signature to your email account:

⌒₊ **Click Signature #1**

⌒₊ **Drag Signature #1 to the desired email account**

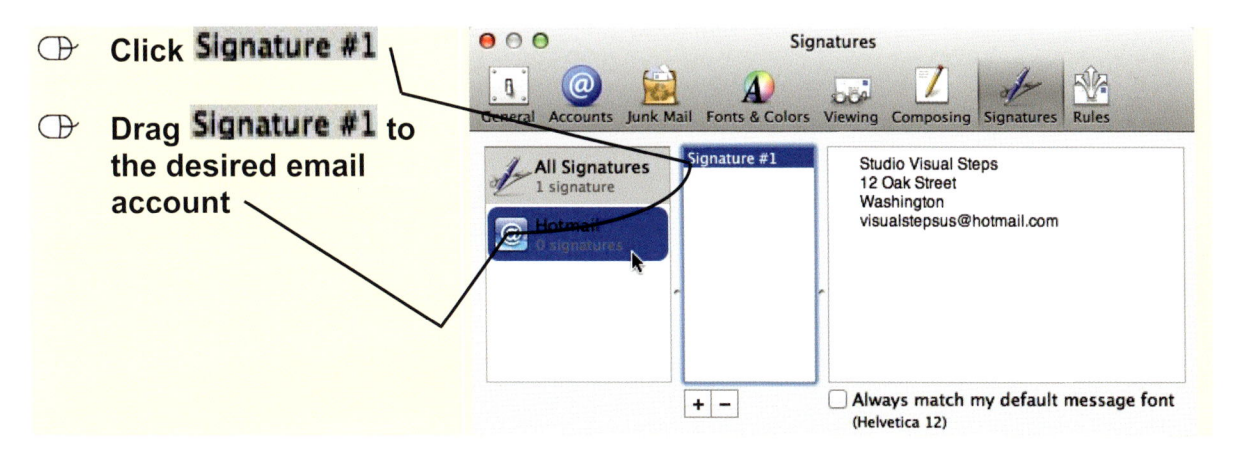

You can add the signature automatically to each new email message, if you want. In this example we will not do this.

☞ **Check the box ☑ by Place signature above** ⟨

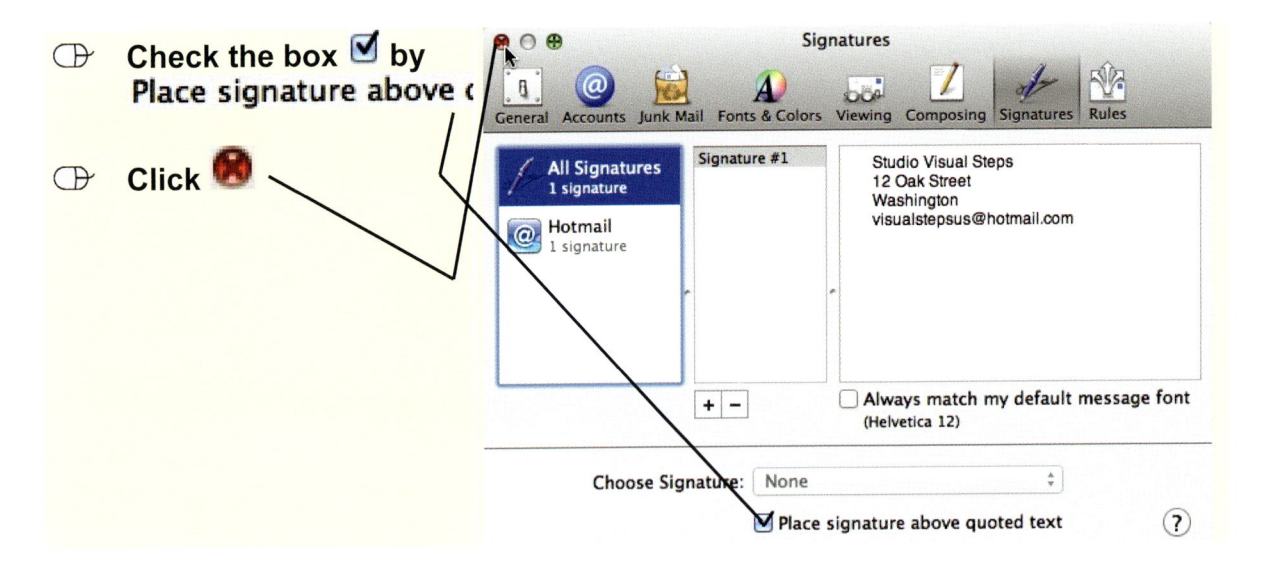

☞ **Click** 🔴

You have created a signature. Now you can manually add this signature to a new email message:

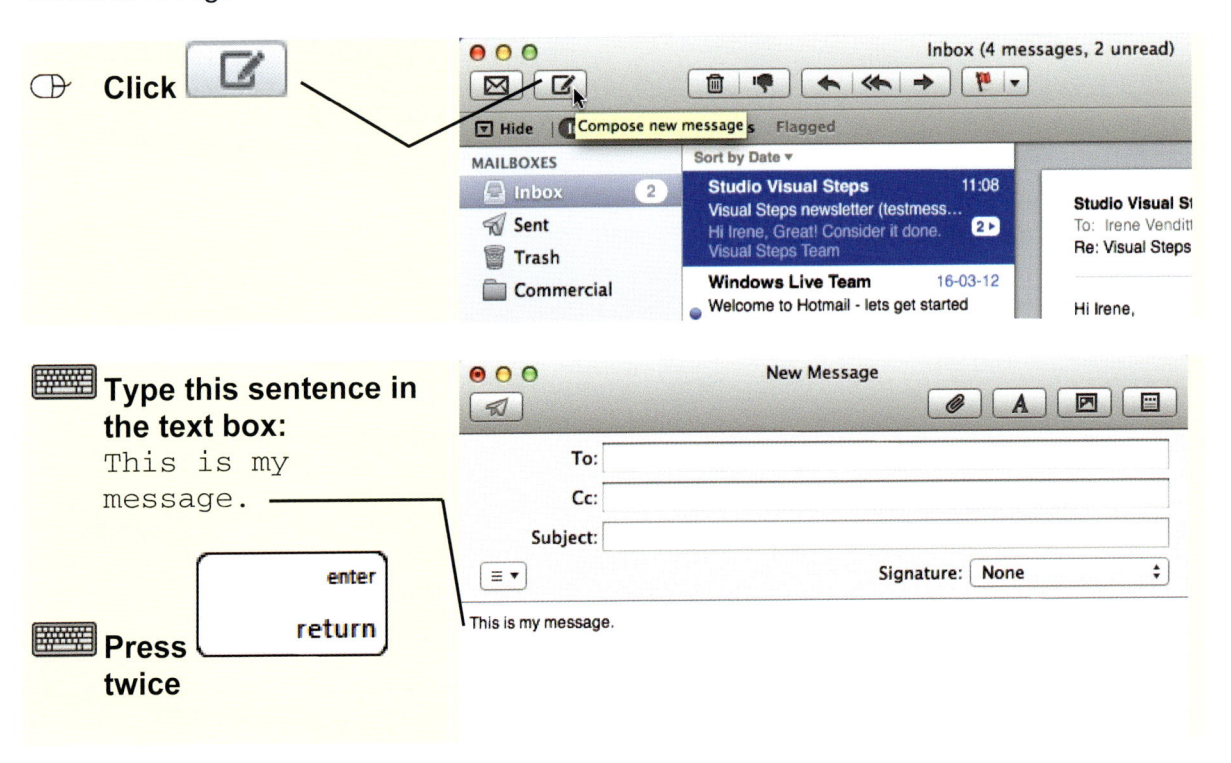

☞ **Click** 🖉

⌨ **Type this sentence in the text box:**
```
This is my
message.
```

⌨ **Press** `enter`/`return` **twice**

Chapter 5 Sending E-mails and Surfing the Internet Made Easier   **185**

Now you can add the signature:

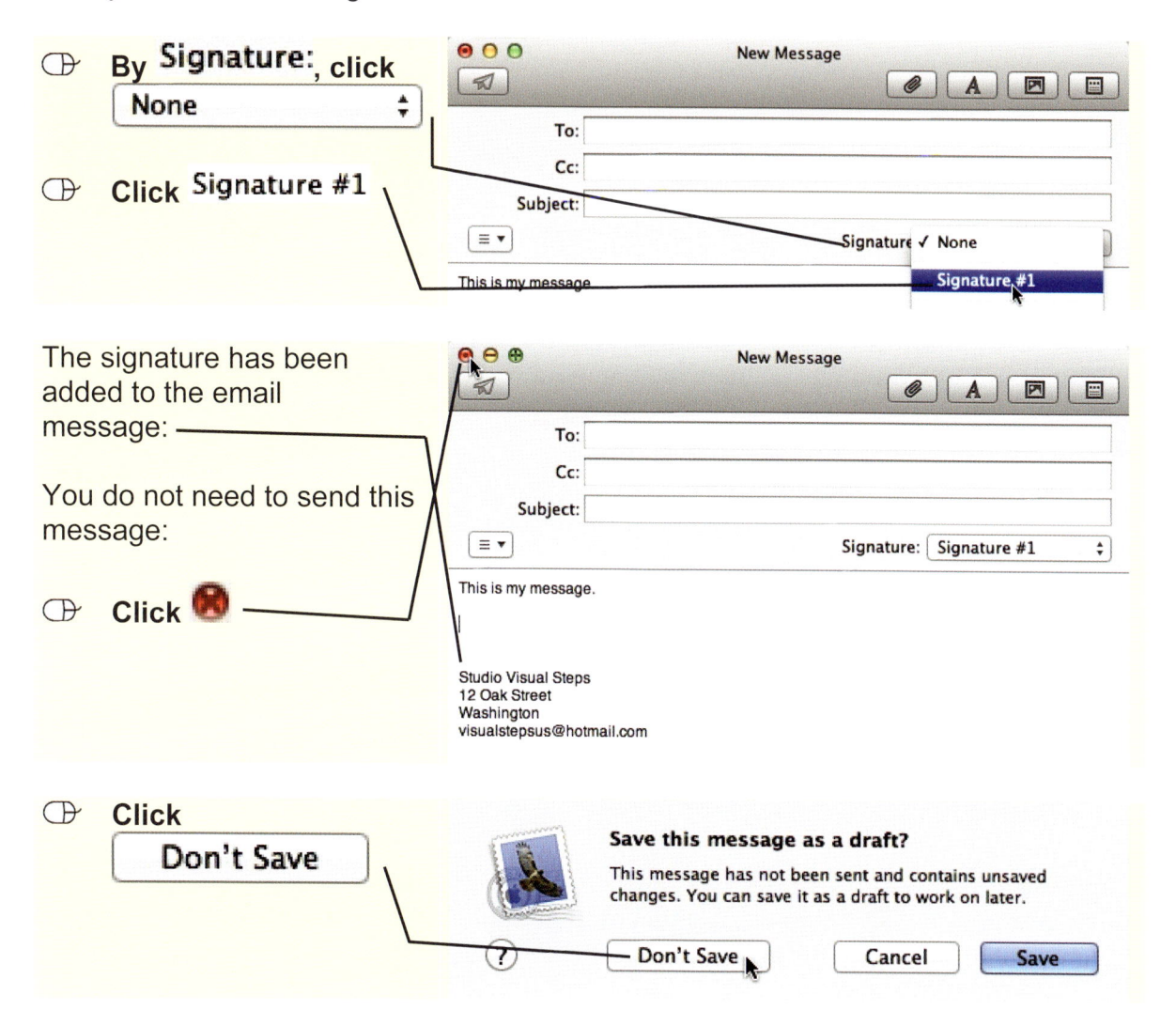

- By **Signature:**, click **None**

- Click **Signature #1**

The signature has been added to the email message:

You do not need to send this message:

- Click 🔴

- Click **Don't Save**

5.4 Searching for Email Messages

If you have many emails stored on your computer, it may be very hard to find a specific message. *Mail* provides a search function that can help you find a message:

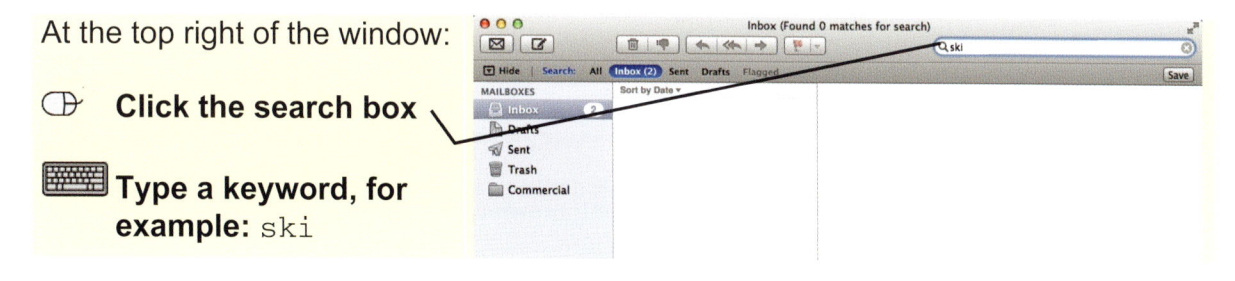

At the top right of the window:

- **Click the search box**

- **Type a keyword, for example:** ski

By default, the mailbox that is currently selected will be searched. But you can also search in another mailbox. In this example you will be searching all of the mailboxes at once:

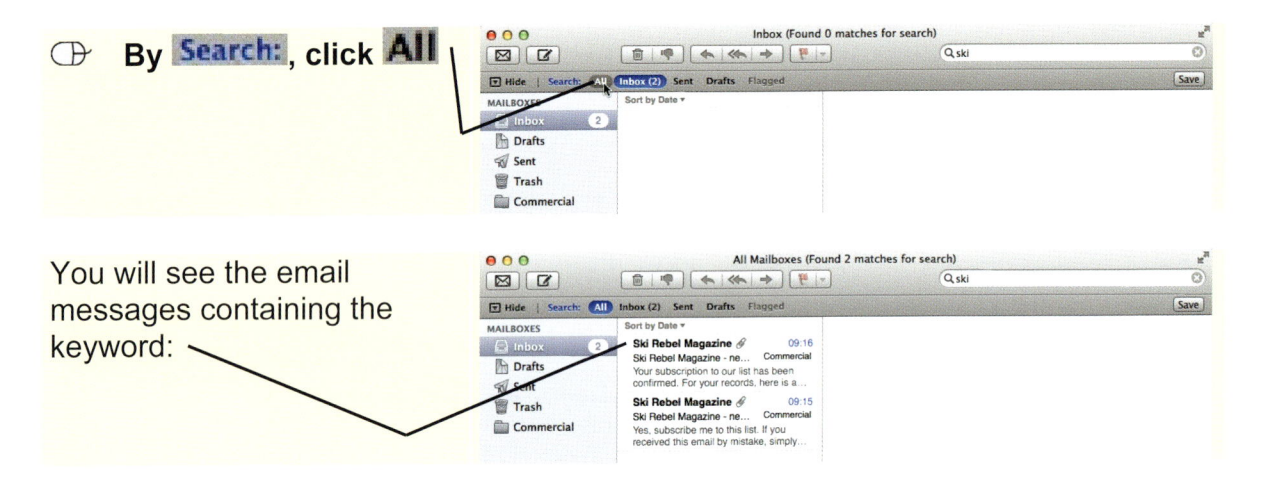

☞ By `Search:`, click `All`

You will see the email messages containing the keyword:

Tip
Searching with multiple keywords
If you search with a single keyword, your search result may yield a very long list of emails. You can try using multiple keywords, each separated by a blank space.

5.5 Deleting an Email Message

In order to keep your mailboxes neat and tidy you can delete the old messages you no longer need. In this example, a conversation containing two messages is deleted:

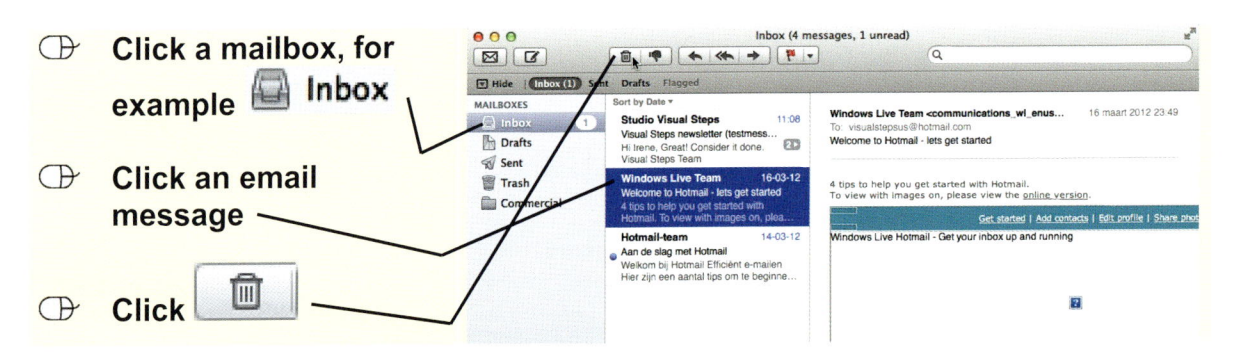

☞ Click a mailbox, for example 🖨 Inbox

☞ Click an email message

☞ Click 🗑

HELP! I only see email messages containing the keyword.
You may just see the emails containing the keyword you entered in the previous section. In that case you will need to close the query first. You do this by clicking ⊗ in the search box `Q ski`   ⊗ .

Chapter 5 Sending E-mails and Surfing the Internet Made Easier **187**

☞ Click 🗑 **Trash**

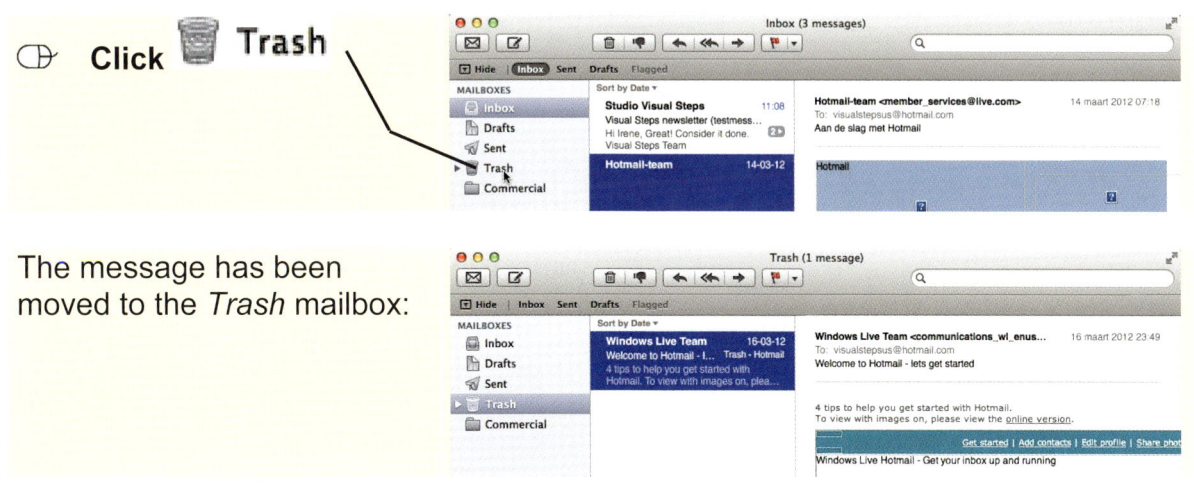

The message has been moved to the *Trash* mailbox:

HELP! I do not see 🗑 Trash.
If the *Trash* mailbox does not appear, you may need to close and open the program again.

☞ Stop *Mail* 👣²

☞ In *Finder*, double-click 📧 **Mail**

💡 **Tip**
The trash will automatically be emptied
The default setting for messages contained in the *Trash* mailbox is that they are automatically deleted after one month. In the *Tips* at the end of this chapter you can read how to change this setting.

This is how to permanently delete all of the messages contained in the *Trash*:

At the top of the window:

☞ Click **Mailbox**

☞ Click **Erase Deleted Items**

☞ Click **In All Accounts...** ⇧⌘⌫

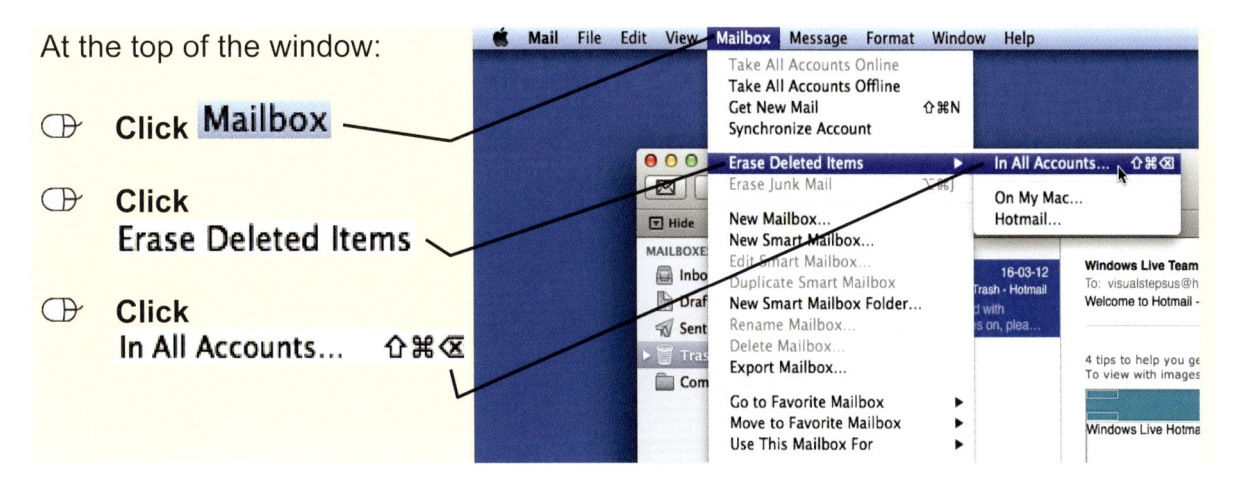

You will see a warning message. If you really want to delete the messages in the *Trash* mailbox:

⊕ Click **Erase**

Now the *Trash* mailbox is empty.

☞ Stop *Mail* ₰₰2

5.6 Organizing Bookmarks in Safari

Mac's built-in browser application is called *Safari*. You can use *Safari* to surf the Internet and view websites. If you want to save a certain website address, you can create a *bookmark* for it. With this bookmark you can quickly open the website later on. After a while, you will have a lot of bookmarks stored in *Safari*. When that happens, it is a good idea to arrange your bookmarks and store them into separate folders. In this way you can keep your bookmarks well organized.

First, we will show you how to create a bookmark and then how to add it to the bookmarks bar:

☞ Open *Finder* ₰₰1

⊕ Click **Applications**

⊕ Double-click **Safari**

Chapter 5 Sending E-mails and Surfing the Internet Made Easier **189**

You will see the *Safari* window:

⊕ **Click the address bar three times**

⌨ **Type:**
www.visualsteps.com

⌨ **Press** `enter return`

You will see the Visual Steps website. You can create a bookmark for this website:

⊕ **Click** 🔗

⊕ **Click** 📖 **Add Bookmark**

In *OS X Lion*:

⊕ **Click** ➕

If the names of the websites on the bookmarks bar are very long, you will only be able to fit a few buttons on the bar. You can shorten the name a bit by using the Backspace key:

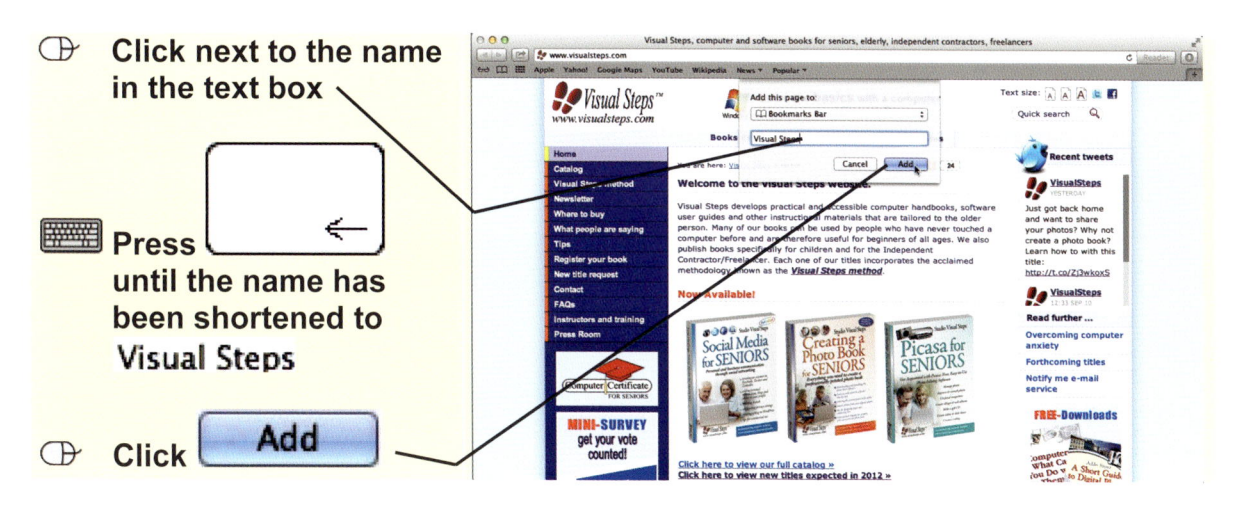

⊕ **Click next to the name in the text box**

⌨ **Press** ⌫ **until the name has been shortened to Visual Steps**

⊕ **Click** **Add**

The **Visual Steps** bookmark has been added to the bookmarks bar:

If you keep adding individual bookmarks to the bar in this way, the bookmarks bar will soon be full. You can prevent this by organizing the bookmarks into folders:

☞ **Click** 📖

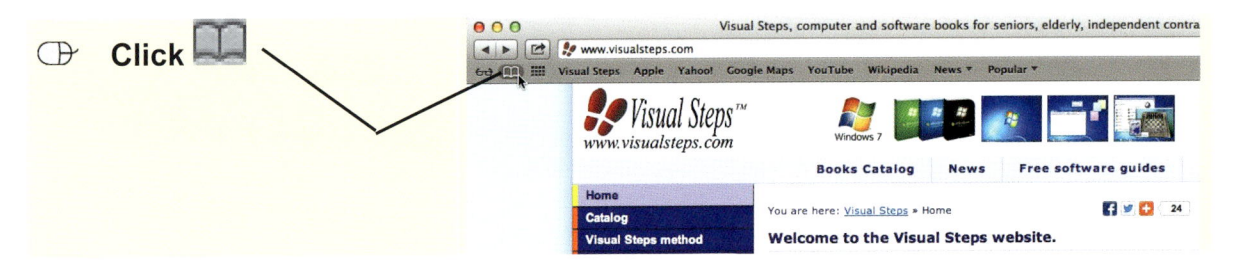

Now the bookmarks library will be opened. This is a window in which you can create, view and organize your bookmarks. Among other things, the bookmarks library contains the browser history, folders with bookmarks and shortcuts to the *Address Book*.

☞ **If necessary, click** 📖 **Bookmarks Bar**

You will see an overview of the bookmarks currently placed on the bookmarks bar:

☞ **Click** ➕

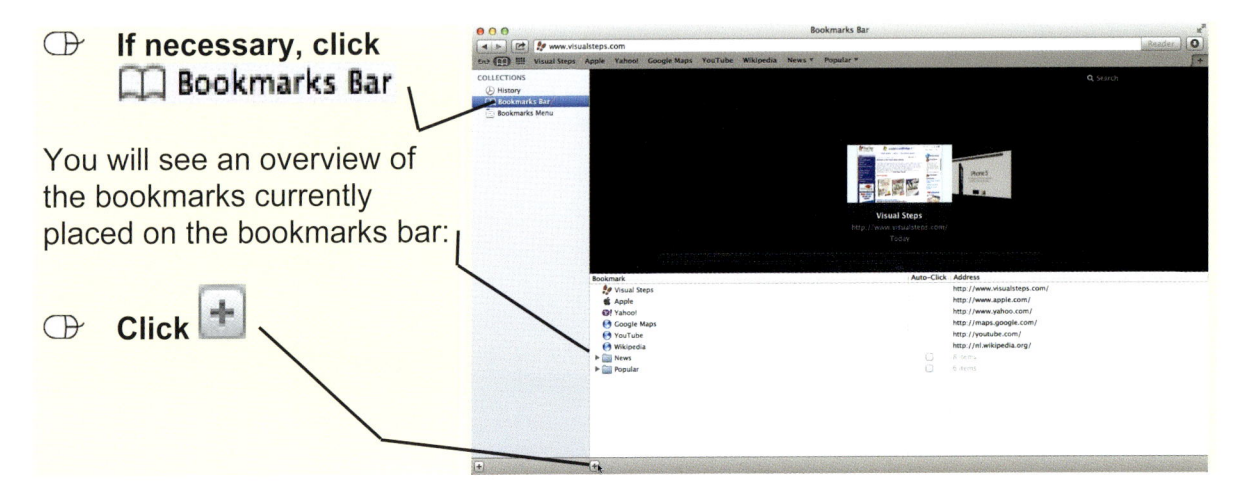

Chapter 5 Sending E-mails and Surfing the Internet Made Easier

A new folder will be added. You can enter a name for this folder:

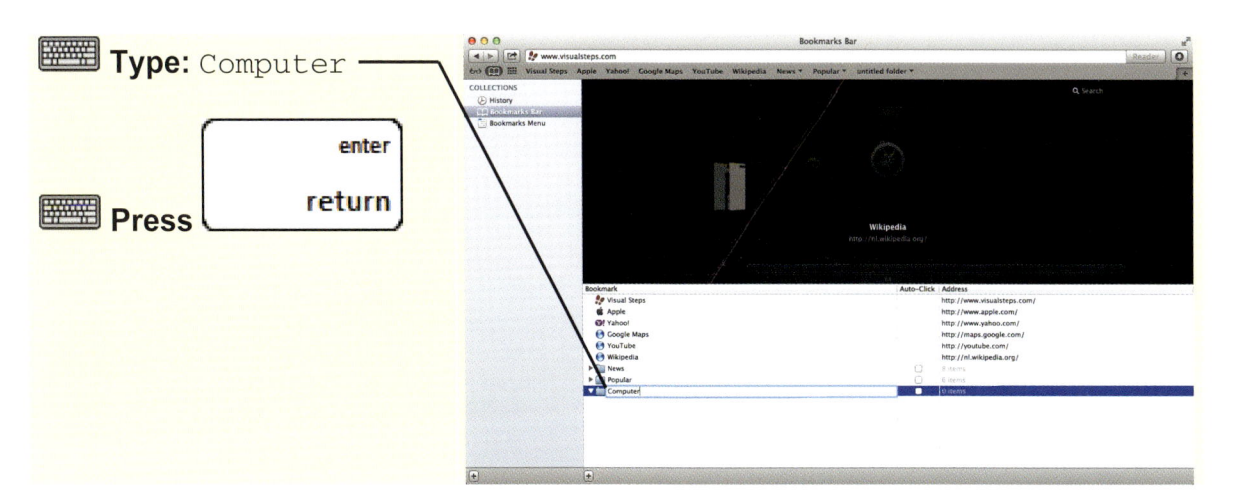

⌨ **Type:** Computer

⌨ **Press** enter / return

The folder is ready for use. Now you can move the bookmark for the Visual Steps website to this folder:

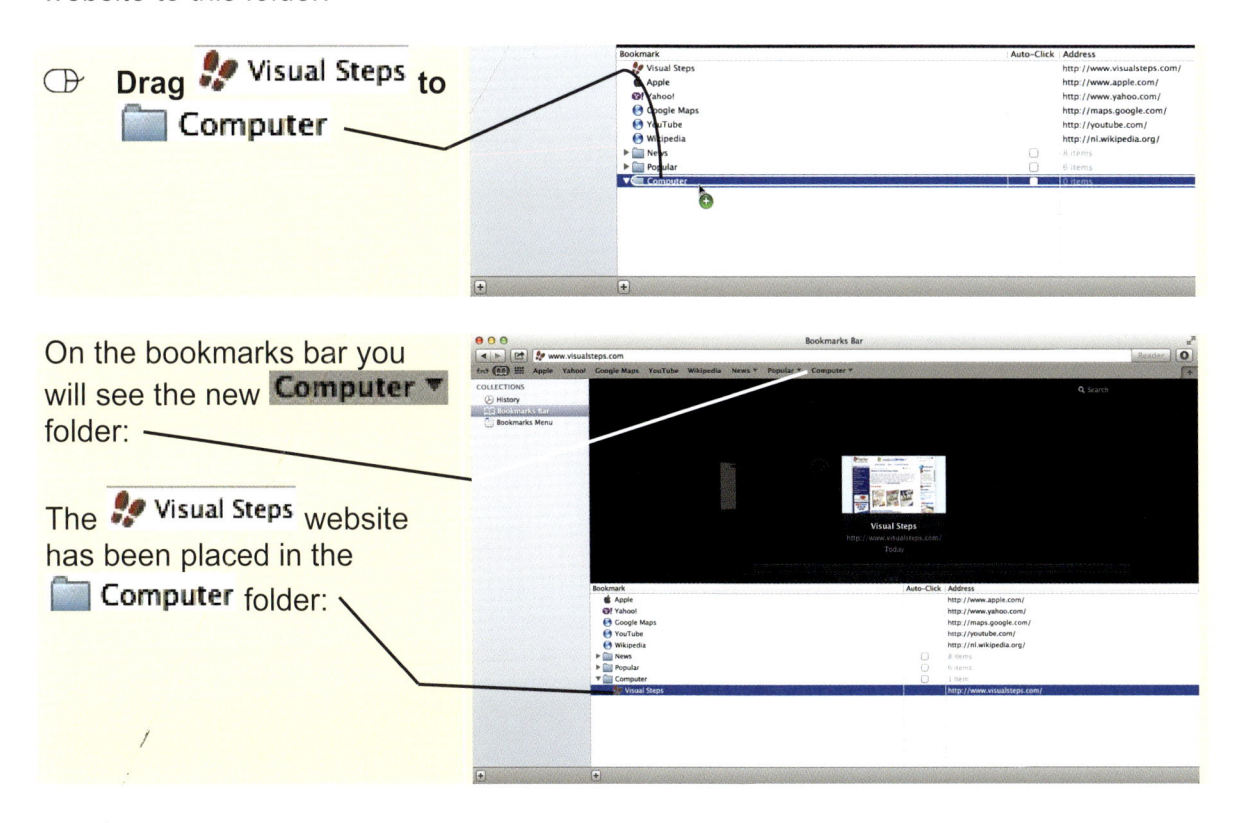

☞ **Drag** Visual Steps **to** Computer

On the bookmarks bar you will see the new **Computer** folder:

The Visual Steps website has been placed in the Computer folder:

💡 Tip
A folder within a bookmarks folder
You can organize your bookmark folders even further, by creating subfolders. For instance, you can divide the *Computer* folder by creating two subfolders called *Mac* and *iPad*:

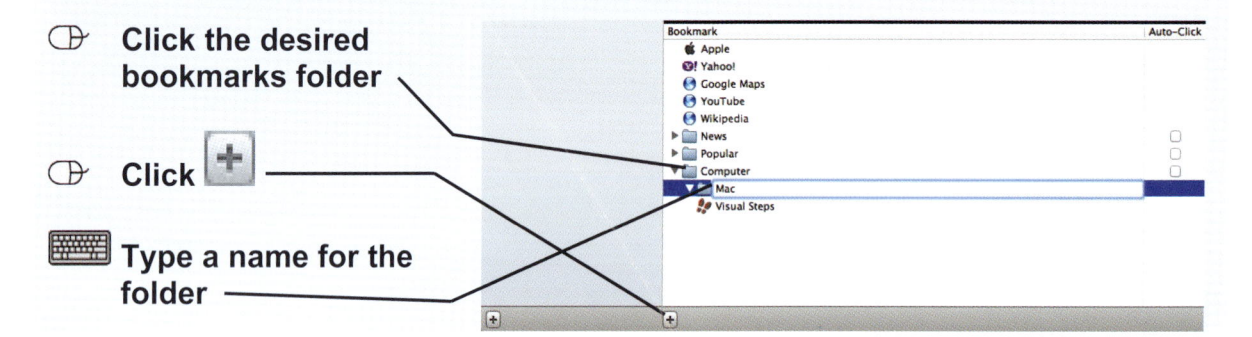

⌨ **Click the desired bookmarks folder**

⌨ **Click** ➕

⌨ **Type a name for the folder**

💡 Tip
Move a folder on the bookmarks bar
On the bookmarks bar, the bookmarks and bookmark folders are arranged in a specific order. But you can rearrange the order yourself, and allow a particular folder or bookmark to appear first or last for example, on the bookmarks bar:

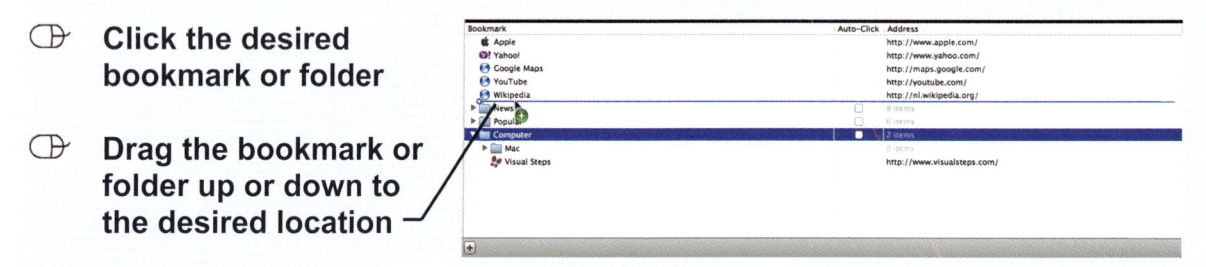

⌨ **Click the desired bookmark or folder**

⌨ **Drag the bookmark or folder up or down to the desired location**

Now the bookmark or folder has been moved to a different spot on the bookmarks bar.

You can close the bookmarks library and return to the website:

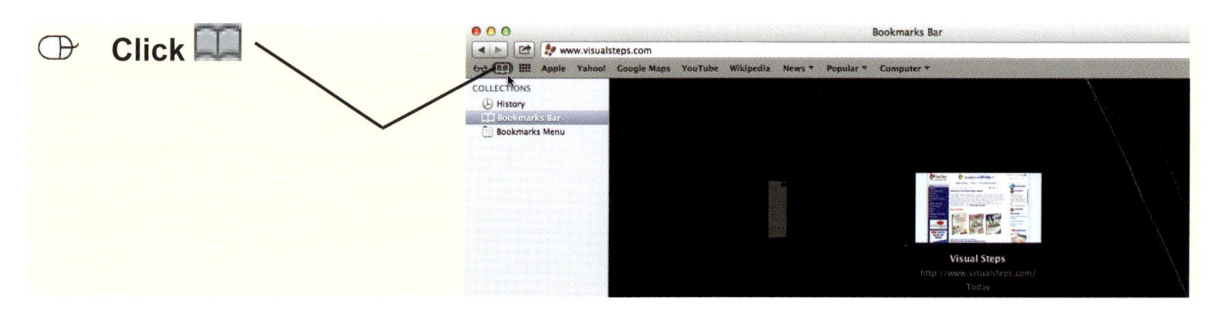

⌨ **Click** 📖

Chapter 5 Sending E-mails and Surfing the Internet Made Easier   **193**

5.7 Adding Bookmarks To the Bookmarks Menu

You can also add a bookmark to the *bookmarks menu*. You can use this menu when you want to go to a website for which you have previously created a bookmark. Using this menu will prevent the bookmarks bar from getting too full.
Here is how you add a bookmark to the bookmarks menu:

☞ Click

☞ Click
 Add Bookmark

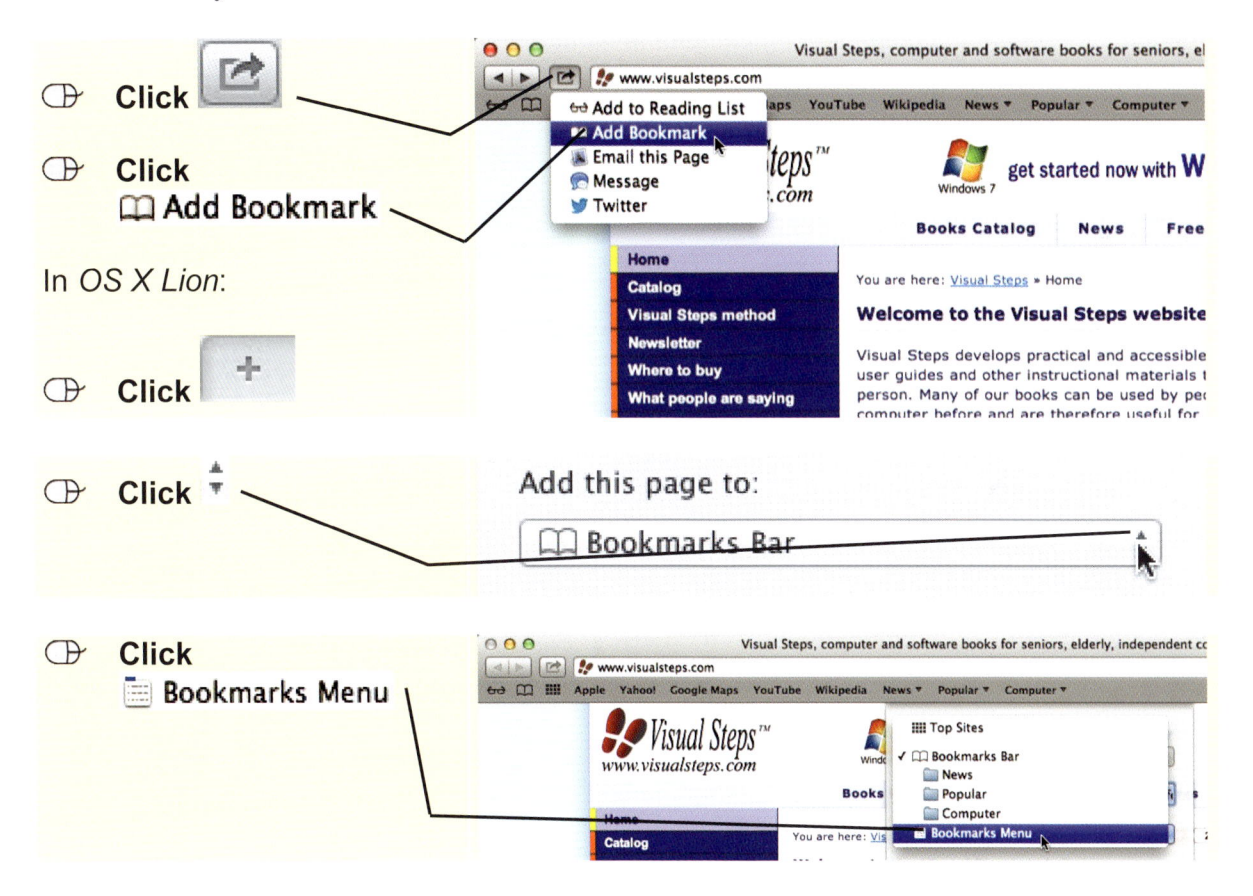

In *OS X Lion*:

☞ Click

☞ Click

☞ Click
 Bookmarks Menu

You can shorten a long name by using the Backspace key:

☞ **Click next to the name in the text box**

⌨ **Press until the name has been shortened to** Visual Steps

☞ **Click** Add

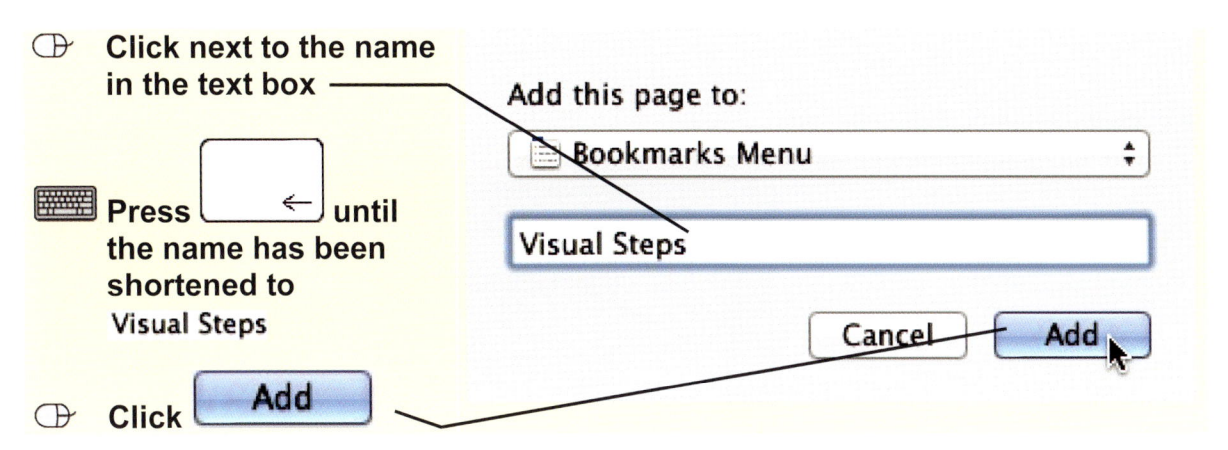

The bookmark has been added to the bookmarks menu. You can open a bookmark from the bookmarks menu like this:

☞ **First, open another website, for example, www.cnet.com website** ℘¹⁰

At the top of the window:

◯ Click **Bookmarks**

◯ Click **Visual Steps**

You will see the *Visual Steps* website:

5.8 Top Sites

Safari dynamically creates a list of the websites you visit most often. These websites are added to the *Top Sites* page. If you want to skip to your favorite website for a moment while reading another web page, you can open *Top Sites* in a new tab. The default setting is for *Top Sites* to open each time you add a new tab.

You need to enable the tab bar:

At the top of the window:

◯ Click **View**

◯ Click **Show Tab Bar**

Chapter 5 Sending E-mails and Surfing the Internet Made Easier **195**

⮕ Please note:
If you see **Hide Tab Bar**, the tab bar has already been enabled.

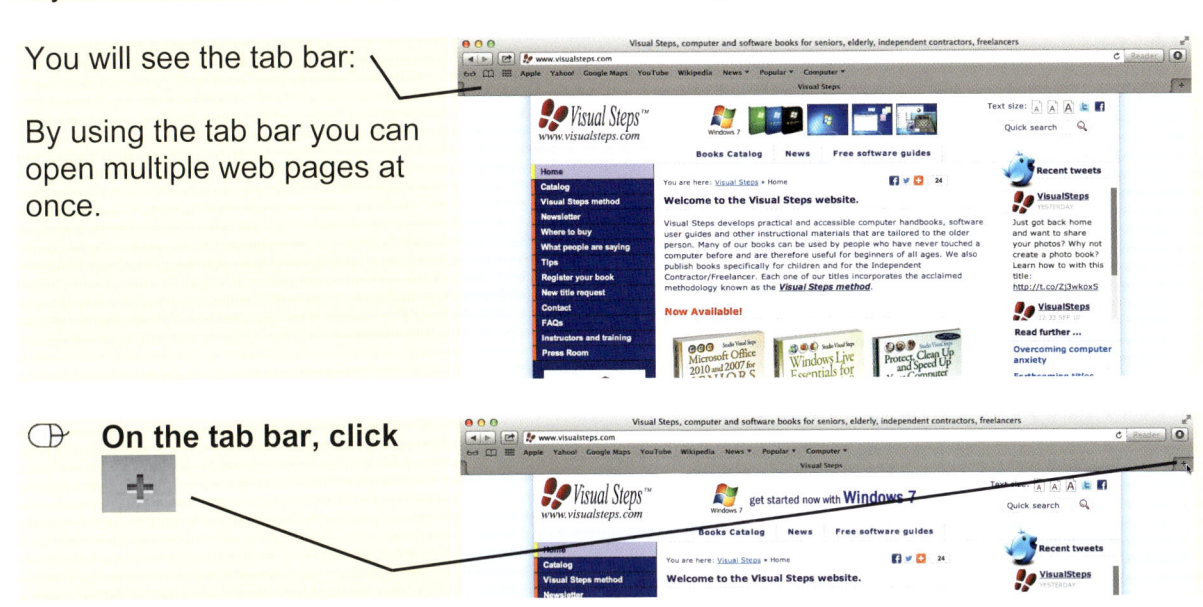

You will see the tab bar:

By using the tab bar you can open multiple web pages at once.

⊕ **On the tab bar, click**
➕

Top Sites will be opened in a new tab:

This page will look different on your own computer. You will see other websites based on your own surfing behavior.

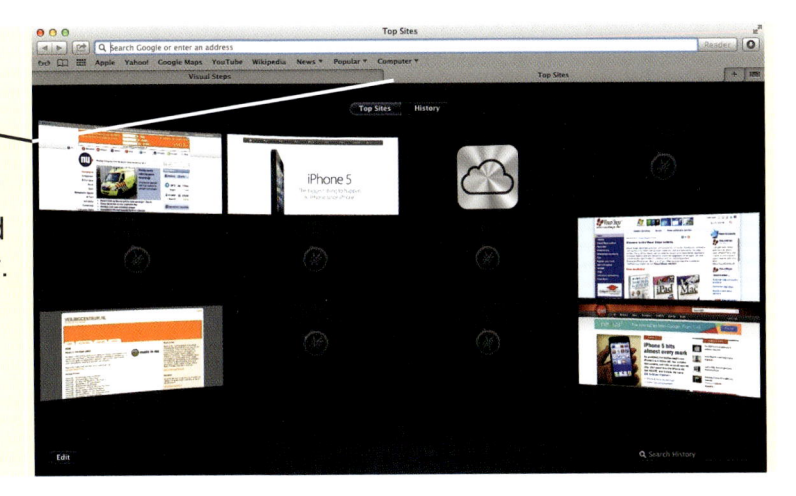

✖ HELP! Top Sites is not opened in a new tab
If *Top Sites* does not open automatically when you add a new tab, you can use the Command key to open it:

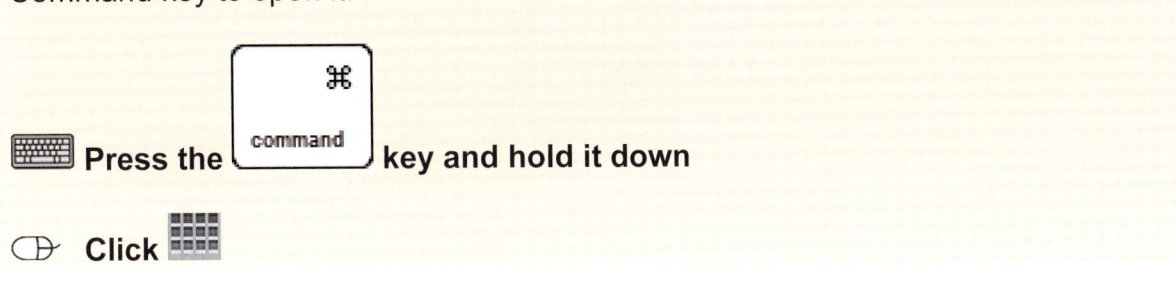

⌨ **Press the** ⌘ **command key and hold it down**

⊕ **Click** ▦

You can close the new tab and then open *Top Sites* in the first tab:

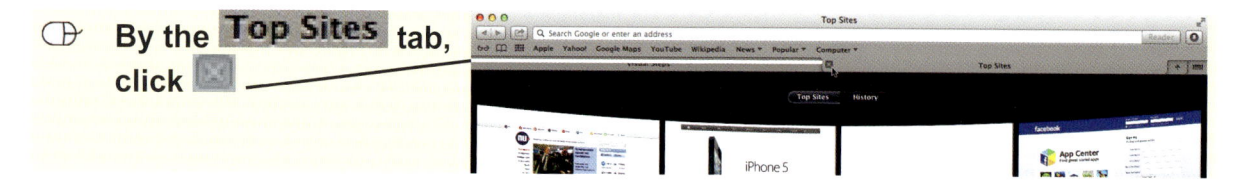

☞ **By the Top Sites tab, click ⊠**

Now you can open *Top Sites* in the current tab:

☞ **Click ▦**

The *Top Sites* page will be opened. You can surf easily to any of the websites shown:

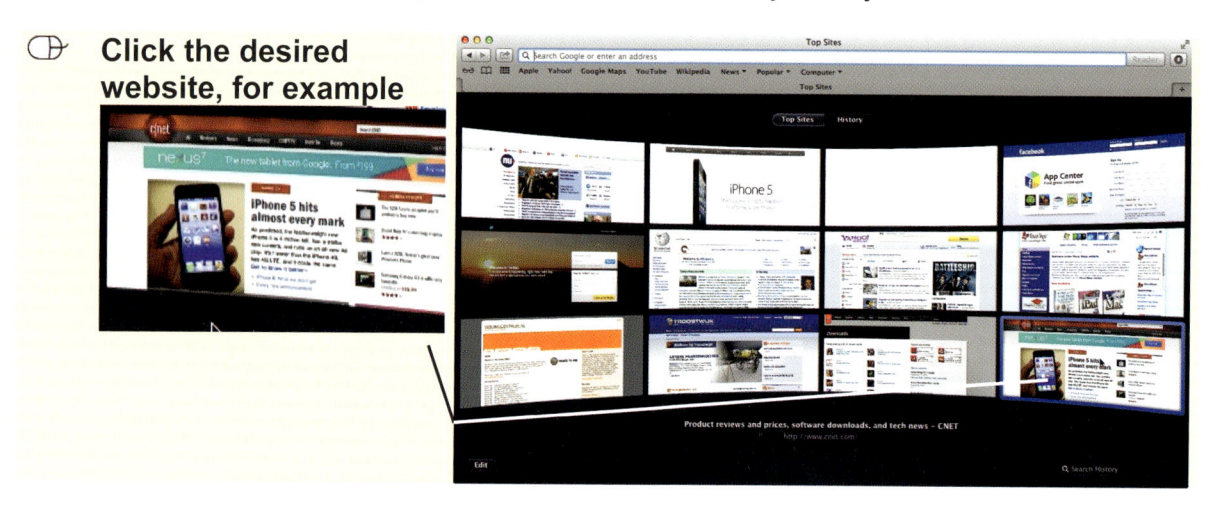

☞ **Click the desired website, for example**

In this example you see the cnet.com website:

This is a new website.

The web page will probably look different now.

☞ **Open the www.visualsteps.com website ⚘10**

Chapter 5 Sending E-mails and Surfing the Internet Made Easier **197**

5.9 Creating a Reading List

Safari has another nice feature called the *Reading List*. If you encounter an interesting page while surfing the net and you want to quietly take a look at the page later on, you can add the page to the *Reading List*. In the *Reading List* your saved web pages are shown in a separate pane. You can read these pages at your own convenience, even without an Internet connection. This is how you add a page to the reading list:

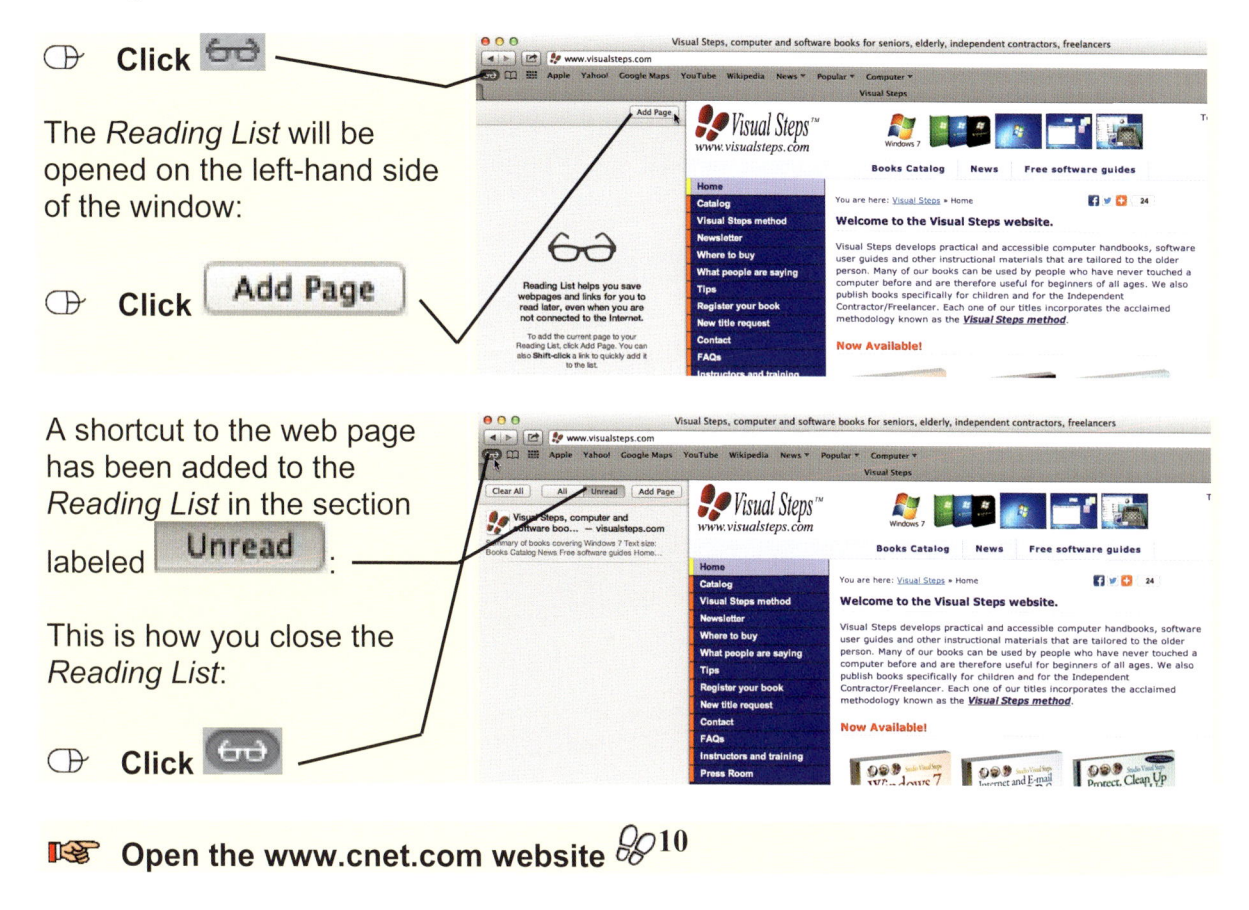

☞ **Click** 👓

The *Reading List* will be opened on the left-hand side of the window:

☞ **Click** `Add Page`

A shortcut to the web page has been added to the *Reading List* in the section labeled `Unread`:

This is how you close the *Reading List*:

☞ **Click** 👓

☞ **Open the www.cnet.com website** 👓 10

Now open a page that you have stored in the *Reading List*:

☞ **Click** 👓

☞ **Click the desired page**

The page will be opened:

You can close the *Reading List*:

⊕ **Click** 👓

After you have viewed the page, the shortcut will be removed from the [Unread] section of the *Reading List*. The shortcut will still be available in the section labeled [All]. In the *Tips* at the end of this chapter you can read how to completely remove the shortcut.

☞ **Stop *Safari*** 👣²

In this chapter you have learned how to use the mailbox feature in *Mail* to help you organize, search and work more efficiently with your email. You have also learned how to add a signature to an email message. In *Safari* you have learned how to manage your bookmarks and how to use the *Top Sites* and *Reading List* features. In short, you have seen how *Safari* can help you to surf and save websites more effectively.

Chapter 5 Sending E-mails and Surfing the Internet Made Easier **199**

5.10 Background Information

Dictionary

Bookmark	A web address stored in a list, so you can easily retrieve the web page later on.
Bookmark bar	A toolbar that contains shortcuts to your favorite websites.
Bookmark library	The pane or window where you can create, view and organize your bookmarks.
Bookmark menu	A menu with shortcuts to your favorite websites.
Conversation	A collection of sent and received email messages revolving around the same subject, which can be displayed together in *Mail*.
Email account	The server name, user name, password and email address used by *Mail* to connect to an email service.
FaceTime	With the *FaceTime* program you can make a video call over Wi-Fi or chat with other *FaceTime* users on a Mac, iPad, iPhone or an iPod touch.
iCloud	Storage space on an *Apple* server. With this service you can access your own documents and data from various devices which have *iOS 5* or higher installed.
iMessage	See *Messages*.
Inbox	The default mailbox in *Mail* that stores your newly-delivered messages.
Mail	A program for sending and receiving email messages.
Mailbox	A folder in *Mail* in which email messages are stored, such as the *Inbox*.

- Continue on the next page -

Messages	A program you can use to send short messages to anyone else using *Messages* on a *Mac* or *iMessage* on an iPhone, iPad or iPod touch. Requires *iOS 5* or higher.
Note	Notes you make in *Mail*, containing information you think important or interesting enough to save.
Notification Center	A feature used to display all the messages you have received on your *Mac*, such as new email messages, in an orderly fashion.
Reading List	A feature that lets you save web pages so you can read them later at your own convenience even without an Internet connection.
Reminders	In *Reminders* you can store important appointments or tasks.
Safari	The *Mac's* default browser application made by *Apple*.
Signature	A text containing name and address information that can be inserted at the end of an email message. A signature is often used in business emails to allow a quick exchange of contact information.
Smart mailbox	In a smart mailbox, messages from other mailboxes are displayed, provided they meet certain criteria. You can define a set of criteria (rules) yourself. In this way you can display all the emails sent by a specific sender, for instance.
Subfolder	A folder within a folder.
Top Sites	A feature exclusive to *Safari*. *Top Sites* keeps track of the websites you visit the most often. You can open these websites with a single mouse click from the *Top Sites* page.
Web browser	A computer program that can display web pages, such as *Safari*.
Wikipedia	An online encyclopedia maintained and edited by Internet users.

Source: Apple Dictionary, www.apple.com, Wikipedia

Chapter 5 Sending E-mails and Surfing the Internet Made Easier **201**

5.11 Tips

💡 Tip
Flag email messages in Mail
In *Mail* you can flag a message with a colored flag. It then becomes easier for you to find this message later on:

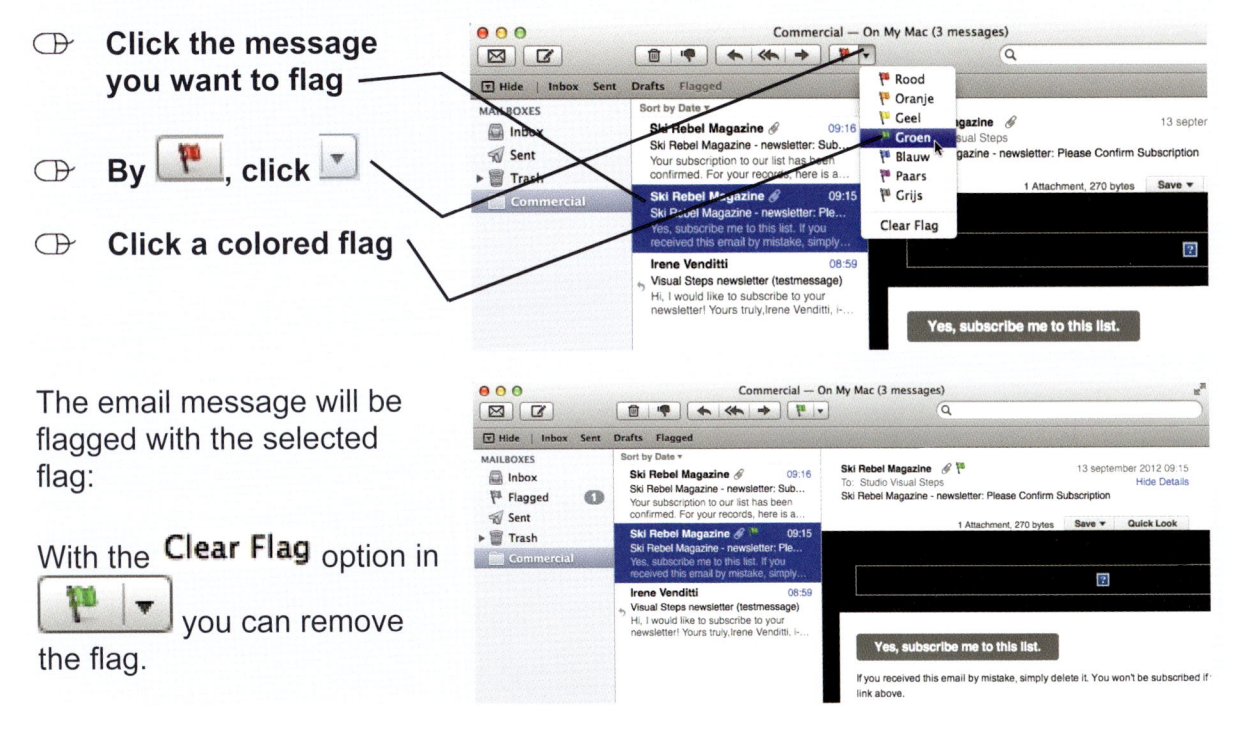

⊕ **Click the message you want to flag**

⊕ **By** 🚩 **, click** ▼

⊕ **Click a colored flag**

The email message will be flagged with the selected flag:

With the **Clear Flag** option in 🚩▼ you can remove the flag.

💡 Tip
Delete a shortcut from the Reading List
If the *Reading List* is getting too long, you can delete some of the shortcuts, like this:

⊕ **Position the mouse pointer on the shortcut you want to delete**

⊕ **Click** ⊗

- Continue on the next page -

The shortcut has been deleted:

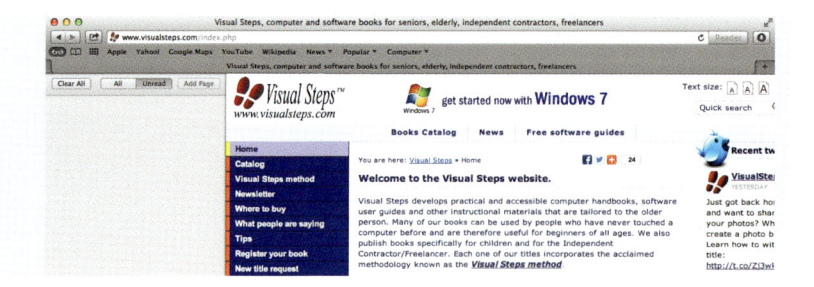

💡 Tip
Jot down a note
On the *Mac* you can jot down a note quickly with the *Notes* program. A note could contain important information or something you want to remember (a new recipe, a website link). This is how you create a note if you are using *Mountain Lion*:

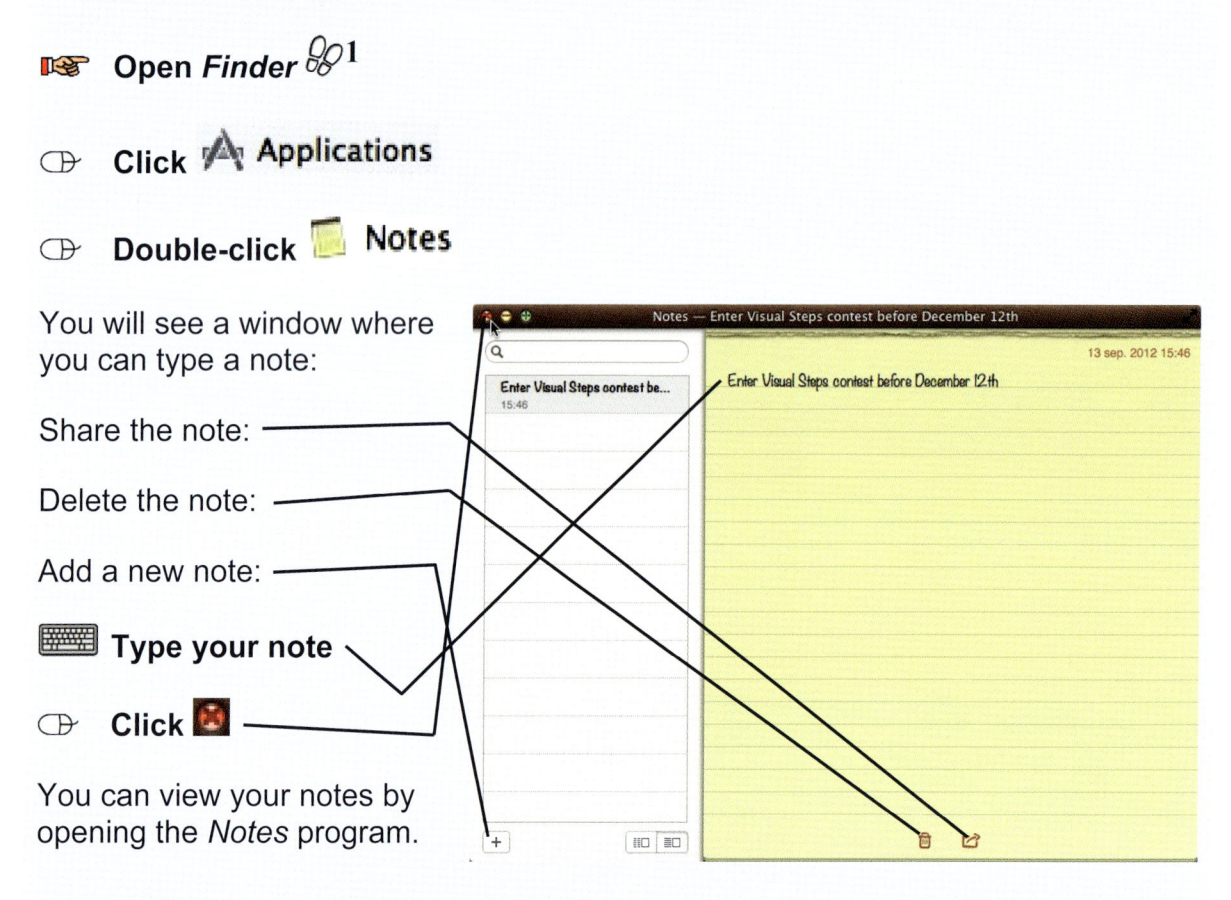

☞ **Open *Finder*** 👣¹

⊕ **Click 🅐 Applications**

⊕ **Double-click 📝 Notes**

You will see a window where you can type a note:

Share the note:

Delete the note:

Add a new note:

⌨ **Type your note**

⊕ **Click** 📤

You can view your notes by opening the *Notes* program.

Notes can work together with *iCloud*, if this service is activated. If you create or edit a note on your *Mac*, the same note along with any recent changes appears on your iPhone, iPad or iPod touch. You can find more information about this subject in the *Bonus Chapter 7 iCloud* on the website accompanying this book
www.visualsteps.com/iphotomac

Chapter 5 Sending E-mails and Surfing the Internet Made Easier **203**

In *OS X Lion* you can also take notes within the *Mail* program:

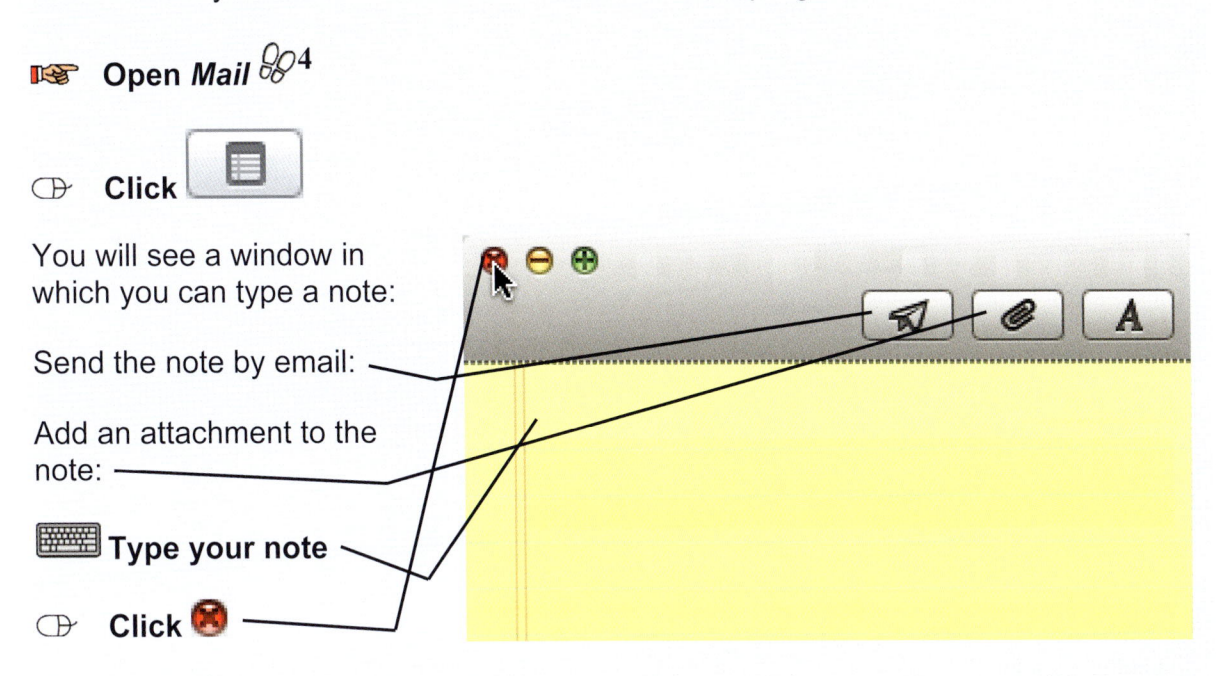

☞ **Open** *Mail* ⚘⁴

☞ **Click** [icon]

You will see a window in which you can type a note:

Send the note by email:

Add an attachment to the note:

⌨ **Type your note**

☞ **Click** 🔴

Notes are collected in *Notes*.

💡 **Tip**
Create a smart mailbox
Along with the regular mailboxes found in *Mail*, you can also create *smart mailboxes.* In a smart mailbox, messages from other mailboxes are displayed, provided they meet certain criteria. You can define a set of criteria (rules) yourself. For instance, you can display all the emails from the same sender:

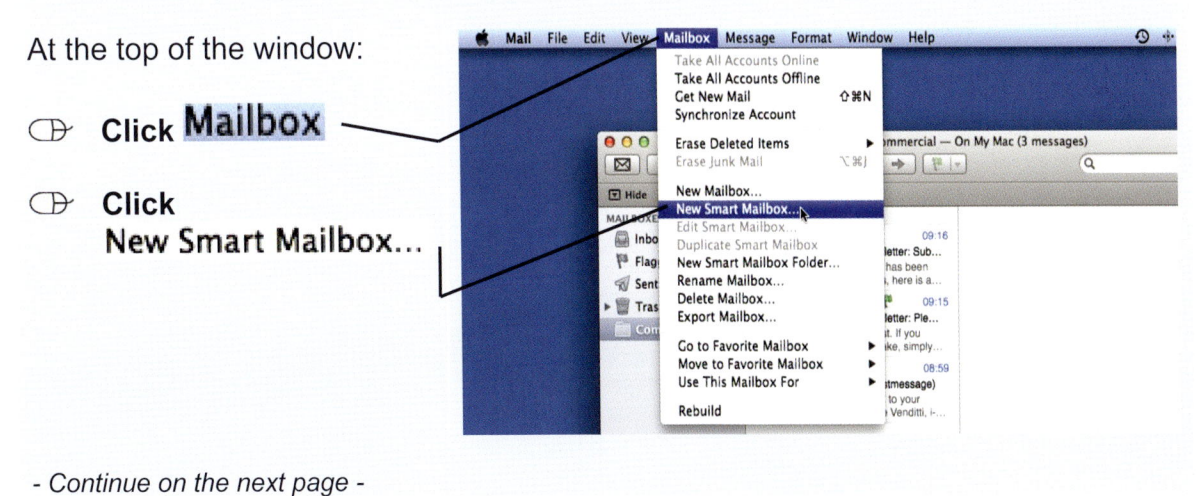

At the top of the window:

☞ **Click Mailbox**

☞ **Click New Smart Mailbox...**

- Continue on the next page -

⌨️ **By** Smart Mailbox Name:, **type the desired name**

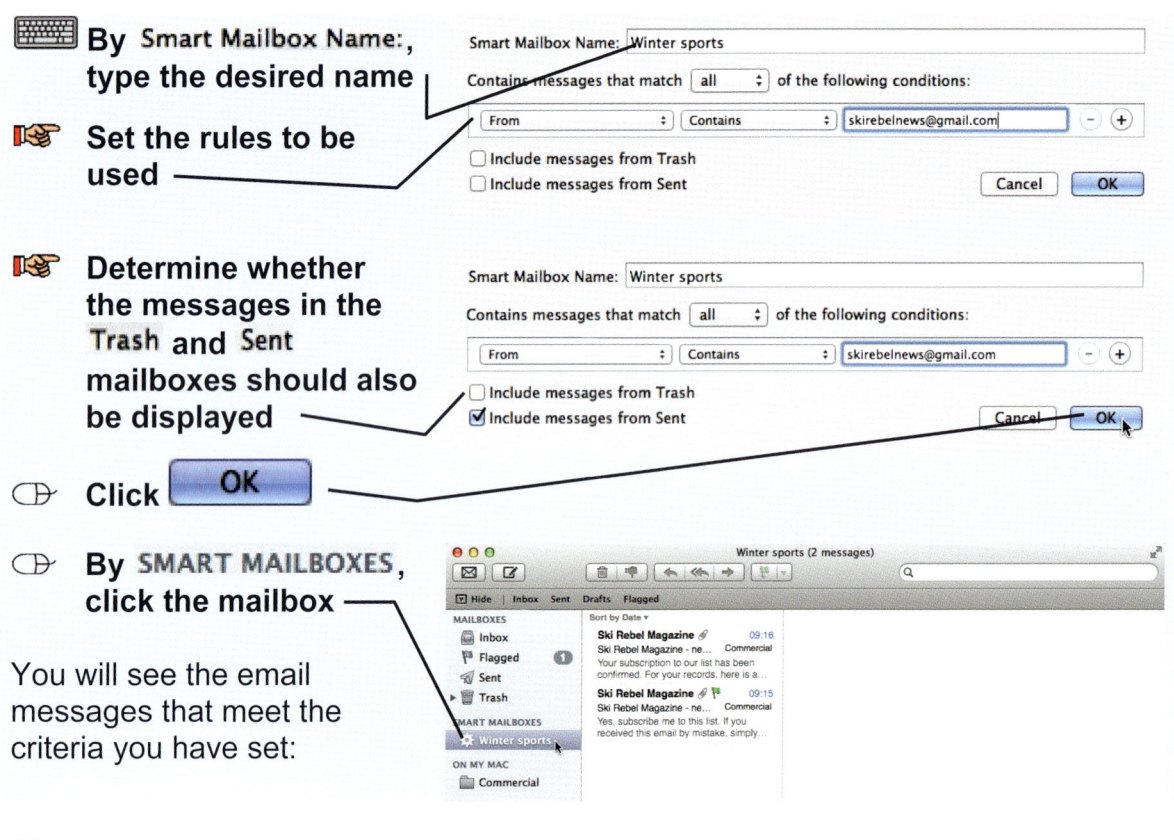

☞ **Set the rules to be used**

☞ **Determine whether the messages in the** Trash **and** Sent **mailboxes should also be displayed**

⃝ **Click** OK

⃝ **By** SMART MAILBOXES, **click the mailbox**

You will see the email messages that meet the criteria you have set:

💡 Tip
Delete a bookmark or folder from the bookmarks bar
If you no longer use a certain bookmark, you can delete it from the bookmarks bar:

⃝ **Click** 📖

⃝ **If necessary, click** 📖 Bookmarks Bar

⃝ **Click the bookmark or folder you want to delete**

⌨️ **Press** ⬅ **(Backspace)**

Now the bookmark or folder has been deleted from the bookmarks bar.

If the bookmark you want to delete is stored in a folder:

⃝ **Double-click the folder**
⃝ **Click the bookmark you want to delete**

⌨️ **Press** ⬅ **(Backspace)**

Chapter 5 Sending E-mails and Surfing the Internet Made Easier **205**

💡 Tip
Reminders in Mountain Lion
You can use *Reminders* in a similar fashion as *Notes*, with the exception that each task or "reminder" is connected to a date and time. This can help you remember something that needs to be done before a certain date, for instance. This is how you add a new task:

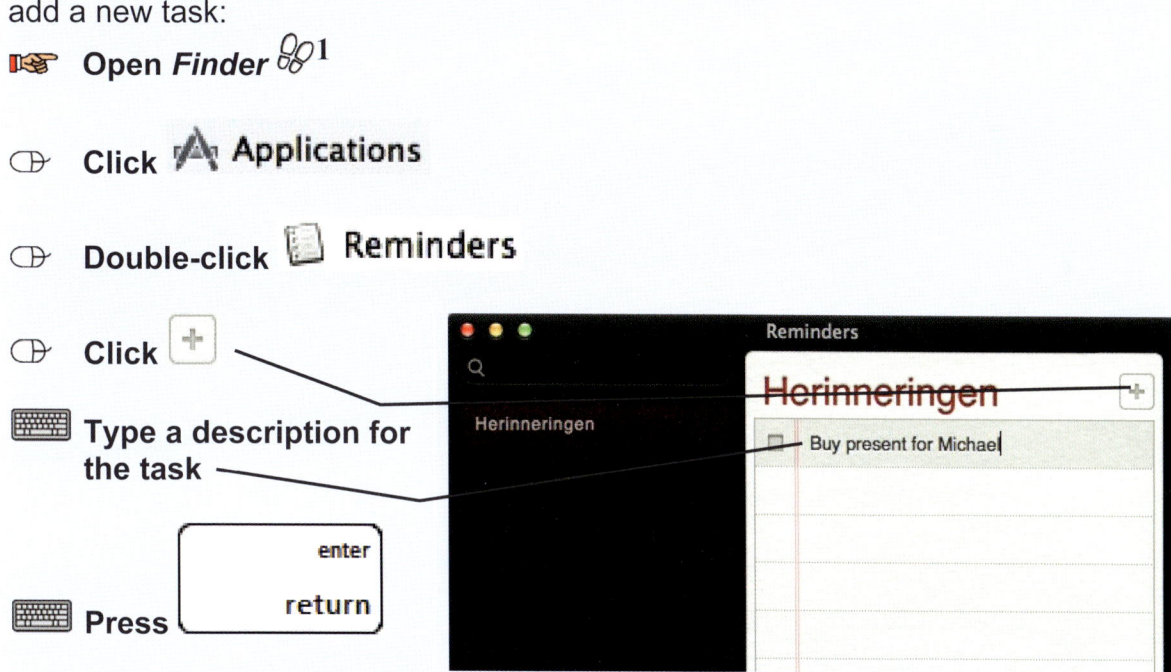

☞ **Open *Finder*** 🐾¹

⊕ **Click** 🅰 **Applications**

⊕ **Double-click** 📔 **Reminders**

⊕ **Click** ➕

⌨ **Type a description for the task**

⌨ **Press** ⏎ enter / return

When you have added a task to the task list, you can also add additional information, such as the day and time for when you want to receive the reminder:

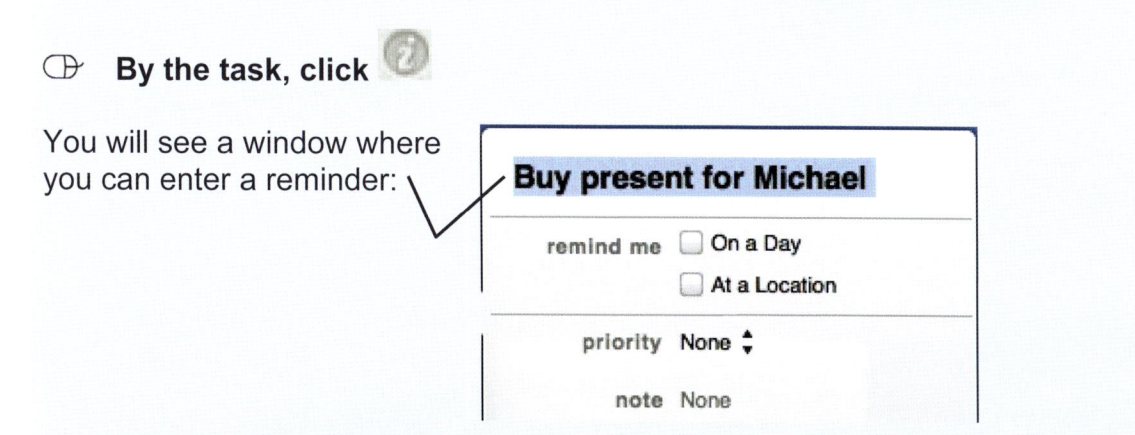

⊕ **By the task, click** ⓘ

You will see a window where you can enter a reminder:

iCloud keeps all your reminders and any changes made to them up-to-date on your Mac, iPad, iPhone and iPod touch. You can find more information about *iCloud* in the *Bonus Chapter 7 iCloud* on the website accompanying this book **www.visualsteps.com/iphotomac**

💡 Tip
Notification Center in Mountain Lion
The *Notification Center* provides a summary of all messages received (alerts) from various programs (apps) on the *Mac*. You can open the notification center like this:

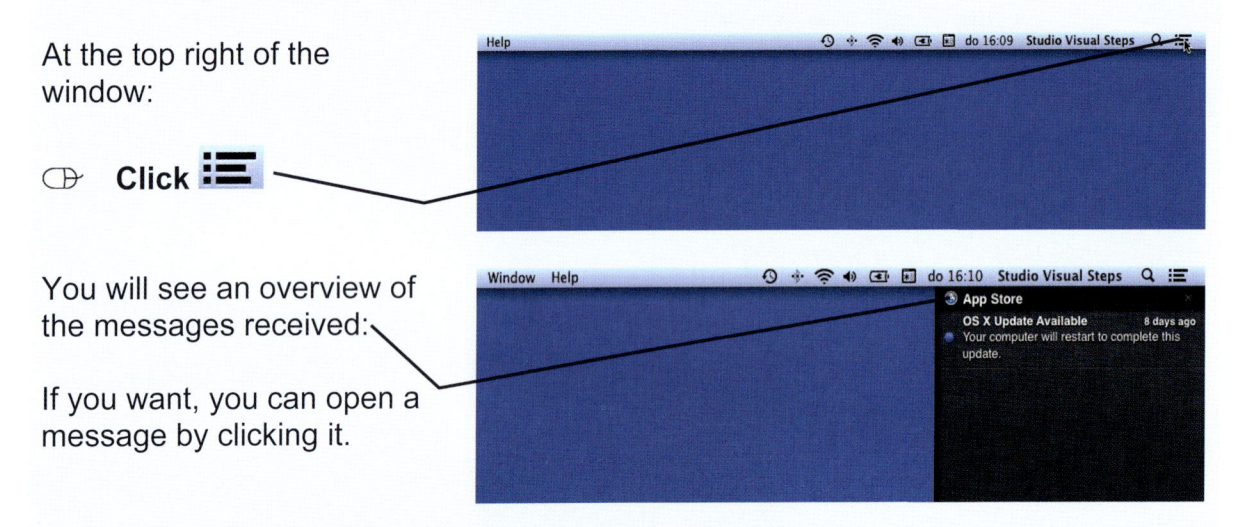

At the top right of the window:

☞ **Click** ≣

You will see an overview of the messages received:

If you want, you can open a message by clicking it.

You can also open the *Notification Center* by dragging two fingers across the trackpad, from right to left.

To change or view the settings, you need to do this:

☞ **Click** ⚙, **Notifications**

You will see this window. For each program you can indicate whether you want to receive a notification and in what form:

Chapter 5 Sending E-mails and Surfing the Internet Made Easier

💡 Tip
Internet calls with FaceTime
With the *FaceTime* program you can make calls using a Wi-Fi connection with other *FaceTime* users on a Mac, iPad, iPhone or an iPod touch.

☞ **Open *Finder*** 📖¹

⌘ **Click** 🅰 **Applications**

⌘ **Double-click** 📷 **FaceTime**

You will see the *FaceTime* window:

If you already have an account, you can sign in right away:

If you do not have an account, you can create one:

After you have signed in you will see the names of your contacts:

⌘ **Click a contact**

⌘ **Click the contact's email address**

If you want to call your contact on an iPhone, you need to select the phone number here.

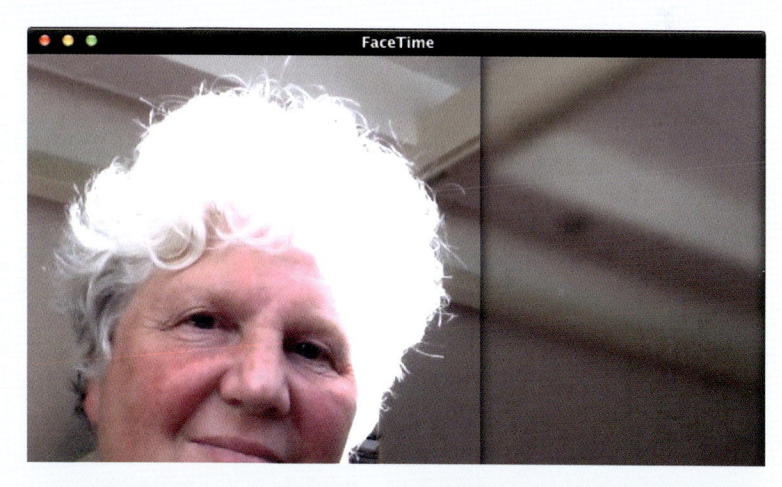

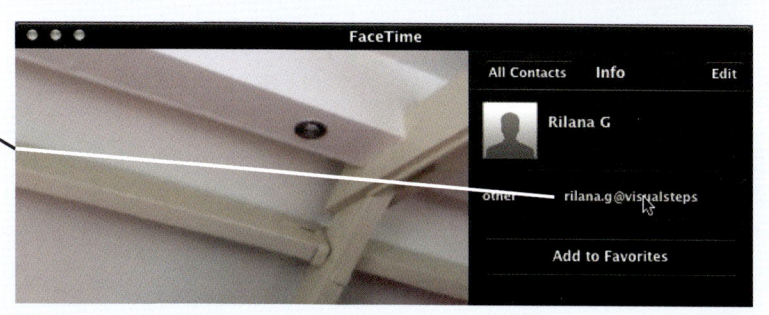

- Continue on the next page -

A connection will be made with your contact. If your contact is already signed in with *FaceTime*, and he or she accepts the call, you can start a video conversation.

💡 Tip
iMessages - Mountain Lion
With *iMessages* you can send messages to anyone using a Mac, iPad, iPhone or an iPod touch with *iOS 5* or higher installed. The messages will be displayed on your *Mac* and on every device you use if you have activated *iCloud*. You can send photos, movies, documents and contact information. If you want to use this program you will need to have an *Apple ID*. If you do not have an *Apple* ID, you can read how to create one in the *Bonus Chapter 8 Creating an Apple ID* on the website accompanying this book **www.visualsteps.com/iphotomac** This is how you send a message:

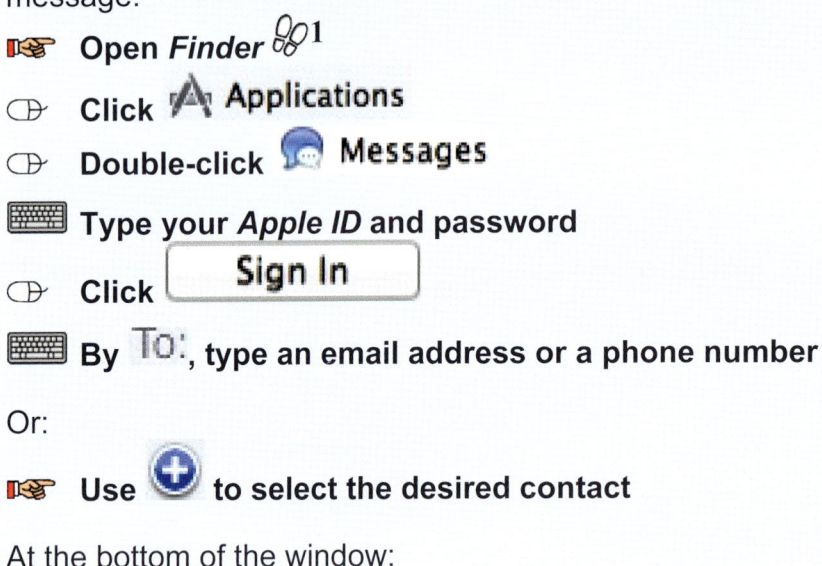

☞ **Open *Finder*** ℘¹

⊕ **Click Applications**

⊕ **Double-click Messages**

⌨ **Type your *Apple ID* and password**

⊕ **Click Sign In **

⌨ **By To:, type an email address or a phone number**

Or:

☞ **Use ⊕ to select the desired contact**

At the bottom of the window:

⌨ **Type a message**

To send the message:

⌨ **Press enter return **

The message will be sent. In this example the recipient has also sent a message back. In this way you can quickly communicate with one another.

6. Managing Data

The computer is an ideal device for managing, storing and securing important data. The *Mac* is equipped with a number of special programs that will help you manage your data in various ways, and make life a whole lot easier.

One of these programs is called *Contacts*. As you can tell by the name, you can use this program to work with people's addresses. You can use the program together with *Mail*, but also as a separate address book.

Besides using an address book, a virtual calendar can come in handy too. With *Calendar* you can keep track of all your appointments and set a reminder to warn you when the specific date and time occurs.

Widgets are tiny and often very useful programs, manufactured by third parties in order to give extra functionality to *Mac*. These small programs usually perform a single task such as one that displays the current weather forecast. You can manage these widgets with the *Dashboard* program.

In this chapter you will learn how to:

- manage addresses;
- manage your calendar;
- manage widgets with *Dashboard*.

Please note:

The screenshots in this chapter are made on a *Mac* running the *Mountain Lion* operating system. If you have a *Mac* running *OS X Lion* you may notice that certain programs have a different name. We will mention this in the relevant section when this occurs.

6.1 Managing Addresses

Almost everyone owns a physical address book containing the addresses of family, friends, acquaintances, local businesses and more. It is often quite a hassle to write down so much data, especially when people move to a new address or there is a change to a phone number. You may have to cross everything out and start over again. As a result, the address book becomes messy and difficult to use. If you use the *Contacts* program you will not need to worry about these things. Furthermore, it will become much easier for you to find specific addresses and keep them updated. You can use *Contacts* together with *Mail*. But you can also use it all on its own, as a separate program. You can even synchronize your contacts with the *iCloud* service. In this way you can open your contact information on other devices such as an iPad or iPhone, if you own one. You can read more about this topic in the *Bonus Chapter 7 iCloud* on the website that accompanies this book:
www.visualsteps.com/popularmac

☞ **Open *Finder*** ⬚¹

⊕ **Click** **Applications**

⊕ **Double-click** **Contacts**

You will see the *Contacts* window. It looks just like a real address book:

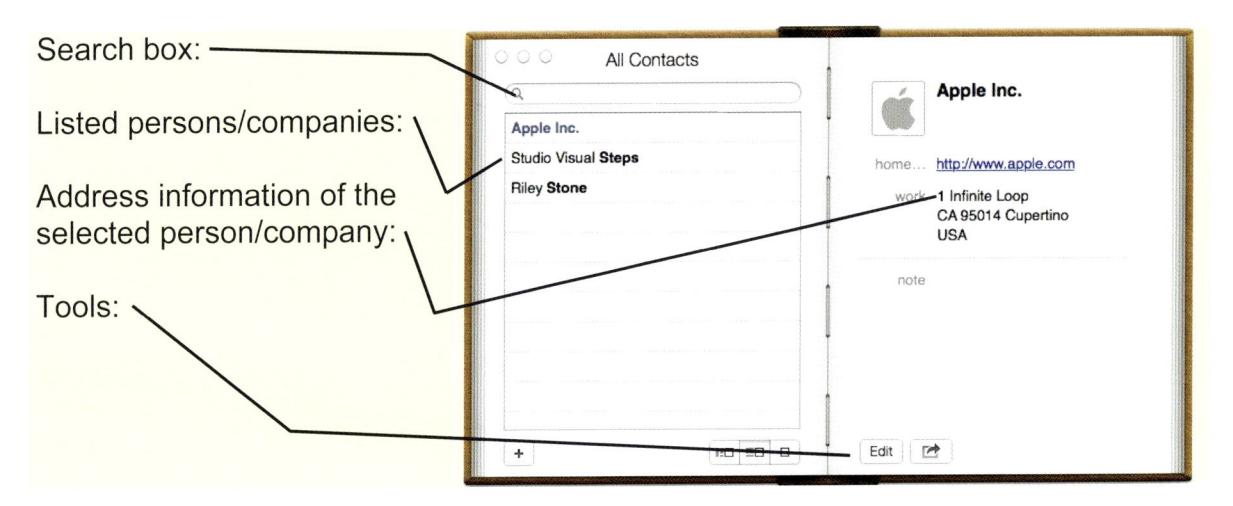

Search box:

Listed persons/companies:

Address information of the selected person/company:

Tools:

Chapter 6 Managing Data **211**

6.2 Adding an Address

When you open *Contacts* for the first time, the program will probably already contain a few of your contacts' addresses. These may be addresses added by *Apple* or addresses you have added yourself in *Mail*. In the *Tips* at the end of this chapter you can read how to add an address through *Mail*.

You can also add an address manually to *Contacts*:

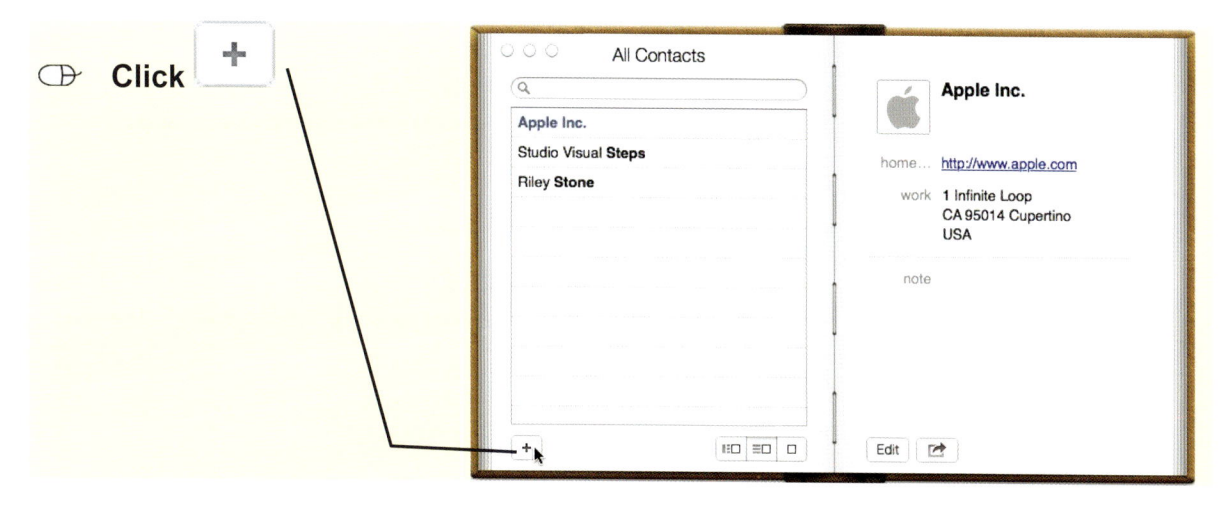

☞ **Click** ➕

A new *card* will be created. This is the name used by the *Contacts* program for a new page with the address and other information from a single contact.

Now you can enter the data for this contact. In this example, you will be adding information about a fictional person:

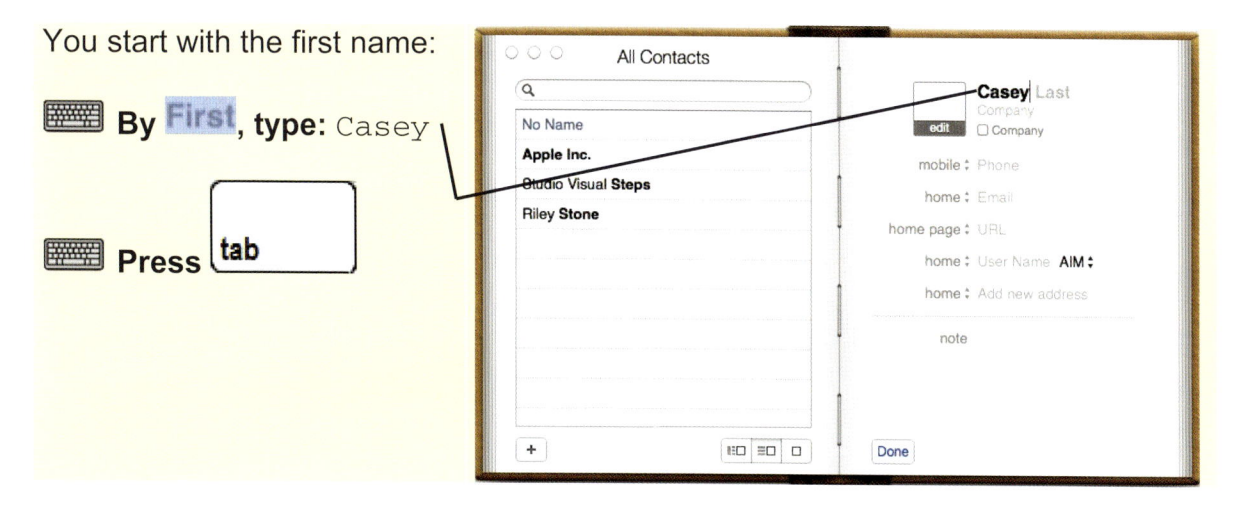

You start with the first name:

⌨ **By** First**, type:** Casey

⌨ **Press** tab

The first name has been entered:

Now you can type the last name:

⌨ By `Last`, type:
Patterson

⌨ Press `tab`

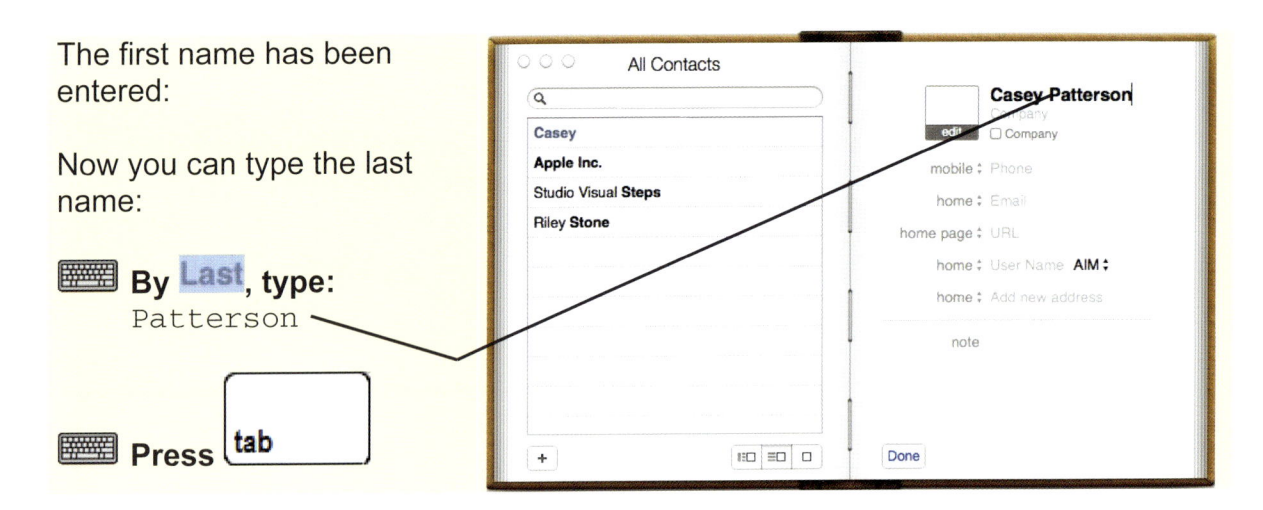

The last name has been entered. You can enter more information in the following text box (or field) in the same manner, step by step. You do not need to fill in every text box. Just enter the information that is relevant to you. You can skip the other fields:

You can skip the company name, for example:

⌨ Press `tab`

You can also simply click any box to start entering the data right away.

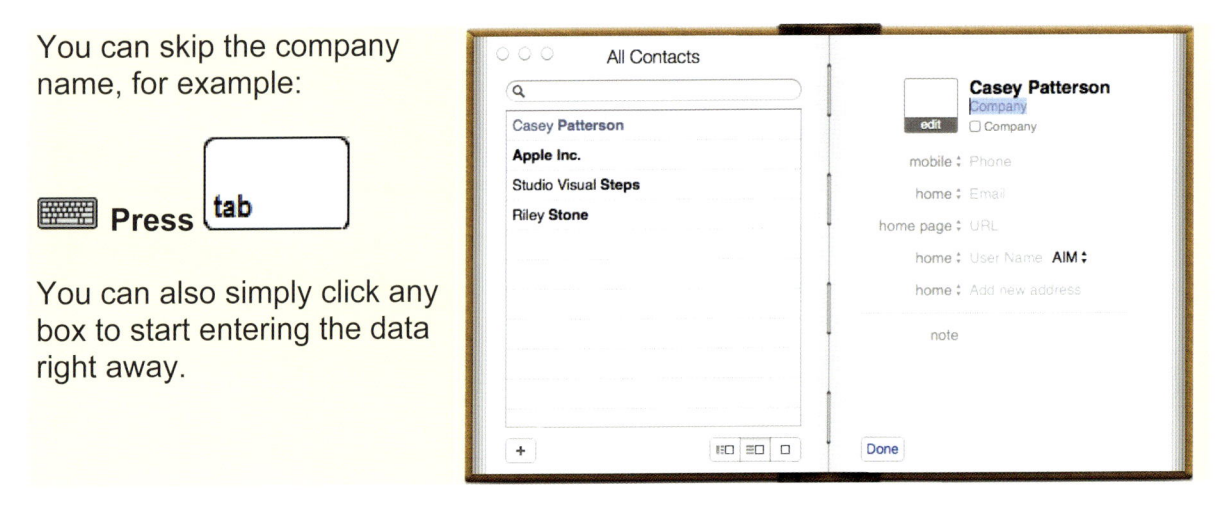

☞ Enter the desired information, for example, a phone number

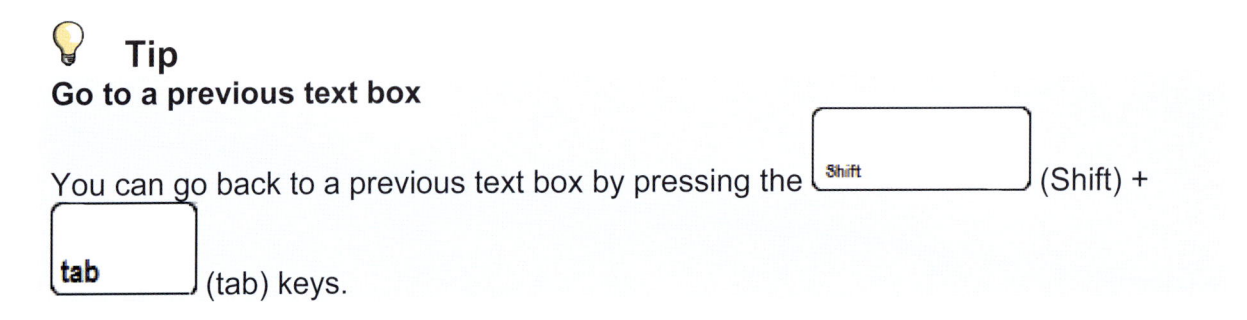

💡 Tip
Go to a previous text box

You can go back to a previous text box by pressing the `Shift` (Shift) + `tab` (tab) keys.

Chapter 6 Managing Data   **213**

For most types of data you can select the type of information that will be displayed:

- ☞ By mobile, click ⇕

You will see a list of options:

- ☞ Click work

☞ Type a phone number, if you want

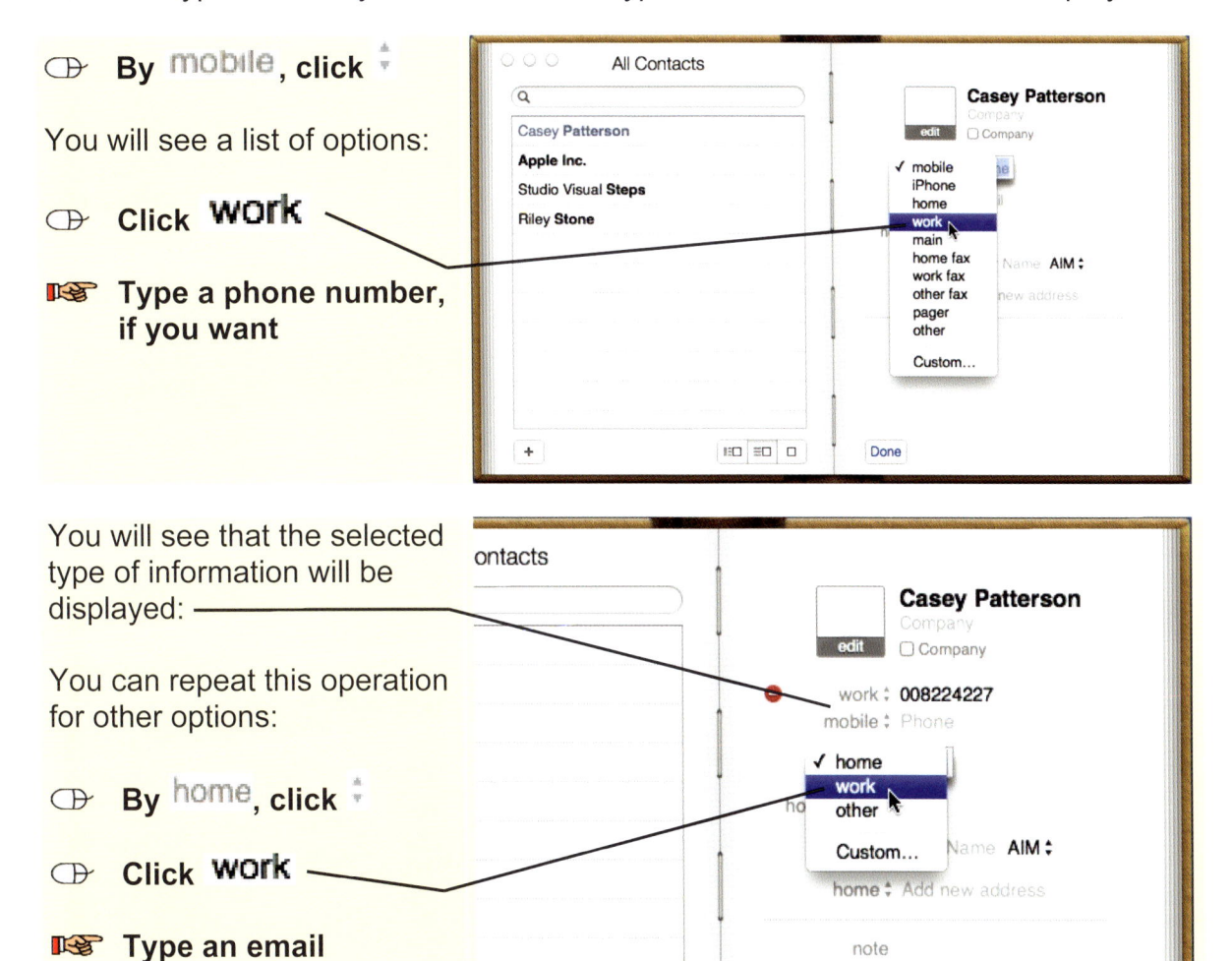

You will see that the selected type of information will be displayed:

You can repeat this operation for other options:

- ☞ By home, click ⇕

- ☞ Click work

☞ Type an email address, if you want

When you have finished entering the data, you need to save the card:

- ☞ Click Done

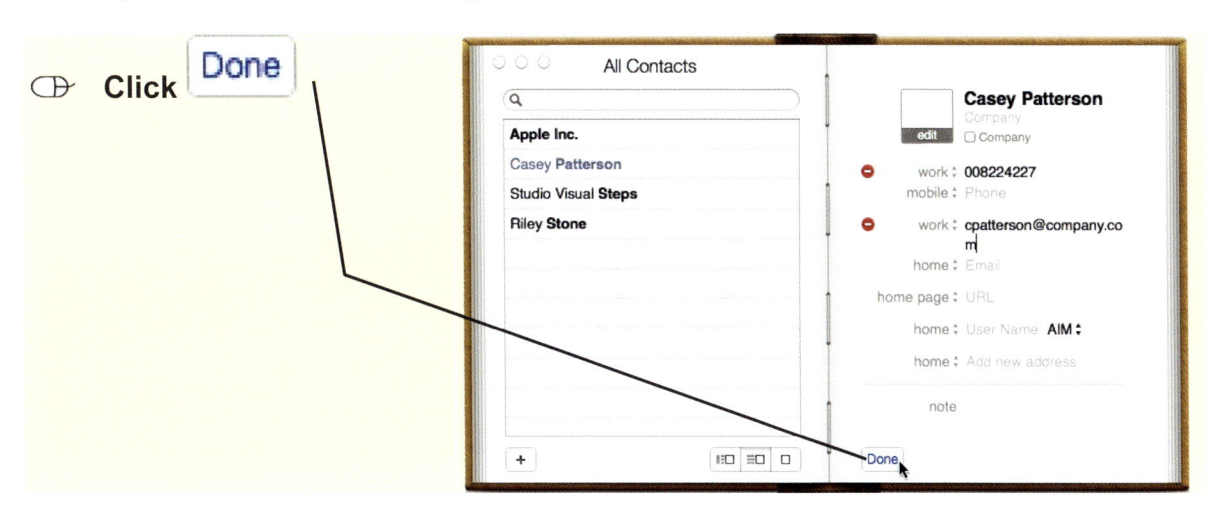

You will see that the card has been added:

Only the fields that were filled in are displayed:

If you want to change the information on the card you click the contact and then click Edit.

6.3 Searching for an Address

There are different ways of looking up information in your address book. The most straightforward manner is to just click the name of a contact in the address book:

☞ **Click the contact you want to view**

You will see the address and perhaps other information for this contact:

If your address book contains many contacts, you can use the search box to find them:

⌨ **Type a person's name in the search box, for instance:** patterson

With each character you type the names of the contacts are filtered:

☞ **Click the desired contact**

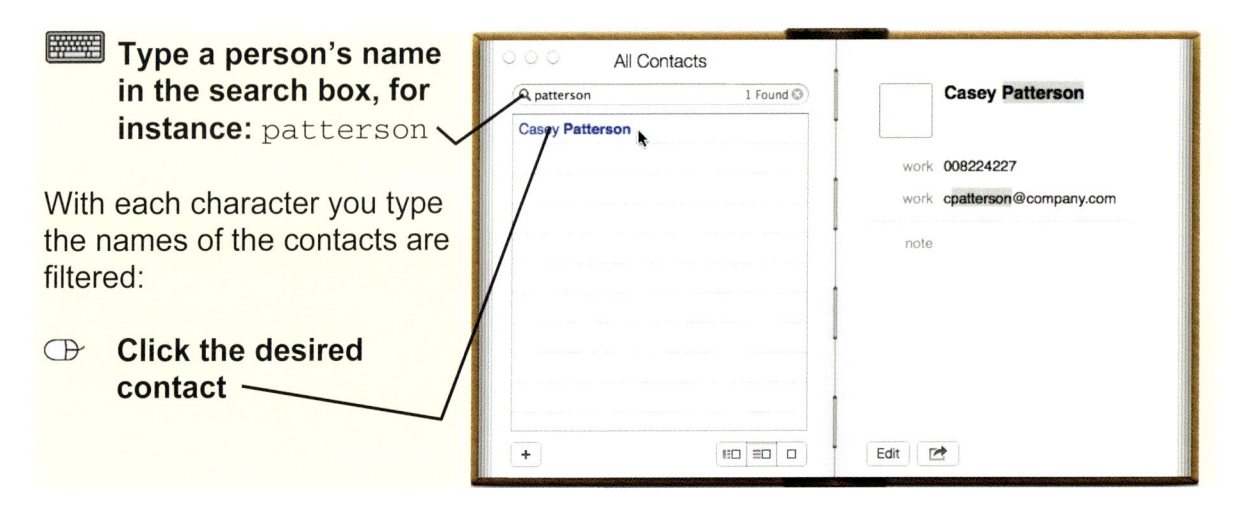

Chapter 6 Managing Data 215

You will see the address and if entered, other information for this contact.

You can close the query:

⊕ Click ⊗

6.4 Deleting a Card

If you no longer need the data from a certain contact, you can delete the contact:

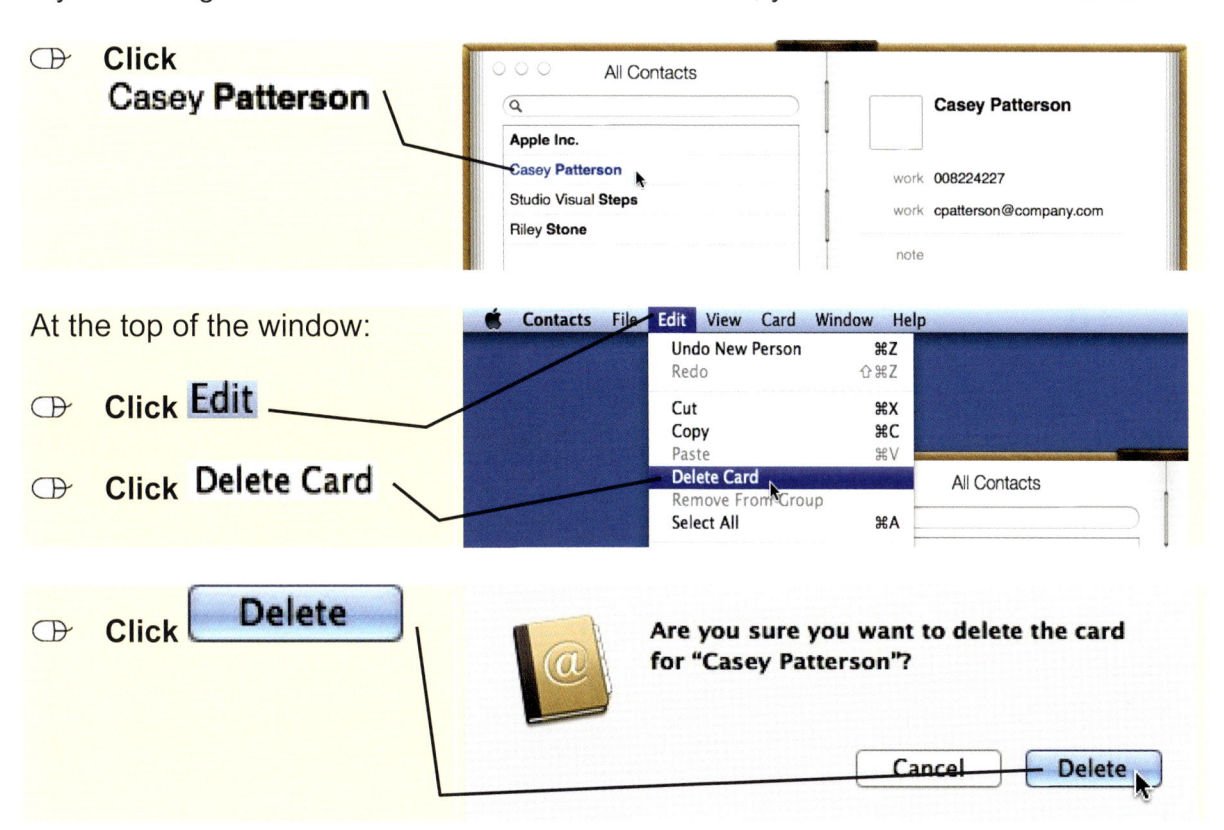

⊕ Click **Casey Patterson**

At the top of the window:

⊕ Click **Edit**

⊕ Click **Delete Card**

⊕ Click **Delete**

The card and all of its data has been deleted.

☞ Stop *Contacts* ⚏²

☞ Close *Finder* ⚏³

6.5 Keeping a Calendar

Not only can you use your *Mac* to manage contact information, you can also use it for managing your appointments. For this task you can use *Calendar*.
This program has several great options. You can keep multiple calendars, for example, a private and a work calendar, and you can set reminders to alert you of important upcoming appointments, birthdays and other events.
This is how you open *Calendar*:

☞ **Open *Finder*** ✤¹

⊙ **Click** 🅰 **Applications**

⊙ **Double-click** 📅 **Calendar**

In *Mountain Lion*:

⊙ **Double-click** 📅 **iCal**

You will see the *Calendar* window. It looks just like a regular paper calendar:

Type of calendar:

Period displayed:

Days and hours:

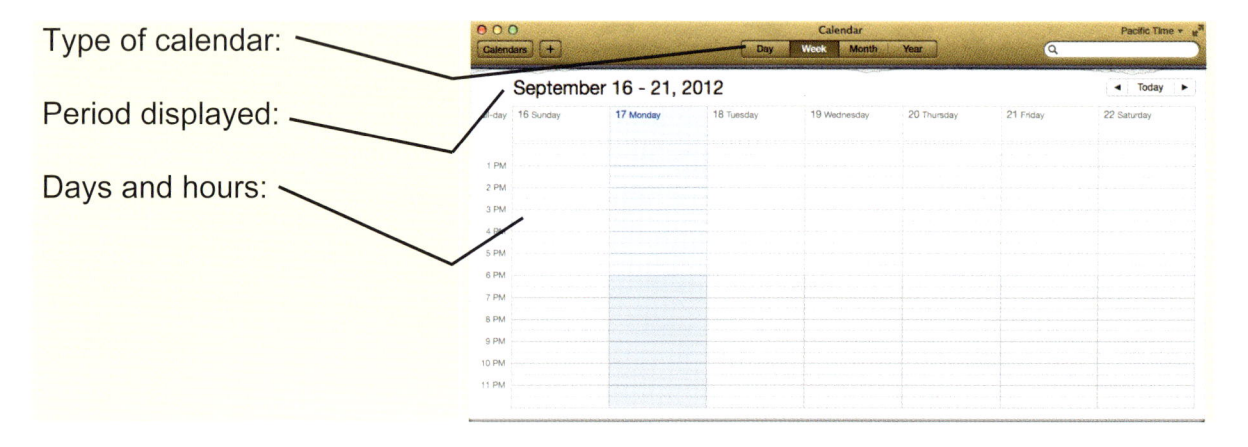

Chapter 6 Managing Data   **217**

6.6 Choosing a Calendar

In *Calendar* you can choose different kinds of calendars. You can select a calendar for personal use or a work-related calendar. In this way you can separate your personal appointments from your work commitments:

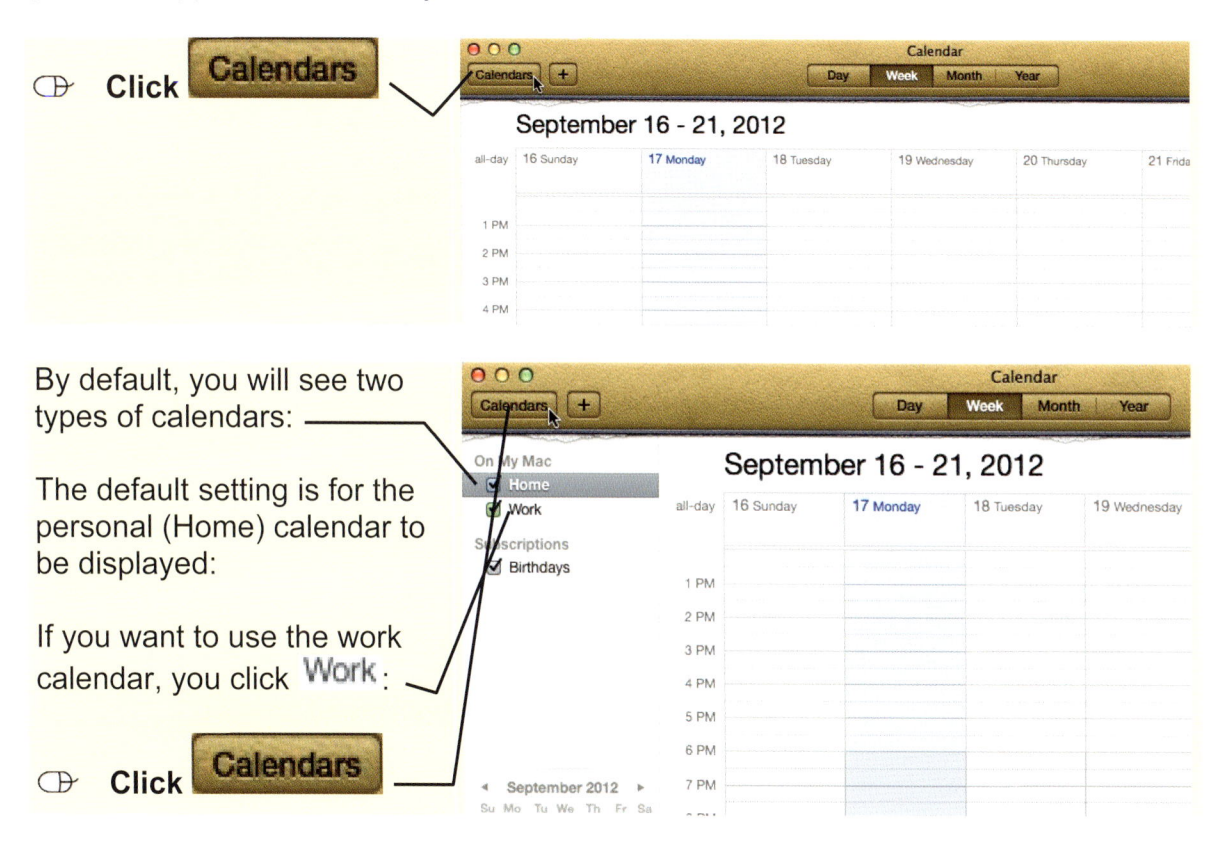

☞ **Click** `Calendars`

By default, you will see two types of calendars:

The default setting is for the personal (Home) calendar to be displayed:

If you want to use the work calendar, you click `Work`:

☞ **Click** `Calendars`

The other choice you can make is whether you want to view your calendar per day, week, month, or year:

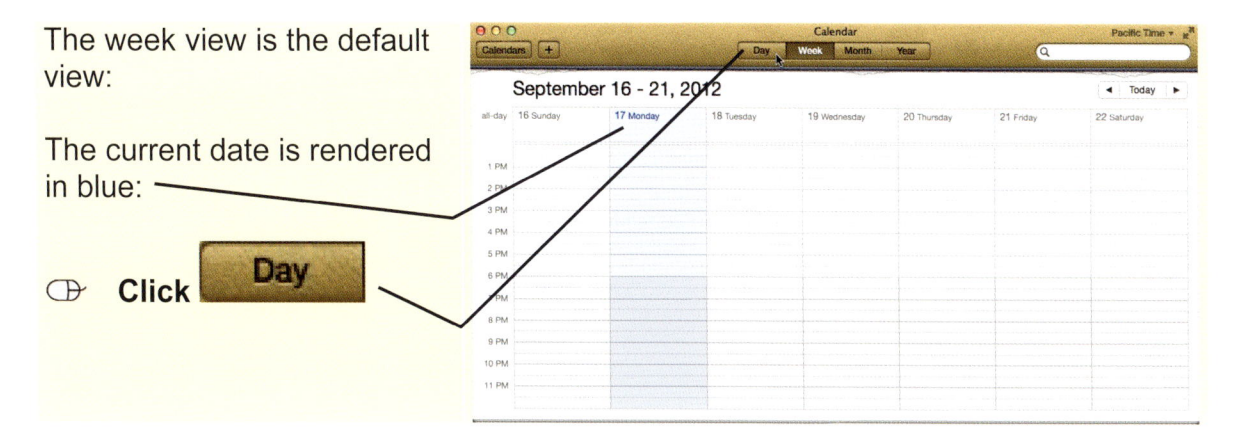

The week view is the default view:

The current date is rendered in blue:

☞ **Click** `Day`

You will see the day view:

☞ Click **Month**

You will see the month view:

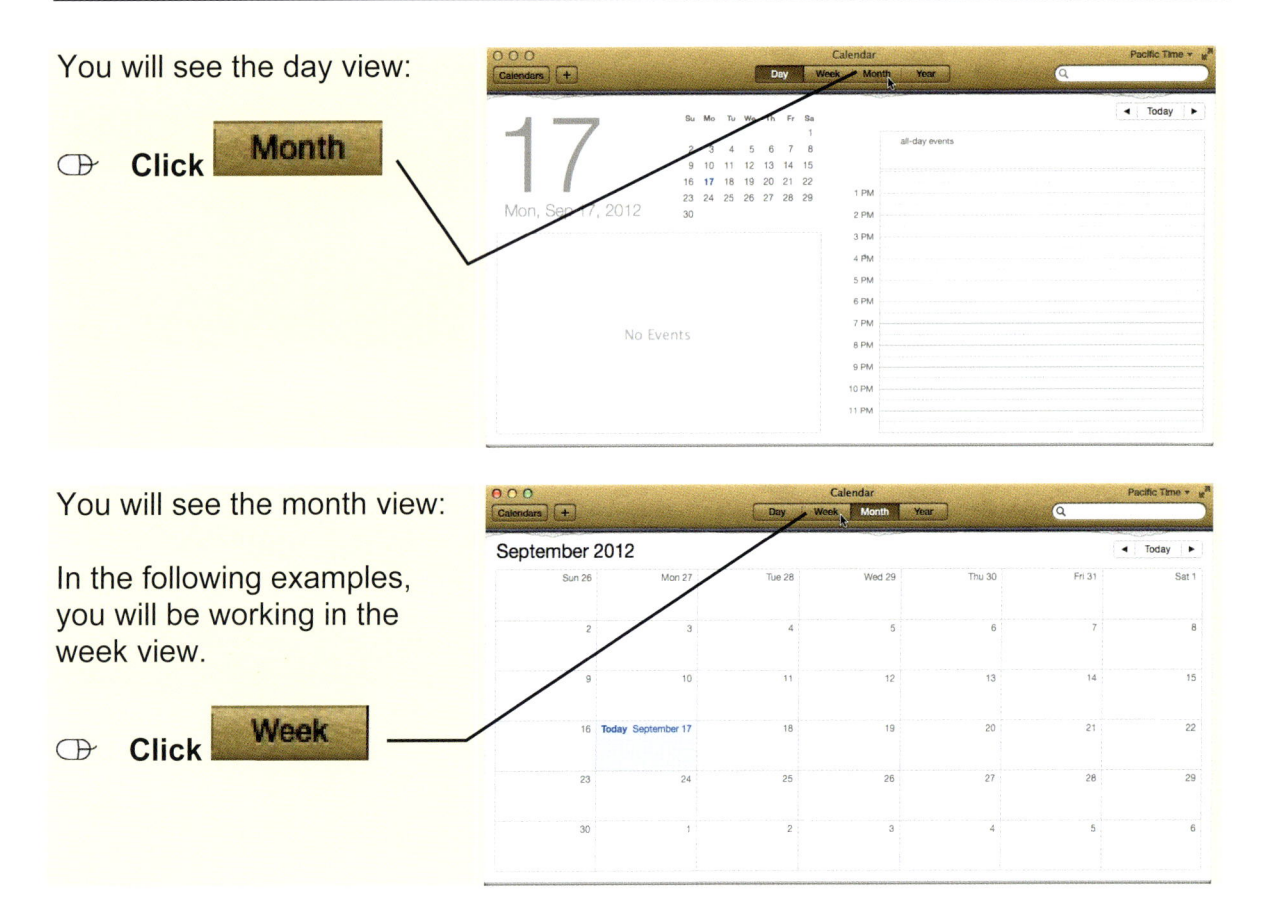

In the following examples, you will be working in the week view.

☞ Click **Week**

💡 Tip
Modify the properties of a calendar
You can change some of the calendar's properties, such as its name and the color:

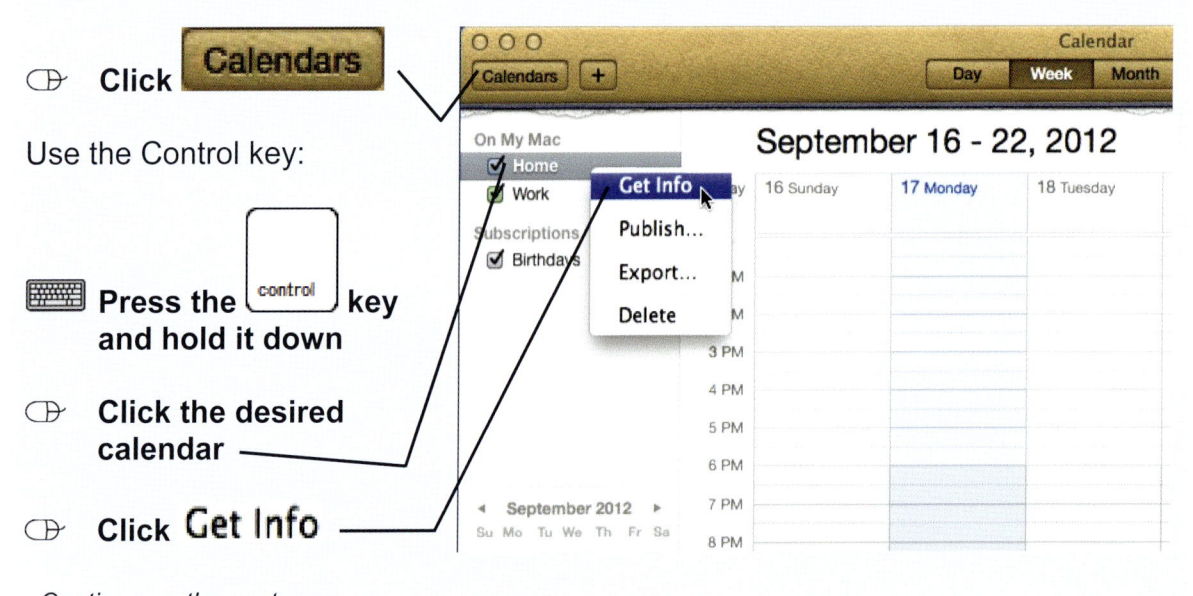

☞ Click **Calendars**

Use the Control key:

⌨ Press the `control` key and hold it down

☞ Click the desired calendar

☞ Click **Get Info**

- Continue on the next page -

Chapter 6 Managing Data

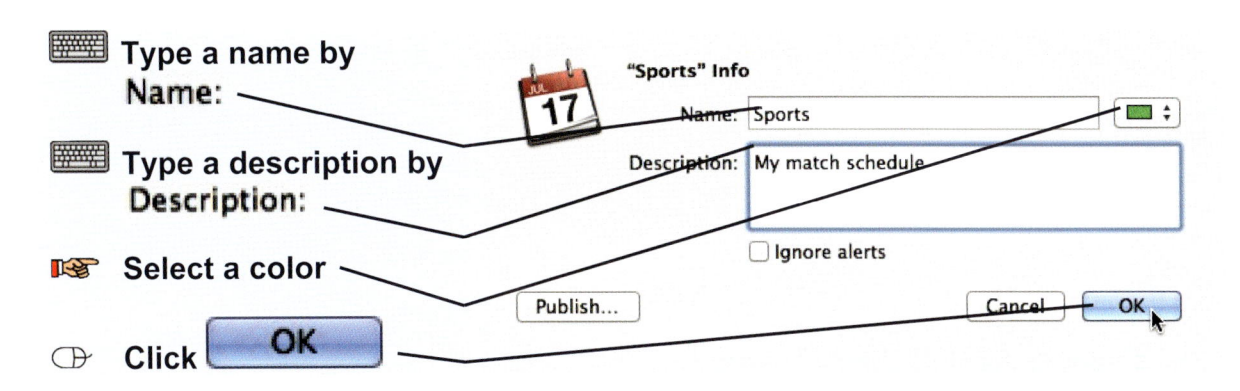

- ⌨ **Type a name by Name:**
- ⌨ **Type a description by Description:**
- ☞ **Select a color**
- ⊕ **Click OK**

6.7 Adding an Event

You can add appointments and activities to your calendar. In *Calendar* these items are called events. This is how you add an event.

Select the day after tomorrow, and set the time between 3:00 p.m. and 6:00 p.m.:

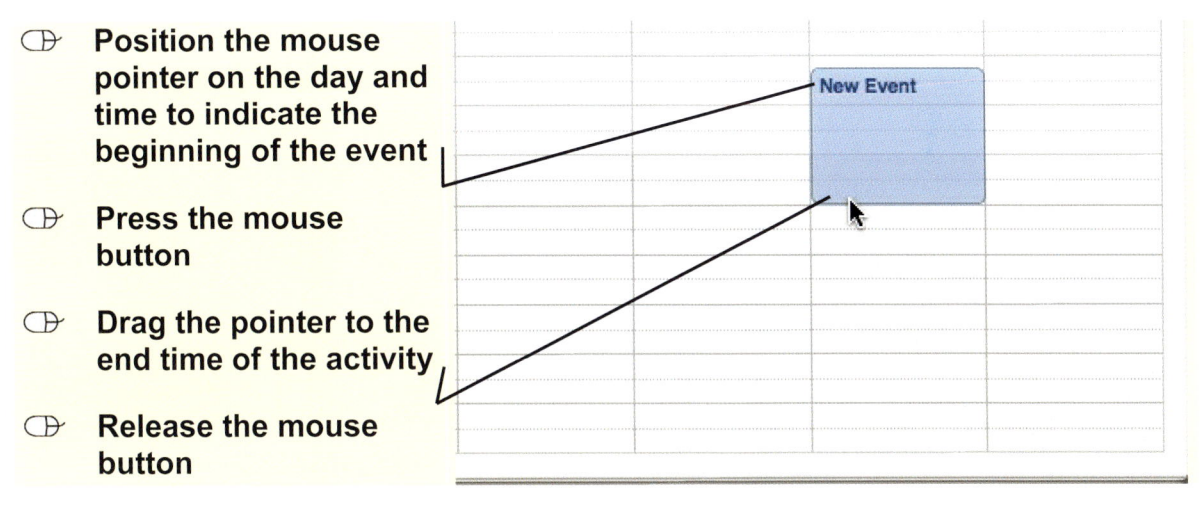

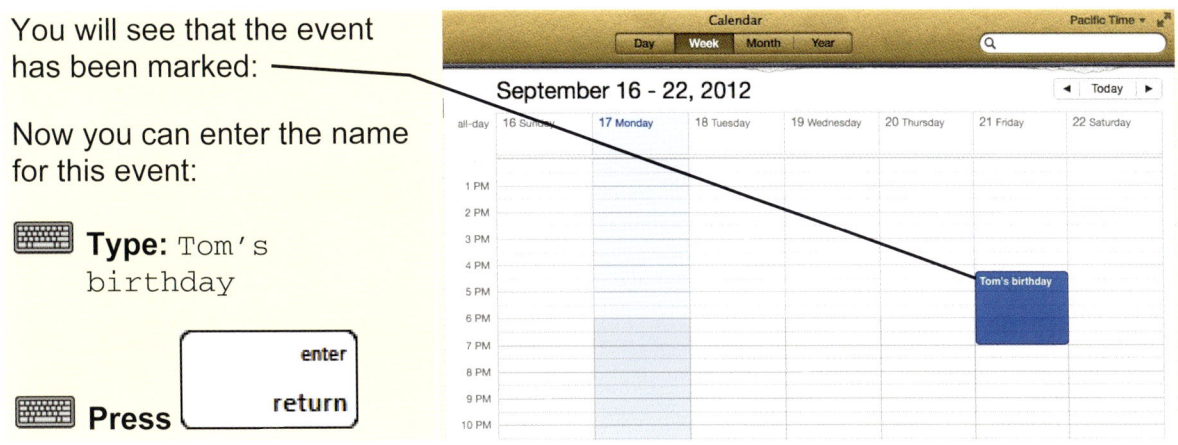

- ⊕ **Position the mouse pointer on the day and time to indicate the beginning of the event**
- ⊕ **Press the mouse button**
- ⊕ **Drag the pointer to the end time of the activity**
- ⊕ **Release the mouse button**

You will see that the event has been marked:

Now you can enter the name for this event:

- ⌨ **Type:** Tom's birthday
- ⌨ **Press enter/return**

The event has been added. There is also another way to add an event:

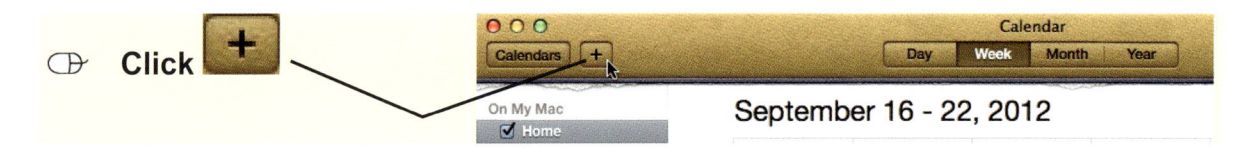

⊕ **Click** ➕

Maybe you will now see a frame with various calendars:

⊕ **If necessary, click the calendar you want to use**

⊕ **If necessary, click ➕ again**

You will see a small window with a text box. You can enter information about an event right there. Type the name of the event, the date and the time of the event, one after the other and separated by blank spaces:

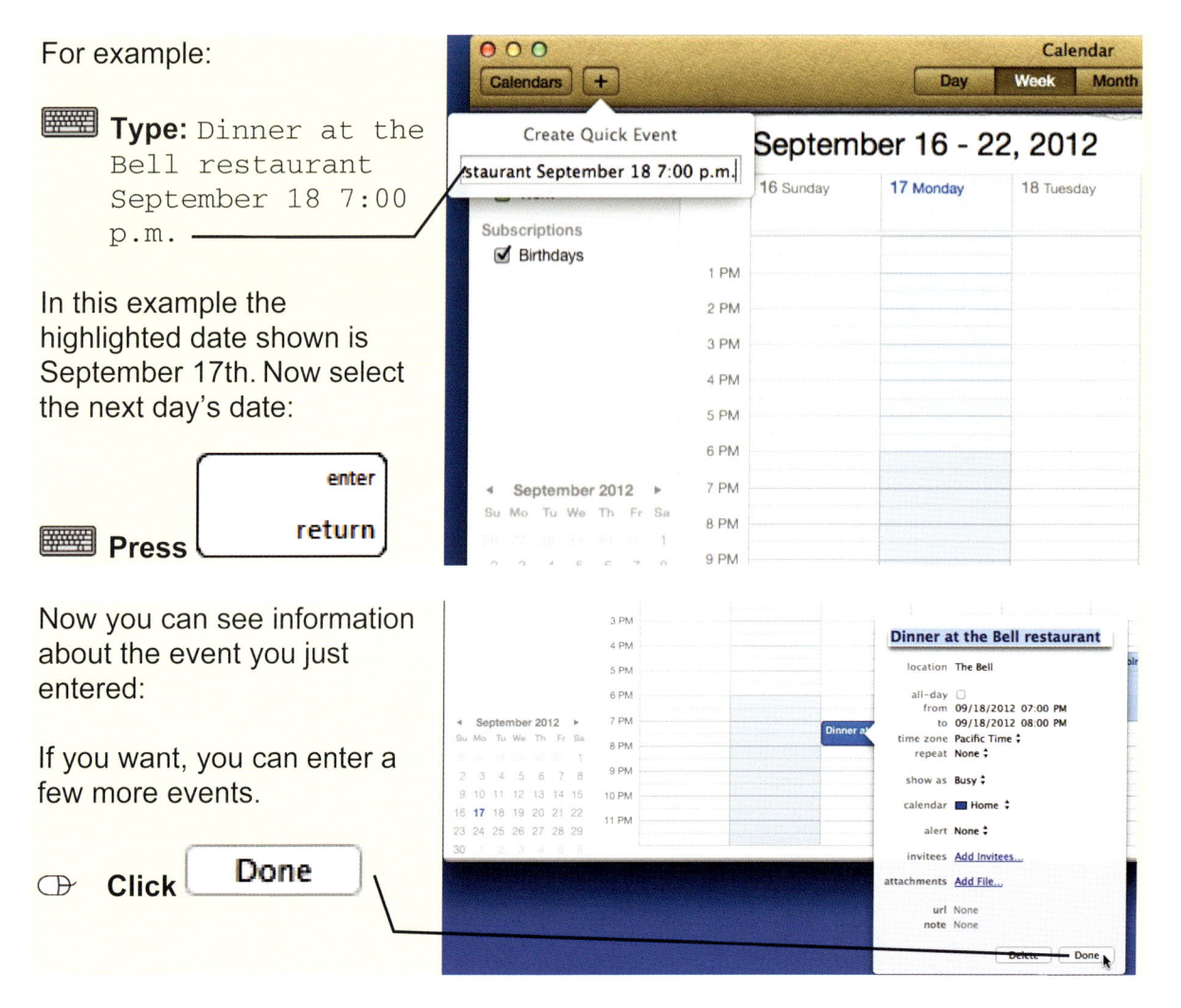

For example:

⌨ **Type:** Dinner at the Bell restaurant September 18 7:00 p.m.

In this example the highlighted date shown is September 17th. Now select the next day's date:

⌨ **Press** enter / return

Now you can see information about the event you just entered:

If you want, you can enter a few more events.

⊕ **Click** Done

Chapter 6 Managing Data   **221**

The event has been added to the calendar. Each new entry has a default duration of one hour. You can edit this duration:

- ☞ **Position the mouse pointer on the lower border of the event**

- ☞ **Press the mouse button**

- ☞ **Drag the pointer to the end time of the event, for example, 9:30 p.m.**

- ☞ **Release the mouse button**

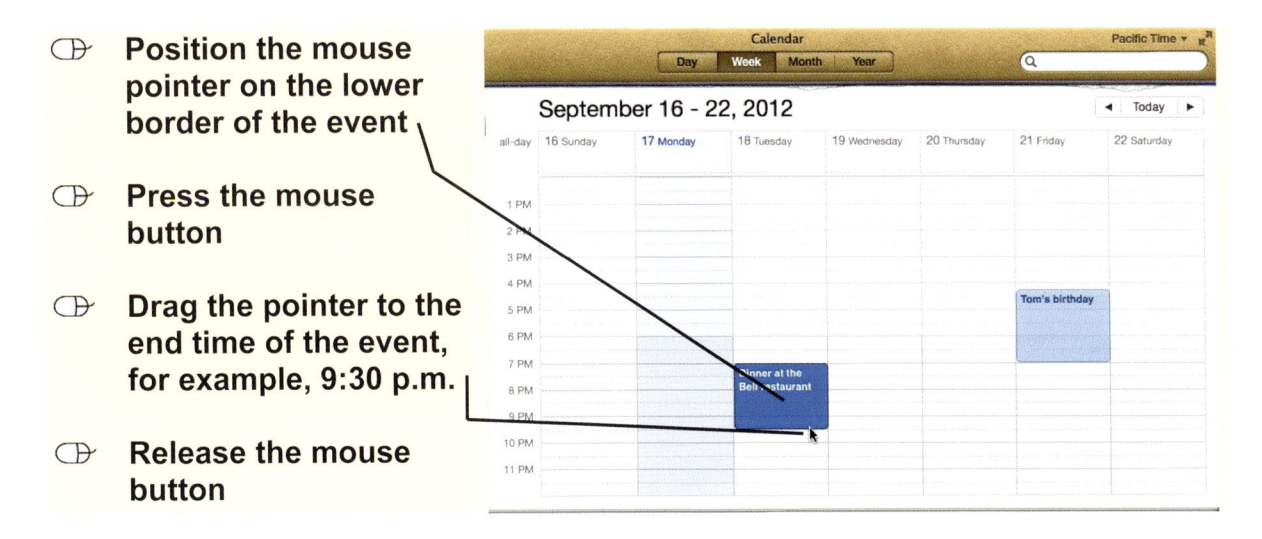

6.8 Editing an Event

You can always edit the information for a certain event. For example, you can add a location. To do this you need to use the Control key:

- ⌨ **Press the `control` key and hold it down**

- ☞ **Click the event**

- ☞ **Click Get Info**

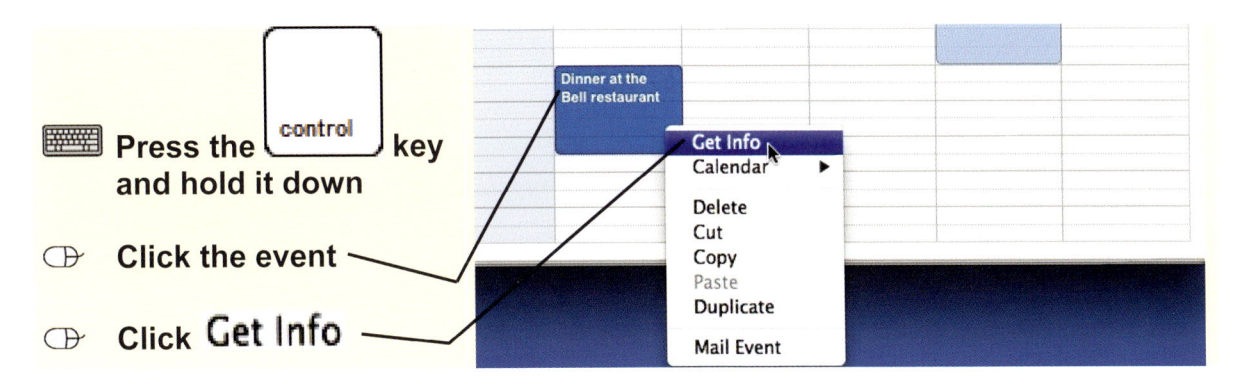

You will see a window in which you can edit or add to the information concerning the event. Let's add a location:

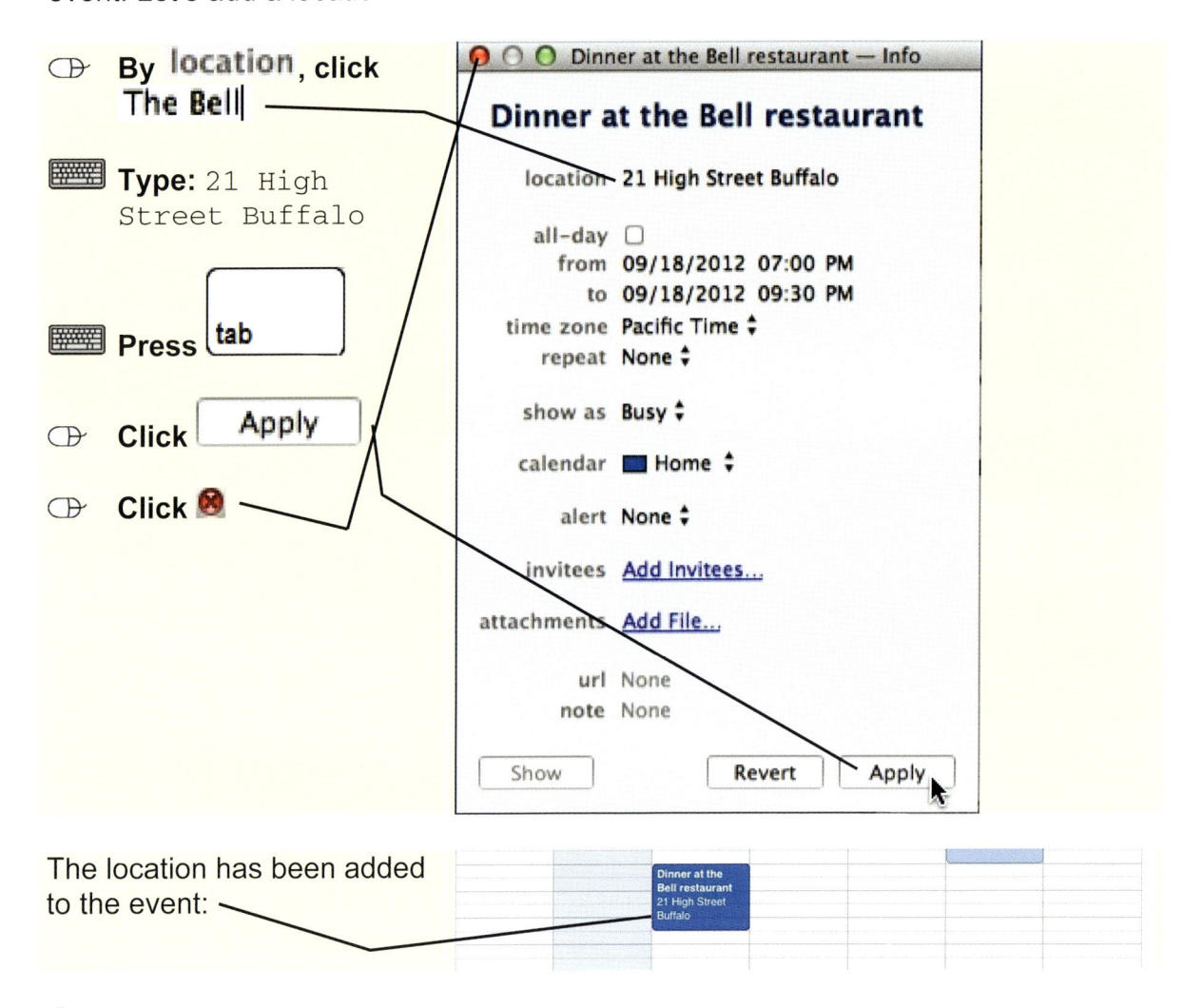

- ☞ By *location*, click `The Bell`

- ⌨ **Type:** `21 High Street Buffalo`

- ⌨ **Press** `tab`

- ☞ **Click** `Apply`

- ☞ **Click** ⊗

The location has been added to the event:

💡 Tip
Delete an event
If an event cannot take place, for example, when an appointment has been cancelled, you can delete this event:

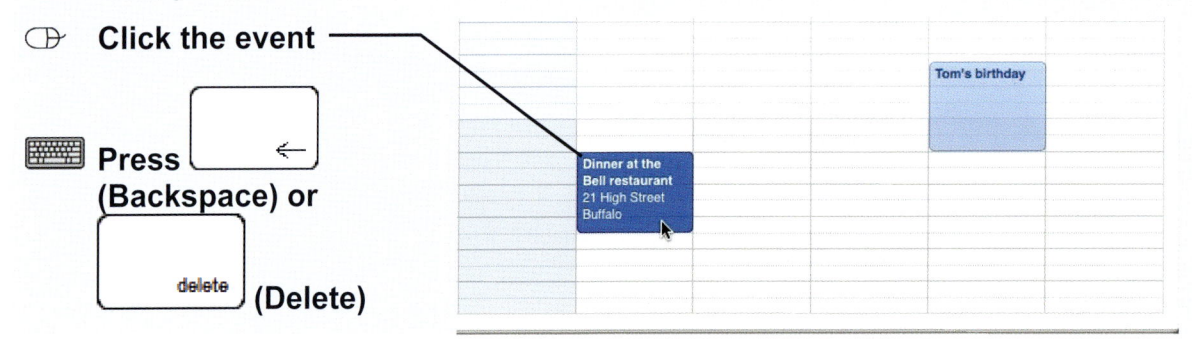

- ☞ **Click the event**

- ⌨ **Press** `←` **(Backspace) or** `delete` **(Delete)**

Chapter 6 Managing Data

6.9 Leaf Through a Calendar

Every now and then, you may want to view your future appointments. You can easily leaf through a calendar to check your appointments:

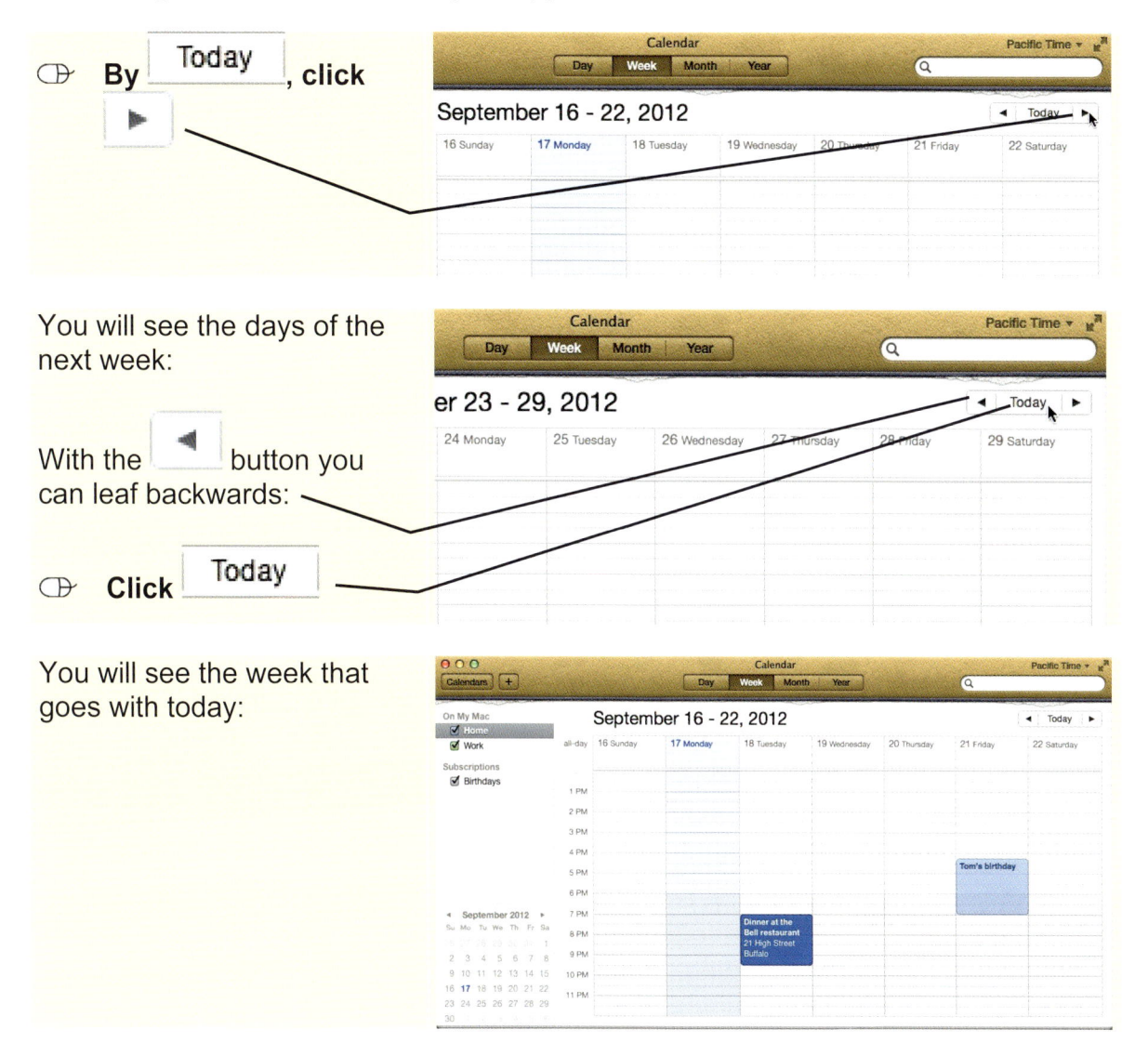

☞ By [Today], click [▶]

You will see the days of the next week:

With the [◀] button you can leaf backwards:

☞ Click [Today]

You will see the week that goes with today:

💡 Tip
Overview per month
You will often get a better insight into your activities if you look at your calendar in the month view:

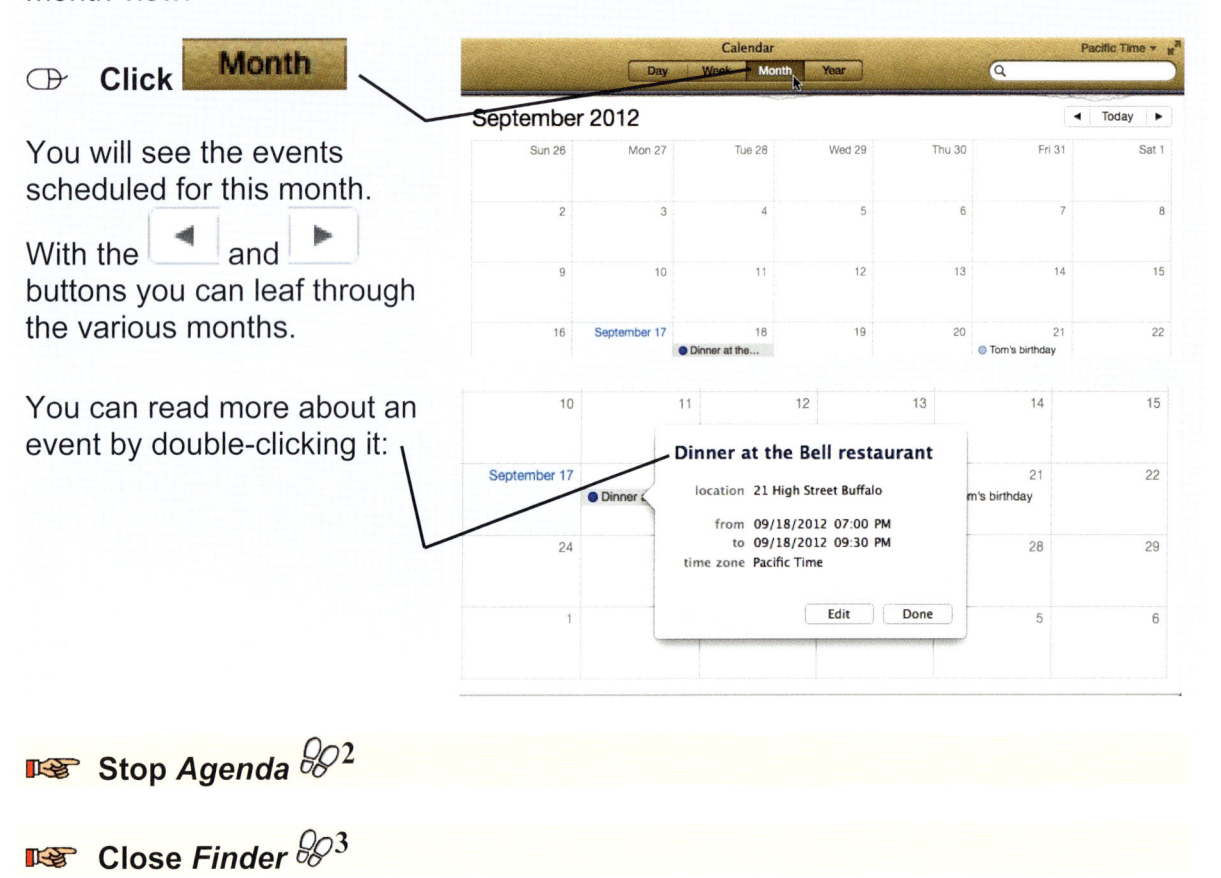

⊕ Click **Month**

You will see the events scheduled for this month.

With the ◀ and ▶ buttons you can leaf through the various months.

You can read more about an event by double-clicking it:

☞ Stop *Agenda* ℘²

☞ Close *Finder* ℘³

6.10 Working with Widgets

Widgets are small programs that provide extra functionality. They can be both fun and useful. There are hundreds of widgets available such as one to display weather forecasts, recipes of the day or news flashes, to name a few.

Your *Mac* already has a few widgets installed. You can view them with the *Dashboard* program:

☞ Open *Finder* ℘¹

⊕ Click **Applications**

Chapter 6 Managing Data 225

⌑ **Double-click** 🌑 Dashboard

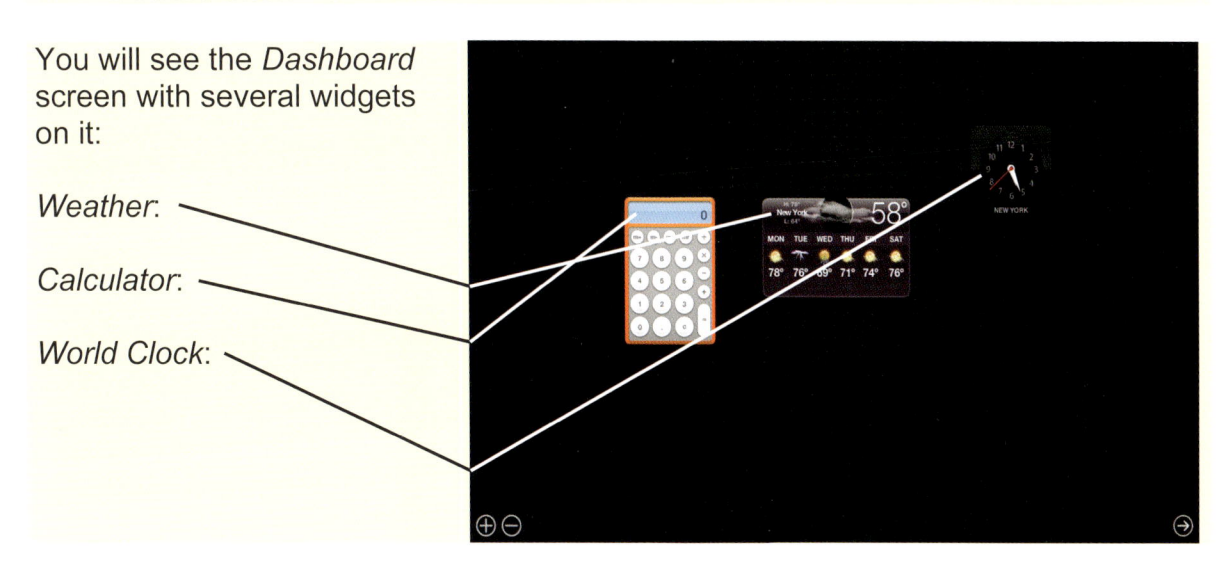

You will see the *Dashboard* screen with several widgets on it:

Weather:

Calculator:

World Clock:

▶ **Please note:**
You may have different widgets installed on your own *Mac*.

▶ **Please note:**
For some of the widgets to work correctly, such as *Weather*, you need to be connected to the Internet. If your computer is not connected to the Internet you will see error messages when you try to use the widget or when the widget tries to download new information.

You can even change the settings for some of the widgets. *World Clock* tells the time in a specific time zone. You can change this time zone, so you can see what time it is in the area where you are going to go on vacation:

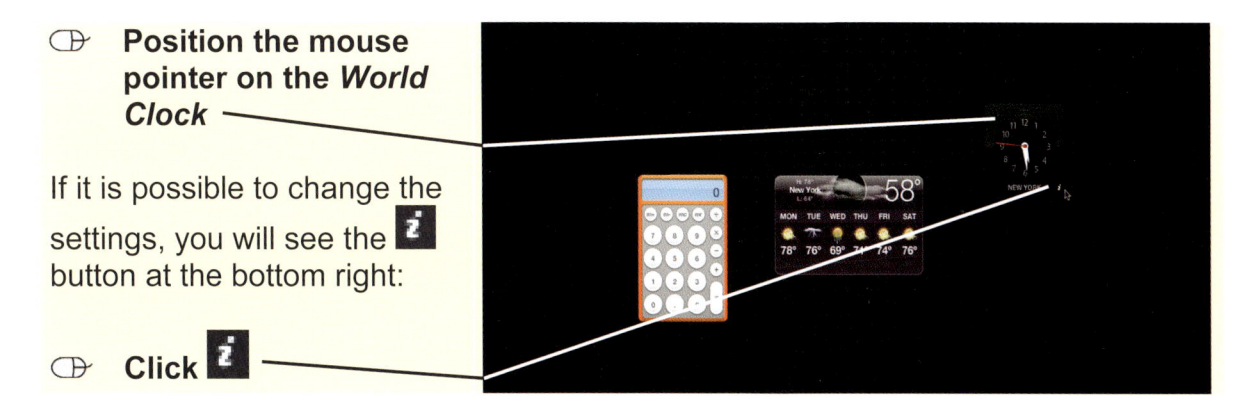

⌑ **Position the mouse pointer on the *World Clock***

If it is possible to change the settings, you will see the *i* button at the bottom right:

⌑ **Click** *i*

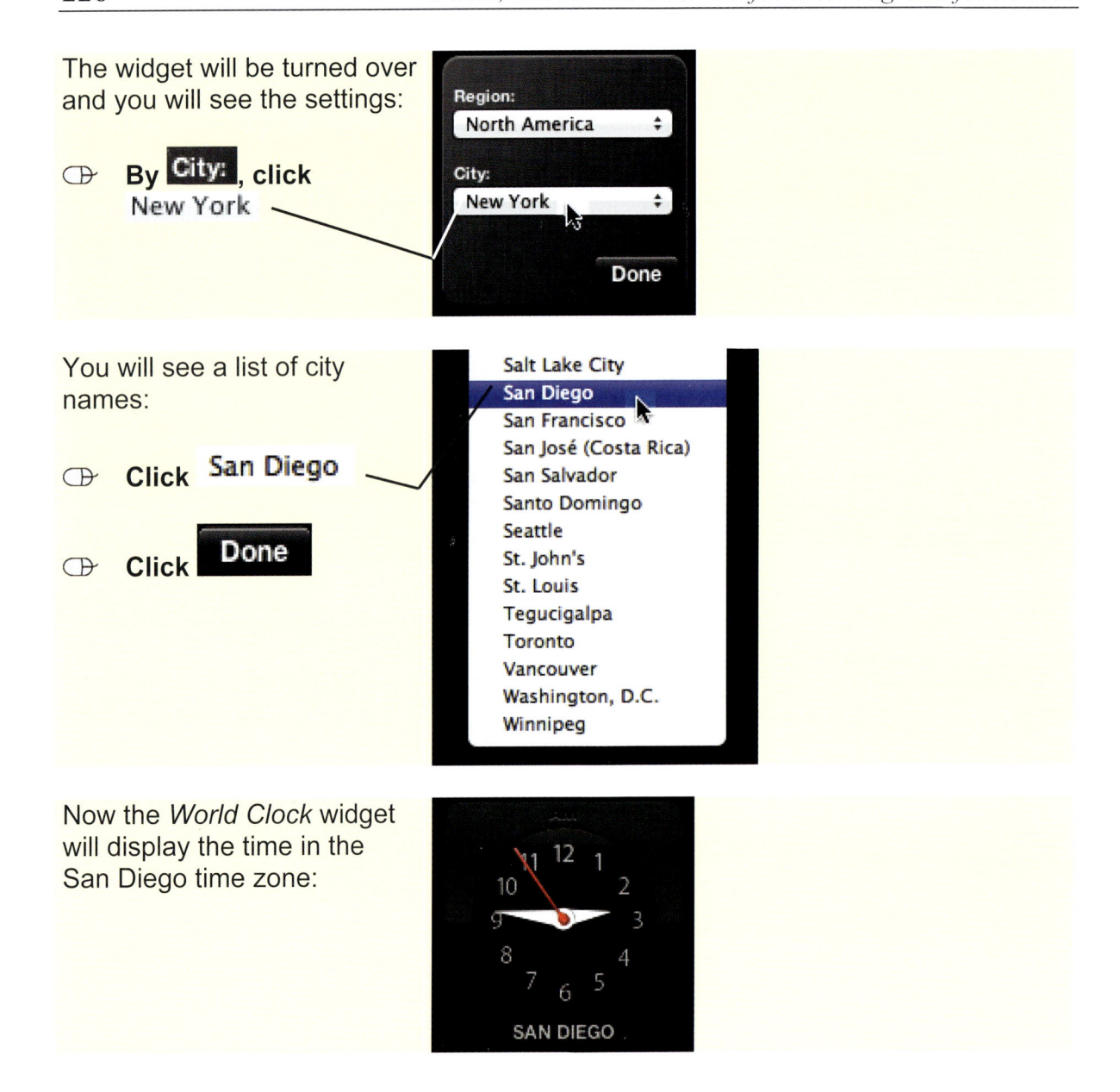

The widget will be turned over and you will see the settings:

☞ **By** `City:`, **click** `New York`

You will see a list of city names:

☞ **Click** `San Diego`

☞ **Click** `Done`

Now the *World Clock* widget will display the time in the San Diego time zone:

6.11 Adding a Widget

Along with the standard widgets displayed in *Dashboard* there are many more widgets you can add. To add the widget called *Tile* Game, go to the bottom left of the screen:

☞ **Click** ⊕

Chapter 6 Managing Data

You will see a screen with widgets you can choose from:

☞ **Click** [tile game icon]

The *Tile Game* widget will be added:

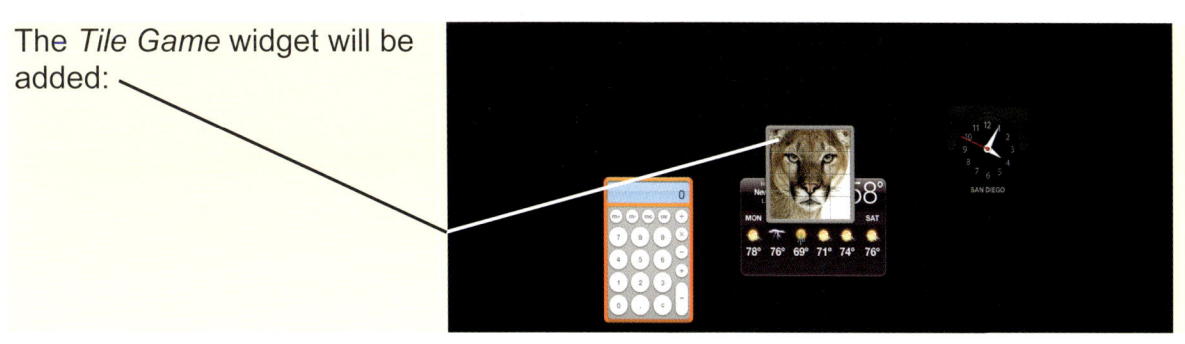

The widget that has been added has been placed on top of one of the other widgets. You can move this widget to a different spot on the *Dashboard*:

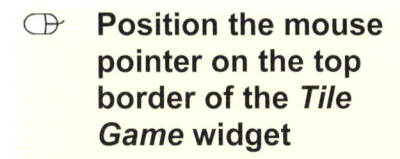

☞ **Position the mouse pointer on the top border of the *Tile Game* widget**

☞ **Drag the widget to the top right of the screen**

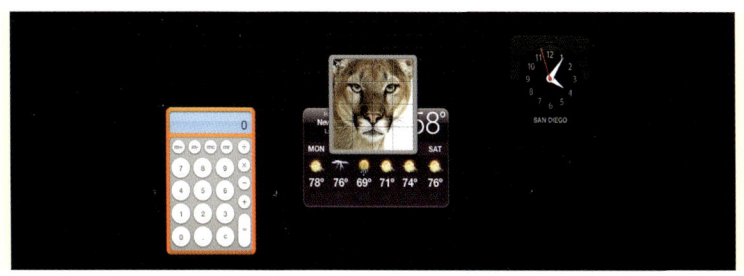

Now the widget has moved to a different spot:

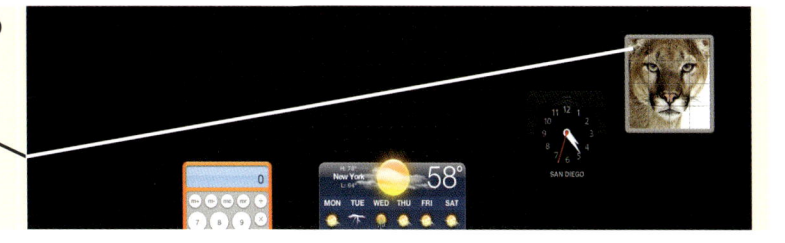

6.12 Closing a Widget

If you do not use a widget you can close it. This way, you create extra space on your *Dashboard*. You can close the *Tile Game* widget. At the bottom left of the screen:

☞ **Click** [minus icon]

You can remove the widget:

- **By the *Tile Game* widget, click** ⊗

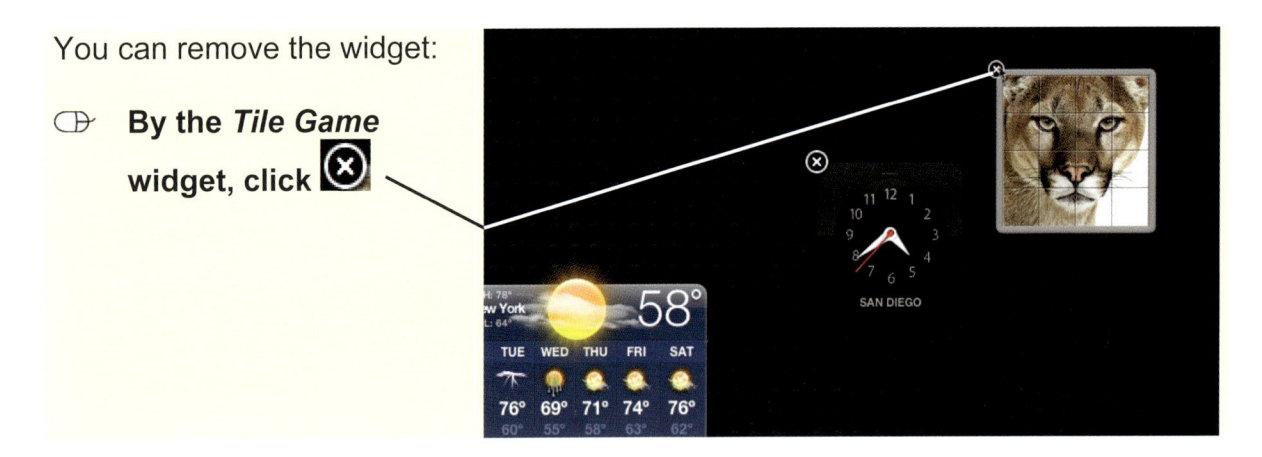

Now the *Tile Game* widget has been removed from the screen.

6.13 Closing the Dashboard

If you do not want to use the widgets any longer you can close the *Dashboard*:

At the bottom right of the screen:

- **Click** ➡

Dashboard will be closed and you will see the desktop again.

☞ **Close *Finder*** ℘³

In this chapter you have learned how to manage contact information in *Contacts* and how to keep a calendar of appointments and upcoming events with *Calendar*. You have also seen how widgets can provide extra functionality to your Mac and be both fun and useful at the same time.

6.14 Visual Steps

By now we hope you have noticed that the Visual Steps method is an excellent method for quickly and efficiently learning more about computers and other devices and their applications. All books published by Visual Steps use this same method. In various series, we have published a large number of books on a wide variety of topics, including *Windows*, *Mac, iPad* and *iPhone,* photo editing, video editing and many other topics.
On the **www.visualsteps.com** website you can click the Catalog page to find an overview of all the Visual Steps titles, including an extensive description. Each title allows you to preview the full table of contents and a sample chapter in a PDF format. In this way, you can quickly determine if a specific title will meet your expectations. All titles can be ordered online and are also available in bookstores across the USA, Canada, United Kingdom, Australia and New Zealand.

Furthermore, the website offers many extras, among other things:
- free computer guides and booklets (PDF files) on all sorts of subjects;
- frequently asked questions and their answers;
- information on the free Computer Certificate that you can acquire at the certificate's website **www.ccforseniors.com**;
- a free notify-me service: receive an email as soon as a new book is published.

6.15 Background Information

Dictionary

Calendar	A program on the *Mac* that is used to enter appointments and upcoming events.
Card	A page in *Contacts* containing the contact's information.
Contact	A person or company whose information is listed in *Contacts*.
Contacts	A program on the *Mac* that is used to manage contact information. You can add new contacts directly to your address book. You can also add a contact through *Mail*.
Dashboard	A program that displays a semi-transparent layer over your desktop so you can see your widgets. You can add, remove or change the settings of a widget with the *Dashboard*.
Widget	A mini program in *Dashboard*. Widgets can be used for all sorts of purposes, such as keeping track of stock prices, viewing a weather forecast, looking up words in a dictionary, etcetera.

Source: Apple dictionary, www.apple.com

6.16 Tips

💡 **Tip**
Add a photo to a card in Contacts
If you want, you can add a photo to a contact's information in the *Contacts* program. Here is how to do that:

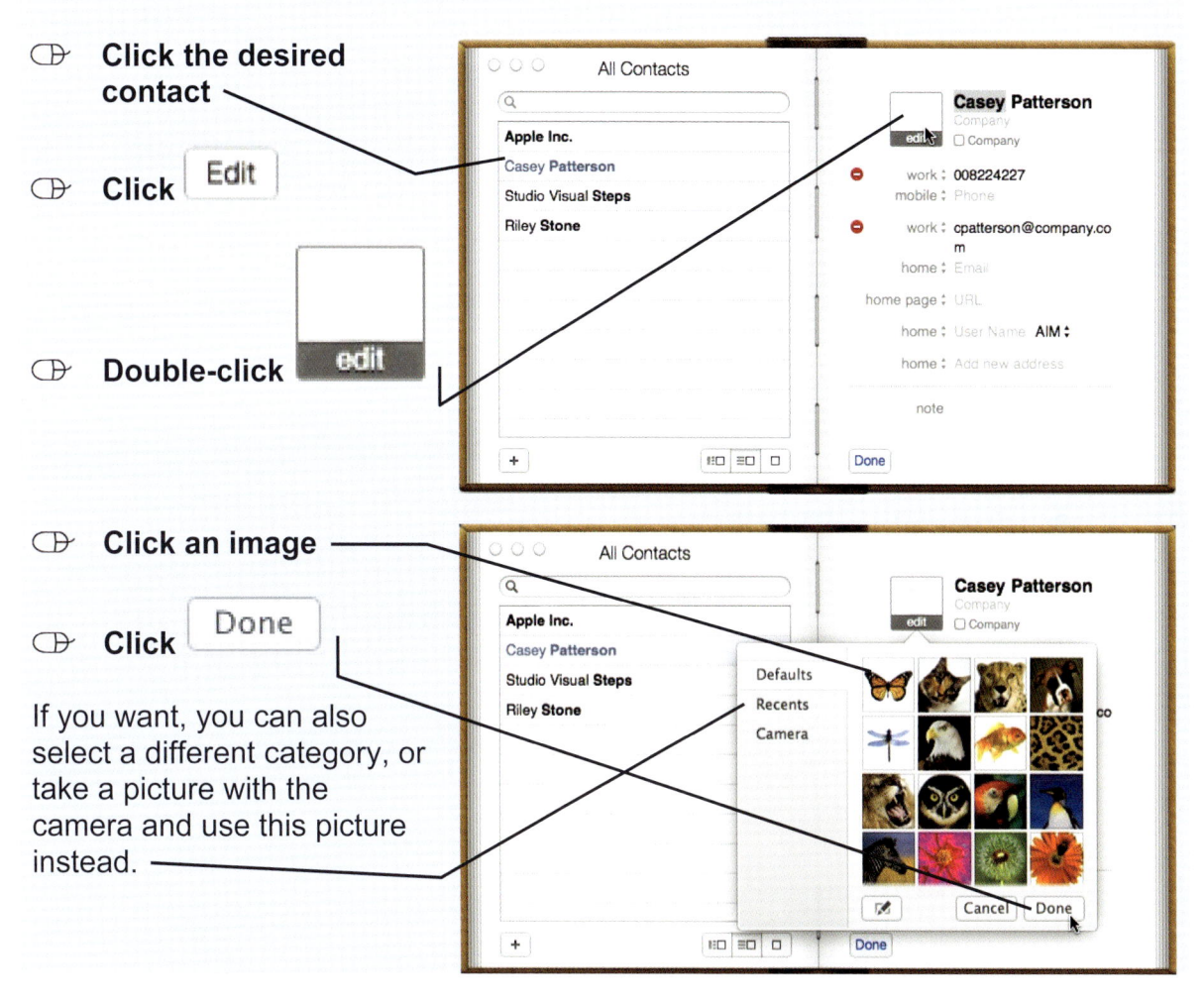

☞ **Click the desired contact**

☞ **Click** `Edit`

☞ **Double-click** `edit`

☞ **Click an image**

☞ **Click** `Done`

If you want, you can also select a different category, or take a picture with the camera and use this picture instead.

💡 **Tip**
Changing the Mail cards
Contacts that have been added in the *Mail* program usually have cards containing just the email information. You will need to add additional information, such as address, phone number or website address with the *Contacts* program.

💡 Tip
Add an address to Contacts through Mail
You can add new contact information directly into *Contacts*, but you can also use *Mail* to get an email address into *Contacts*. Here is how to do that:

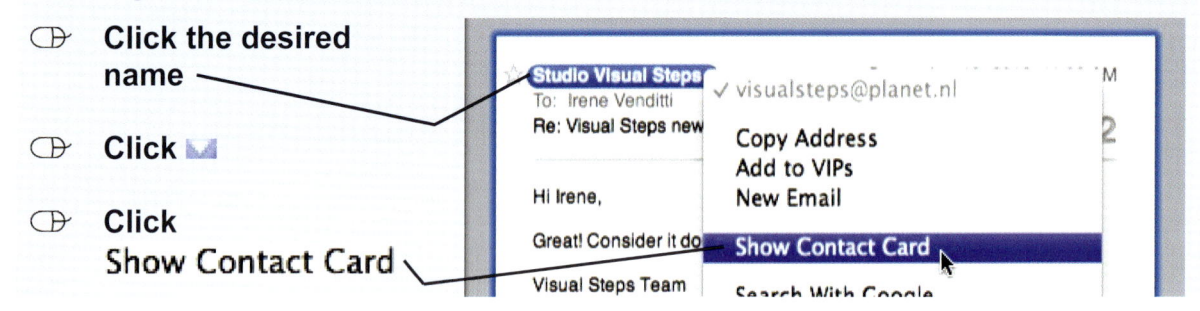

- ☞ **Click the desired name**
- ☞ **Click** ✉
- ☞ **Click Show Contact Card**

💡 Tip
View longer time periods in Calendar
By default, only part of the hours of a day is displayed in the program. If you want to view more hours, you can change the settings:

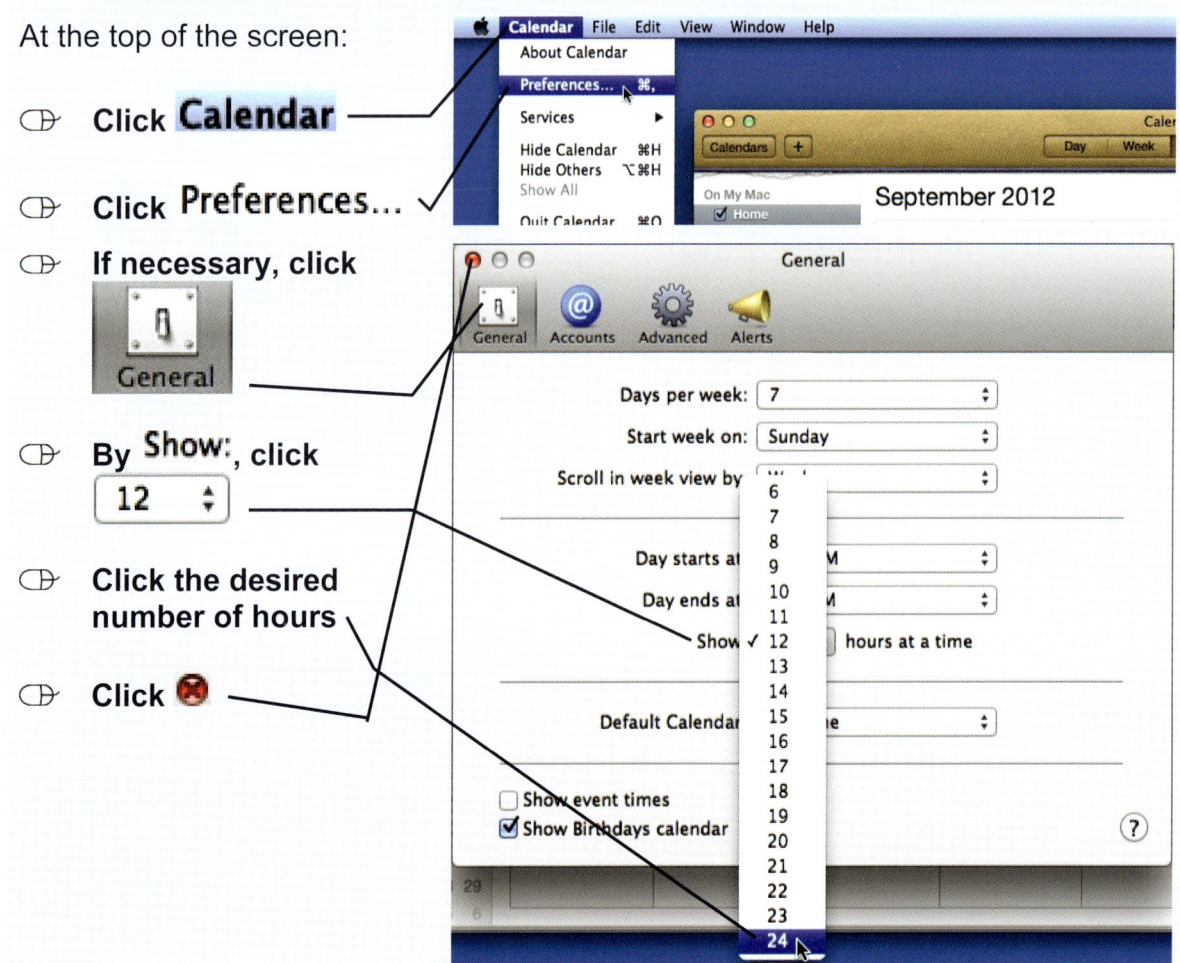

At the top of the screen:

- ☞ **Click Calendar**
- ☞ **Click Preferences...**
- ☞ **If necessary, click General**
- ☞ **By Show:, click 12**
- ☞ **Click the desired number of hours**
- ☞ **Click** 🔴

Chapter 6 Managing Data 233

💡 Tip
Download widgets
Your *Mac* already contains several useful widgets, but there are many more available. Hundreds of additional widgets for a variety of different purposes can be found on the Internet. This is how you download a widget. At the bottom left of the window:

☞ **Click** ➕ , **More Widgets...**

Safari will open and you will see the page on the *Apple* website where you can download more widgets:

In the table on the page:

☞ **By Category, click a category**

☞ **By Widget, click a widget**

If you click **More Info...** you will see more information about this widget:

To download:

☞ **Click Download 1.1MB**

👉 **Follow the instructions in the next few windows**

Notes

Write your notes down here.

Appendices

A. How Do I Do That Again?

The actions and exercises in this book are marked with footsteps: ⏱1
In this appendix you can look up the numbers of the footsteps and read how to carry out a certain action once more.

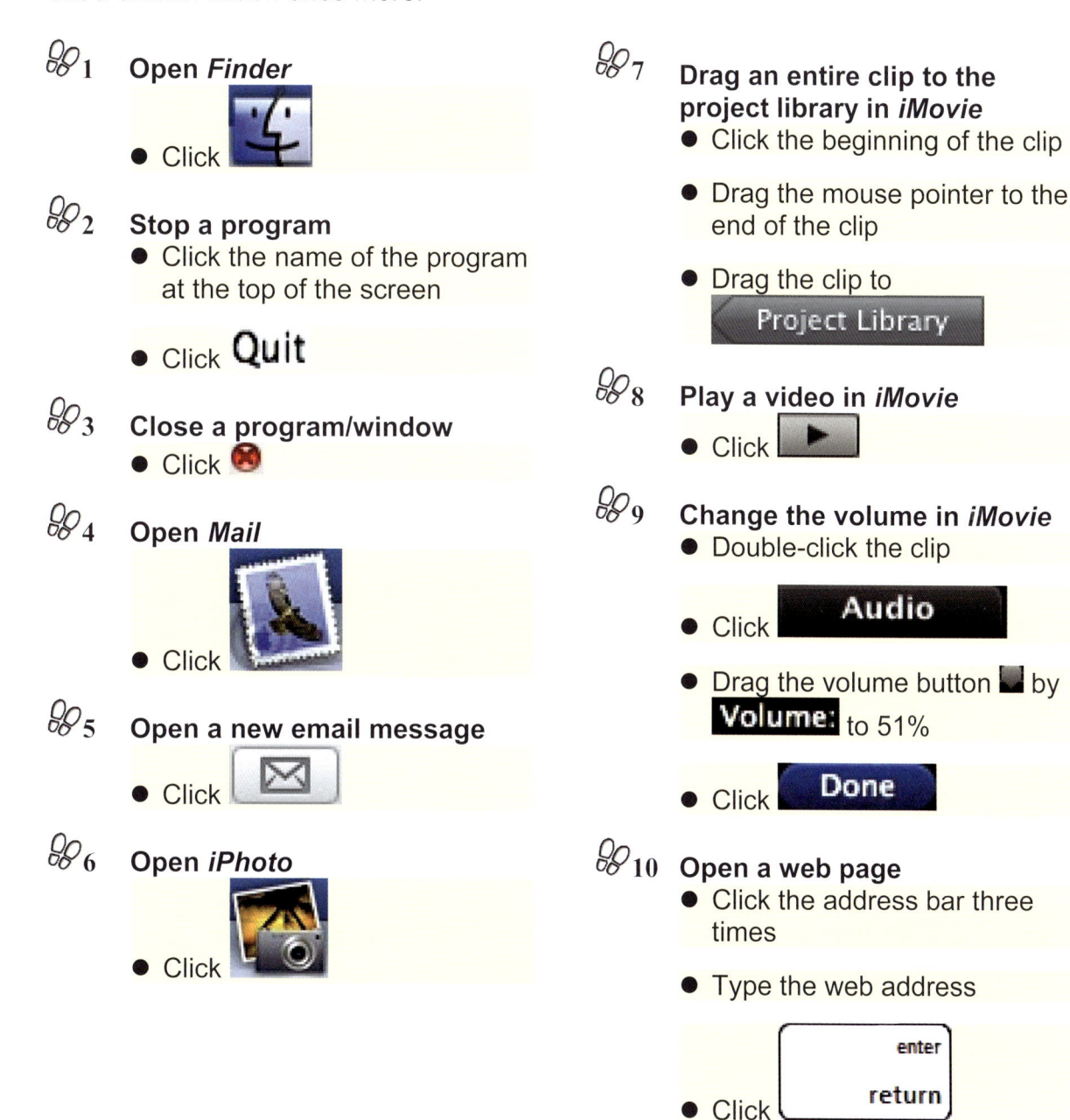

⏱1 **Open *Finder***
- Click

⏱2 **Stop a program**
- Click the name of the program at the top of the screen
- Click **Quit**

⏱3 **Close a program/window**
- Click

⏱4 **Open *Mail***
- Click

⏱5 **Open a new email message**
- Click

⏱6 **Open *iPhoto***
- Click

⏱7 **Drag an entire clip to the project library in *iMovie***
- Click the beginning of the clip
- Drag the mouse pointer to the end of the clip
- Drag the clip to **Project Library**

⏱8 **Play a video in *iMovie***
- Click

⏱9 **Change the volume in *iMovie***
- Double-click the clip
- Click **Audio**
- Drag the volume button by **Volume:** to 51%
- Click **Done**

⏱10 **Open a web page**
- Click the address bar three times
- Type the web address
- Click **enter / return**

11 Delete a file
- Drag the file on top of

12 Open *Safari*
- Click

13 Return to the photo overview
- Click **Photos**

14 Select part of a clip
- Position the mouse pointer on the left-hand border of the yellow frame
- Press the mouse button and drag the pointer to the desired spot
- Release the mouse button

15 Copy and paste a frame
- Click the desired frame
- Click **Edit**
- Click **Copy**
- Click the spot where you want to paste the frame
- Click **Edit**
- Click **Paste**

16 Open *Launchpad*
- Click

17 Rotate a photo
- Double-click a photo
- Click **Edit**
- Click **Rotate** three times

18 Add a task to a list of tasks
- Click a task
- Drag the task to the box on the right-hand side, below the first task

B. Download and Install Codecs

In order to properly play video files on the *Mac* it is important to have the right codecs installed. Codecs are pieces of software that encode and decode the data in a video file. This makes it possible for video programs to work with the various video file formats. Without the proper codecs, some video files cannot be opened by a video program.

If the proper codec has not yet been installed on your *Mac*, you will see the window below. This means you need to download and install the codecs:

☞ **Click**
   Tell Me More

The document "Mill.avi" could not be opened. A required codec isn't available.

To see if additional software is available that will enable QuickTime Player to open the movie, click Tell Me More.

[Tell Me More] [OK]

Safari will open and you will see a page on the *Apple* website containing additional information about these codecs.

Video file types are manufactured by different companies who have their own copyrights to these file types. That is why you will need to download the codecs from various websites.
The exercise file used in this book is a video file of the *AVI/DivX* type. You can visit the corresponding website:

☞ **In the row by DivX, click DivX**

Format	File extension(s)	Codec or component	Link to website
Windows Media	.wmv, .wma, .wm, .asf, .wvx, .wax, .wmx, .asx, .avi	Flip4Mac WMV Components for QuickTime	Telestream
DivX	.divx, .avi	DivX for Mac	DivX
MPEG-2	.mpg, .mpeg, .m2v	QuickTime MPEG-2 Playback Component. Supports program and elementary streams on Mac OS X 10.4.10 through Mac OS X 10.6.8.	Apple Inc.
MXF	.mxf	MXF Import QT	Hamburg Pro Media
Digital Picture Exchange	.dpx	Codec components for digital film formats such as Kodak Cineon, SMTPE DPX, ARRIRAW, and Phantom Cine Raw Files.	Glue Tools
REDCODE RAW	.R3D	RED QuickTime codec	RED
AJA Kona	Not applicable	AJA Macintosh QuickTime Codec	AJA Video Systems

239

⊗ HELP! I do not see any windows.

If you do not see this website you can open the www.divx.com website in *Safari*.

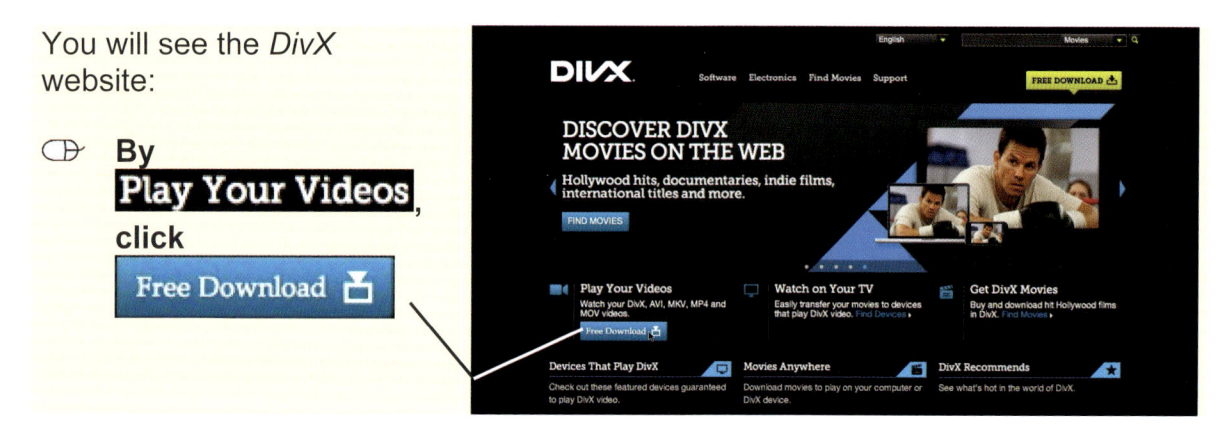

You will see the *DivX* website:

☞ By **Play Your Videos**, click **Free Download**

If you see a white window:

☞ Click ⊠

Now you will see the next window. First, you are going to check whether the file containing the codecs is already being downloaded:

Here you can see that the codecs are being downloaded:

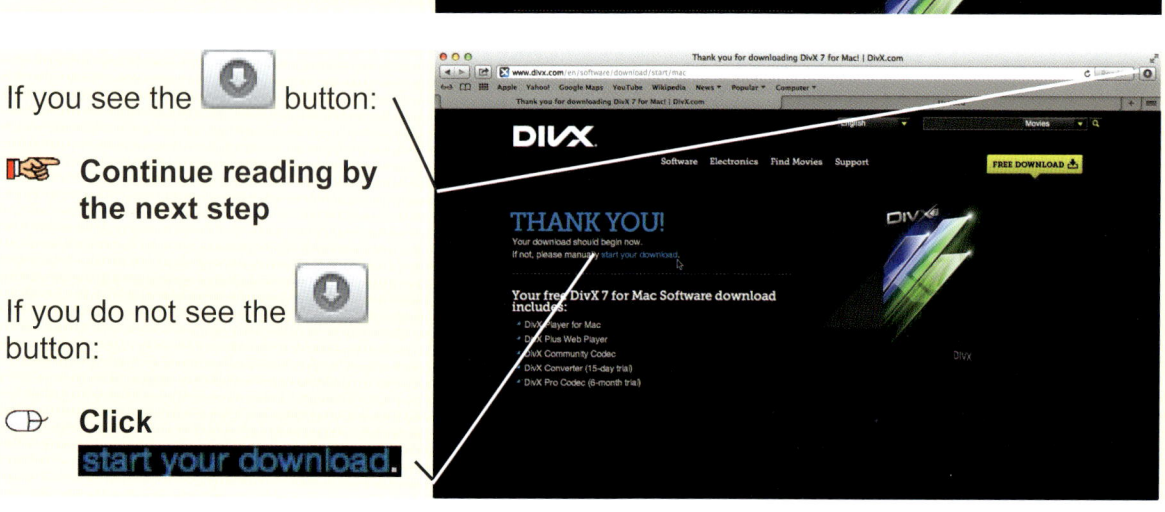

If you see the 🔽 button:

☞ Continue reading by the next step

If you do not see the 🔽 button:

☞ Click **start your download**.

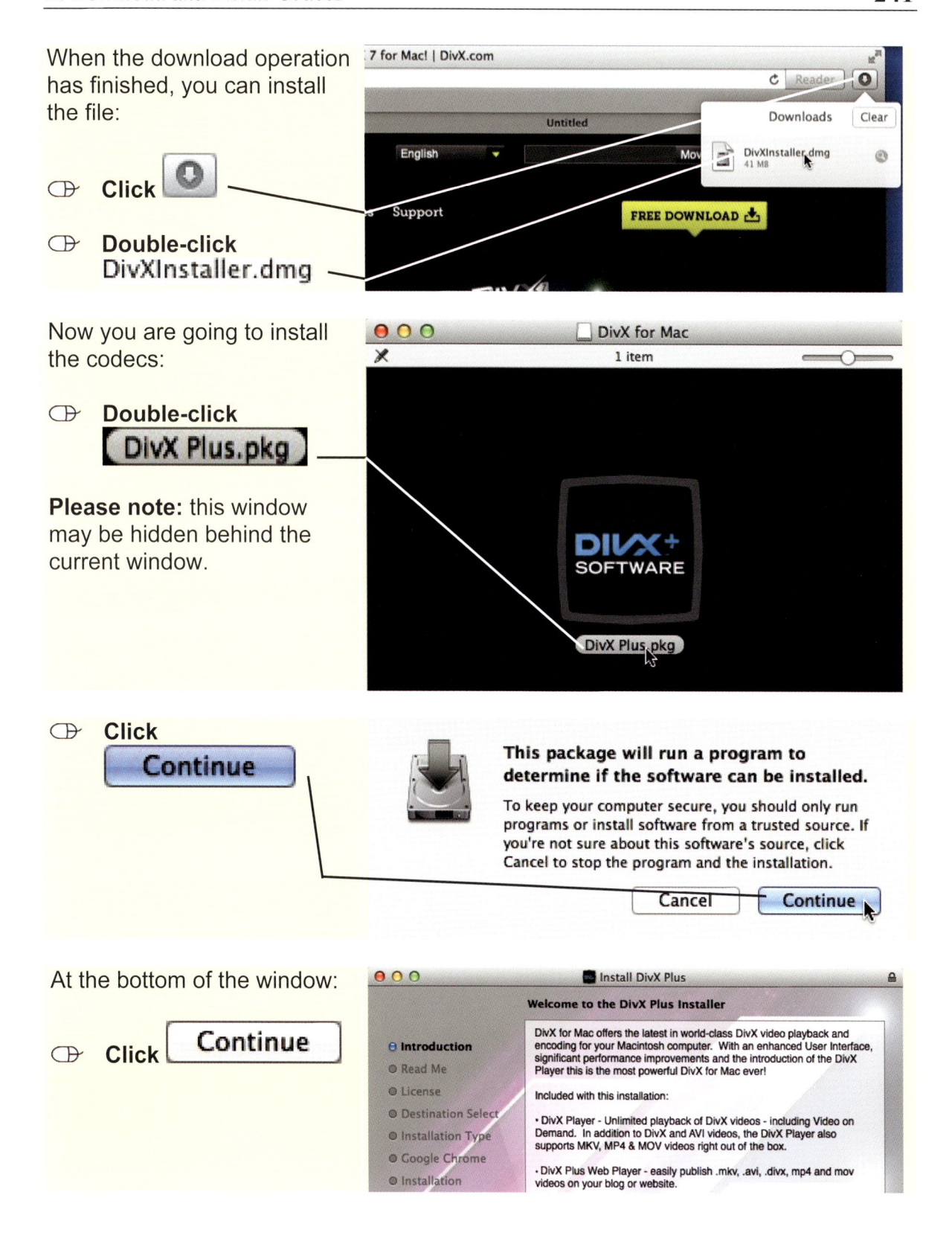

B. Download and Install Codecs **241**

When the download operation has finished, you can install the file:

⊕ **Click** [download icon]

⊕ **Double-click** *DivXInstaller.dmg*

Now you are going to install the codecs:

⊕ **Double-click** [DivX Plus.pkg]

Please note: this window may be hidden behind the current window.

⊕ **Click** [Continue]

At the bottom of the window:

⊕ **Click** [Continue]

At the bottom of the window:

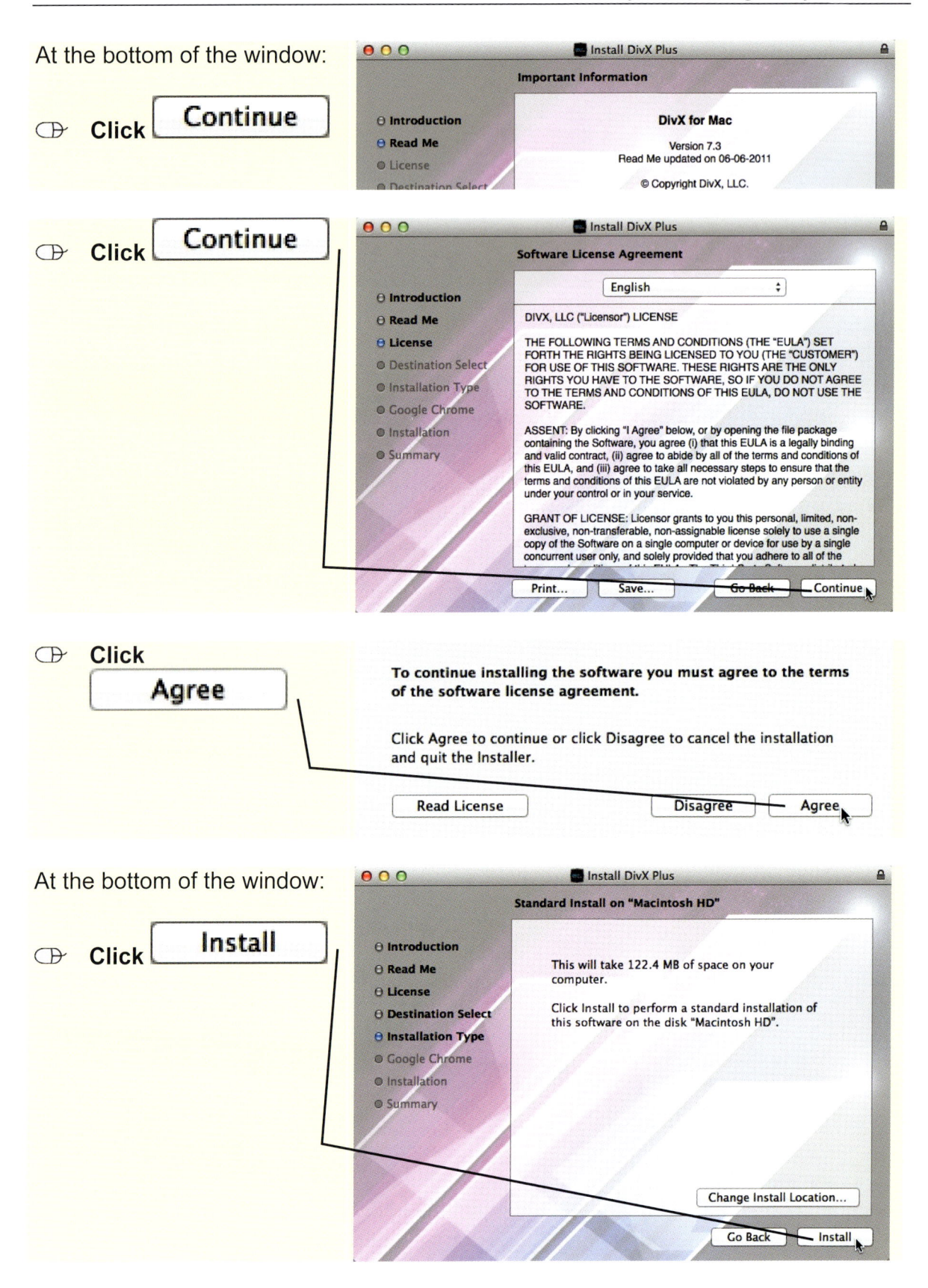

☞ Click [Continue]

☞ Click [Continue]

☞ Click [Agree]

At the bottom of the window:

☞ Click [Install]

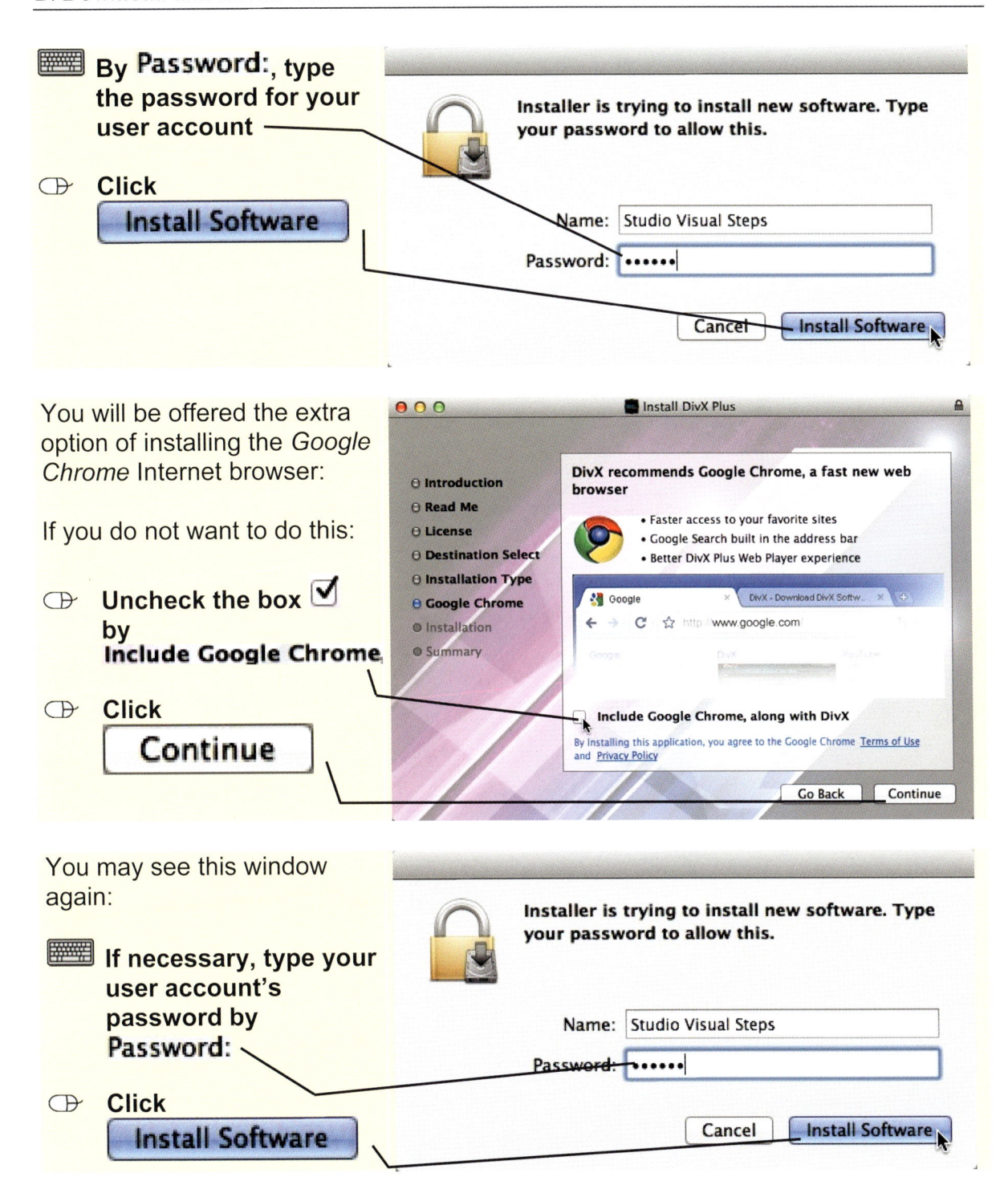

B. Download and Install Codecs **243**

⌨ **By `Password:`, type the password for your user account**

☞ **Click `Install Software`**

You will be offered the extra option of installing the *Google Chrome* Internet browser:

If you do not want to do this:

☞ **Uncheck the box ☑ by `Include Google Chrome`**

☞ **Click `Continue`**

You may see this window again:

⌨ **If necessary, type your user account's password by `Password:`**

☞ **Click `Install Software`**

The codecs will be installed. After a while you will see this window:

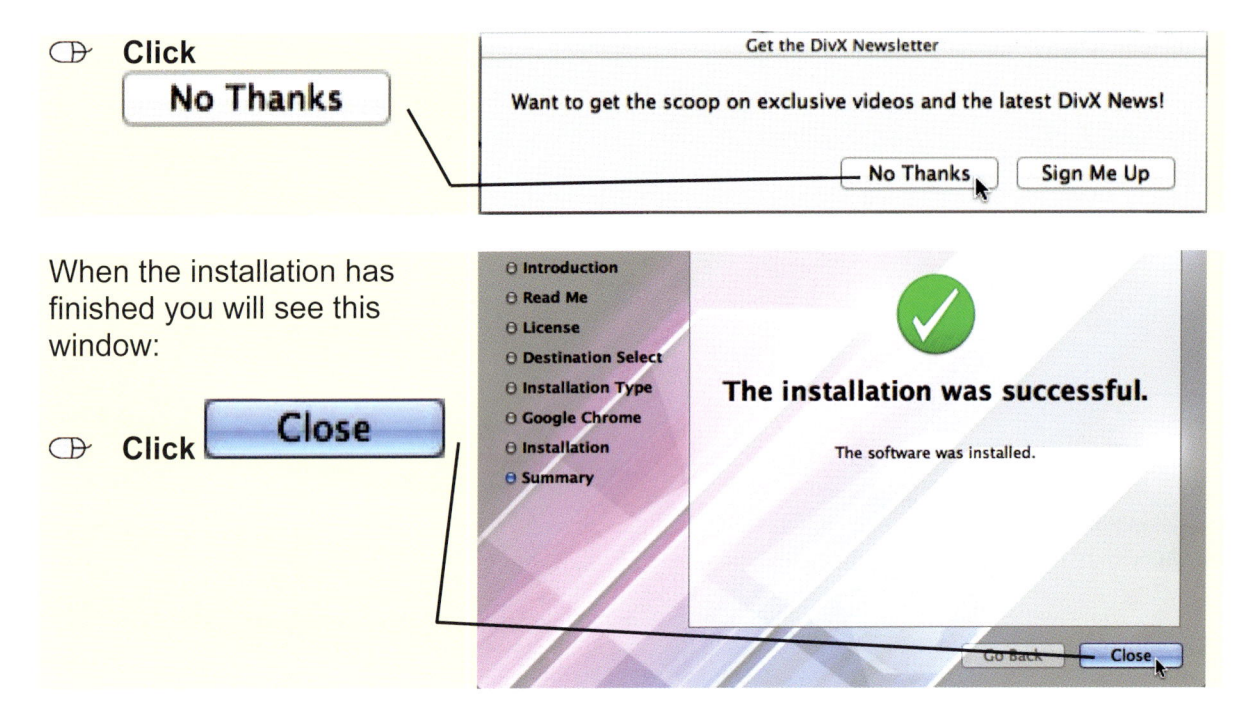

⊕ **Click** No Thanks

When the installation has finished you will see this window:

⊕ **Click** Close

Along with the codes, a number of programs have been installed, among which is the *DivX Player*. This is a video player.

☞ **Close all open programs** ℘³

↪ **Please note:**
You can also download and install other codecs from the *Apple* website. The procedure for downloading and installing codecs may vary according to the type of codec.

↪ **Please note:**
You will often need to re-start your computer after having installing the codecs, in order to activate them. If you still have problems opening your video files after having installed the codecs, then re-start the computer and try again.

↪ **Please note:**
Sometimes a video program will still not function correctly after you have installed the proper codecs. You could check if there is a more recent version of the program concerned, and download and install this version. You can also try to use a different video program to work with the video file. There are various types of video software available that will allow you to perform certain tasks, such as video editing.

C. Download Practice Files

If you want to follow the examples in *Chapter 1 Working with Photos* and *Chapter 2 Working with Video*, you will need to use various practice files. You can download these practice files from the website accompanying this book.

☞ **Open the www.visualsteps.com/iphotomac/practice web page** ℘¹⁰

The web page containing the practice files will be opened. First you are going to download the practice files for *Chapter 1 Working with Photos*:

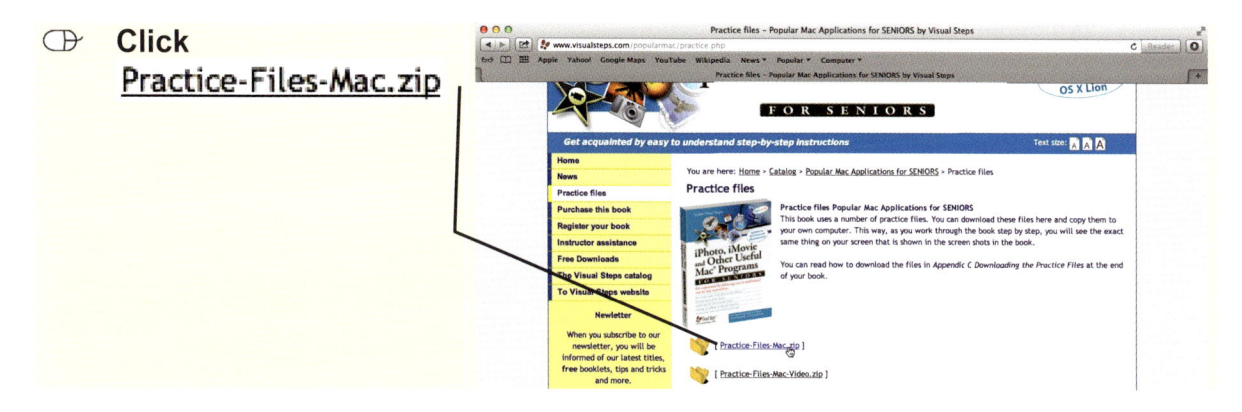

⊙ Click **Practice-Files-Mac.zip**

The practice files will be downloaded right away.

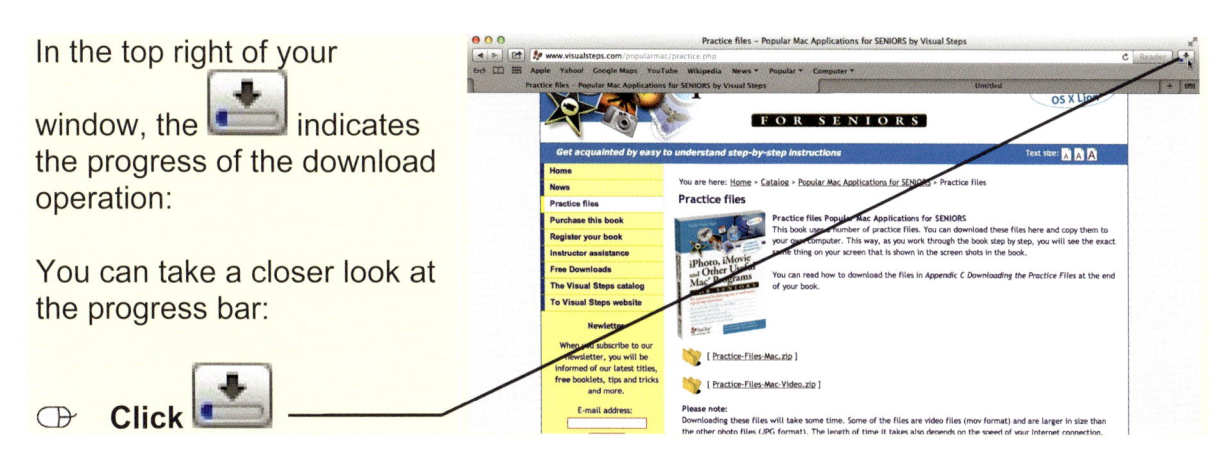

In the top right of your window, the ⬇ indicates the progress of the download operation:

You can take a closer look at the progress bar:

⊙ Click ⬇

Here you can see a better view of the download process and how much time is needed for completion:

Downloads — Practice-Files-Mac.zip — 19.9 MB of 28 MB (94 KB/sec) — 1 minute remaining

The files have been downloaded. The folder with the practice files will be stored in the *Downloads* folder on the *Mac*. Now you can delete the folder from this list. If you do this, the folder will only be deleted from the download list; the actual files will still remain in the *Downloads* folder.

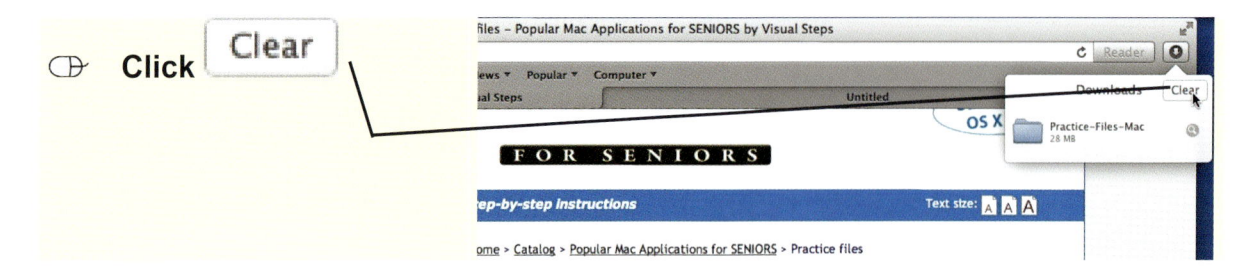

☞ Click **Clear**

If you want to use the practice files in *iPhoto*, you will need to import these files into the program. This is how you do that:

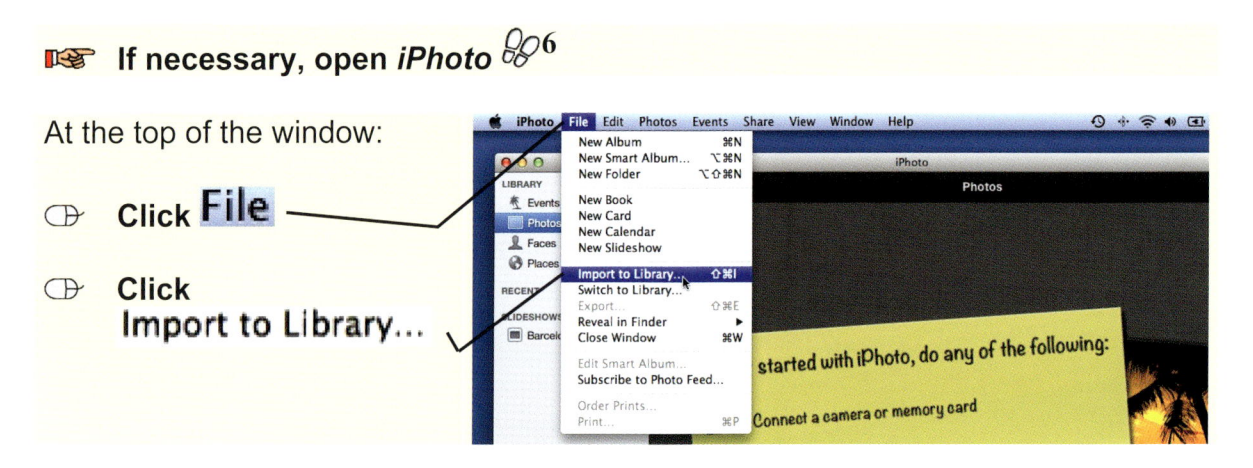

☞ If necessary, open *iPhoto* ℰ⁶

At the top of the window:

☞ Click **File**

☞ Click **Import to Library...**

The practice files have been stored in the *Downloads* folder:

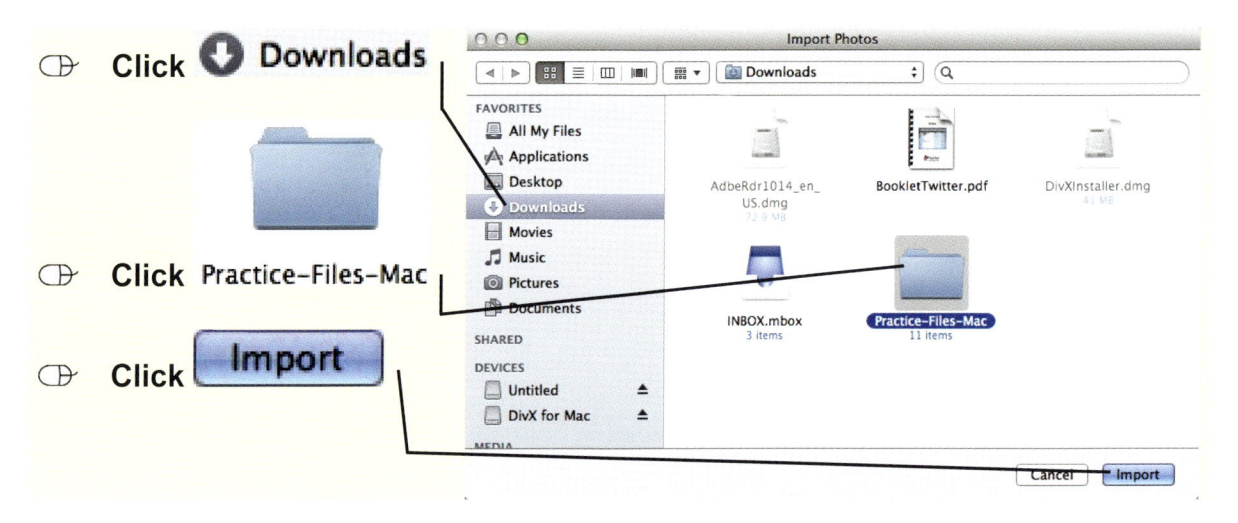

☞ Click **⬇ Downloads**

☞ Click **Practice-Files-Mac**

☞ Click **Import**

C. Download Practice Files   **247**

Now the photos have been imported in *iPhoto*. You will find them under the label ⊙ **Last Import**.

☞ **If necessary, stop *iPhoto* ⏱²**

Now you can download the practice files for *Chapter 2 Working with Video*:

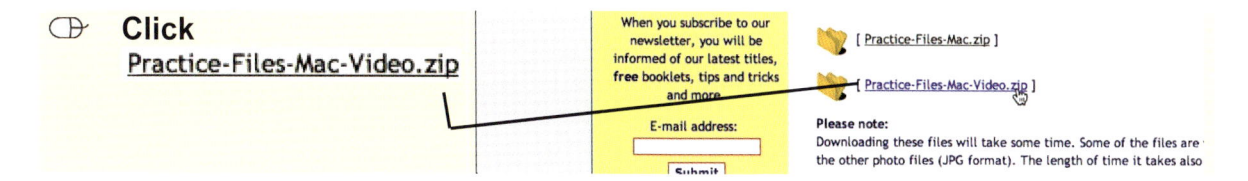

☞ **Click Practice-Files-Mac-Video.zip**

The practice files will be downloaded right away. When the download process has completed, you can delete the folder from the list:

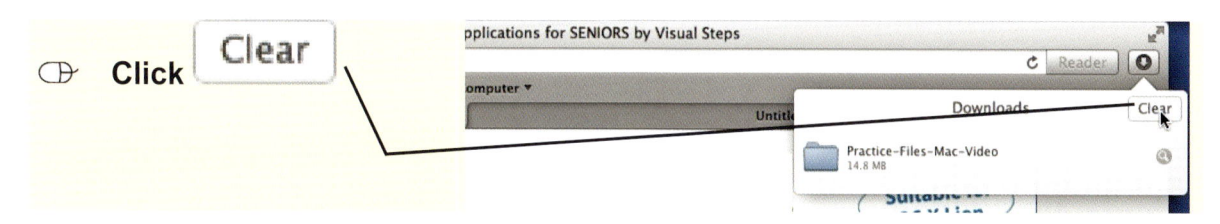

☞ **Click Clear**

Now you can stop *Safari*:

☞ **Stop *Safari* ⏱²**

D. Open a Bonus Chapter

On the website accompanying this book you will find several bonus chapters. These are PDF files. This is how you open the files on the website accompanying this book:

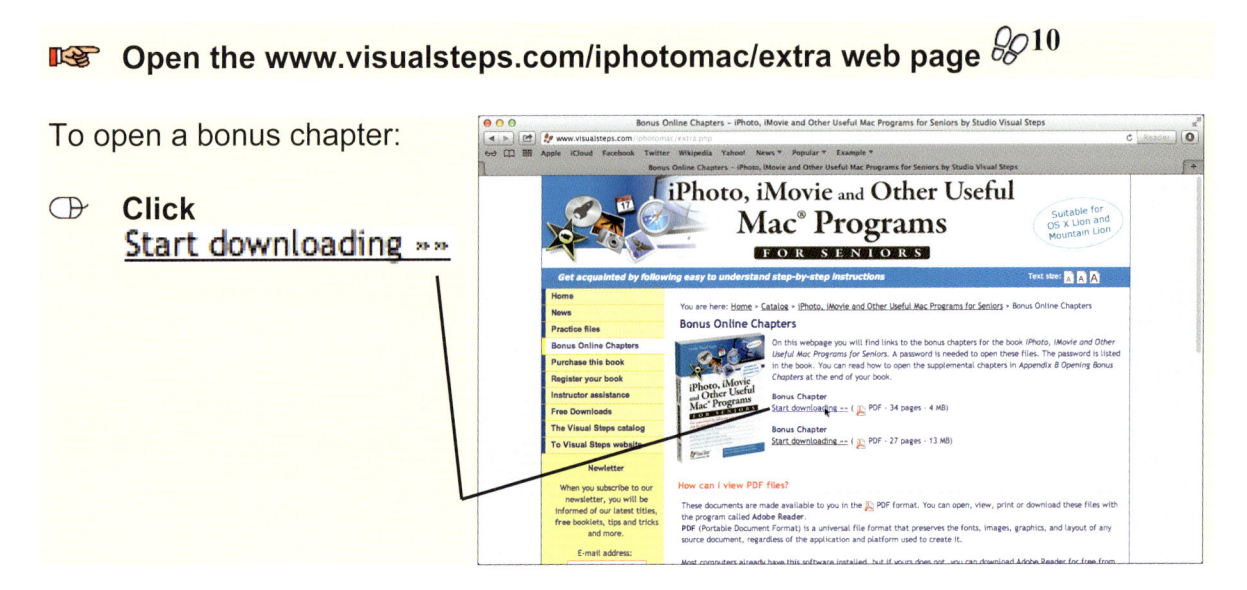

☞ **Open the www.visualsteps.com/iphotomac/extra web page** 🐾10

To open a bonus chapter:

⊕ **Click Start downloading »»**

The PDF files have been secured with a password. You need to enter a password to open them:

⌨ **Type:** 985632

⌨ **Press** `enter / return`

The bonus chapter will be opened. You can work through this bonus chapter in the same way as you did with the chapters in the book. After you have read or printed the bonus chapter you can close all the windows.

E. Index

A

Album	56
adding photos	28
creating	25
delete	36
remove photo	29
Adding	
address	211, 232
album to playlist	139
apps to *Launchpad*	154
bookmarks to bookmarks menu	193
event	219
images	50
multiple tracks at once	138
multiple video files	87
music	97
photos to album	28
photos to card in *Contacts*	231
photos to video project	92, 93
signature email message	182
songs to playlist	135
text	50
titles	94
tracks to iPod	145
transition	95
widget	226
Addresses	
adding	211, 232
managing	210
searching	214
App	173
downloading	166
installing	166
removing	170
Aspect ratio	116

B

Backup	171, 173
Bonus chapter	248
Bookmarks	188, 199
to bookmarks menu	193
Bookmarks	
bar	199, 204
library	199
menu	199
Burning a DVD	106, 118

C

Calendar	216, 230
overview per month	224
Camera	
deactivate	22, 77
remove	22, 77
Card	230
deleting	215
CD importing	123
Changing	
font	54
order of playlist	140
Mail cards	231
size of photo	47
Choosing a calendar	217
Closing	
Dashboard	228
widgets	227
Codecs	70, 116, 239
Combining apps in *Launchpad*	158
Comments	56
Compress	116
Contact	230
Contacts	230
adding photo	231
Conversations	180, 199
Copy multiple files to iPod	152

Creating
- album — 25
- backup — 171
- mailboxes in *Mail* — 176
- playlist — 135
- *Reading List* — 197
- slideshow — 30
- smart mailbox — 203
- smart playlist — 143
- video file — 101
- videos with *iMovie* — 78

Cropping a photo — 48, 93

D

Dashboard — 230
- closing — 228

Deactivate
- camera — 22, 77
- SD card — 77

Deleting
- album — 36
- bookmark from bookmarks bar — 204
- card — 215
- email — 186
- event — 222
- folder from bookmarks bar — 204
- mailboxes — 180
- music — 100
- playlist — 145
- shape — 51
- shortcut from *Reading List* — 201
- text object — 52
- tracks iPod — 152

Disk Utility — 153, 162, 173

Displaying conversations — 180

Downloading
- app — 166
- codecs — 70, 239
- practice files — 245
- widgets — 233

DVD player — 116

DVD playing — 112

E

Editing
- event — 221
- photos in *Preview* — 42
- video clip — 83

Email
- account — 56, 199
- adding signature — 182
- delete — 186
- searching — 185

Enable sound check in *iTunes* — 151

Enhancing a photo — 45

Event — 56, 116
- adding to calendar — 219
- editing — 221
- delete — 222

External hard drive — 173

F

Facebook — 60
FaceTime — 199, 207
Facial recognition *iPhoto* — 68
Finalize — 116
- video project — 103

Flag email messages — 201
Folder within bookmarks folder — 192
Font changing — 54
Frame rate — 116

G

GPS coordinates — 56

I

iCloud — 199
iDVD — 69, 116
- burning a DVD — 106

Image Capture — 56, 57
iMessages — 199, 208
iMovie — 72, 116
- creating videos — 78
- starting new project — 78

E. Index

Import 56, 117
Importing
    CD 123
    photos 18, 21
    video file into project 80
    video files from camera 72
    videos from SD card 82
Inbox 199
Installing
    app 166
    codecs 70, 239
Internet radio 150
iPad 56
iPhone 56
iPhoto 17, 56, 117
    facial recognition 68
    options 62
iPod
    adding tracks 145
    copy multiple files 152
    delete tracks 152
iTunes 121, 150
    enable sound check 151
    opening 122
    playing music 125

J

Jot down a note 202

K

Keeping a calendar 216

L

Launchpad 173
    adding apps 154
    combining apps 158
    removing apps 154
Leaf through calendar 223
Library 121, 150
    viewing information 128
Listening to radio 147

M

Mail 175, 199
    creating mailboxes 176
Mailbox 199
    within a mailbox 179
Managing
    addresses 210
    data 209
Messages 200
Modifying
    information on a track 129
    properties of calendar 218
Moving
    email to standard mailboxes 179
    folder to bookmarks bar 192
    video clip 91
Music 121
    adding 97
    deleting 100
    programs 98

N

New project in *iMovie* 78
Note 200
    jot down 202
Notification Center 200, 206

O

Opening
    bonus chapter 248
    iTunes 122
Options *iPhoto* 62
Organizing bookmarks *Safari* 188
Overview per month 224

P

PAL 117
PDF documents viewing 64
Photo(s)
    changing size 47
    cropping 48, 93

enhancing	45
importing	18
rotating	23, 43
sending	37, 63
upload	60
use templates	58
Photo Booth	66
Playing	
DVD	112
music in *iTunes*	125
playlist	141
video	104
Playlist	150
adding album	139
adding songs	135
changing the order	140
creating	135
deleting	145
playing	141
remove track	140
Practical applications	153
Practice files	245
Preview	17, 56
editing photos	42
viewing photos	41
Project *iMovie*	78
Proportional (aspect ratio)	56

Q

QuickTime	150
Player	69, 104, 117

R

Radio	147, 150
Rating tracks	131
Reading List	200
creating	197
delete shortcut	201
Reminders	200, 205
Remove	
apps	154, 170
camera	22
photo from album	29
track from playlist	140
Resolution	117
Restore	
file from backup copy	174
previous version	44
Rip	150
Rotating a photo	23, 43

S

Safari	175, 200
organizing bookmarks	188
Saving a slideshow	34
SD card	56, 117
deactivate	77
import videos	82
removing	77
Searching	
address	214
email	185
songs	133
with *Spotlight*	164
Selecting	
multiple email messages	179
trailer	79
Sending	
emails	175
photo by email	37, 63
Shape deleting	51
Share a movie	119
Shuffle	150
Signature	200
Slideshow	56
creating	30
music	32
saving	34
select photos	36
viewing a theme	31
Smart playlist	133, 142, 150
creating	143
Smart mailbox	200, 203
Social media	62
Specific search	134
Spotlight	153, 164, 173

Starting new project in *iMovie*	78
Subfolder	200
Surfing the Internet made easier	175

T

Take pictures with *Photo Booth*	66
Text object deleting	52
Time Machine	153, 173
creating a backup	171
Titles adding	94
Top Sites	194, 200
Track(s)	150
rating	131
Trailer	117
Transition	117
adding	95

U

Upload photos to Internet	60
Use templates for photos	58
Using smart playlists	142

V

Video clip	
editing	83
moving	91
Video editing	117
Video file	
adding	87
creating	101
importing	80
Viewing	
information *Library*	128
PDF documents	64
photos with *Preview*	41
Visual Steps	229

W

Web browser	200
Webmail service	56
Widgets	209, 230
adding	226
closing	227
downloading	233
working with	224
Wikipedia	200
Working with	
Disk Utility	162
music	121
photos	17
video	69
widgets	224
Writable DVD	117

Y

YouTube	119

Z

Zooming	53

iPhone for SENIORS

iPhone for SENIORS
Get started quickly and at your own pace

Author: Studio Visual Steps
ISBN 978 90 5905 158 4
Book type: Paperback
Nr of pages: 304 pages
Accompanying website:
www.visualsteps.com/iphone

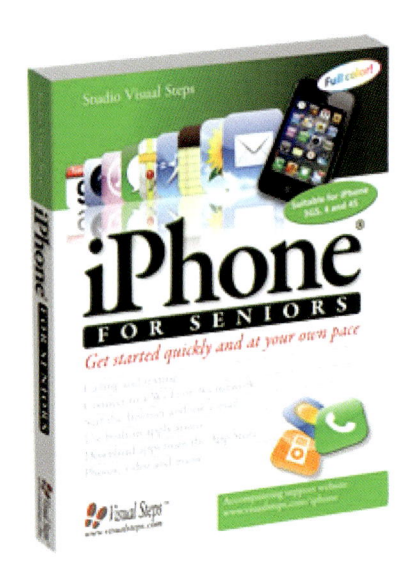

The iPhone is a complete, fully functional multimedia device, adored by millions of fans. In this comprehensive book you will get acquainted with the core features of the iPhone as well as many of the additional options that are available. You work in your own tempo, step by step through each task. The clear and concise instructions and full-color screenshots will tell you exactly what to do. The extra tips, notes and help sections will help you even further to get the most out of your iPhone.
You can use the iPhone 3GS, 4, 4S and 5 not only to make phone calls, but also to send e-mails and surf the Internet. The iPhone is bundled with many standard apps (programs) that enable you to take pictures, shoot videos, listen to your favorite music and even maintain a calendar. Would you like to know how to view your current location and plan a route to get to somewhere else? In this user friendly book you will learn all about this topic and how to use the other built-in apps as well.
Once you have learned about the standard apps and options of the iPhone, you can take a look at the App Store with thousands of other apps available for free or for a small charge. You can find everything from recipes, horoscopes, fitness and health information, card games, photo editing applications, and much more. Whatever your interests, there is bound to be an app for you. Explore and discover the possibilities of this handy device with this practical book!

Learn how to:
- making phone calls and sending text messages
- connect to a Wi-Fi or mobile data network
- surf the Internet and use email
- use built-in applications
- download apps from the App Store
- photos, video and music

Social Media for SENIORS

Social Media for SENIORS
Personal and business communication through social networking

Author: Studio Visual Steps
ISBN 978 90 5905 018 1
Book type: Paperback
Nr of pages: 224 pages
Accompanying website:
www.visualsteps.com/socialmedia

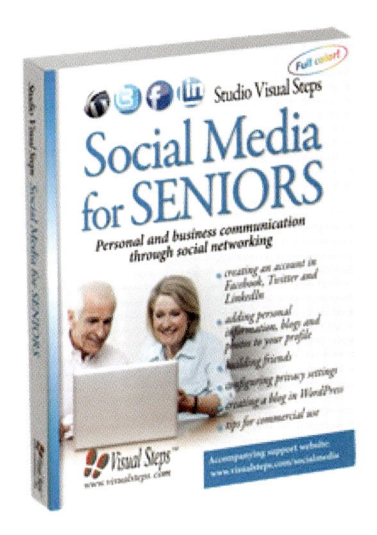

For millions of people, Facebook, Twitter, LinkedIn and other social media websites have become an integral part of everyday life for both private and commercial purposes.
You can hardly find a company, club, newspaper or television program that does not have its own page on Facebook or Twitter. For many celebrities, clubs and sports organizations, such a page has proved to be an indispensable form of communication.
The user-friendly computer book **Social Media for Seniors** will acquaint you with Facebook, Twitter, LinkedIn and WordPress. You will learn how to create an account and how to enter all the necessary information. Next you will learn how to update your status by creating messages that can include hyperlinks, photos and videos. You will then be ready to add or invite friends or contacts to your page. Finally, we will discuss some of the important elements to consider when configuring the privacy settings.
Do you own a company, or are you involved in a club organization? You will also get valuable commercial tips about using your page for communicating with your customers or members. These days, social media pages can play a major part in your business!

Topics covered in this computer book:
- create an account in Facebook, Twitter and LinkedIn;
- add personal information, blogs and photos to your profile;
- build friends;
- configure privacy settings;
- create a blog in WordPress;
- with tips for commercial use.

iPad for SENIORS

iPad for SENIORS
The book that should have come with the iPad

Author: Studio Visual Steps
ISBN 978 90 5905 108 9
Book type: Paperback, full color
Nr of pages: 296 pages
Accompanying website:
www.visualsteps.com/ipad

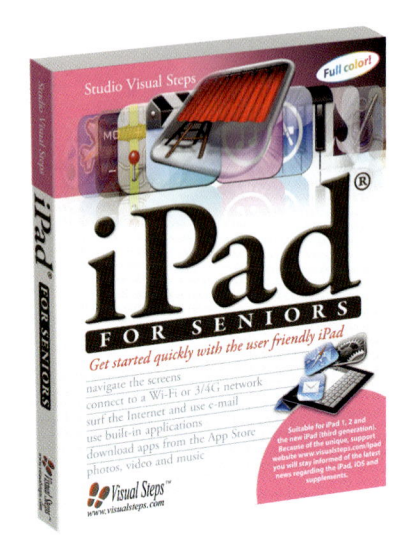

This comprehensive and invaluable **iPad for SENIORS** book will show you how to get the most out of your iPad. The iPad is a user friendly, portable multimedia device with endless capabilities. Use it to surf the Internet, write e-mails, jot down notes and maintain your calendar.

But these are by far not the only things you can do with the iPad. This practical tablet computer also comes with built-in apps (applications) that allow you to listen to music, take pictures and make video calls. You can even use it to plan routes.

In the Apple App Store you can choose from hundreds of thousands of apps to add extra functionality to your iPad. Many apps can be downloaded for free or cost practically nothing. Perhaps you are interested in new recipes, horoscopes, fitness exercises, news from around the world or podcasts? There is literally an app to do almost anything. With this step-by-step book you can learn how to take complete advantage of this technology. Before you know it, you won't believe you ever lived without an iPad. Your world will open up and become a lot bigger!

You will learn how to:
- navigate the screens
- connect to a Wi-Fi or mobile data network
- surf the Internet and use e-mail
- use built-in applications
- download apps from the App Store
- work with photos, video and music